Fascist Italy and Nazi Germany

Fascist Italy
and Nazi Germany

Comparisons and contrasts

EDITED BY

RICHARD BESSEL

The Open University

CAMBRIDGE
UNIVERSITY PRESS

Published by the Press Syndicate of the University of Cambridge
The Pitt Building, Trumpington Street, Cambridge CB2 1RP
40 West 20th Street, New York, NY 10011-4211, USA
10 Stamford Road, Oakleigh, Melbourne 3166, Australia

First published 1996
Reprinted 1997

Printed in Great Britain at the University Press, Cambridge

A catalogue record for this book is available from the British Library

Library of Congress cataloguing in publication data

Fascist Italy and Nazi Germany: comparisons and contrasts/edited by
Richard Bessel.
    p. cm.
    Based on the conference Fascism in Comparative Perspective,
organised in March 1993, held at St Peter's College, Oxford.
    Includes index.
    ISBN 0 521 47129 X (hc) – ISBN 0 521 47711 5 (pbk)
    1. Fascism – Italy – History. 2. Italy – Politics and govern-
ment – 1922–1945. 3. Italy – Economic conditions – 1918–1945.
4. National socialism. 5. Germany – Politics and government –
1918–1933. 6. Germany – Politics and government – 1933–1945.
7. Germany – Economic conditions – 1918–1945.
    I. Bessel, Richard.
    DG571.F298   1996
    320.5′33′0945 – dc20 95-30622CIP

ISBN 0 521 47129 X hardback
ISBN 0 521 47711 5 paperback

WV

Can Fascist Italy and Nazi Germany be compared? Not long ago, the answer seemed obvious: they could be and they were. Nationalist rhetoric, hostility to the Left and to parliamentary government, and the glorification of violence seemed to invite comparison. More recently, doubts have arisen. As Marxist-inspired class paradigms lose their attraction and greater attention is paid to the terrible consequences of Nazi racism, it has been questioned whether Nazi Germany can be compared with anything.

This collaborative volume meets the challenge of comparing the two movements. It contains ten essays, two each on five central themes: the rise of the Fascist and Nazi movements; the relation of the regimes to workers, women, and war; and how the regimes may be viewed in a long-term perspective. The essays take stock of recent research, advance fresh theories about the histories of Nazism and Fascism, and provide a basis for informed comparison of two regimes central to twentieth-century history.

CONTENTS

NOTES ON THE CONTRIBUTORS

TOBIAS ABSE is Lecturer in Modern European History at Goldsmiths' College, University of London. He is the author of *Sovversivi e fascisti a Livorno: Lotta politica e sociale (1918–1922)* (Milan, 1991), and numerous articles on various aspects of twentieth-century Italian history, especially Fascism and the labour movement. His most recent publication is 'Italy: A New Agenda', in Perry Anderson and Patrick Camiller (eds.), *Mapping Europe's Left* (London, 1994).

RICHARD BESSEL is Senior Lecturer in History at the Open University and co-editor of the journal *German History*. His publications include *Political Violence and the Rise of Nazism: The Storm Troopers in Eastern Germany, 1925–1934* (New Haven and London, 1984); (ed.) *Life in the Third Reich* (Oxford, 1987); and *Germany after the First World War* (Oxford, 1993).

GABRIELE CZARNOWSKI is completing her *Habilitation* in Berlin on the theme of 'Abortion in National Socialism'. Her publications include *Das kontrollierte Paar. Ehe- und Sexualpolitik im Nationalsozialismus* (Weinheim, 1991); 'Frauen als Mutter der "Rasse". Abtreibungsverfolgung und Zwangseingriff im Nationalsozialismus', in Gisela Staupe and Lisa Vieth (eds.), *Unter anderen Umständen. Zur Geschichte der Abtreibung* (Dresden and Berlin, 1993), pp. 58–72; and 'Abortion as Political Conflict in the United Germany', *Parliamentary Affairs. A Journal of Comparative Politics*, vol. 47 (1994), pp. 252–67.

MICHAEL GEYER is Professor of History at the University of Chicago. His publications include *Aufrüstung oder Sicherheit. Die Reichswehr in der Krise der Machtpolitik 1924–1936* (Wiesbaden, 1980); *Deutsche Rüstungspolitik 1860–1980* (Frankfurt/Main, 1984); and (ed., with John W.

Boyer), *Resistance against the Third Reich, 1933–1990* (Chicago and London, 1994).

MacGREGOR KNOX is Stevenson Professor of International History at the London School of Economics and Political Science. He is author of *Mussolini Unleashed, 1939–1941. Politics and Strategy in Fascist Italy's Last War* (Cambridge, 1982) and a variety of articles on aspects of Fascist and Nazi foreign and military policies, and is co-editor of *The Making of Strategy: Rulers, States, and War* (Cambridge, 1994).

CARL LEVY is Lecturer in European Politics in the Department of Social Policy and Politics, Goldsmiths' College, University of London. His publications include (ed.) *Socialism and the Intelligentsia, 1880–1914* (London, 1987); (ed.) *Italian Regionalism* (Oxford, 1996); and many articles on comparative European social and intellectual history.

ADRIAN LYTTELTON is Professor of Contemporary European History at the University of Pisa. His publications include *The Seizure of Power: Fascism in Italy 1919–1929* (2nd edn., London and Princeton, 1988); (ed.) *Italian Fascisms* (London, 1973); 'The Middle Classes in Liberal Italy', in John Davis and Paul Ginsborg (eds.), *Society and Politics in the Age of the Risorgimento* (Cambridge, 1991); and 'The National Question in Italy', in Mikuláš Teich and Roy Porter (eds.), *The National Question in Europe in Historical Context* (Cambridge, 1993).

MARK ROSEMAN is Senior Lecturer in Modern History at Keele University. His publications include *Recasting the Ruhr 1945–1948. Manpower, Economic Recovery and Labour Relations* (Oxford, 1992); *Neither Punitive nor Powerless. Western Europe and the Division of Germany 1945–1948. A Reappraisal* (Birmingham, 1993); and (ed.) *Generations in Conflict. Youth Revolt and Generation Formation in Germany 1770–1968* (Cambridge, 1995).

TILLA SIEGEL is Professor for the Sociology of Industrialised Countries at the Johann Wolfgang Goethe-Universität in Frankfurt/Main. Her publications include *Leistung und Lohn in der nationalsozialistischen 'Ordnung der Arbeit'* (Opladen, 1989); (together with Thomas von Freyberg), *Industrielle Rationalisierung unter dem Nationalsozialismus* (Frankfurt/Main and New York, 1991); 'Welfare Capitalism – Nazi Style', in *International Journal of Political Economy*, vol. 18, no. 1 (1988); 'It is only Rational – an Essay on the Logics of Social Rationalization', in *International Journal of Political Economy*, vol. 25 (1995).

BERND WEISBROD is Professor of Modern European History at the University of Göttingen. His main subjects are the social history of Victorian Britain (pauper and delinquent children, social reform and social policy) and twentieth-century German history (industrial relations, political culture, postwar history). He has recently published two collections of essays on the regional culture of postwar Lower Saxony: *Grenzland. Beiträge zur Geschichte der deutsch-deutschen Grenze* (Hanover, 1992); and *Rechtsradikalismus. Politische Kultur und politischer Regionalismus in der Nachkriegszeit* (Hanover, 1995).

PERRY WILLSON is Lecturer in Italian History and Language at the University of Edinburgh. A member of the Editorial Collective of *Gender and History* and of the Editorial Board of *Modern Italy*, her recent publications include *The Clockwork Factory: Women and Work in Fascist Italy* (Oxford, 1993). In 1992–3 she held a Jean Monnet Fellowship at the European University Institute in Florence.

PREFACE

This volume has its origins in a conference on 'Fascism in Comparative Perspective', organised in memory of Tim Mason in March 1993. The conference was held at St Peter's College, Oxford, where Tim Mason taught between 1971 and 1984. I would like to take this opportunity to thank the German History Society, the Association for the Study of Modern Italy, History Workshop, the Royal Historical Society, the British Academy, and the German Academic Exchange Service for their generous support, without which the conference could not have been held. I would also like to thank St Peter's College, Oxford, for providing so congenial a conference venue, and all the participants who helped make it a success. I hope that this volume is a fitting tribute to a fine historian and friend to whom a great many people owe a great deal.

ABBREVIATIONS

AWI	Arbeitswissenschaftliches Institut der Deutschen Arbeitsfront
BGB	Bürgerliches Gesetzbuch
CDU	Christlich-Demokratische Union
CSU	Christlich-Soziale Union
DAF	Deutsche Arbeitsfront
DC	Democrazia Cristiana
DFW	Deutsches Frauenwerk
DVU	Deutsche Volks-Union
ENI	Ente Nazionale Idrocarburi
ETZ	Ehetauglichkeitszeugnis
GIL	Gioventù Italiana del Littorio
IMI	Istituto Mobiliare Italiano
IRI	Istituto per la Ricostruzione Industriale
MSI	Movimento Sociale Italiano
NEP	New Economic Policy
NSDAP	Nationalsozialistische Deutsche Arbeiterpartei
NSF	Nationalsozialistische Frauenschaft
NSV	Nationalsozialistische Volkswohlfahrt
ONB	Opera Nazionale Balilla
OND	Opera Nazionale Dopolavoro
ONMI	Opera Nazionale per la Maternità ed Infanzia
OVRA	Opera Volontaria per la Repressione Antifascista
PCI	Partito Comunista Italiano
PDS	Partei des Demokratischen Sozialismus
PDS	Partito Democratico della Sinistra
PNF	Partito Nazionale Fascista
PSI	Partito Socialista Italiano
RMD	Reichsmutterdienst
RMdI	Reichsministerium des Innern

RMJ	Reichsministerium der Justiz
SA	Sturmabteilungen
SD	Sicherheitsdienst
SiPo	Sicherheitspolizei
SOLD	Sezione Operaie e Lavoranti a Domicilio
SPD	Sozialdemokratische Partei Deutschlands
SS	Schutzstaffel

INTRODUCTION: ITALY, GERMANY
AND FASCISM

RICHARD BESSEL

> Fascism is the plague of the twentieth century, and we are living
> in the twentieth century.
> Nikolai Ryabov, chairman of the Russian Central Election
> Commission, 13 December 1993[1]

In one of the last pieces he wrote, Tim Mason posed the question:
'Whatever happened to "Fascism"?' Typically for Tim Mason, he was
not simply outlining an important historiographical problem; he also
was making an impassioned plea – a plea that fascism as a general concept not be dropped from our vocabulary. It was an expression of his
concern, reinforced at the Philadelphia conference on 'Re-evaluating the
"Third Reich" ' in April 1988 which he had attended, about 'the decline
of the "Fascist" paradigm'.[2] As he noted, general comparative questions
framed within discussion of fascism no longer occupied centre stage in
the study of Nazi Germany:

> most of the interesting new work is concerned specifically with Ger-
> many, Nazism, and the Third Reich, especially with the relationship
> between institutional structures and policy-making, on the one
> hand, and with biological politics (racism and eugenics), on the
> other. The most extreme peculiarities of German Nazism have thus
> slowly and silently come to dominate our moral, political and

Throughout this book 'fascism' (and cognates) is used to refer to the phenomenon in
the generic sense, while 'Fascism' (and cognates) is used to refer specifically to the
Italian case.
[1] Quoted in *The Independent*, 'Fascism stalks Russia', by Andrew Higgins, 14 Dec. 1993,
p. 1.
[2] Papers from this conference have been published in the valuable collection edited by
Thomas Childers and Jane Caplan, *Reevaluating the Third Reich* (New York and
London, 1993). Tim Mason's article, 'Whatever Happened to "Fascism"?', first published in *Radical History Review*, no. 49 (Winter 1991), was republished as an appendix
to the Childers and Caplan collection, pp. 253–62.

professional concerns. When referred to at all at the Philadelphia
conference, 'Fascism' seemed to have become old hat.[3]

For Tim Mason, this tendency carried the danger (as Jane Caplan put
it) of 'a retreat from engagement with the most fundamental moral and
political questions that could be asked of this period of history'.[4] If historical research into this period were going to address such questions,
it needed to be capable of generating general conclusions, and not just
to describe events of a specific time and place.

Concern to reach general conclusions from the profoundly disturbing
and destructive events which took place in Europe – and in Italy and
Germany in particular – between 1918 and 1945 was precisely what
had inspired earlier debates about 'fascism'. 'Fascism' as a subject of
theoretical and comparative analysis was a product of a largely Marxist-
inspired debate, in which the relations of capital, labour and the state,
and questions of class, occupied centre stage. It had its origins in contemporary writings during the 1920s and 1930s, as Marxists and non-
Marxists alike struggled to make sense of the threatening phenomena
with which they were faced in interwar Europe; and it had formed a
central theme in the historiography of twentieth-century Europe during
the 1960s and 1970s. During the 1980s, however, it largely disappeared
from view under a mass of individual studies of Fascist Italy and Nazi
Germany which largely neglected to make comparative glances across
the Alps. Yet at the same time the opening up of new subjects of enquiry
and the gaining of valuable new insights – not least from the work of
historians of everyday life, researchers using oral evidence to understand
working-class attitudes, feminist historians examining policies towards
and the experiences of women, and military historians examining how
the Fascist and Nazi regimes made war – provided potentially fruitful
bases upon which to make new generalisations. New pieces of the jigsaw
were uncovered in astounding quantity; the task was somehow to put
them together to make a coherent picture.

At least so it seemed before the political earthquake which began with
the breaching of the Berlin Wall. The events of the past few years – the
ending of the Cold-War division of Europe, the reunification of Germany, the crumbling of the postwar political system in Italy, the collapse
of Marxist–Leninist socialism in Europe – now give the history of Nazi
Germany and Fascist Italy, and of fascism generally, a different frame
from what had seemed the case a decade ago. Of course, there had been

[3] Mason, 'Whatever Happened to "Fascism"?', in Childers and Caplan (eds.), *Reevaluating the Third Reich*, p. 255.
[4] Jane Caplan, 'In Memoriam: Tim Mason 1940–1990', *Radical History Review*, vol. 49
(Winter 1991), p. 87.

rumblings of change before 1989: implicitly with the post-modernist and 'linguistic turn' among historians who cast growing doubts upon the explanatory power of a structural history of society which would capture the reality of a coherent past and 'create a progressive imaginary';[5] and explicitly, for example, with the debates which were sparked by Martin Broszat's plea for the 'historicisation' of German National Socialism.[6] However, the profound political changes since 1989 have made it apparent that the postwar, post-fascist era in Europe is past, and it consequently is time to look at the phenomenon of fascism anew.

If, in this post-postwar context, Tim Mason's call to take 'Fascism' seriously as a conceptual and comparative tool is not to be regarded as the cry of those somehow hoping to resurrect the intellectual world of the 1960s, then we need to look at the history of Europe during the first half of the twentieth century with new eyes. That history, of which the history of Fascism and Nazism forms a major part, no longer appears safely buried. This may be seen on a number of planes. The most obvious – and therefore perhaps easiest to misunderstand – is the political. Whether or not one regards the Republikaner in Germany, the Alleanza Nazionale in Italy, or the Front national in France as 'fascist' parties, their growth and, most notably in Italy, the fact that they have become serious players on the national political stage indicate that important changes in historical and political consciousness have taken place in Europe over the past decade. And were that not enough, the spectre of the Russian Liberal Democratic Party and its leader Vladimir Zhirinovsky, to say nothing of figures even further to the Right, and the parallels often drawn between pre-Nazi Germany and post-Communist Russia (or 'Weimar Russia', as it sometimes has been labelled), should make us question whether the fascist ghost was entirely laid to rest in 1945 as so many had hoped.

We no longer can assume – as many silently had done hitherto – that post-fascist, Cold-War Europe was a permanent fixture, separating us irrevocably from the doubts, dangers, hopes and horrors unleashed by two world wars. The unspoken assumption that Europeans had learned the lessons of history, that after the catastrophes of the first half of the

---

[5] See the special issue on 'German Histories: Challenges in Theory, Practice, Technique', *Central European History*, vol. 22, no. 3/4 (1989), especially the introductory article by Michael Geyer and Konrad H. Jarausch, 'The Future of the German Past: Transatlantic Reflections for the 1990s'.

[6] The key text is Martin Broszat's essay, first published in *Merkur*, no. 39 in 1985, 'Plädoyer für eine Historisierung des Nationalsozialismus', reprinted in Hermann Graml and Klaus-Dietmar Henke (eds.), *Nach Hitler. Der schwierige Umgang mit unserer Geschichte. Beiträge von Martin Broszat* (Munich, 1986), pp. 159–73. The clearest discussion of the historiographical issues involved may be found in Ian Kershaw, *The Nazi Dictatorship. Problems and Perspectives of Interpretation* (3rd edn, London, 1993), pp. 180–96.

century the heirs of the Enlightenment (whether liberal or Marxist) finally had triumphed, has been shattered. Europeans face the disturbing possibility that their twentieth century is ending where it began: in Sarajevo.

This, it would seem, might offer some basis for looking comparatively at Fascism and Nazism in a new light. The end of the Cold War has both liberated us from old politically motivated and essentially unproductive Cold-War paradigms (for example, by allowing us to look anew at theories of totalitarianism without being weighted down by Cold-War baggage) and given the theme of fascism a new urgency and relevance. And, to be sure, there were from the start good reasons why the two phenomena deserved comparison. After all, both were radical ideological and political negations of the Enlightenment; both came to power in countries deeply shaken by economic, political and psychological crises in the wake of the First World War; both were militantly opposed to parliamentary democracy; both aggressively assaulted the Left; both glorified the role of violence in politics and war; and both led their respective countries to ruin.

However, the challenges posed by the terrible violence unleashed by German National Socialism, which really had no parallel in the history of Fascist Italy, and the centrality to Nazism of race and the Nazis' monstrous attempt to racially restructure Europe through campaigns of war and mass murder, inevitably raise the question: can Italian Fascism and German National Socialism meaningfully be compared at all? Many observers, when faced with the enormity of Nazi crimes, have effectively denied that Nazi Germany can be compared with anything, and suggest that to make such comparisons amounts at best to a fundamental misunderstanding of the essence of Nazism and at worst to a dereliction of the historian's moral duty. A particularly fluent and uncompromising view of the singularity of the Nazi project has been presented by Michael Burleigh and Wolfgang Wippermann, who conclude their book *The Racial State* with an unequivocal assertion of the 'extreme peculiarities of German Nazism':

> The main object of social policy remained the creation of a hierarchical racial new order. Everything else was subordinate to this goal, including the regime's conduct of foreign affairs and the war. In the eyes of the regime's racial politicians, the Second World War was above all a racial war, to be pursued with immense brutality until the end, that is until the concentration camps were liberated by invading Allied armies. All of these points draw attention to the specific and singular character of the Third Reich. It was not a form of regression to past times, although the regime frequently instru-

mentalised various ahistorical myths to convey the idea of historical normalcy. Its objects were novel and *sui generis*: to realise an ideal future world, without 'lesser races', without the sick, and without those who they decreed had no place in the 'national community'. The Third Reich was intended to be a racial rather than a class society. This fact in itself makes existing theories, whether based upon modernisation, totalitarianism, or global theories of Fascism, poor heuristic devices for a greater understanding of what was a singular regime without precedent or parallel.[7]

If the essence of Nazism was about race and racialist politics, and if the attempt to murder the entire Jewish population of Europe was 'novel and *sui generis*', an act of singular barbarity, what value can there be in a comparative approach to fascism? Is the attempt to draw comparisons between Italian Fascism and German National Socialism therefore condemned to be limited to matters of secondary importance and concern, matters which ultimately may deflect us from understanding the greatest tragedy of the twentieth century?

There are no easy answers to these questions. It is an historical fact that Nazi Germany committed crimes which are without parallel in modern European history, just as it is an historical fact that Nazism developed and succeeded in a country facing problems which, while they may have been extreme, paralleled those which had arisen elsewhere – not least in Italy. Furthermore, the assertion that a particular history or development was 'novel and *sui generis*' itself implies comparison, if only to establish that claims about similarities are misplaced; assertion of difference or singularity involves no less an element of comparison than does assertion of similarity or identity. Precisely herein lies the challenge of any attempt to compare and contrast Fascism and Nazism: to explain their histories while ignoring neither the points of genuine comparison nor the singularity of Nazi crimes. To focus on just one or the other would be to write only half a history, and thus would offer poor heuristic devices for understanding either of these destructive political phenomena.

This volume offers a modest attempt to deliver what its title promises: comparisons and contrasts between Fascist Italy and Nazi Germany. That is the rationale for the structure of the book – two essays on each of five key themes in the history of Fascism and Nazism – which forms an explicit attempt to offer bases for comparison. This is not to say that all, or even most, aspects of Italian Fascism had their parallels in

[7] Michael Burleigh and Wolfgang Wippermann, *The Racial State. Germany 1933–1945* (Cambridge, 1991), pp. 306–7.

German National Socialism or vice versa; in many respects it is the contrasts between the two which are more striking. But framing the project as a whole is a concern to view Fascism and Nazism within a comparative perspective and to take seriously the challenge posed by Tim Mason with which this introduction began.

The concerns raised by Tim Mason shortly before his death provided the starting point for this volume in a double sense: on an intellectual plane, the contributors to this collection share the concern to understand and account for the destructive phenomena of Italian Fascism and German National Socialism in ways whose explanatory power is not limited to these specific times and places and thus remain, ultimately, antiquarian. On another, personal plane, this collection is testimony to the debt which we owe to Tim Mason. This book arises out of a conference on 'Fascism in Comparative Perspective' which was held in Tim Mason's memory in April 1993 at St Peter's College, Oxford, the college where he taught from 1971 until 1984.[8] The structure of the conference, and consequently the structure of this volume, was shaped by the main themes in Mason's work: Crisis of Bourgeois Society, Fascism and Workers, Fascism and Women, Fascism and War, and Post-Fascist Societies and Modernisation. While obviously not offering a comprehensive treatment of the subject – something which no single volume could pretend to do – this book aims to present both a basis for informed discussion of what was specific to Italian Fascism and German Nazism as well as of what they had in common, and for an informed general comparative discussion of 'fascism'.

In the first pair of essays, which address what lay behind the collapse of democratic politics which preceded the Fascist or Nazi takeovers, Adrian Lyttelton (examining Italy) and Bernd Weisbrod (examining Germany) make different assessments of the 'crisis of bourgeois society' – and even the extent to which one usefully can deploy such a term. Both focus particularly on the role, and the widespread acceptance, of violence in politics as a key element in the breakdown of parliamentary government and of bourgeois society and in the success of the Fascist and Nazi movements. While Lyttelton is at pains to stress that a crisis *in* bourgeois society (of which the rejection of parliamentary government in favour of Fascist violence was a powerful symptom in Italy) is not the same thing as a crisis *of* bourgeois society, the argument is taken further in the German case: there, as Bernd Weisbrod sees it, the conventional morals of bourgeois society were shattered, and Hitler was able to destroy its last defences in a way that Mussolini never could.

---

[8] For a report of the conference, see Eve Rosenhaft, 'Fascism in Comparative Perspective', *German History*, vol. 12, no. 2 (1994), pp. 197–202.

However, when observing, as Weisbrod notes, that in Germany 'the civilising mission of bourgeois society mutated into a racist project', we should not assume that this was simply a sign of the uniqueness of Nazism. Instead, it is worth considering the intriguing suggestion by Adrian Lyttelton, which turns the commonly held assumption on its head: namely that it may have been Italian Fascism, rather than German Nazism, which, by virtue of its absence of racialist politics, was the exception among fascist movements.[9]

The historical and historiographical contrasts are particularly evident in the two contributions which focus on the position of workers in and the relationship of workers to the Fascist and Nazi regimes. This subject was at the centre of Tim Mason's work, and should – at least from a Marxist perspective – offer ideal grounds for comparison. After all, both regimes took power in violent campaigns against a Left which saw itself as the political representative of the working class; both regimes left capitalist modes of production intact – even if capitalist producers were subject to increasing government regulation; and both regimes expended considerable energy in trying to counter the internationalist Marxist message and to integrate workers into the 'national community', if with varying degrees of success. It is here that the usefulness or otherwise of a 'class-conflict' paradigm most obviously presents itself – as questions, if not as answers: to what extent did workers continue to regard themselves as such and, consequently, resist the blandishments of regimes which, through combinations of bribery and repression,[10] sought to eliminate class divisions and integrate workers into a 'national community'?

The challenges posed by the two histories are very different – something which Tobias Abse addresses squarely in his contribution when he asserts that, in contradistinction to German workers under Nazism, Italian workers formed 'a working class which broke with the regime, not one that followed – or appeared to follow – the dictator to the bitter end'. The challenges facing the historian examining what happened to German workers under Hitler are quite different to the challenges facing

[9] In this context, it is worth considering the suggestion by Charles Maier, in his foreword to the book of the 1988 Philadelphia conference, that 'if a new "biological" paradigm emerges, one extrapolated less from German particularity than Western pseudoscientific hierarchies, does not the new historiography on the Left allow for the rehabilitation of a new generic fascism based on eugenic categories or even dehumanized technocratic longings?' See Charles S. Maier, 'Foreword', in Childers and Caplan (eds.), *Reevaluating the Third Reich*, p. xv.

[10] On this theme, see Carola Sachse, Tilla Siegel, Hasso Spode and Wolfgang Spohn, *Angst, Belohnung, Zucht und Ordnung. Herrschaftsmechanismen im Nationalsozialismus* (Opladen, 1982), and especially Tim Mason's introductory essay, 'Die Bändigung der Arbeiterklasse im nationalsozialistischen Deutschland. Eine Einleitung'.

the historian of Italian workers under Mussolini. Whereas Abse is able to trace the *tradizione sovversiva* among Italian workers, a tradition which Fascism could not destroy and which emerged with the mass strikes in Milan and Turin in March and April 1943, nothing comparable can be found in the behaviour of German workers during the Second World War. While Weimar Germany had had a big and well-organised trade-union movement and the largest Communist Party outside the Soviet Union, after 1933 German workers did not rise up to challenge the Nazi regime in the way that their Italian counterparts ultimately challenged the Fascists. Why? Answers may be found in the more advanced techniques employed by German employers and the Nazi regime to rationalise work and integrate workers, to vastly greater levels of repression, to the attraction of a racism which privileged German workers and gave them their little stake in the 'racial state', or to the fear of what was in store once the Russians arrived and took their revenge. More than that, however: in her contribution on the attitudes of workers in Nazi Germany Tilla Siegel emphasises not only the explicit postures towards (or against) the Nazi regime (which has generated an enormous literature over the past couple of decades), but also the social norms, values and rationalisations which governed workers' everyday behaviour and which – often obliquely – framed their relationships to the Nazi regime.

If the key contrast between the Fascist and Nazi regimes is the latter's fixation upon race and its determination to put racialist ideology into practice, then this contrast surfaces particularly clearly in the pair of essays which focus on women and their experiences. While Perry Willson presents a general overview of women in Fascist Italy, their role in the production process as well as their position as objects of the regime's pronatalist policies, Gabriele Czarnowski concentrates on Nazi policies towards marriage and the treatment of women in their reproductive role as objects of Nazi racial policy. To be sure, the Italian and German stories certainly have important parallels: Victoria de Grazia's observation that 'Mussolini's regime stood for returning women to home and hearth, restoring patriarchal authority, and confining female destiny to having babies' would not be out of place if applied to the Third Reich, and both Fascism and Nazism were 'integrally authoritarian and anti-feminist'.[11] However, there was a vital difference: whereas the Fascist regime was concerned to prevent women from experiencing emancipation and promoted pronatalist policies, the Nazi regime went some

[11] Victoria de Grazia, *How Fascism Ruled Women. Italy 1922–1945* (Berkeley, Los Angeles and Oxford, 1992), pp. 1, 3.

terrible steps further, in – as Czarnowski makes clear – applying policies guided by a racial ideology, with terrible consequences.

Perhaps the feature which Italian Fascism and German National Socialism most clearly shared was their affirmation, in theory and in practice, of violence and war. In this the left-wing opponents of fascism were absolutely right: fascism meant war. Violence and war undeniably were at the core of the Fascist and Nazi projects. Both ideologies and both regimes glorified war; both launched wars; and both met their ends in war. However, their military performance and the wars they pursued were very different. Both the similarities and the differences are examined in the pair of articles which focus on the Fascist and Nazi pursuit of war. MacGregor Knox takes an explicitly comparative approach in which he analyses the different war-fighting capabilities of the two countries and seeks to locate the reasons for these differences in their different traditions of military training, and in their different economic and political structures. Michael Geyer, on the other hand, focuses on the period when Nazi Germany became in effect incomparable: the years from 1938 to 1941, when Germany launched wars of incomparable violence – wars which set the Nazi regime apart from Fascist Italy. By taking this as his focus, Geyer critically examines one of the main theses expounded by Tim Mason, namely that of the 'inner crisis' and 'crisis of social reproduction', and probes the ways in which war and terror served as an 'attractor' for the ambitions of large segments of the German population.

The more time which elapses between the end of Fascist Italy and Nazi Germany, the more tempting – indeed necessary – it is to view the Fascist and Nazi periods not just in and of themselves but also as the pre-histories of what came afterwards. Both regimes contained considerable continuities with the parliamentary systems which preceded them, and both obviously created preconditions for the political, economic and social orders which succeeded them. How are we to place the histories of Italian Fascism and German Nazism into a longer-term perspective? To what extent did the experiences of the Fascist and Nazi regimes pave the way for the prosperous parliamentary democracies which developed in West Germany and Italy after 1945? To ask such questions, whether implicitly or explicitly, is to raise the issue of modernisation, and whether the Fascist and Nazi regimes – perhaps contrary to their aims – in effect served to modernise Italian and German societies. Such questions have never been easy to address. However, as Carl Levy and Mark Roseman demonstrate in their contributions to this volume, German reunification and the re-creation of the German nation-state on the one hand and the crumbling of the postwar political order of the Italian Republic on the other – processes both of which began at the end of the 1980s – have made the drawing of longer-term perspectives both more complicated and more pressing. For the first time since 1945 there is a unified German nation-state in the centre of Europe and an open admirer of Mussolini in the Italian government.

As both Levy and Roseman discuss in their essays, there has been a growing temptation in recent years to view the Fascist and Nazi dictatorships as 'modernising' – a temptation which is highly contentious and fraught with politically charged dangers of misunderstanding the phenomena being discussed.[12] To venture onto this historiographical terrain means unavoidably confronting the 'moral, political and professional concerns' which were at the core of Tim Mason's work. Here the differences thrown up by the histories of the two regimes are striking; the total defeat suffered (achieved?) by Nazi Germany and the unparalleled crimes committed in its name, as well as the postwar division of the country, no doubt made it far more difficult either to regard neofascism as a respectable political force or to look to the Nazi past as a source of postwar success than has been the case with Italy, where the leader of the neo-fascist Alleanza Nazionale managed to enter government coalition. The issue in Germany has not been so much *whether* to reject the Nazi past but *how* to reject it; in Italy, as Levy demonstrates, the issue has never been so clear, and recently it has become cloudier than ever. In both countries, however, there has been a growing appreciation that the Fascist and Nazi past cannot be bracketed out of the longer political or social-historical narrative. If the histories of Italy and Germany, or of twentieth-century Europe as a whole for that matter, are to be read as histories of 'modernisation', then the relationship of the processes of 'modernisation' to the Fascist and Nazi periods needs to be understood and explained.

Of course, drawing genuinely comparative conclusions is, and no doubt will remain, difficult and problematical. The histories we write, our historical knowledge, are dominated by national frameworks – framed by national constitutions, politics, economies, cultures and documentation. Furthermore, when attempting to compare and contrast modern Italian and modern German history we are building upon two national historiographies which, as Eve Rosenhaft observed in her report of the conference from which this book has emerged, 'have pro-

[12] As, for example, A. James Gregor, *Italian Fascism and Developmental Dictatorship* (Princeton, 1979), and Rainer Zitelmann, 'Die totalitäre Seite der Moderne', in Michael Prinz and Rainer Zitelmann (eds.), *Nationalsozialismus und Modernisierung* (Darmstadt, 1991), pp. 1–20. For a strong critique of the idea that National Socialism was 'modernising', see Hans Mommsen, 'Nationalsozialismus als vorgetäuschte Modernisierung', in Walter H. Pehle (ed.), *Der historische Ort des Nationalsozialismus. Annäherungen* (Frankfurt/Main, 1990), pp. 31–46.

ceeded on distinct and largely separate trajectories, in terms both of the objects studied and interpretative techniques'.[13] The distinctness and separate trajectories are apparent in the contributions to this volume, but so is the need to draw meaningful comparisons between phenomena which clearly were not unrelated. To return, in closing, to the concerns raised by Tim Mason shortly before his death:

> If we can now do without much of the original contents of the concept of 'Fascism', we cannot do without comparison. 'Historicization' may easily become a recipe for provincialism. And the moral absolutes of Habermas, however politically and didactically impeccable, also carry a shadow of provincialism, as long as they fail to recognize that fascism was a continental phenomenon, and that Nazism was a peculiar part of something much larger. Pol Pot, the rat torture, and the fate of the Armenians are all extraneous to any serious discussion of Nazism; Mussolini's Italy is not.[14]

If all histories are unique, if comparison is avoided, then there is little sense in studying history except for amusement and as an antiquarian pastime. And there can be few subjects where the need, the moral imperative, to avoid antiquarianism can be greater than the study of fascism. For if 'Fascism is the plague of the twentieth century', then we who 'are living in the twentieth century' need to understand it, both to comprehend what has shaped our world and to help us prevent the plague from spreading again.

[13] Rosenhaft, 'Fascism in Comparative Perspective', p. 201.
[14] Mason, 'Whatever Happened to "Fascism"?', p. 260.

I

THE 'CRISIS OF BOURGEOIS SOCIETY' AND THE ORIGINS OF FASCISM

ADRIAN LYTTELTON

I want to start by discussing the general problem of the comparability of Fascism and National Socialism, and of the processes at work in German and Italian society. It should be obvious that what I have to say on this notoriously difficult question makes no pretence to completeness. The major objection to any exercise in comparison which assumes that Italian Fascism and German National Socialism are members of the same class is that it ignores the terrible specificity of Nazism and, in particular, of Nazi racialism, and thereby banalises or trivialises it.[1] But I believe that we can recognise the autonomy and centrality of Nazi racial anti-Semitism, for which we can find no equivalent in Italian Fascism, without denying that there exist powerful similarities in methods of action and organisation and in the structures of power. Moreover these surface similarities reflect underlying affinities of mentality and belief, in the attitude towards violence, the mystique of leadership, and the unqualified adherence to a Darwinist vision of the struggle between nations for survival. One should talk of 'affinity' and not of 'identity', and it is well known that there is a critical difference, insofar as the Nazi language is one of racial community, whereas the Fascists insist on the primacy of the state. But the common element in the two is the aim to create a new level of national cohesion through a new regime, which would radically reverse the process of decline attributed to liberal and materialist 'decadence'. Compared with other forms of 'mere' nationalism, a distinguishing characteristic is the stress on the need to eliminate the 'internal enemy' as a precondition for success in the international

---

[1] Saul Friedlander, *Reflections of Nazism: an Essay on Kitsch and Death* (trans. Thomas Weyr) (New York, 1984), pp. 121–2. See also Karl Dietrich Bracher, 'Il nazionalsocialismo in Germania: problemi d'interpretazione', in Karl Dietrich Bracher and Leo Valiani (eds.), *Fascismo e nazionalsocialismo* (Bologna, 1986).

struggle.[2] One further comment should be made on anti-Semitism. It would be wrong to reduce racial anti-Semitism to a reflection of anti-communism or anti-internationalism. But there is an easy and logical passage from one to the other, which even Italian Fascism ended by taking. Finally, it should be noted that Italian Fascism was decidedly the exception – even in western Europe – so far as the marginal role of anti-Semitism is concerned, and that this must be explained by the unique degree of integration of the Italian Jews in the national community.

Now I come to the second and perhaps even more difficult point about comparability. How is it possible to compare 'the crisis of bourgeois society' in Italy and Germany? My short answer is that it is not, or rather that in order to do so we need a more flexible and differentiated vocabulary. I believe that it is only by attending to the different meanings of 'nation', 'state', and 'society' that we can arrive at an adequate analytical framework which will permit us to understand both the points of contact and the differences between the two crises and their outcomes. Again, it is not possible here to do more than offer a sketch for such a framework. Michael Mann has argued convincingly that discussion of the state and capitalism must start from the premise that the capitalist mode of production inserted itself into a system of states whose organisation and rules of competition were antecedent to it.[3] Without taking into account this prior existence of states, we will certainly not be able to situate the third term, 'nation', in its historical context with accuracy. The category of 'latecomers', developed by Gerschenkron as a tool for understanding the differing growth patterns of industrial economies, encompasses both Italy and Germany. But some are later than others, and Italy was, at a rough estimate, a good forty years behind Germany in its induction into sustained industrial growth. Instead, the formation of the nation-state took place more or less contemporaneously, with Italy in fact enjoying a small but significant lead. This difference between the timing of industrial growth and political change is important. Whereas in Germany national unification came after the beginnings of modern industrial growth and the integration of a national market through the *Zollverein*, in Italy it was the task of the national state to create the preconditions for these developments. If we look at the classic analyses of the state–society relationship in Italy and

---

[2] For a similar viewpoint, see Ian Kershaw, *The Nazi Dictatorship. Problems and Perspectives of Interpretation* (3rd edn, London, 1993), pp. 34–9. The importance of the myth of rebirth, or 'palingenesis', for Fascist ideology is stressed by Roger Griffin, *The Nature of Fascism* (London, 1993), pp. 32–45.

[3] Michael Mann, *States, War and Capitalism* (Oxford, 1988), pp. 118–20, 139–41.

Germany in the period 1890–1914 we find, I think, that their diagnosis is almost diametrically opposed: in Germany what is striking is the persistence of many elements of the political old regime in a rapidly modernising society, in Italy the strains set up by the existence of a parliamentary government and an active, fiscally ambitious state in a backward society. Naturally this contrast needs to be heavily shaded and three qualifications seem particularly relevant:

1. The efficiency of the state administration naturally tended to reflect conditions in civil society, rather than the formal nature of the political system.
2. The extension of the suffrage also corresponds with social development: Italy was forty years behind Germany in the introduction of universal suffrage.
3. In both nations uneven development – the backward south in Italy, but also the backward east in Germany – critically affects the argument.

How could two political cultures arrive at fascism from such different starting-points? Was not the difference in paths and stages of development reflected in a radically different posture towards modernisation? If modernisation has been the basic process of the epoch, and if Fascism was modernising while Nazism was archaising, how can the two regimes possibly have been of the same genus? One might suggest, for a start, that the perceived discordance between the political system and civil society is a common feature, even if the terms of the discordance are reversed. Secondly, as late-coming nation-states Italy and Germany shared some problems: nationalists in both countries felt the need for a 'surplus' of cohesion to enable them to catch up with the leaders. Hence they shared an exaggerated sensitivity to threats from 'anti-national' forces, Socialist or Catholic. In addition, we have to see that the 'catching-up' process – or modernisation if you like – altered the original terms of the state–society equation. While in northern Italy economic growth and the capacity for association or self-organisation of civil society was so highly developed by the time of the First World War that state structures and personnel came to seem backward by comparison, Germany acquired a highly modern constitution with Weimar. But it is just this 'evening-up', harmonising, or even reversal, of the original relationship which gives reaction its urgency. In Italy, the threat to old social structures becomes sufficiently intense to require the restoration of an authoritarian state; in Germany the threat of political modernity has to be countered by the mobilisation of archaic social and cultural sentiments.

Let me make some further comments on the Italian case. It was perhaps the crucial mistake of the Left to have confused a crisis *in* bourgeois society for the definitive crisis *of* bourgeois society – a mistake that was endlessly repeatable, given that crises are inherent in the structure of capitalism. Antonio Gramsci's famous comparison between the West and Russia, which emphasised the superior resilience of civil society in the West,[4] attains at least a retrospective insight. It was easy in Italy to deduce the definitive crisis of bourgeois society from the crisis of the liberal state. The perception of the inadequacy of state and party structures to cope with modernisation, the beginnings of mass politics, and the imperatives of international conflict was shared by many observers already in the prewar years, 1911–14. On the other side, the intelligent Right – from Pareto to Mussolini – did not see the structure of capitalism or bourgeois society as the essential problem in need of reform. Mussolini believed, even, that the NEP would lead to a restoration of capitalism in Russia.[5] Worldwide capitalism, indeed, was 'scarcely at the beginning of its history'.[6] Rather, it is the crisis of an inadequate liberal state which endangers the continuance of bourgeois society, and it can only be overcome by appealing to national values, which are also under threat. For Pareto, strikes are not a problem; they are perfectly legitimate.[7] Why, then, did he (together with Mosca) denounce, long before the war, the new 'feudalism' of the unions? Because it was a symptom of the decadence of the liberal elite, unwilling to use force even to uphold its own laws. In Pareto, of course, there is a critique of state interventionism in the economy; but his theory of 'demagogic plutocracy' really focuses attention on the collusion of apparently opposed political elites. He is a critic of capitalism, but not on economic grounds. The danger is that unrestrained capitalist innovation carries with it a moral disintegration which threatens the maintenance of the political order necessary to ensure its survival. The balance between politics and economics is disturbed. The entrepreneurs inhabit 'Cosmopolis', while only peasants and other backward classes remain sincerely loyal to the nation-state. As wealth increases, idealism decreases. Money softens, and soft individuals produce a soft state. The balance can only be rectified by violence, war or revolution. But in a world increasingly dominated by the speculators and their allies, where is the motive force

---

[4] *Selections from the Prison Notebooks of Antonio Gramsci* (ed. Quentin Hoare and Geoffrey Nowell Smith) (2nd edn, London, 1992), p. 238.

[5] Benito Mussolini, *Opera omnia* (ed. Eduardo and Duilio Susmel) (Florence, 1951–1980), vol. XVI, pp. 119–21. As early as 15 Jan. 1921 Mussolini wrote: 'That nothing communistic is left in Russia is henceforward beyond dispute.' He elaborated this theme further in numerous articles: e.g. *ibid.*, vol. XVII, pp. 204–5 (2 Nov. 1921): 'Russia is now a perfectly capitalist state ... a "bourgeois" government like all the others'.

[6] *Ibid.*, vol. XVIII, pp. 404–5, 15 Sept. 1922.

[7] Vilfredo Pareto, *Mythes et idéologies* (ed. Giovanni Busino) (Geneva, 1966), p. 216.

for violence to come from? It can only come from those classes who are losing out in the inflationary race for wealth – mostly the pre-industrial classes but also including small investors and state employees. At the international level, Pareto, like Veblen, sees Germany as advantaged by the relative weight and vigour which these classes have retained, and a war provoked by Germany may put an end to the plutocratic cycle. Why this digression on Pareto? Because no other writer stated with such brutal clarity the grounds on which bourgeois observers legitimised Fascist violence:

1. It substitutes for the action of the state, controlled by a do-nothing humanitarian elite.
2. Their readiness to use violence identifies the Fascists as the counter-elite whose emergence Pareto had predicted and justified. Before the war he had seen the revolutionary syndicalists as the most likely candidates, but then, of course, Fascism owed much to syndicalism both in terms of personnel and of theory. Truly, 'the victory of Fascism confirms splendidly the results of my sociology ... I can therefore rejoice both personally and as a scientist.'[8]

Mussolini viewed violence in this period in a very Paretian way, but to mobilise the violence of the Fascist movement required a different sort of legitimation. There is a problem about the rationality of Fascist violence. It is a dangerous mistake to imagine that Fascist violence was necessarily irrational.[9] The question of rationality depends on which actors one considers. From the standpoint of the agrarians, violence was a rational response to the threatened collapse of social norms and property relationships. From the standpoint of the political leaders of the *squadristi* it could be a rational path to social promotion. This kind of hard-headed and hard-hearted calculation was by no means incompatible with a romantic halo of gallantry, as the example of Italo Balbo makes plain. The *condottiere* is one of the Fascists' more significant self-images. Of course, the *condottiere* had to be on the right side, that of the nation, even if he served for pay and might change masters or become one himself. But there is some evidence that for the mass of the *squadristi* violence was a less rational response. Originally, the early *squadristi* who came prevalently from urban middle-class backgrounds

[8] Vilfredo Pareto, *Correspondance 1890–1923* (ed. Giovanni Busino) (Geneva, 1975), vol. II, p. 1114 (13 Nov. 1922). See also Richard Bellamy, *Modern Italian Social Theory: Ideology and Politics from Pareto to the Present* (Cambridge, 1987), p. 33.
[9] See Adrian Lyttelton, 'Fascism and Violence in Post-War Italy: Political Strategy and Social Conflict', in Wolfgang J. Mommsen and Gerhard Hirschfeld (eds.), *Social Protest, Violence and Terror in Nineteenth- and Twentieth-century Europe* (London, 1982), pp. 270–2.

responded to the call of the 'nation in danger', or 'the victory betrayed', fuelled by a more diffuse sense of fear and social resentment engendered by relative deprivation caused by inflation.[10] One could certainly argue that the repression of working class and peasant activism and the restoration of economic differentials were rationally chosen goals of collective action which over a long term achieved a high level of fulfilment. It was another mistake of the Left, even in some of its most intelligent exponents, to imagine that the petty bourgeois were always the dupes of the capitalists. Their support was purchased in material as well as symbolic ways. But if one does assume, as I think one should, that the fear for national values and national integrity was in many instances sincere, then one might see the *squadristi* as acting on the basis of inadequate information, both about the existing political situation, and about the aims of their own leaders. In this sense, one could identify a distinct element of irrationality in the violence of the *squadristi*, even where it had clearly defined political goals. This often betrayed itself in a strong sense of disillusionment, usually directed at the lack of radicalism of the movement and its failure to live up to its stated ideals of impartiality between the classes. Emilio Gentile, in the first volume of his projected history of the Fascist party, has drawn attention to the creation of a new collective mentality in and through the movement, in which the deficiencies of ideology were made good by ritual.[11] Without the secondary psychological gains which this made possible, disillusionment might have been more frequent.

One might suggest that there was also a 'supply-side' explanation of Fascist violence, which does have strong analogies with the German experience, though more with that of the Freikorps and the other formations of the immediate postwar period than with the SA. By this I refer to the existence of groups who resisted demobilisation. There were, first, the *arditi*, specialists in violence, with a high degree of initiative, who found in the futurism of Marinetti and Mario Carli the ideology they needed. This combined militant nationalism with an outward rejection of bourgeois norms of behaviour. Secondly, there was the larger pool of ambitious, under-employed ex-officers, who prepared, staffed and organised the violent expansion of the movement in 1920–1. Clearly, one cannot treat the existence of such groups as a sufficient explanation for violence in abstraction from the political and cultural context. But it was perhaps a necessary condition. Fascism, as distinct from some other hypothetical form of reaction, simply could not have existed with-

[10] For an example, see Mario Piazzesi, *Diario di uno squadrista toscano 1919–1922* (Rome, 1981), p. 141.
[11] Emilio Gentile, *Storia del Partito Fascista 1919–1922: Movimento e Milizia* (Rome and Bari, 1989), pp. 526–34.

out these men. The *ardito* is the prototype, ideologically and symboli-
cally, of the Fascist. In what sense are these individuals the product of
the crisis of bourgeois society? One can come nearer to the truth if one
poses the question in Italian, because in Italian 'borghese' also means
'civilian'. They were, essentially, the product of war, and of a war such
as had never been known before, and they formed not so much a marginal as a transitory social group, occupying the particular postwar con-
juncture. They challenged the ethics and mores of civil society in the
name of the myth of the nation. In his effort to escape from the stultify-
ing polarity of 'modern' and 'backward', Tim Mason coined a wonder-
ful phrase – 'a novel barbarism' – to describe Fascism.[12] This novelty
found its sources directly in the war and cannot be understood otherwise. Fascism was inspired by the modernity of war, not the modernity
of peace, and can perhaps best be understood, if one looks at its whole
historical trajectory, as the attempt to impose on a peacetime society
the techniques of wartime mobilisation. Technology, in this perspective,
was seen as an extension of the 'will to power', and as a means to renew
the 'primacy of politics'.

However, if it was only the Great War which brought into being this
potential for internal violence, the ideological frameworks within which
violence was given a meaning preceded its outbreak. One of the most
significant features of these ideologies is their assumption of the con-
vertibility of external and internal violence, war and civil conflict. War
is perceived as an opportunity for changing the rules of politics. War
will restore a proper hierarchy of political ends, in which the power of
the sacralised nation must take the highest place and relegate all partial
political interests to a lower plane of significance. The 'primacy of politics' can only be restored through the primacy of war. In this connection, it might be better to talk about the internal *significance* of war,
rather than the internal *causes* of war, since the crisis of the liberal state
in Italy should not be seen in isolation, but as part of the wider crisis
of the international order. Finally: 1918 marked both the apotheosis of
the nation-state as an organising principle in Europe and the emergence
of powerful internationalist challenges. Here one should remember that
the first nationalist mobilisation of the postwar period was in response
to Wilsonianism, although it was only an episode compared with the
continuity of anti-socialism. So the nation-state and its power was
exalted as never before, and threatened as never before.

I do not, of course, intend to deny that there was a social crisis of
the utmost gravity in Italy after the end of the war, only to maintain

[12] Tim Mason, 'Italy and Modernization: a Montage', *History Workshop. A Journal of
Socialist and Feminist Historians*, no. 25 (spring 1988), p. 139.

that 'the crisis of bourgeois society' may not be the only or the best way to describe the overall situation. The extreme diversity of Italy's social constitution makes any unified description difficult; even the war did not, in my view, bring about a full nationalisation of politics, and local motives remained of primary importance. What is most evident is a general crisis of agrarian hegemony, at least in northern and central Italy. This was no longer confined to the classic terrain of agrarian class conflict in the Po Valley, but spread to the previously tranquil *mezzadria* regions of central Italy. Tuscany, whose landlords had enjoyed a reputation for enlightened paternalism, was the theatre of some of the worst Fascist violence.[13] With the crisis of the *mezzadria*, a whole paradigm of social peace was shattered. In this upheaval, however, it is possible to discern the advance of a new *borghesia agraria*, at the expense of older landowning groups, in which the nobility still played a central role. Such was the case in Bologna, studied by Anthony Cardoza.[14] The postwar crisis, it is important to note, had been prepared by a long process of erosion of the traditional patterns of patronage and deference. A writer in the *Agricoltore cremonese* in 1913 observed that 'all the philanthropic substratum of the old relationships has ended, all the ancient customs have ended. Every servile or affective tie has been broken.'[15] This almost echoes Marxian language about capitalism stripping away the veils of sentiment from economic reality. One could say that for the agrarians it was the full realisation of bourgeois society which produced the crisis.

The industrial bourgeoisie was more divided and less committed to violence than the agrarians. The shock of the factory occupations was certainly profound, but once it had passed the industrial leadership showed a greater degree of confidence that the restoration of 'normality' could be achieved without outside assistance. It is not that the industrialists condemned violence (their press made many apologies for it), but it was seen typically as a necessity of limited scope and duration.[16] The viewpoint of the leaders of industry, however, was different from that of small industrialists in the provinces, who often shared the viewpoint of the agrarians.

According to Jens Petersen, the figures on Fascist membership show that the composition of the movement drew more on the older middle classes, and the better-educated, and less petty-bourgeois than the

---

[13] Angelo Tasca, *Nascita e avvento del fascismo* (Bari, 1965), pp. 177–9.

[14] Anthony L. Cardoza, *Agrarian Elites and Italian Fascism: the Province of Bologna 1901–1926* (Princeton, 1982), pp. 10, 450.

[15] C. Fumian, 'Aspetti culturali e politici dell'imprenditorialità agraria Lombarda, 1900–1920', in Istituto lombardo per la storia del movimento di liberazione, *Cultura e società negli anni del fascismo* (Milan, 1987), p. 369.

[16] See Adrian Lyttelton, *The Seizure of Power: Fascism in Italy 1919–1929* (2nd edn, London and Princeton, 1988), p. 212.

NSDAP.[17] However, some recent research has queried the 'petty bourgeois' prevalence in the Nazi movement.[18] In the Italian case, it certainly is worth paying particular attention to the crisis of the professions, or, in Robert Michels' terms, 'the intellectual classes'.[19] This struck at the heart of the liberal state. Giovanni Papini, in one of his more lucid moments, wrote in October 1919 of the end of the prevalence of the 'media borghesia liberale e discorritrice' – which can roughly be translated as 'the chattering classes'. With its decline, 'we have a struggle between Mammon and Caliban, between plutocracy and the proletariat . . . Whichever class wins liberty will be sacrificed . . . The intellectuals who side with one or the other will have ever less influence in the world. The rich buy them while they have the need, the poor distrust them.'[20] Mosca believed that the 'decimation' of the technical and professional classes had put an end to the hopes of a renewal of the elite.[21] Not only the intellectuals in the narrow sense but new and old professions feared the loss of their independent role and status. The fears and resentments which surfaced were not altogether new; the professions were chronically overcrowded and intellectual unemployment was no novelty.[22] But in the postwar situation the crisis in career expectations was aggravated by the shock of inflation and the loss of savings. This crisis was most keenly felt by the younger generations, the war generation and the postwar generation. In the Fascist province of Ferrara, almost one in five of the lawyers practising in the early 1930s had joined the party as a student.[23] As many as 12–13 per cent of all university and secondary school students were members of the Fascist movement, a far higher proportion than in any other social group.[24] Moral and material causes (the war experience and the inability of fathers to assure career opportunities for their sons) combined to produce a 'generation gap'. Subjectively, this was often lived out as a repudiation of bourgeois values, but in reality it was only some bourgeois values which were rejected. To a certain extent, of course, adolescent revolt was regarded as normal anyway; but what Fascism achieved was the institutionalisation of a permanent adolescence.

[17] Jens Petersen, 'Elettorato e base sociale del fascismo italiano negli anni venti', *Studi storici*, vol. XVI, no. 3 (1975), pp. 657–8.

[18] See Richard F. Hamilton, *Who Voted for Hitler?* (Princeton, 1982), pp. 420–1.

[19] Robert Michels, *Sozialismus und Faschismus in Italien* (Munich, 1925), p. 257.

[20] Giovanni Papini and Giuseppe Prezzolini, *Storia di un'amicizia, 1900–1924* (Florence, 1966), p. 317.

[21] Bellamy, *Modern Italian Social Theory*, p. 48.

[22] Marzio Barbagli, *Educating for Unemployment: Politics, Labor Markets, and the School System: Italy 1859–1973* (trans. Robert H. Ross) (New York, 1982), *passim*.

[23] Gabriele Turi, 'La presenza del fascismo e le professioni liberali', in Istituto lombardo, *Cultura e società*, p. 25.

[24] Petersen, 'Elettorato e base sociale', pp. 659–60.

One other aspect of the relationship between Fascism and the professions deserves comment. On the whole, Fascism attracted greater support from the lesser and newer professions. Lawyers were, after all, the backbone of the political class in the liberal state. Many joined the Fascist movement, but relatively their importance declined. On the other hand it seems – though more research is needed – that engineers, surveyors, veterinarians, and agronomists saw in the Fascist movement the chance not only to confirm their status *vis-à-vis* the working class, but to improve their status in relation to the older professions.[25] It is among these groups that one could perhaps find an attitude which could be described as 'reactionary modernism', to adopt Jeffrey Herf's label.[26] But the specific meanings would be somewhat different from those of the German case. There is no real equivalent to the atmosphere of cultural pessimism which enveloped the German discussion. At a slightly lower social level, teachers, municipal doctors (*medici condotti*) and communal employees complained of their precarious status and dependence on local notables and politicians. Among these groups there were many converts from socialism to Fascism. The price paid by these groups, in most cases not too unwillingly, was bureaucratisation, achieved through the medium of the Fascist *sindicati*. This encompassed artists and writers as well. The *inquadramento* of the professions required legal and administrative constraint as well as consent. But the defence of professional associations and their freedom was undermined by their lack of co-ordination and effective political representation. It is ironic that a movement which originally presented itself as the revolt of heroic individualism against bureaucrats and professional politicians should have ended by creating a political machine which vastly expanded both these roles.

Can one speak of a crisis of bourgeois society as the result of the establishment of Fascist power? The anti-bourgeois rhetoric of Fascism in the late 1930s must be read as a confession of failure. The bourgeoisie – defined as a 'political and moral category'[27] – had conducted a successful passive resistance to the imperatives of a militaristic modernisation. The spectre of a revival of the violent traditions of *squadrismo* was conjured up, for its value as a demonstration of the readiness to break with bourgeois norms, in the hope (not altogether unfounded) of

---

[25] See Mariuccia Salvati, *L'inutile salotto: l'abitazione piccolo-borghese nell'Italia fascista* (Turin, 1993), p. 166.

[26] Jeffrey Herf, *Reactionary Modernism: Technology, Culture and Politics in Weimar and the Third Reich* (Cambridge and New York, 1984).

[27] Renzo De Felice, *Mussolini il Duce*, vol. II, *Lo Stato totalitario, 1936–1940* (Turin, 1981), p. 98.

galvanising the younger generations into enthusiasm.[28] In the negative image of the bourgeois spirit presented by Fascism, one can discern a curious mixture of pre-modern and modern traits. The two most notorious initiatives of the campaign, that against the use of 'Lei' as a form of address and the attack on celibacy and the decline of the birth-rate, illustrate this ambivalent nature of the Fascist stereotype. On the one hand, the use of 'Lei' was attacked as a survival of courtly, deferential and pre-modern styles of behaviour; traditional social deference was perceived as an obstacle to, not as a reinforcement of, the modern virtues of military and political obedience, founded on a hierarchy of merit and an equality of submission. On the other hand, the seeds of demographic decadence were attributed to an excess of the spirit of rational calculation, and to the imitation of the more advanced bourgeois societies.

If these considerations indicate the limited impact of Fascism on bourgeois mores, one cannot, however, ignore the consequences for the bourgeoisie of the destruction of the 'public sphere': loss of autonomy, loss of self-confidence and a tendency to retreat into the intimate sphere of the family as a refuge. Yet this sphere of intimacy was more difficult to defend from public intrusion than in the past.[29] In this sense, Fascism accompanied and greatly accentuated features which have been held to be typical of an emerging mass society.[30]

---

[28] Simona Colarizi, *L'opinione degli italiani sotto il regime, 1929–43* (Rome and Bari, 1991), pp. 282–7.

[29] See Salvati, *L'inutile salotto*, p. 162.

[30] See the classic work of Jürgen Habermas, *Storia e critica dell'opinione pubblica* (Rome and Bari, 1988), pp. 183–8. (German edition: Jürgen Habermas, *Strukturwandel der Öffentlichkeit* (Neuwied, 1962).)

2

THE CRISIS OF BOURGEOIS SOCIETY IN INTERWAR GERMANY

BERND WEISBROD

When he began writing about Nazi Germany thirty years ago, Tim Mason might have been happy to proceed from the assumption that the crisis of bourgeois society which lay at the heart of the Nazi take-over was really a crisis of class domination, and that fascist rule was, in the Bonapartist tradition, a political alternative to the democratic impasse of class struggle – although he warned from the start that a price had to be paid by the ruling class for this 'primacy of politics'.[1] However, already in 1979, at the famous Ruskin College Workshop, he spelled out the three areas in which his kind of work would leave behind great deficits: the role of Hitler, the historical meaning of the Holocaust, and the motivation of rank-and-file Nazis in their quest for power.[2] Thanks to more recent research we have come a long way since then.[3] Yet, no less than when Tim Mason first pointed it out, what lies at the heart of these three deficits still needs addressing: a new reading of 'bourgeois political attitudes and ideologies in the twentieth century' – not of 'unique individuals and their utterly distinctive ideology' but their political common denominator so to speak, the collective fears and hopes which gave rise to Hitler, allowed the Holocaust to happen and fuelled the determination of the Nazi rank-and-file.[4]

---

[1] See his famous exchange with some East German historians in *Das Argument* (1966), translated as 'The Primacy of Politics: Politics and Economics in National Socialist Germany', in S. J. Woolf (ed.), *The Nature of Fascism* (London, 1968), pp. 165–95.

[2] Tim Mason, 'Open Questions in Nazism', in Raphael Samuel (ed.), *People's History and Socialist Theory* (London, 1981), pp. 205–10.

[3] See the distillation of a number of outstanding works by Ian Kershaw in his *Hitler* (London, 1992). On the rank and file, see Richard Bessel, *Political Violence and the Rise of Nazism: The Storm Troopers in Eastern Germany 1925–1934* (New Haven and London, 1984). The centrality of the Holocaust has now been firmly re-established after the misconceived efforts of Ernst Nolte at its 'historicisation' in the *Historikerstreit*; see Charles S. Maier, *The Unmasterable Past. History, Holocaust, and German National Identity* (Cambridge, Mass., and London, 1988).

[4] Mason, 'Open Questions', p. 209. Another *desideratum* spelled out in the wake of the 'Historikerstreit', a comparative approach to fascism, is squarely addressed in this

This may provide a good starting point for a reappraisal of the crisis
of bourgeois society in the light of one of the possible readings of the
'ends and beginnings' of the Third Reich which Tim Mason offered in
a posthumous text: the emergence of distinctively new attitudes to politics and public life in the aftermath of the First World War.[5] Obviously
such an, admittedly, rather loose definition of a general crisis in bourgeois society feeds very much on its own 'consciousness of crisis'.[6] Other
approaches certainly are possible and should be considered: for
example, as Tim Mason suggested, it would be worthwhile to probe the
hegemonic importance of integrative ideologies such as nationalism and
social Darwinism in the 'undisguised self-image' of struggle and competition which mobilised German society for a 'Third Reich'.[7] However,
in terms of the basic components of the crisis of bourgeois society, and
for the sake of comparison, we ought to look more directly at the processes in which bourgeois value systems were being eroded in the aftermath of the First World War and remade in the transition from the
Weimar Republic to the 'Third Reich'. This may not give us precise
answers to questions of bourgeois rule and governance, the interplay of
interests or of power alliances – all of which have been given their due
consideration.[8] Nevertheless, I would argue, the crisis of bourgeois
society is a story to be told less in terms of political power than of political culture – or, to put it another way, less in terms of its structure,
incomplete or otherwise, than in its contested meaning.

This is no easy task, especially if we want to trace the erosion and
redefinition of the common-sense value systems of bourgeois society in
their political representations. Three elements stand out here: (1)
notions of property (i.e. *Besitz*), (2) notions of learning and expertise
(i.e. *Bildung*), and (3) notions of civilised behaviour (i.e. *Anstand*).
These three elements comprised the canon so to speak of 'bourgeois
behaviour as way of life' (*Bürgerlichkeit als Lebensform*) – not necessarily
restricted to the bourgeoisie as an economic or social class but as a value

---

volume. See also Tim Mason, 'Whatever Happened to Fascism?', *Radical History
   Review*, no. 49 (1991), pp. 89–98.
[5] See Tim Mason, 'Ends and Beginnings', *History Workshop. A Journal of Socialist and
   Feminist Historians*, no. 30 (1990), pp. 134–50.
[6] Among writers and intellectuals such a sense of crisis is, of course, easier to detect.
   See T. Koebner (ed.), *Weimars Ende. Prognosen und Diagnosen in der deutschen Literatur
   und politischen Publizistik 1930–1933* (Frankfurt/Main, 1982).
[7] Mason, 'Open Questions', pp. 209–10; Mason, 'Ends and Beginnings', p. 139.
[8] For further reading see Eberhard Kolb, *The Weimar Republic* (London, 1988); Detlev
   J. K. Peukert, *The Weimar Republic. The Crisis of Classical Modernity* (London, 1991);
   Hans Mommsen, *Die verspielte Freiheit. Der Weg der Republik von Weimar in den Untergang 1918 bis 1933* (Berlin, 1989); Heinrich-August Winkler, *Weimar 1918–1933. Die
   Geschichte der ersten deutschen Demokratie* (Munich, 1993). See also the contributions
   to Ian Kershaw (ed.), *Weimar: Why Did German Democracy Fail?* (London, 1990).

system based on economic security and independence, personal merit and achievement as well as on social and moral responsibility. This still offered a wide variety of political options and was in many ways subject to the great denominational divide in German society which added a decidedly Protestant bias to the bourgeois value system. However, it held together a German society permeated by a growing sense of national self-esteem in the run-up to the First World War.[9] In these areas, it is argued here, some central assumptions about the legitimising rationale and the conventional morals of bourgeois society were challenged and redefined in the wake of the war. More than the loss of the Kaiser as father-figure or the catastrophic defeat, the erosion in underlying bourgeois values shifted the ground under Weimar's political culture and, at the same time, redefined the relationship between German civil society and the German state.

It is well known that the political formation of bourgeois society came under threat during the Weimar period: from the breakdown of bourgeois party politics, the retreat from open forms of public communication in favour of secretive channels of influence, the demise of the 'politics of the notables' (*Honoratiorenpolitik*) and the advent of a new youthful political style of mass mobilisation.[10] This is a complicated story, which cannot be explained in terms of a simple backlash to the red mob running wild (as in Ernst Nolte's rehash of the anti-Bolshevik propaganda of the early 1920s).[11] By the end of the Weimar period the red spectre had long lost what little relevance it may have had in the early years of the Republic. What needs to be explained is why the transformation of political legitimacy could still feed on a general feeling of anxiety that cut across most sectors of bourgeois society. An examination of the common-sense notions of *Besitz*, *Bildung* and *Anstand* singled out above might clear the ground for some tentative explanations.

[9] For the untranslatable concept of *Bürgerlichkeit* as 'Habitus', see Jürgen Kocka, 'Bürgertum und Bürgerlichkeit als Problem der deutschen Geschichte vom späten 18. zum frühen 20. Jahrhundert', in Jürgen Kocka (ed.), *Bürger und Bürgerlichkeit im 19. Jahrhundert* (Göttingen, 1987), pp. 21–63. See also the informative introduction (by David Blackbourn) to David Blackbourn and Richard J. Evans (eds.), *The German Bourgeoisie. Essays on the Social History of the German Middle Class from the Late Eighteenth to the Early Twentieth Century* (London, 1991), pp. 1–45.

[10] On the erosion of the political configuration of bourgeois society which started well before the war, see especially Hans Mommsen, 'The Decline of the Bürgertum in Late Nineteenth- and Early Twentieth-Century Germany', in Hans Mommsen, *From Weimar to Auschwitz* (Cambridge, 1991), pp. 11–27. On the breakdown of bourgeois party politics, see Larry Eugene Jones, *German Liberalism and the Dissolution of the Weimar Party System 1918–1933* (Chapel Hill, 1988).

[11] See the critique by Wolfgang Schieder, 'Der Nationalsozialismus im Fehlurteil philosophischer Geschichtsbetrachtung. Zur Methode von Ernst Noltes "Europäischen Bürgerkrieg" ', *Geschichte und Gesellschaft*, vol. 15 (1989), pp. 89–114.

Because of recent statistical findings about voting behaviour we have become reluctant to take at face value the arguments advanced by contemporary observers such as Theodor Geiger (who in fact did address such general feelings of anxiety and – equally importantly – other items of historical software like economic mentalities).[12] In the recent effort to recast the Nazi Party as a genuine people's party, the 'social panic in the middle classes' that these observers identified should not be forgotten. Given the rate of voter and membership turnover, it is not surprising that, as Geiger observed many years ago, the Nazi Party managed to make inroads into the *Arbeitermittelstand* (respectable working class) and even appeared to challenge the Centre Party as a genuine 'people's movement' (*Volksbewegung*) cutting across all social strata.[13] It even broke into some otherwise immune and fiercely hostile socialist and Catholic milieux – such as in remote parts of Thuringia or the Black Forest where the fragile social infrastructure, working-class and bourgeois alike, had more or less evaporated.[14] Much more significant, however, is the fact that it won majority status in Protestant home towns and in the countryside and did extremely well in university towns and the fashionable quarters of the big cities.[15] It was, as even Jürgen Falter concedes, in essence a successful *Sammlungsbewegung* (catch-all movement) of that bourgeois–Protestant electorate which already in 1925 had lined up behind Hindenburg as the candidate of the 'Reichsblock' against the Weimar candidates of the 'Volksblock'.[16]

This political tradition was clearly galvanised by the panic experienced for different reasons among the propertied or 'old' middle classes

---

[12] Theodor Geiger, *Die soziale Schichtung des deutschen Volkes. Soziographischer Versuch auf statistischer Grundlage* (Stuttgart, 1932; repr. Darmstadt, 1972). See also his 'Panik im Mittelstand', *Die Arbeit*, vol. 7 (1930), pp. 637–9.

[13] The vast literature is best summed up in Jürgen W. Falter, *Hitlers Wähler* (Munich, 1991), and Thomas Childers, *The Nazi Voter. The Social Foundations of Fascism in Germany, 1919–1933* (Chapel Hill, 1983). See also the special issue on 'Die NSDAP als faschistische "Volkspartei"', *Geschichte und Gesellschaft*, vol. 19 (1993).

[14] See, for example, Oded Heilbronner, 'Der verlassene Stammtisch. Vom Verfall der bürgerlichen Infrastruktur und dem Aufstieg der NSDAP am Beispiel der Region Schwarzwald', *Geschichte und Gesellschaft*, vol. 19 (1993), pp. 178–201; F. Walter, 'Sachsen – ein Stammland der Sozialdemokratie?', *Politische Vierteljahresschrift*, vol. 33 (1991), pp. 207–31; F. Walter, 'Thüringen – einst Hochburg der sozialistischen Arbeiterbewegung?', *Internationale Wissenschaftliche Korrespondenz zur Geschichte der Arbeiterbewegung*, vol. 28 (1992), pp. 21–39.

[15] In Peter Fritzsche, *Rehearsals for Fascism. Populism and Political Mobilization in Weimar Germany* (New York and Oxford, 1990), the *Bürger* mobilisation appears more as the backbone of the Nazi movement than merely its statistical *Mittelstandsbauch* ('middle-class belly'). See also Rudy Koshar, *Social Life, Local Politics and Nazism. Marburg, 1880–1935* (Chapel Hill and London, 1986) for bourgeois 'grassroots Nazism'; Richard F. Hamilton, *Who Voted for Hitler?* (Princeton, 1982) for successes in fashionable districts; and Thomas Childers (ed.), *The Formation of the Nazi Constituency* (London, 1986).

[16] Falter, *Hitlers Wähler*, p. 374.

in agriculture, trade and industry on the one hand and the professional or 'new' middle classes on the other – groups which were differentiated most obviously by their different economic mentalities. As Geiger saw it, to overcome that great divide was indeed one of the main aims of National Socialism.[17] To be sure, directing the struggle against the 'Marxist' working class gave it a political goal, an end to class conflict. However, it was more than just the fragmentation and failure of bourgeois party politics in the face of this task that made the promise of the '*Volk* community' (*Volksgemeinschaft*) so attractive; it was the perceived fragmentation of bourgeois society itself.

We know that panics have to do more with perceptions than with real life. As Heinrich August Winkler and others have shown, the economic crisis in the 'old *Mittelstand*' was blown up out of all proportion as a threat posed by modernity to the 'moral economy' of the home-town tradition and a secure and privileged life in ordered estates.[18] Its material claims reflected only the status insecurity which resulted from a basic loss in confidence in the traditional value systems of property ownership and work and from the perceived loss of political leverage and social respect in the Weimar system. This feeling of threatened identity was at the heart of the great longing for a strong state which would re-establish these value systems and remake civil society in their image.

However, the importance of 'pre-industrial' mentalities should not be overestimated here. The propertied petty bourgeoisie was quite open to bribery and yet hardly steeped in etatist concepts of corporate society; and among those in white-collar jobs and facing the completely new problem of mass unemployment, especially among the older generation, the lack of traditional self-esteem was widespread.[19] In the end, the much trumpeted German 'special path' (*Sonderweg*) might have less relevance here than the postwar experience of a total loss of trust in even the basic assumptions about well-established bourgeois life: neither *Besitz*, *Bildung* nor *Anstand* seemed to guarantee 'the well-ordered bourgeois existence' (Theodor Geiger) which alone could provide the societal trust necessary for the cohesion of a politically fragmented bourgeois society.[20]

---

[17] Geiger, *Soziale Schichtung*, pp. 117–22.

[18] Heinrich August Winkler, *Mittelstand, Demokratie und Nationalsozialismus. Die politische Entwicklung von Handwerk und Kleinhandel in der Weimarer Republik* (Cologne, 1972).

[19] For a critical reappraisal, see F. Lenger, 'Mittelstand und Nationalsozialismus? Zur politischen Orientierung von Handwerkern und Angestellten in der Endphase der Weimarer Republik', *Archiv für Sozialgeschichte*, vol. 29 (1989), pp. 173–98. The international dimension is discussed in H. Müller, G. Raulet and A. Wirsching (eds.), *Gefährdete Mitte? Mittelschichten und politische Kultur zwischen den Weltkriegen: Italien, Frankreich und Deutschland* (Sigmaringen, 1993).

[20] See D. Mehnert and K. Megerle (eds.), *Politische Teilkulturen zwischen Integration und Polarisierung. Zur politischen Kultur der Weimarer Republik* (Opladen, 1990).

The betrayal of this basic trust was due mainly to an inflation which played havoc not only among holders of government bonds but also in the status hierarchies of the civil service and other fixed-income professional groups.[21] It is now generally recognised that, despite the semblance of full employment, wage earners generally suffered disproportionately from the inflationary gap between money wages and prices and the breakdown of commodity markets.[22] However, the independent incomes of the 'rentier class' virtually disappeared, income differentials narrowed and even the owners of real property, the true profiteers from inflation, had to adjust to the diminution of their assets: the value of wills in the late 1920s fell to well below one quarter of the prewar level.[23] It may be less than convincing to argue that inflation rang the death knell for the middle classes generally; their property and income base was much too diverse for that to have been the case. However, it did turn the value system of bourgeois society upside down.

Rises in emigration, suicide and crime statistics give a clear indication of the underlying *Angst* which increased especially among the middle classes, the self-styled champions of respectability. They experienced a completely new uncertainty of property-related morals: speculation was rampant and fast-moving pleasure-seekers in the big cities provoked nervous irritation. Even property owners in the countryside, who in many respects did best out of the inflation, could lay claim to the status of 'winners as losers' in their fight against price controls.[24] In the ensuing political and legal wrangling about the revaluation of debts incurred during the inflation, different kinds of property owners were pitted against one another in fierce conflict. Principles of 'equity and good faith' in private contracts were suspended, and with them went all trust in a state whose taxation policies fell heavily on wage and salary earners,

---

[21] For the almost inflationary expansion of inflation studies, see the collections of essays in Otto Büsch and Gerald D. Feldman (eds.), *Historische Prozesse der deutschen Inflation 1914 bis 1924* (Berlin, 1979), and by Gerald D. Feldman, Carl-Ludwig Holtfrerich, Gerhard A. Ritter and Peter-Christian Witt (eds.): *Die deutsche Inflation. Eine Zwischenbilanz* (Berlin, 1982); *Die Erfahrung der Inflation im internationalen Zusammenhang und Vergleich* (Berlin, 1984); *Die Anpassung an die Inflation* (Berlin, 1986); *Konsequenzen der Inflation* (Berlin, 1989). All recently wrapped up in Feldman's *magnum opus*: *The Great Disorder. Politics, Economics and Society in the German Inflation, 1914–1924* (Oxford, 1993).

[22] See the discussion in K. Hartwig, ' "Anarchie auf dem Warenmarkt". Die Lebenshaltung von Bergarbeiterfamilien im Ruhrgebiet zwischen Kriegswirtschaft und Inflation (1914–1923)', in Klaus Tenfelde (ed.), *Arbeiter im 20. Jahrhundert* (Stuttgart, 1991), pp. 241–74.

[23] See Charles S. Maier, 'Die deutsche Inflation als Verteilungskonflikt: soziale Ursachen und Auswirkungen im internationalen Vergleich', in Büsch and Feldman (eds.), *Historische Prozesse*, pp. 329–42.

[24] See Robert G. Moeller, *German Peasants and Agrarian Politics, 1914–1924. The Rhineland and Westphalia* (Chapel Hill, 1986), esp. Chap. 5.

who saw their tax deducted immediately while other taxpayers were able to drag their feet.[25]

Most important of all, however, was the psychological impact of the working-class experience of a constant threat of irregular income and intermittent employment coming to be shared by bourgeois society at large: the erosion of the material and cultural mainstays of an aspired-to lifestyle, the loss of status security, the shortening of time horizons, the break-up of interpersonal networks, the lack of trust in the law. In short, this spelled the undermining of the very essence of 'bourgeois' existence, the very ideal of bourgeois social identity: security. This, in turn, created the widespread inflationary trauma which prevailed right into the depression of the 1930s, when any suggestion of reflation was defeated on any political pretext.[26]

In terms of political discontent there was no clear-cut target. In the course of the inflation the bourgeois parties lost whatever credibility they might still have salvaged from the revolutionary period. The frustration with bourgeois party politics arising from the blatant injustices of inflationary redistribution gave rise to a plethora of regional and special-interest parties whose support, in most cases, pre-figured the patterns of subsequent Nazi electoral successes.[27] In this respect the incubation period for disenchantment with bourgeois politics reached well back to the inflation period.

The general feeling of anxiety also galvanised the traditional 'anti-modernism' of the middle classes into the militant anti-Semitism and nationalism which reached its first peak in the years of the inflation. The anti-Semitic propaganda of the *völkisch* movement and conservatives alike drew heavily upon the inflation image of the money-changing and immoral city-dweller, an image which had first appeared with the figure of the war profiteer.[28] In this respect Hitler was just one of a

---

[25] See David B. Southern, 'The Impact of Inflation: Inflation, the Courts and Revaluation', in Richard Bessel and E. J. Feuchtwanger (eds.), *Social Change and Political Development in Weimar Germany* (London, 1981), pp. 55–76.

[26] See Jürgen von Krüdener, 'Die Entstehung des Inflationstraumas. Zur Sozialpsychologie der deutschen Hyperinflation 1922/23', in Feldman *et al.* (eds.), *Konsequenzen der Inflation*, pp. 213–86. See also the articles by Knut Borchardt and Gerhard Schulz in Gerald D. Feldman (ed.), *Die Nachwirkungen der Inflation auf die deutsche Geschichte 1924–1933* (Munich, 1985), pp. 233–96, on the long-term effects upon economic policy options.

[27] See Larry Eugene Jones, 'Inflation, Revaluation, and the Crisis of Middle-Class Politics: a Study in the Dissolution of the German Party System', *Central European History*, vol. 12 (1979), pp. 143–68. See also Thomas Childers, 'Inflation, Stabilization and Political Realignment in Germany 1924–1928', in Feldman *et al.* (eds.), *Die deutsche Inflation*, pp. 409–31.

[28] Strangely there still is no thorough study of anti-Semitism during the inflation. For the historical background see the classic account by Peter Pulzer, *The Rise of Political Anti-Semitism in Germany and Austria* (revised edn, London, 1988); and Shulamit

number of those 'inflation saints' who promised redemption through a
new moral order which would compensate for personal 'devaluation'
and humiliation by restoring pride of place to the *Volk*.[29]

Although everything seemed to revert more or less to normal after
the stabilisation crisis of 1923/4 – which brought high unemployment
and wages below those of 1913, tax incentives for capital formation and
a bourgeois government[30] – the sense of insecurity remained. It was
easily mobilised again when depression struck, threatening property first
in agriculture, which had come through the inflation debt-free, and subsequently in every trade and business. Mass unemployment rightly
assumes prominence in the story of the Great Depression. However, in
the German context it was perhaps less the working-class experience of
revolutionary strike action than the middle-class experience of inflation
which fuelled the panic of bourgeois society.[31]

Inflation thus triggered primarily a crisis in notions of *Besitz*, a crisis
which produced a long-lasting political disorientation among the 'economic bourgeoisie'. However, the spectacle of profits gleaned from
speculation and of immoral life-styles also called bourgeois concepts
of *Bildung* and *Anstand* into doubt. The relationship between personal
performance and reward was severed, and nowhere was this felt more
seriously than in the world of the professions. The impact of the
inflation on the 'educated estate' (Geiger's *Stand der Gebildeten*) might
have had its most devastating effect on the different sectors of the
Bildungsbürgertum, which in the German tradition was the incarnation
of the very ideal of bourgeois society.

The professional crisis which ensued[32] might even have been more a
crisis of the received value systems of *Bildung* and its central role in
bourgeois society than a material threat, at least to those already well
established in the professions. However, this must be seen against the

Volkov, *The Rise of Popular Antimodernism in Germany. The Urban Master Artisans, 1873–
1896* (Princeton, 1978).

[29] For discussion of some of the less politically minded inflation saints, see Ulrich Linse,
Barfüßige Propheten. Erlöser der zwanziger Jahre (Berlin, 1983). See also Ian Kershaw,
The 'Hitler Myth': Image and Reality in the Third Reich (Oxford, 1987), pp. 13–47.

[30] On bourgeois stabilisation, see Claus-Dieter Krohn, *Stabilisierung und ökonomische Inter-
essen. Die Finanzpolitik des Deutschen Reiches 1923–1929* (Düsseldorf, 1974).

[31] Significantly, despite the increase in the Communist vote, there was no real danger of
revolutionary upheaval. The Nazi scaremongers still fed on the pervasive notion of a
'Marxist' threat which in many respects was permeated with the anxiety of the 'inflation
trauma'. This helps to explain the inherent contradictions in the Nazi take-over,
especially with regard to economic policy; on this, see Avraham Barkai, *Das Wirtschaftssystem des Nationalsozialismus. Ideologie, Theorie, Politik 1933–1945* (Frankfurt/Main,
1988).

[32] This has only recently been fully investigated by Konrad Jarausch, in *The Unfree Professions. German Lawyers, Teachers and Engineers, 1900–1950* (Oxford, 1990). See also
Feldman, *Great Disorder*, pp. 527 55.

time-honoured German tradition of the *Bildungsbürgertum*: distinction lent by *Bildung* and the superiority of German *Kultur* over western *Zivilisation* were regarded as its most treasured national assets. In Wilhelmine Germany they had allowed the *Bildungsbürgertum* to identify its own self-image of social privilege and patriotic duty with a vision of the German *Sonderweg* which could now be shown to have failed disastrously.[33]

In real terms, civil servants, members of the free professions, and academics generally did not fare worse than other groups in the aftermath of the inflation; on the contrary, they fared rather better. The most vociferous of the Republic-haters, the German professors, even improved upon their privileged prewar position: already by 1924 full professors, whose income differentials had been slashed during the inflation, had increased their prewar advantage over average industrial wages by 30 to 70 per cent; and in 1930, when mass unemployment really began to bite, they still enjoyed real incomes at 40 per cent above the prewar level.[34] Yet this failed appreciably to endear the Republic to them.

Since the inflation had more or less wiped out independent incomes from capital, the *Bildungsbürger* who had subscribed heavily to war loans out of a sense of patriotic duty felt deeply wronged by their beloved Fatherland. However, inflation had also produced deep-seated anxiety about status differentials in all the professions, and especially in the civil service – the model of the German type of state-led professionalisation.[35] Inflation had drastically undermined the material position of the upper echelons of the civil service, and caused small-town civil servants to protest against cost-of-living bonuses for their colleagues in the cities.[36] It had destroyed the security of career patterns and hierarchies on which German professions had so prided themselves, and left an entire

---

[33] See the classic study by Fritz K. Ringer, *The Decline of the German Mandarins. The German Academic Community, 1890–1933* (Cambridge, Mass., 1969). For the historians' role in this tradition, see Bernd Faulenbach, *Ideologie des deutschen Weges. Die deutsche Geschichte in der Historiographie zwischen Kaiserreich und Nationalsozialismus* (Munich, 1980). See also Hans-Ulrich Wehler, 'Deutsches Bildungsbürgertum in vergleichender Perspektive – Elemente eines "Sonderwegs"?', in Jürgen Kocka (ed.), *Bildungsbürgertum im 19. Jahrhundert. Teil IV: Politischer Einfluß und gesellschaftliche Formation* (Stuttgart, 1989), pp. 215–37.

[34] See C. Jansen, *Professoren und Politik: Politisches Denken und Handeln der Heidelberger Hochschullehrer* (Göttingen, 1992), p. 29.

[35] Charles E. McClelland, *The German Experience of Professionalization. Modern Learned Professions and their Organization from the Early Nineteenth Century to the Hitler Era* (Cambridge, 1991).

[36] Andreas Kunz, *Civil Servants and the Politics of Inflation in Germany, 1914–1924* (Berlin, 1986); Andreas Kunz, 'Variants of Social Protest in the German Inflation. The Mobilization of Civil Servants in City and Countryside', in Feldman *et al.* (eds.), *Die Anpassung an die Inflation*, pp. 323–54.

generation of aspiring young academics in the lurch even when the
stabilisation re-established much of the previous balance.

For the student generation, the threat of proletarianisation rested on
the very real and shocking experience of the devaluation of the monthly
cheque and the personal degradation involved in the pursuit of
Bildung.[37] Students had to deal with a complete 'devaluation' of their
expectations and the promise of deferred security; the young generation
in fact had lost all sense and concept of 'civility as way of life'
(*Bürgerlichkeit als Lebensform*).[38] As well as the political pressures of the
new republic, demographic pressure led to an academic intake slightly
less exclusive in gender and class terms, and eventually contributed to
hitherto unknown levels of unemployment among academic recruits to
the labour market during the depression. However, levels of unemployment in the region of 20 to 25 per cent were spectacular only when
viewed against the previously privileged position of young academics;
they were hardly unusual for the majority of the population. Within the
civil service, traditionally the main employer of young professionals,
they merely reflected the breakdown of the state's system of probation-
ary employment.

Thus the state had failed its natural defenders yet again. By lowering
thresholds for entry into *Ersatz* professions – such as teaching and engineering – it engendered fears of a 'democratisation of the professions'
(*Berufsdemokratisierung*) and, of course, of 'double-earning' (*Doppel-
verdienertum* – the employment of both husband and wife). Nevertheless,
the professions during the Weimar period could hardly be described as
anything other than undemocratic and male-dominated. Despite a slight
broadening of the social and sexual base of the intake, self-recruitment
prevailed. Professional *Angst*, therefore, was politically diffuse although
generally aimed at the state as provider of professional privilege. There
were, however, large numbers of Jews in big-city, non-civil-service professions – between 30 and 50 per cent of Berlin doctors and about 26
per cent of all Prussian lawyers[39] – although the Jewish middle classes
themselves were caught up in the general experience of decline.[40]

[37] For an excellent summary, see Konrad H. Jarausch, *Deutsche Studenten 1800–1970*
(Frankfurt/Main, 1984), pp. 129–45.
[38] For a succinct account of the 'devaluation' effect of inflation on bourgeois values also
in terms of its philosophical implications, see K. Löwith, *Mein Leben in Deutschland vor
und nach 1933* (Stuttgart, 1986), p. 61.
[39] Avraham Barkai, 'Die Juden als sozioökonomische Minderheitengruppe in der Weimarer Republik', in Walter Grab and Julius H. Schoeps (eds.), *Juden in der Weimarer
Republik* (Stuttgart, 1986), pp. 330–46 (here p. 337).
[40] See Donald L. Niewyk, *The Jews in Weimar Germany* (Baton Rouge, 1980), pp. 11–
42; Donald L. Niewyk, 'The Impact of Inflation and Depression on the German Jews',
Leo Baeck Institute Yearbook, vol. 28 (1983), pp. 19–36. There was less of a decline for
the economic elite; see Werner E. Mosse, *Jews in the German Economy. The German–
Jewish Economic Elite, 1820–1935* (Oxford, 1987), pp. 323–79.

Yet even where there was no open Nazification of professional bodies the Nazis managed to mobilise the pervasive feeling among the *Bildungsbürgertum* of failed expectations and of the need for 're-professionalisation'.[41] Nowhere was this so evident as in the 'self-Nazification of the young *Bildungsbürgertum*' (Jarausch), which gave the Nazis majority support in the fiercely anti-Semitic student body well before 1933.[42] The lure of the Nazi promise drew upon the perceived obligation of the state to re-establish that which was deemed lost, i.e. bourgeois order in terms of the value-system of the professions. This entailed the guarantee of social distinction in, and national superiority of, a society ordered in estates.

Thus, quite contrary to the Nazis' quasi-revolutionary rhetoric, the promise of the *Volksgemeinschaft*, with its notions of a 'trusteeship' of every estate in the name of the people, fed precisely on the German tradition of a civil-service culture of duty and security. In fact, Nazi propaganda seems to have played less on allegedly pre-modern mentalities than on a combination of special-interest appeals to occupational estates and the evocation of patriotic duty and national solidarity, a combination especially (but not exclusively) successful among the middle classes.[43] The German professions had never been self-regulating to the degree known in Great Britain. This was due mainly to the prominent position of the professional civil service (*Berufsbeamtentum*), of the educated civil servant, for whom the Nazis clearly found 'the right language'.[44] However, even for rather 'unfree' professions the Nazi regulation of the professions was an extraordinary price to pay for the promise of remaking bourgeois society in their image. It eventually made them into 'accomplices' (Jarausch) in more than just deprofessionalisation.

To seek political redress from the state shows the inherent weakness of independent bourgeois value systems such as *Besitz* and *Bildung*. Above the level of party orientation, the political culture of bourgeois

---

[41] This point is made quite clear by Konrad Jarausch in *Unfree Professions*, pp. 92–111, and in 'Die Krise des deutschen Bildungsbürgertums im ersten Drittel des 20. Jahrhunderts', in Kocka (ed.), *Bildungsbürgertum IV*, pp. 180–205 (esp. p. 199).

[42] See Michael H. Kater, *Studentenschaft und Rechtsradikalismus in Deutschland 1918–1933. Eine sozialgeschichtliche Studie zur Bildungskrise in der Weimarer Republik* (Hamburg, 1975). See also Geoffrey J. Giles, *Students and National Socialism in Germany 1919–1945* (Princeton, 1985).

[43] See Thomas Childers, 'The Middle Classes and National Socialism', in Blackbourn and Evans (eds.), *The German Bourgeoisie*, pp. 318–37. See also Thomas Childers, 'The Social Language of Politics in Germany: The Sociology of Discourse in the Weimar Republic', *American Historical Review*, vol. 95 (1990), pp. 331–58.

[44] See Jane Caplan, 'Speaking the Right Language: The Nazi Party and the Civil Service Vote', in Childers (ed.), *The Formation of the Nazi Constituency*, pp. 182–201; Jane Caplan, *Government without Administration. State and Civil Service in Weimar and Nazi Germany* (Oxford, 1988), pp. 102–30.

society in crisis thus revealed its character as a civil-service culture rather than a civic culture. It was characterised by the idea that the formation of society was basically a state exercise and that, consequently, bourgeois society could also be dismantled and remade by the state. This is also why German civil society, weak and fragmented as it was, aspired to the status of a surrogate state, which the Nazis kindly granted in the guise of the *Volksgemeinschaft*.

Nevertheless this still does not explain why the anxieties and expectations noted above should manifest themselves in a mode of politics which called the most basic bourgeois value system – i.e. 'civilised' behaviour – into doubt. This was not a matter of *Weltanschauung* or party programmes, or of illiberalism or irrationality, but of the simple fact that the threat and use of violence was at the very core of the Nazi movement right from the beginning.[45] Not only was this plain for all to see and part and parcel of the self-motivation of Nazi activists; it also was bound up with the death cult of a movement which waved its blood-stained banner in front of society at large as a symbol of its bid for power.

From the Abel collection of autobiographical essays we know how Nazi 'old fighters' responded to that evocation of masculine camaraderie in the famous party rallies as well as in countless everyday brawls on street corners.[46] The violent disposition of the activists set them apart from respectable society, and was intended to do so. Theirs was a distinctly un-bourgeois counter-world. Yet we know much less about the appeal that this determined show of physical prowess had for onlookers, male and female, and on an insecure bourgeois society generally. How was it that the Brownshirts, despite their brawling and bad manners, still could be regarded in bourgeois circles with a combination of approval and disdain, as Friedrich Meinecke observed in September 1930?[47]

We need to explain the obvious fascination with this almost Sorelian cult of violence.[48] It is not just the amount of physical violence displayed by Nazi activists which is astonishing; it also is the tacit acceptance of

---

[45] For the legacy of violence in the Nazi movement, see Bessel, *Political Violence*; Richard Bessel, 'Violence as Propaganda: The Role of the Storm Troopers in the Rise of National Socialism', in Childers (ed.), *The Formation of the Nazi Constituency*, pp. 131–46.

[46] See Peter H. Merkl, *Political Violence under the Swastika. 581 Early Nazis* (Princeton, 1975); Peter H. Merkl, *The Making of a Stormtrooper* (Princeton, 1980).

[47] Friedrich Meinecke, 'Nationalsozialismus und Bürgertum', *Politische Schriften und Reden. Gesammelte Werke*, vol. II (Darmstadt, 1955), p. 442 (first published in *Kölnische Zeitung*, no. 696, 21 Dec. 1930).

[48] Bernd Weisbrod, 'Gewalt in der Politik. Zur politischen Kultur der Gewalt in Deutschland zwischen den beiden Weltkriegen', *Geschichte in Wissenschaft und Unterricht*, vol. 43 (1992), pp. 391–404.

this violence by those who flocked to Nazi ranks as members or voters but whose bourgeois value system ruled out any such violent behaviour on their own part, to say nothing of those political actors who counted on the Nazis' co-operation in the final bid for power. The judiciary, the military and the Reich government were reluctant to follow the lead of some state governments, such as that of Prussia, whose police administration repeatedly urged a clamp-down on the NSDAP on account of its violent record and unconstitutional behaviour. The state's monopoly of force thus was being slowly eroded and the legal safeguards for the constitutional order slowly transformed from 'the protection of the Republic' into some sort of authoritarian 'protection of the state', while political expediency ruled out any permanent dissolution of the SA by means of emergency decrees.[49]

When looking at voting behaviour and the effects of propaganda we must assume that, apart from its escalation in mid-1932, the public show of violence – the 'propaganda of the deed' – fed on its own success. Nazi political violence was targeted very carefully not just at the professed enemy, in particular in the spectacular head-on collisions with the Communists on their own territory; it also was aimed at a much larger audience which was willing in effect to delegate the use of violence.[50] As we know, the SA hardly ever ventured into hostile working-class districts without some sort of police protection, and they carefully avoided attacking the police outright. They secretly aspired to the place of the police, and they successfully played on the insecurity of policemen who, in their efforts to keep the Nazis at bay, were increasingly left in the lurch by the courts and the political authorities.[51] Accordingly, when it reported about the casualties which resulted from political confrontations the bourgeois press tended to give the Nazis the benefit of the doubt.[52]

[49] See Gotthard Jasper, *Der Schutz der Republik. Studien zur staatlichen Sicherung der Demokratie in der Weimarer Republik 1922–1930* (Tübingen, 1963). See also Robert M. W. Kempner, *Der verpaßte Nazi-Stopp. Die NSDAP als staats- und republikfeindliche hochverräterische Verbindung. Preußische Denkschrift von 1930* (Frankfurt/Main, 1983).

[50] This context usually takes second place in discussion of the escalation of violence. See Eike Hennig, 'Politische Gewalt und Verfassungsschutz in der Endphase der Weimarer Republik', in R. Eisfeld and I. Müller (eds.), *Gegen die Barbarei. Essays Robert M. W. Kempner zu Ehren* (Frankfurt/Main, 1989), pp. 107–30. For the Communist politics of territorial self-defence, see also Eve Rosenhaft, *Beating the Fascists? The German Communists and Political Violence 1929–1933* (Cambridge, 1983).

[51] See Peter Leßmann, *Die preußische Schutzpolizei in der Weimarer Republik. Streifendienst und Straßenkampf* (Düsseldorf, 1989). See also Richard Bessel, 'Policing, Professionalisation and Politics in Weimar Germany', in Clive Emsley and Barbara Weinberger (eds.), *Policing Western Europe: Politics, Professionalisation and Public Order, 1850–1940* (New York, 1991), pp. 187–218.

[52] See Thomas Childers and E. Weiss, 'Voters and Violence: Political Violence and the Limits of National Socialist Mobilization', MS.

Political violence in the Weimar Republic thus involved a very complicated process of public negotiation, which relied heavily on a kind of
popular approval for a successful challenge to the state's monopoly of
force.[53] The breakdown of political authority was as much its consequence as its precondition. However, at its root lay not just a problem
of disturbed young activists or the ideologies dished out to them. There
are signs, like the numerous SA revolts, that the violent road to power
was in part the self-propelled drive of a frustrated rank and file which
got out of hand. Yet its extent and public impact were also defined to
some extent by the degree to which it was condoned, tacitly or openly,
in bourgeois society at large. The climate of violence created by the
Nazis fed on an expert show of self-victimisation. This activated the
frustrated expectations and fears of large sectors of bourgeois society
which simultaneously abhorred the concomitant 'uncivilised behaviour'.
Political violence in Weimar Germany, just as race riots today, was as
much a problem of substance as of form.

During the Weimar period the fascination with violence had permeated bourgeois society ever since its wholesale arming in response
to the postwar strike movement. The breadth of this anti-revolutionary
mobilisation, especially in small towns and the countryside, has long
been underestimated. It quickly imitated and easily surpassed the short-
lived exercise of workers' control in forms of self-administration, mass
demonstrations and the display of arms.[54] Citizens' councils were established, political strikes and boycotts organised by trades and professions
and, most importantly, an entire generation of students was recruited
into battle as hundreds of thousands stood at the ready in the law-and-
order troops of the *Einwohnerwehren*. Not only did they exercise 'a form
of vigilantism directed towards social and regime control' which united
the fragmented middle classes in an effective *Sammlungsbewegung*; they
also provided first-hand experience of 'successful middle-class political
action . . . intimately associated with the use [or threat] of force [which]
was to have fateful consequences'.[55]

---

[53] On this double-bind effect of political violence, see Norbert Elias, 'Die Zerstörung des
staatlichen Gewaltmonopols in der Weimarer Republik', in Norbert Elias, *Studien über
die Deutschen. Machtkämpfe und Habitusentwicklung im 19. und 20. Jahrhundert*
(Frankfurt/Main, 1989), pp. 282–94.

[54] See the long-overdue redressing of the balance in Hans-Joachim Bieber, *Bürgertum in
der Revolution. Bürgerräte und Bürgerstreiks in Deutschland 1918–1920* (Hamburg, 1992).

[55] James M. Diehl, *Paramilitary Politics in Weimar Germany* (Bloomington, 1977), p. 59.
See also Peter Bucher, 'Zur Geschichte der Einwohnerwehren in Preußen 1918–1921',
Militärgeschichtliche Mitteilungen, no. 10 (1971), pp. 15–59; and Jens Flemming, 'Die
Bewaffnung des "Landvolks". Ländliche Schutzwehren und agrarischer Konserva-
tismus in der Anfangsphase der Weimarer Republik', *Militärgeschichtliche Mitteilungen*,
no. 26 (1979), pp. 7–36.

The memory of this bourgeois vigilantism which arose behind the lines where the Freikorps fought their bloody battles provided the script to which Nazi activists were playing in the death agony of the Weimar Republic. The Freikorps might have provided some bourgeois Germans with heroic compensation for having missed the war, and many Nazi 'old fighters' could pride themselves on such *Ersatz* baptisms of fire. However, the majority of the postwar generation had to make do with the late Weimar surge in hero worship and the concomitant denunciation of the Weimar home front. The intriguing image of the betrayed fighter returning to an ungrateful home was, however, more an officer's myth than a reflection of reality.[56] Yet this image could be fused to the collective memory of bourgeois vigilantism in the postwar generation's search for a purpose when the 'beautiful' tales of the real war were told. Whatever the relevance of the erotic aestheticism of literary death in the trenches or the militant concepts of political philosophy – *pace* Ernst Jünger and Carl Schmitt – the threat and use of force was far from alien to the postwar experience of bourgeois society.[57]

Before they sought out Communists on Germany's streets, the Nazis' political show of violence had drawn on the experience of the *Landvolk* movement, whose embattled farmers and trades people had resorted to violent boycotts and the occasional bombing of tax offices in defence of their property already in 1928/9.[58] At the same time, and paradoxically, it played on the counter-revolutionary passion for holding the line in defence of (bourgeois) law and order. Nazi activists offered, in effect, a very un-bourgeois – but oh so manly – denunciation of the rational politics which obviously had failed to defend even the most basic assumptions about the security of a bourgeois way of life. With its hallmarks, the notions of *Besitz* and *Bildung*, in tatters, the Nazi exercise in self-victimisation could be read as a cover-story for the general despair and political disorientation in bourgeois society at large. In this

[56] See Richard Bessel, 'Militarismus im innenpolitischen Leben der Weimarer Republik: Von den Freikorps zur SA', in Klaus-Jürgen Müller and Eckardt Opitz (eds.), *Militär und Militarismus in der Weimarer Republik* (Düsseldorf, 1978), pp. 193–222; Richard Bessel, 'The Great War in German Memory: The Soldiers of the First World War, Demobilization, and Weimar Political Culture', *German History*, vol. 7 (1988), pp. 20–34.

[57] There is a vast literature on this subject. On Carl Schmitt, see Joseph W. Bendersky, *Carl Schmitt. Theorist for the Reich* (Princeton, 1983); on Ernst Jünger, see Jeffrey Herf, *Reactionary Modernism: Technology, Culture and Politics in Weimar and the Third Reich* (Cambridge, 1984), pp. 70–108.

[58] For the link with the violent Freikorps tradition, see Ernst von Salomon, *Der Fragebogen* (Hamburg, 1951). See also Jürgen Bergmann and Klaus Megerle, 'Protest und Aufruhr der Landwirtschaft in der Weimarer Republik (1924–1933). Formen und Typen der politischen Agrarbewegung im regionalen Vergleich', in Jürgen Bergmann et al. (eds.), *Regionen im historischen Vergleich. Studien zu Deutschland im 19. und 20. Jahrhundert* (Opladen, 1989), pp. 200–87.

fundamental respect it seems that the violent Nazi appeal to bourgeois vigilantism was the most successful of a number of otherwise much more sophisticated but politically frustrated efforts at forming a bourgeois *Sammlungsbewegung* during the Weimar period.

This is not to deny the importance of fundamental political issues and promises, such as the defence of national honour against reparations or the brutal suppression of class conflict, for the Nazi appeal to bourgeois society in the alleged 'battle against Marxism' – the shorthand for everything the Republic stood for. However, the Nazis were successful in orchestrating the anti-republican consensus because they 'worked with the grain of bourgeois political sentiment'[59] or – in Tim Mason's words – in tune with everyday 'bourgeois political attitudes'. They spoke to the bourgeois experience of insecurity in property relations, status differentials, performance and reward as well as law and order, and they did so in a way reminiscent of postwar bourgeois vigilantism.

It was the 'historical regression' of bourgeois society involved in this exercise, as Franz Neumann saw it,[60] which was probably the clearest indication of the depth of the crisis. It involved – as does every effective attempt to control *Angst* – a serious and self-destructive double-bind: every such promise of law and order entailed a further threat of insecurity and danger.[61] This seems also to have been the secret of the 'squadrismo' in Italy, which not only offered a 'safety valve' for the pent-up violent pressures in postwar society but also promised a return to law and order to those scared by it.[62] Only a comparative history of fascism of the kind Tim Mason had in mind will bring out this common dimension in the postwar crisis of bourgeois society which, in the German case, set the stage for an irrevocable break in the history of civilisation.

Hitler, dressed up as the saviour of bourgeois society, would eventually destroy its last defences. His rhetoric of self-sacrifice drew on the sub-conscious death wish of a morally emasculated society.[63] In this process the conventional morals of bourgeois society were finally and utterly shattered: only the most primitive purging rituals like the mur-

---

[59] David Blackbourn, 'The German Bourgeoisie', in Blackbourn and Evans (eds.), *The German Bourgeoisie*, p. 30.

[60] See Franz Neumann, 'Anxiety and Politics', in Franz Neumann, *The Democratic and Authoritarian State: Essays in Political and Legal Theory* (Glencoe, Ill., 1957), pp. 270–300.

[61] See August Thalheimer, 'Über den Faschismus', *Gegen den Strom*, vol. 3 (1930), in Wolfgang Abendroth (ed.), *Faschismus und Kapitalismus. Theorien über die sozialen Ursprünge und die Funktion des Faschismus* (Frankfurt/Main, 1967), p. 33.

[62] See Adrian Lyttelton, 'Fascism and Violence in Post-War Italy: Political Strategy and Social Conflict', in Wolfgang J. Mommsen and Gerhard Hirschfeld (eds.), *Social Protest, Violence and Terror in Nineteenth- and Twentieth-century Europe* (London, 1982), pp. 257–74 (p. 263). See also his chapter in this volume.

[63] See J. P. Stern, Hitler. *The Führer and the People* (London, 1975).

derous Röhm *Putsch* or the all-engulfing obsession with the enemy within – and eventually without – could keep at bay the fears which had been set free by the numerous transgressions of the basic bourgeois value systems of *Besitz*, *Bildung* and 'civilised behaviour'. The civilising mission of bourgeois society mutated into a racist project, which not only destroyed the European Jews among others but also dashed all hopes of its own perfectibility.

However, that is a different story, and certainly not just an elite affair – although the 'one-dimensional' German elite rightly attracts much criticism for its moral indifference and functional perfection.[64] There also was a strong element of popular appeal in the charismatic leadership of the 'Third Reich' and even to some degree in the Gestapo terror which could feed on a surplus of denunciations. Nevertheless, 'the decomposition of conscience' (Norbert Elias) involved in all this, the underlying decomposition of the most basic tenets of bourgeois society, grew out of the crisis it experienced in the wake of the Great War. It was there that the fundamental values of *Besitz*, *Bildung* and 'civilised behaviour' were first called into question; it was there that bourgeois society learned to look to a new state to remake civil society in its image; and it was there that violence was experienced as a successful political force.

[64] See Rainer C. Baum, *The Holocaust and the German Elite. Genocide and National Suicide in Germany, 1871–1945* (London, 1981). However, see also Z. Bauman, *Dialektik der Ordnung. Die Moderne und der Holocaust* (Hamburg, 1992).

3

ITALIAN WORKERS AND ITALIAN FASCISM

TOBIAS ABSE

The Italian working class's experience of Fascism was very different from the German working class's experience of Nazism. The sort of questions that Tim Mason asked himself in the Epilogue to the English edition of *Social Policy in the Third Reich*, the questions that led him to doubt the value of his earlier analyses centred on class relations, do not need to be asked in the Italian instance. This was a working class which broke with the regime, not one that followed – or appeared to follow – the dictator to the bitter end. If 'the behaviour of the German population, civilian and military, from early 1943 to May 1945' might be described as 'incomprehensible',[1] the same cannot be said of their Italian counterparts. This difference in behaviour between the two working classes might be attributed in part to the differing levels of efficiency reached by the two dictatorships – Mussolini's Italian Fascism was an authoritarian regime which made a large number of compromises with existing political and economic elites, compromises which went far beyond any the Nazis made, and it had no real equivalent to the Gestapo or the SS, for the OVRA was little more than a slightly better organised version of the political section that had always existed within the traditional police. Therefore repression did not reach German levels: if political murders of anti-Fascists occurred in 1920–5 and again in 1943–5, for the bulk of the regime's existence *squadrismo* gave way to very traditional police methods; imprisonment and internal exile, not death, were the standard penalties for political dissidence. Therefore, there is a certain plausibility in Mason's argument that 'the crucial difference lay in the capillary character and the greater executive power of the various German administrative machines'.[2]

---

[1] Tim Mason, *Social Policy in the Third Reich. The Working Class and the 'National Community'* (Providence and Oxford, 1993), p. 276.

[2] Mason, *Social Policy*, p. 277.

However, the difference in response cannot be attributed purely to the relative levels of violence. The Fascist regime lasted nearly twice as long as the Nazi one, and a generation of inefficient dictatorship might have had as depoliticising an effect as twelve years of extremely intense repression. Therefore, it seems reasonable to argue that the Italian working class's experience of and response to Fascism can be understood only in the context of Italy's unique tradition of working-class militancy throughout the twentieth century.[3] This was something which Mason, despite his brave forays into comparative history towards the end of his life, never fully accepted – perhaps because of grave intellectual doubts about any thesis based on different national traditions and national political cultures as containing some risk of conflation into the very notion of innate racial characteristics that his whole historical/political project opposed. No discussion of the Italian working class and its peculiarities ought to ignore the tradition of *sovversivismo* that preceded the foundation of the Italian Socialist Party in 1892, let alone the Italian Communist party in 1921 – a tradition that grew out of the artisan radicalism of the nineteenth-century Anarchists and Republicans and preceded industrialisation[4] although it has frequently taken aggressively *operaista* (workerist) forms in subsequent decades. *Sovversivismo*, although condemned by Gramsci, has arguably been the dominant trend on the Italian Left in the twentieth century; the more respectable tradition of reformist Socialism embodied in Filippo Turati eventually imploded with the misdeeds of Bettino Craxi, and the PDS are Social Democrats only by adoption. *Sovversivismo* may well have been strengthened by the Fascist experience; it was certainly not eradicated by it. The much greater degree of alienation from both state and nation prevalent amongst Italian workers before Fascism illustrated by the pacifist line taken by the Italian Socialist party during the First World War was very important: if 1918 had a legacy for National Socialism as Mason so frequently argued, then the experience of 1915–18 was even more fundamental in the Italian case. French and British Socialists joined war cabinets; the Noskes of the SPD would have been only too willing to accept such an invitation had the Kaiser been willing to issue it; but Turati knew that any such deal would have destroyed his credibility with his members and voters.

---

[3] I develop this theme at greater length in my contribution to Stefan Berger and David Broughton (eds.), *The Force of Labour: The Western European Labour Movement and the Working Class in the Twentieth Century* (Oxford, 1995), pp. 137–70.

[4] Carl Levy, 'Italian Anarchism 1870–1926', in David Goodway (ed.), *For Anarchism: History, Theory and Practice*, (London and New York, 1989), pp. 25–78; Nunzio Pernicone, *Italian Anarchism 1864–1892* (Princeton, 1993).

In this context it is hardly surprising that Italian Fascism never really gained any widespread consensus of support amongst the industrial working class of northern and central Italy, with the sole, if extremely interesting, exception of Trieste (where the Fascists rallied a large section of the ethnically Italian workers alongside the Italian petty bourgeoisie in an alliance against the Slav workers who were more inclined to the political Left). The exception reinforces the general argument. Trieste, it must be remembered, was not only ethnically divided, it had also been under Habsburg, not Italian, rule before 1918 and its political culture owed more to the rival nationalisms of Austria-Hungary than to the anti-statist, anti-militarist traditions of the Italian workers' movement. The industrial cities were the strongholds of anti-Fascist resistance in the undeclared civil war of 1921–2, when the *Arditi del Popolo* of Livorno, Piombino and La Spezia fought back against the Fascist squads with far more organisation and determination than the leaderless and largely unarmed *braccianti* (landless labourers) of Ferrara and Reggio Emilia. Many historians have been too ready to assume that the behaviour of the rank and file can be deduced from the proclamations of party leaderships – that the rank and file in the militant cities of northern and central Italy followed to the letter the absurd pacifism of the Milanese middle-class intellectual Filippo Turati, who from the safety of a parliamentary forum solemnly instructed Socialists to turn the other cheek to the tide of Fascist barbarism, or the equally absurd sectarian bombast of the Neapolitan engineer Amadeo Bordiga that Communists should form no alliances in the fight against Fascism. It did not. Even if the only national dynamic behind an armed united front against the Fascists came from the Anarchists, whose leader Errico Malatesta argued for it throughout 1921–2, at the local level *sovversivi* of every stripe – Socialists, Communists, Anarchists, Syndicalists, Republicans – rallied to the defence of their neighbourhoods and fought the Fascists square by square, street by street, turning whole districts of cities like Livorno into 'no go' areas for the Fascists and their allies in the security forces. When attention was drawn to this phenomenon by the much maligned maverick Renzo Del Carria a quarter of a century ago,[5] the mainstream of professional historians tended to ignore his revaluation because of the dogmatic if heterodox Marxist-Leninist theorisation that accompanied it. However, my own more archivally based work on Livorno confirmed the validity of many of his observations, and further empirical confirmation from archival sources for Del Carria's unfootnoted assertions can be found in the more general

---

[5] Renzo Del Carria, *Proletari senza rivoluzione: Storia delle classi subalterne italiane dal 1860 al 1950* (Milan, 1966), vol. II, pp. 188–225.

descriptions of the *Arditi del Popolo* embedded in Claudio Natoli's *La Terza Internationale e il fascismo*, a work that contains rather more local and social history in tandem with its high political and institutional themes than its title might suggest.[6] It is of course true that there is no direct correlation between industrialisation and the presence of the *Arditi del Popolo*, that they were strongest in cities and towns where there was a strong Anarchist or Syndicalist tradition and that, although their rank and file used 'proletari' as a self-definition, they included many artisans, with the far from industrial city of Parma being the scene of the most dramatic and successful armed urban resistance to the Fascists in August 1922. Nonetheless, the extent of violent working-class resistance to Fascism has been underestimated in many general accounts of the 1918–22 crisis because of the agrarian lens through which the postwar crisis has been so frequently viewed.

What of working class participation in the Fascist movement? Insofar as there has been any serious investigation of the social composition of the squads in industrial and urban areas – and it must be said that the Italian Fascist movement has not been subjected to the kind of rigorous scrutiny that Richard Bessel, Conan Fischer and Detlef Mühlberger have conducted in the German instance[7] – there is no evidence of mass working-class membership outside the city of Trieste. My own investigations of the social composition of the early Livornese Fascists found the working class to be seriously under-represented by comparison with the census data, with the petty bourgeoisie constituting the largest single group amongst the *squadristi*.[8] Trieste was a border city which was bitterly divided between Italians and Slavs and had in any event been incorporated into the Italian kingdom only after the Armistice of November 1918. Whilst data cited by Lyttelton for Carrara suggest large numbers of marble quarrymen joined the Fascists,[9] this does not prove a great deal since quarrying was more or less the only occupation in this

---

[6] Claudio Natoli, *La Terza Internationale e il fascismo, 1919–1923: Proletariato di fabbrica e reazione industriale nel primo dopoguerra* (Rome, 1982).

[7] Conan Fischer, *Stormtroopers. A Social, Economic and Ideological Analysis, 1929–1933* (London, 1983); Richard Bessel, *Political Violence and the Rise of Nazism. The Storm Troopers in Eastern Germany 1925–1934* (New Haven and London, 1984); Detlef Mühlberger, 'Germany', in Detlef Mühlberger (ed.), *The Social Basis of European Fascist Movements* (London, New York and Sydney, 1987), pp. 40–139; Detlef Mühlberger, *Hitler's Followers. Studies in the Sociology of the Nazi Movement* (London, 1991).

[8] Tobias Abse, 'The Rise of Fascism in an Industrial City: The Case of Livorno 1918–1922', in David Forgacs (ed.), *Rethinking Italian Fascism: Capitalism, Populism and Culture* (London, 1986), pp. 68–9.

[9] Adrian Lyttelton, *The Seizure of Power: Fascism in Italy 1919–1929* (London, 1973), p. 71 and, especially, p. 454, where he notes that in October 1921 1,270 of the 1,600 members of the Carrara *fascio* were workers.

locality and larger numbers of quarrymen were violently anti-Fascist[10] – Carrara was a traditional Anarchist stronghold, so further questions about unemployment or previous criminality would need to be answered if we are ever to furnish a more nuanced explanation of why a minority of this occupational group in this particular locality joined the Fascists.

How closely linked was the rise of Fascism with the economic class struggle in the factories and other industrial workplaces? As Natoli emphasises at the national level and studies such as my own have pointed out at the local level, the rise of Fascism went hand in hand with a counter-attack by the industrialists on the working-class gains of the *biennio rosso* of 1919–20.[11] The years 1921–2 saw a whole series of lock-outs and mass redundancies in which political militants, whether Communists, Socialists or Anarchists, were singled out for dismissal. Whilst the exact details of the collusion between employers and Fascist squads in industrial cities and regions need further detailed empirical investigation of the type I undertook in my case-study of Livorno, any notion that the struggle inside the factory can be divorced from the struggle on the streets is either hopelessly naive or reeks of bad faith; one of the more wearisome aspects of Forsyth's recent one-sided monetarist interpretation of *The Crisis of Liberal Italy* lies precisely in this area.[12] There may well have been genuine economic reasons for employers to seek wage cuts or lay-offs in 1921–2 – firms such as Ansaldo and ILVA were in considerable difficulty – but the precise course of events cannot be divorced from the politics of the period. Workers' bargaining power within the factory was enhanced by the paramilitary strength of the *Arditi del Popolo* on the streets and, conversely, any defeat of the *Arditi del Popolo* at the hands of the Fascists or the security forces or a combination of the two paved the way for an attack on workers' conditions inside the factory. In the Livornese case, mass redundancies and wage cuts followed the Fascist conquest of the city in the aftermath of the defeat of the 'Legalitarian General Strike' and the enforced resignation of the Socialist council in August 1922 . The pattern was broadly similar in cities like Milan and Genoa.

Having surveyed working-class reactions to the rise of Fascism in Italy, it is essential to turn to the experience of workers under the

[10] Antonio Bernieri, 'La nascita del fascismo a Carrara', in *La Toscana nel regime fascista (1922–1939)* (Florence, 1971), pp. 677–703.
[11] Claudio Natoli, *La Terza Internazionale*, pp. 205–22 and 242–60; Tobias Abse, *Sovversivi e fascisti a Livorno: Lotta politica e sociale (1918–1922)* (Milan, 1991), esp. pp. 169–245; Ivo Biagianti, *Sviluppo industriale e lotte sociali nel Valdarno superiore (1860–1922)* (Florence, 1984), pp. 369–411; Pietro Bianconi, *Il movimento operaio a Piombino* (Florence, 1970), pp. 131–63; Antonio Bianchi, *Lotte sociali e dittatura in Lunigiana storica e Versilia (1919–1930)* (Florence, 1981), pp. 137–230.
[12] Douglas J. Forsyth, *The Crisis of Liberal Italy. Monetary and Financial Policy 1914–1922* (Cambridge, 1993), esp. pp. 236–94.

regime. This has become an historiographical minefield, where historians of the Italian working class have to contend not only with Renzo De Felice,[13] whose revisionist approach to the Fascist period provoked some of Tim Mason's most effective work on an Italian theme, but also with younger, less avowedly apologetic and more anthropologically influenced historians such as Luisa Passerini and Maurizio Gribaudi, who have sought to cast some doubt on traditional accounts which emphasised the dogged and stubborn resistance of the industrial working class to the blandishments of the regime.[14] With remarkable prescience Denis Mack Smith forecast long ago that De Felice's sprawling multi-volume biography of Mussolini would serve as 'a monument to the *Duce*'. Whilst De Felice's status and influence – a status and influence that will undoubtedly increase given the congruence between some of his theses and those of Gianfranco Fini, the self-styled post-Fascist leader of Alleanza Nazionale – within the patronage networks of Italian academic and cultural life make trenchant critical interventions such as those by Mason a constant necessity, the bulk of Italian historians engaged in serious work on Fascism have little regard for him, even if they do not always find it politic to say so. De Felice's claims about working-class consensus for the regime during the 1930s are closely entangled with claims about working-class living standards. In fact, it has now been shown beyond reasonable doubt, by Paul Corner amongst others, that working-class living standards declined during the Fascist period, not just during the depths of the Great Depression but from the imposition of *Quota Novanta* if not earlier.[15] Moreover, we have a detailed point-by-point refutation of De Felice's tendentious claims about increasing living standards during the 1930s in the meticulous work of Anna Cento Bull on the province of Bergamo, which also demonstrates the degree of dissidence present amongst workers, even female textile workers, in a province dominated by a white, Catholic, and not a red, Socialist sub-culture in the early 1930s.[16]

Luisa Passerini's work is far more interesting and original than that of De Felice and accordingly merits a rather fuller discussion. She is

[13] Renzo De Felice, *Mussolini il rivoluzionario, 1883–1920* (Turin, 1965); *Mussolini il fascista*. vol. I, *La conquista del potere 1921–1925* (Turin, 1966); *Mussolini il fascista*, vol. II, *L'organizzazione dello Stato fascista 1925–1929* (Turin, 1968); *Mussolini il Duce*, vol. I, *Gli anni del consenso 1929–1936* (Turin, 1974); *Mussolini il Duce*, vol. II, *Lo Stato totalitario 1936–1940 (Turin, 1981); Mussolini l'alleato, 1940–1945*, vol. I, *L'Italia in guerra, 1940–1943* (Turin, 1990).

[14] Luisa Passerini, *Fascism in Popular Memory: The Cultural Experience of the Turin Working Class* (Cambridge, 1987); Maurizio Gribaudi, *Mondo operaio e mito operaio. Spazi e percorsi sociali a Torino nel primo novecento* (Turin, 1987).

[15] Paul Corner, 'Italy', in Stephen Salter and John Stevenson (eds.), *The Working Class and Politics in Europe and America 1929–1945* (London and New York, 1990), pp. 154–71.

[16] Anna Cento Bull, *Capitalismo e fascismo di fronte alla crisi. Industria e società bergamasca 1923–1937* (Bergamo, 1983), pp. 142–66.

Italy's leading oral historian and one of the first Italian historical researchers to engage with important issues connected with subjectivity and the nature of memory, questioning rather naive views of memory as a pristine, unpolluted source of evidence that had previously been widespread amongst those attracted by 'history from below'. Her work undoubtedly has a stronger purchase on many aspects of everyday life amongst the working class than that of those historians, such as Spriano, who had concentrated on the history of working-class organisations rather than that of the working class itself, or than that of the 'operaisti', like Maione or Musso, who have concentrated on factory struggles and statistics on strikes and class composition to the virtual exclusion of everything else.[17] Passerini draws attention to previously rather neglected aspects of working-class culture, such as the way workers sang parodies of the Fascist songs or devised comic versions of the main Fascist slogans as well as to the symbolic significance of the struggles over colours in the Fascist period, when both red and black became politicised to a greater extent than had previously been the case. She shows how workers' attitudes towards work and the role work played in the constitution of the workers' own identity changed as deskilling started to erode traditions of craft pride. Furthermore, her extremely courageous and original work on abortion in the Fascist period shows how oral history can be used as a tool to investigate previously hidden areas of human, particularly women's, experience.

While it would be mistaken to dismiss completely her cogent arguments about the ambivalence of humour, which could be a safety valve as well as a sign of disaffection, the general tendency of Passerini's work is to suggest a high degree of working-class acceptance of, or complicity with, Fascism. Her quotation without critical comment of the judgment of the liberal intellectual Benedetto Croce – whose own record in relation to the Fascists was very far from consistent, arguably giving him the sort of bad conscience that would be all too ready to project his guilt on to others for whom dissidence would have been a much riskier option – that 'the working class accepted it: certainly no more, but neither any less than the others'[18] is one of the most overt examples of this. Frequently her own stance, influenced by anthropology and psychoanalysis, leads her to take a rather condescending attitude to the Torinese workers, as if they were members of some primitive tribe or deeply disturbed patients rather than a class with their own political

[17] Paolo Spriano, *Storia del Partito comunista italiano* (5 vols., Turin, 1967–75); Giuseppe Maione, *Il biennio rosso. Autonomia e spontaneità operaia nel 1919–1920* (Bologna, 1975); Stefano Musso, *Gli operai di Torino (1900–1920)* (Milan, 1980).
[18] Passerini, *Fascism in Popular Memory*, p. 188.

traditions.[19] She accepts De Felice's argument about working-class consensus in 1929–34 at face value, whilst showing no qualms about attacking Marxist historians, whether 'traditional Marxists' such as Spriano or 'the historical accounts of the New Left' such as Quazza.[20] Since Passerini freely admits that she is 'more concerned with drawing out forms of cultural identity and shared traditions than with the factual aspects of social history' and willingly concedes that 'the group of interviewees is not representative in the sense that this term is used in sociological research',[21] the most reasonable judgment one can make is that her work needs to be put in the broader context provided by other more conventional historical source material[22] rather than the wide range of anthropological, psychoanalytical, cultural and literary theory that she finds so much more appealing.

Gribaudi's *Mondo operaio e mito operaio*, whilst making use of oral-history methods and of concepts derived from social anthropology, is not so original in its approach as Passerini's work. Indeed it could be seen as merely an application of mainstream anti-Marxist Anglo-Saxon social science to an Italian milieu previously studied by Marxists. Although it contains a lot of interesting demographic material about the geographical origins of the Torinese working class and argues for the importance of the neighbourhood rather than the factory in the formation of Torinese working-class culture, its main impact on the debate about Italian workers and Fascism has derived from its contention that a younger generation of workers were attracted by the modernising aspects of Fascism – by motorcycles, cars, aeroplanes, sport, cinema and radio – and began to develop a new set of individualistic and consumerist values in place of the collective orientation of the older generation within the working-class community. Although Gribaudi makes some perfectly valid points about the attitudes of eleven individuals at a particular point in their lives, a number of serious objections could be raised to the attempt to turn this vivid testimony into the basis for wide-ranging generalisations about changes in workers' attitudes. First, Turin – the most modern industrial centre of the time – was not typical of industrial Italy as a whole. Second, eleven is a rather small sample, particularly if we remember that it is not a random sample and that all these individuals knew each other in their youth. Third, all members of

[19] This can be seen in her judgment that: 'The inescapable fact remains that we are confronted by a real and ruthless impoverishment of working class culture. We see it reduced to stunted forms of expression': Passerini, *Fascism in Popular Memory*, p. 125.

[20] *Ibid.*, p. 6.

[21] *Ibid.*, pp. 8, 10.

[22] In the Torinese case Giulio Sapelli, *Fascismo, grande industria e sindacato. Il caso di Torino 1929–1935* (Milan, 1975) is a useful corrective, particularly to Passerini's attempt to distance FIAT from Fascism.

the group were male – so it is not valid as evidence about the female half of the population. Fourth, the attitude of members of the group seems to have changed on marriage, since without the high disposable income characteristic of a particular phase in the lifecycle (i.e. being single), such a consumerist orientation was no longer possible. Fifth, Gribaudi makes no effort to explain how the old subversive tradition survived within the working-class quarters of Turin and re-emerged in the 1940s; the re-emergence signalled by the mass strikes of 1943–5 does not really tally with the radical rupture between the generations on which he places so much weight.

Whilst a discussion of the controversies aroused by the views put forward by De Felice, Passerini and Gribaudi form an unavoidable preliminary in any discussion of the relationship between the working class and the regime, any further exploration of this theme that seeks to ascertain the extent to which the *tradizione sovversiva* survived between 1922 and 1943 has to address a number of more general issues: the extent to which the mass organisations of the Fascist regime, such as the Fascist trade unions, the Fascist youth organisation and the Fascist leisure organisation, changed workers' attitudes; the effects of Taylorism and rationalisation (so important in the German case), insofar as they affected Italian industry, on the working class; and the extent to which Fascism was able to create a new working class from peasants or women without prior political traditions.

The Fascist mass organisations were designed to facilitate the integration of the lower classes – the industrial workers and peasants – into the nation-state, the project in which the Liberals had shown themselves such failures before 1922. Of all the Fascist mass organisations, the Fascist trade unions were the most obvious means through which the industrial proletariat might have been won over to the new regime. The Pact of Palazzo Vidoni between the employers and the regime, together with the anti-strike legislation of 1926, had left the Fascist trade unions as the only legal representatives of the Italian working class. However, the Fascist trade unions did not profit from this legal monopoly to any great extent. It is true that they tried to assert their autonomy between 1926 and 1928, often denouncing the employers and occasionally calling strikes to demonstrate their potential power, but the employers were able to ignore their empty threats and appeal directly to Mussolini, who was not prepared to risk his alliance with the industrialists for the sake of the pride of Fascist trade-union bureaucrats. Once the unified corporative organisation was divided into seven separate bodies in 1928, the Fascist unions were left virtually impotent, whatever vestigial beliefs in workers' participation may have lingered on in the minds of former Syndicalists within the bureaucracy. The drastic wages cuts in 1927 had weakened the Fascist unions early in their existence, and the decrees which sanctioned additional pay cuts in 1930 and 1934 further undermined their credibility in the eyes of their potential constituency on the factory floor. The massive growth in unemployment in the industrial centres during the 1930s was another indication of the unions' powerlessness; Corner argues that unemployment remained around 50 per cent for years in some provinces,[23] and unions that can neither defend wages nor defend jobs have no possible source of legitimacy. While the trade-union bureaucrats would have liked to have posed as the workers' champions, if only to increase their own prestige in relation to the leaders of other Fascist organisations, the regime gave them little opportunity to do so and frequently did deals with major employers over their heads – as was the case in Turin, where Agnelli preferred to deal with the Fascist party rather than with the Fascist unions. Whilst desperate workers may have turned to the Fascist unions as well as to other Fascist organisations in search of financial assistance in the early 1930s, this is not a reflection of any genuine consensus around bodies which had signally failed to defend either their wages or their jobs.

While the Fascist trade unions were the mass organisation which targeted the workers as workers, the Fascist youth organisations – the ONB (Opera Nazionale Balilla) until 1937, the GIL (Gioventù Italiana del Littorio) after 1937 – were likely to have had by far the greatest impact on working-class children brought up under Fascism. Whilst the population of certain agricultural provinces of southern Italy had a minimal contact with Fascist youth organisations, the same cannot be said of the industrial north. By June 1939 70 per cent of six- to twenty-one-year-olds in Turin were members of Fascist youth organisations.[24] Amongst the ninety-four Italian provinces Turin had the tenth place, Genoa the eleventh and Milan the fourteenth in terms of the percentage of the relevant age group joining the GIL in May 1939.[25] However, it would be wrong to assume that, because a large percentage of working-class youth had been through the Fascist youth organisations at some stage in their lives, they had been turned into devoted Fascists. Two reports on youth organisations in the province of Turin drawn up by the provincial party secretary in the 1930s make interesting reading in this connection. In November 1931 it was reported to Starace that 'unfortunately instead of diminishing, the detachment between Fascism and the youth sector seems to be growing . . . [There] is an aversion to what Fascism

---

[23] Corner, 'Italy', p. 160.
[24] Edward R. Tannenbaum, *Fascism in Italy. Society and Culture 1922–1945* (London, 1973), p. 139.
[25] T. H. Koon, *Believe, Obey, Fight. Political Socialization of Youth in Fascist Italy, 1922–1943* (Chapel Hill and London, 1985), p. 183.

represents and a repulsion for the idea of coming closer and understanding what Fascism really means.' In 1937 the provincial secretary sounded equally depressed: 'The young Fascists are deserting the meetings ... Only the books are full of members, but the truth is that the young no longer go to the groups.' Nor was Turin atypical – the situation was the same elsewhere in the industrial north, as this 1936 report from the Ligurian province of Savona, commenting on recent ceremonies involving the youth groups, makes abundantly clear: 'The Fasci Giovani were a joke from all points of view ... Discipline did not exist and I was forced to resort to severe punishment to get them to show up at meetings.'[26] Tannenbaum has emphasised that in the larger towns working-class youths belonged to different branches of the Fascist youth organisation from their middle-class contemporaries because of the geographical divisions between the classes. Tannenbaum also emphasises that even in the late phase, after 1939 when GIL membership was mandatory regardless of parents' wishes, this was only so for those still at school.[27] (Previously, working-class parents with leftist sympathies, less concerned about their children's career prospects than middle-class professionals, had been amongst the most obstructive.) This meant that vast numbers of working-class teenage boys, who left school before their middle-class counterparts, escaped its influence.

The third of the Fascist mass organisations that might have had a major effect on the working class and its attitude to the regime was the Fascist leisure organisation, the Opera Nazionale Dopolavoro (OND). The OND had the largest membership of any of the mass organisations, representing a very important part of the attempt to create a consensus for the regime, especially in the 1930s.[28] Under the inspiration of Mario Giani, a former director of Italian Westinghouse who claimed to have been influenced by American examples, the Fascist trade unions had originally seen the provision of workers' leisure facilities as a means of competing with the Socialists, who had built up an extensive network of cultural and educational organisations. The competition was in no sense a fair one; when in the early 1920s Fascist violence forced the closure of many of the Socialist clubs and societies, those buildings and facilities that had not been physically destroyed by the squads were often re-opened as part of this new Fascist Dopolavoro. In April 1925 Mussolini agreed to the Fascist unions' demands to set up a national Dopolavoro organisation, the OND, with Mario Giani at its head, but took its

[26] All quotations taken from Koon, *Believe, Obey, Fight*, p. 114.
[27] Tannenbaum, *Fascism in Italy*, p. 160.
[28] The membership figures were 280,000 in 1926, 2,780,000 in 1936 and 5 million in 1940: Renzo De Felice, *Mussolini il duce*, vol. I, *Gli anni del consenso, 1929–1936* (Turin, 1974), p. 198.

effective control away from the Fascist trade unions lest what he regarded as an unruly element, with a dangerous ex-Syndicalist component, use it to threaten his power base. The new organisation initially had a productivist and largely apolitical image, which gained it the support of employers, at least in principle, although few rushed to set up Dopolavoro sections in their own plants. In April 1927 Augusto Turati, the Fascist party Secretary, became OND leader, sacked Giani and turned the OND into a fully fledged auxiliary of the Fascist party. However, its image remained a rather austerely productivist rather than actively political one during the late 1920s and it was only in the 1930s under Achille Starace's direction that it became primarily recreational, concentrating on sports rather than technical instruction, and gained a genuine mass membership as a consequence. It ought to be stressed that its greatest success was amongst the salaried petty bourgeoisie rather than the working class, but nearly 40 per cent of the industrial work force, a minority but a very significant minority, had been recruited into the Dopolavoro by 1939. Despite its rhetoric about breaking down class divisions, it is worth noting that a number of its activities, including the more expensive sports such as skiing and motorcycling, were only really open to its non-working-class members. Nonetheless, the outings and sports activities organised by the Dopolavoro proved genuinely popular with large numbers of workers, who enjoyed the chance to visit other parts of Italy or to play football, a game whose popularity rose under Fascism, aided by the two Italian world cup victories of the 1930s.

However, these activities did not turn workers into ideologically convinced supporters of the Fascist regime. Corner puts this argument very forcefully, observing that 'Fascism had nothing to offer beyond the odd film or theatre production, generally of very low quality which the workers dismissed immediately as *roba dei fascisti* (more or less "Fascist rubbish"). This dismissal was based often less on ideological grounds than on the fact that the rhetorical material of Fascism was, in most cases, boring and laughable. Where it was not, it was not explicitly Fascist and therefore did nothing to reinforce the image of Fascism.'[29] The Dopolavoro had a minimal effect on the female section of the working class. As Perry Willson points out: 'The testimonies of female employees, however, suggest that they remained largely excluded from this shop-floor culture, and the Fascists' campaign to "nationalise the masses" through the OND had little impact on this half of the population'.[30] From the Fascist point of view yet another problem for the

[29] Corner, 'Italy', p. 164.
[30] Perry R. Willson, *The Clockwork Factory: Women and Work in Fascist Italy* (Oxford, 1993), p. 210.

Dopolavoro was that a number of large employers took it over for their
own ends, seeking to use sports or welfare provision as a means of bind-
ing the work force to the management rather than to the regime. De
Grazia has shown in some detail that this was the case at FIAT, which
was almost as distrustful of the OND as it was of the Fascist unions,[31]
and Willson demonstrates that the Fascist Dopolavoro only became an
active force at Magneti Marelli from 1934 onwards, and that even then
welfare facilities, such as the nursery, were kept separate as management
initiatives.[32]

At first sight it might be presumed that Fascism had a further weapon
in reserve against the working class: that – by promoting class collaboration between workers and employers to raise productivity within each
factory and by promoting greatly intensified competition between individual workers or small work teams seeking to maximise their bonuses
at the expense of other individual workers or work teams – Taylorism,
Fordism and other methods of scientific management might perhaps
have destroyed the older working-class traditions based on collective
identity and a shared antagonism to the employer, associated with *sovversivismo*. However, the issue of scientific management provides us
with yet another contrast between Italy and Germany. Despite the widespread discussion of Taylorism and Fordism all over interwar Europe,
not least in Italy, such methods were only introduced on a large scale
in Germany. It has been argued by Accornero that the prerequisites for
the introduction of scientific management are weak unions and a good
supply of unskilled workers.[33] If this theory had any validity, Fascist
Italy – with its powerless Fascist unions and mass migration of unskilled
rural workers towards the urban areas, regardless of Fascist legislation
against it – would have provided ideal conditions for the introduction
of scientific management. This was not the case. As Sapelli has pointed
out, 'Italy was far from providing fertile ground for the spread of scientific management methods. There were numerous problems'.[34] Among
these were the relatively low degree of industrial concentration, the limited size of the type of industry suitable for the introduction of mass
production methods, the large numbers of small and medium-sized
firms still using backward production methods and unable to modernise
owing to their diversified product range, the revaluation of the lira in

[31] Victoria de Grazia, *The Culture of Consent: Mass Organization of Leisure in Fascist Italy*
(Cambridge, 1981), pp. 74–81.
[32] Willson, *The Clockwork Factory*, pp. 164–211.
[33] A. Accornero, 'Dove cercare le origini del taylorismo e del fordismo', *Il Mulino*, vol.
241 (1975).
[34] Giulio Sapelli, *Organizzazione, lavoro e innovazione industriale nell'Italia tra le due guerre*
(Turin, 1978), p. 122.

1927 which had compelled firms in every sector to cut costs, and the problems of the financial markets which weighed heavily on small firms. Serious attempts to implement Fordism and Taylorism in Italy were confined to a handful of large industries – FIAT in Turin, the Olivetti typewriter factory at Ivrea and the Magneti Marelli light engineering factory at Sesto San Giovanni being the major examples. Even in the automobile sector, Americanisation was a conscious choice rather than an inevitable necessity; FIAT engaged in it but Alfa Romeo maintained traditional work methods. Rationalisation in Italian firms usually meant simply the use of bonus incentive systems such as the notorious Bedaux system and the speeding up of the work tempo rather than any more far-reaching re-organisation of production methods. Drastic cost cutting without the introduction of scientific management methods, such as that carried out after 1927 in the textile industry (still one of Italy's leading manufacturing sectors in this period), hardly served to promote social peace and individualism. Instead, despite political repression, it led to strikes and unrest amongst hitherto largely apolitical and unorganised women workers as productivity was raised by transparently exploitative methods such as making each worker operate more than one machine. The failure of the Fascist mass organisations to achieve a significant transformation of attitudes within the traditional working-class areas of northern and central Italy – southern Italy was not noted for either the size of its working class or the effectiveness of its mass organisations – and the minimal impact of scientific management in Italy demonstrate that neither political indoctrination nor changes in the labour process yielded the same dividends for the Fascist regime that such develop-ments yielded for the Nazis during the Third Reich (perhaps because neither was pursued with the same vigour as in the German case).

However, there was another means by which continuities in the working-class tradition might have been broken: namely the recruitment of a new working class. The case of Porto Marghera (near Venice) dem-onstrates what might have been possible if the regime had had more time or better economic conditions than history actually accorded it.[35] Thus it will serve to show that the argument being advanced in this essay does not proceed from the premise that all workers or even all Italian workers are naturally class conscious, let alone revolutionary, but merely that a tradition of class-conscious militancy established in Italy in particular pre-Fascist circumstances was not broken under Fascism because of the specific limitations which economic as well as political circumstances placed on the capacity of the Italian Fascist regime to change its own society. Between 1920 and 1945 Porto Marghera

[35] Francesco Piva, *Contadini in fabbrica. Il caso Marghera 1920–1945* (Rome, 1991).

experienced rapid large-scale industrialisation of a type that created a large factory proletariat where none had existed before. This great transformation occurred not during the Liberal epoch that had seen the growth of such centres of *sovversivismo* as Piombino or Sesto San Giovanni, but during the Fascist regime, even if the plans had been drawn up in 1917. Despite the original claims by the scheme's promoters that Porto Marghera's factories and shipyards would draw on Venice's skilled workers and artisans, the labour force for the new plants was largely recruited from the peasantry of the Terraferma. Only in the Cantiere Breda was any substantial use made of Venetian labour, and even there the former Arsenalotti were very much in the minority – a mere 21.8 per cent of the work force during the 1928–45 period, although this figure has to be compared with the minuscule 7.8 per cent in the Montecatini fertiliser plant during the period 1924–45. Although some of the Venetians at the Breda were *sovversivi* who had played an active role during the *biennio rosso*, their views had very little impact on the new peasant workers; there were no strikes in Marghera between 1927 and 1943. Not only was this new proletariat immune from the influence of radical urban workers or artisans, but the local peasantry from which the vast majority of the labour force was drawn was one with no tradition of agrarian class struggle. The peasantry of the Brenta–Dese zone were in the main very small leaseholders or very small proprietors with 5 hectares or less. The trend towards the parcellisation of these land holdings, which continued unchecked during the interwar period, meant that there was no mass flight from the land to the new industrial centre during the 1920–45 period. The bulk of the factory workers of peasant origin retained their link with the land, commuting from their farms on their bicycles rather than settling in the new speculative housing built near the factories. During the interwar years the factory proletariat of Marghera was not a stable group but one characterised by very high rates of labour mobility amongst skilled as well as unskilled workers. The high turnover was in part the product of the cyclical nature of industry in the area. All Italian shipyards were very dependent on commissions, and the new one at Marghera was not in a strong position to compete with more established shipyards elsewhere in the country at a time of stagnant or falling demand. For reasons connected with the agricultural cycle, a similar pattern prevailed at the Montecatini fertiliser works.

The employers were lucky that the peasants of the Terraferma fitted into these patterns and had little desire for permanent factory employment. Factory work was originally seen as an occupation for younger sons who were surplus to the farm's labour requirements, although as Marghera became more established the balance shifted within the next generation of peasant families as factory employment with its regular wage came to be seen as the best employment for elder sons and agricultural tasks were passed on from one younger brother to another in order to preserve the existence of the family farm. Both agricultural work on the family farm and factory work at Marghera fitted into a wider pattern: overcrowding on the farms had meant many peasants from this zone had been engaged in a wide variety of paid employment. The logic of the market had entered into their lives before the foundation of Marghera, but the peasant family household remained the central focus of their existence until the eventual flight from the land after 1945.

The case of Marghera shows the geographical limits outside which the collective ethic at the root of all varieties of the red sub-culture failed to penetrate the working class. Perhaps by 1945 the Marghera working class was a class in itself but it was not yet a class for itself. These workers had no experience of free trade unions before they entered the factory and the Fascist unions at Marghera were both weak and, insofar as they had any autonomy from the employers, formed a lobby for the unemployed workers of Venice against the peasant-workers of the Terraferma. Therefore it is not surprising that the newly recruited workers of Marghera understood the factory in a very partial and personalised way which owed much to the agrarian environment of their childhood and youth, and had little grasp of the overall production process or of power relations within the factory; they attributed arbitrary powers to their immediate superiors and deceived themselves into believing that the factory owners were remote but benevolent figures unaware of the abuses committed in their name. Given such a misunderstanding of their everyday working lives, the lack of genuine anti-Fascism and frequent adherence to the cult of the *Duce* should occasion no astonishment; political anti-Fascism was unlikely to make any impact on workers without a sense of collective identity rooted in workplace antagonisms.

The experience of Marghera was exceptional. For most of the Fascist period the size of the industrial working class was contracting rather than expanding – the only general expansion came in the late 1930s, with re-armament and autarky in the years immediately preceding the war that was to destroy the regime itself. Women workers in the interwar years cannot be seen as a 'new' proletariat analogous to the peasant workers of Marghera. In the first place it was contrary to the general ideological thrust of Fascism to encourage women to work outside the home. Although Willson argues that both widespread Fascist recognition of the inability of most working-class families to survive on one male breadwinner's wage and pressure from the capitalist backers of the regime, who wanted to employ cheap female labour, meant that this policy was applied to working-class women to a much lesser extent than to middle-class women, she acknowledges that Fascism did 'create some obstacles to working class women's access to the wage-labour market'.[36] Moreover, whilst Willson raises many questions about official census figures that show a slight decline in the numbers of women working between 1921 and 1936, she does not actually suggest any overall increase in full-time female industrial employment in this period. A second factor that militated against women being a new proletariat in the sense that the Marghera peasant-workers were, and thus becoming more susceptible to Fascist influence, was the influence of the family in the formation of their political ideas. Whilst Willson accepts that 'where the Church moulded women's political ideas, it was a conservative influence', she argues that 'in the formation of political ideas the Church was often subordinate to the family'.[37] As Willson suggests in a crucial formulation, that offers considerable support to the notion of a *tradizione sovversiva* being put forward in this essay, 'It is evidence of the strength of commitment to certain political beliefs that they could be passed down from generation to generation even under Fascist repression. The family was crucial in this. Women who did get politically involved almost invariably formed their ideas at home.'[38] Whilst female workers in rural areas without pre-existing traditions of political militancy were less likely to become politicised by factory experiences than male ones – although even here one has to recall the radicalising effect of cost-cutting on female textile workers in the early 1930s referred to above – in industrial centres of *sovversivismo* like Sesto San Giovanni women's political views were likely to be heavily influenced by leftist conceptions held by their fathers, brothers or husbands. Willson suggests that the experience of Magneti Marelli shows that even if participation in the Resistance amongst female factory workers may have taken different forms from that of male workers, it was nonetheless extremely significant and that women cannot be seen as outside, or hostile to, the general trend within the northern industrial working class at the time.

The Second World War affected Italian workers in a multiplicity of ways. Of these, the expansion of the war industries is perhaps the most obvious. However, it should be emphasised that the switch from peace-time to war-time production in Italy had to a large extent started in 1936, not 1940, with the invasion of Abyssinia, not the fall of France.[39]

---

[36] Willson, *The Clockwork Factory*, p. 7.
[37] *Ibid.*, p. 240.
[38] *Ibid.*
[39] The remainder of this essay draws heavily on my chapter on 'Italy' in Jeremy Noakes (ed.), *The Civilian in War: The Home Front in Europe, Japan and the USA in World War II* (Exeter, 1992), which develops many of these ideas at greater length and with more illustrative detail.

In the years 1935–9 11.8 per cent of Italy's national income had been spent on war preparations, compared with 12.9 per cent in Nazi Germany, and the mere 6.9 per cent in France and 5.5 per cent in Britain. Admittedly Italy pushed this up to 18.4 per cent of national income in 1939–40, but such a level of mobilisation was not really sustainable. The agreement between Agnelli and Mussolini to plan the development of war production reached on 24 October 1940 only achieved its targets in 1942. Italy's war economy proved less successful in the Second World War than in the First. If the 1938 figure for industrial production is represented as 100, 1940 saw Italy achieve 110, before falling back disastrously to 89 in 1942 and 70 in 1943.[40]

The most conspicuous phenomenon associated with the outbreak of war as far as the working class was concerned was not a switch from car-production to tank-production at FIAT, which had already started in 1936, but the entrance of large numbers of women into a labour market from which the Fascists had consciously sought to exclude them during the interwar years (even if, as Willson points out, the practice had often diverged from the theory). It is no accident that on 5 June 1940 previous Fascist legislation discriminating against women was rescinded and replaced by a decree allowing the substitution of female for male personnel in the public administration. This had results in a wide variety of sectors; women were seen driving trams as well as staffing the post offices. Even in large factories like FIAT in Turin or Pirelli and Falck in Milan, where at least some of the male work force were protected from the call-up, the lower grades included an increasing number of women, generally the wives and daughters of men who had been sent to the front. Women were the most mobile and marginal segment of the labour force and could be taken on and dismissed with equal rapidity. Nonetheless, this blatant exploitation cannot be seen as the whole story. Miriam Mafai has emphasised the subjective as well as the objective dimension of the female entry into the Italian labour force during the war, stressing the feelings of independence and personal responsibility it generated, especially amongst those women whose husbands or male relatives were away at the front.[41]

Food, or rather the lack of it, was a crucial aspect of the Italian working-class experience of the Second World War. The appearance of rationing, which started in May 1939 with restrictions on the serving of coffee in bars, was a sign of the imminence of war. Pasta rationing came

[40] Valerio Castronovo, 'L'industria di guerra 1940–1943', in Francesca Ferratini Tosi, Gaetano Grassi and Massimo Legnani (eds.), L'Italia nella seconda guerra mondiale e nella resistenza (Milan, 1988), pp. 237–56.
[41] Miriam Mafai, Pane nero. Donne e vita quotidiana nella seconda guerra mondiale (2nd edn, Milan, 1989).

in the autumn of 1940 and as the war went on the situation deteriorated with further restrictions in 1941. In the autumn of 1941 bread was rationed – 200 grams per head per day. This gave rise to much discontent and the regime reacted in November by increasing the bread ration for various categories it considered to be more deserving (or perhaps to possess greater potential for rebelliousness): for instance, the ration for miners and dockers was raised to 500 grams. The dire economic situation made such politically expedient decisions difficult to sustain for any length of time and in March 1942 the standard bread ration was reduced to 150 grams a head. War increased the gap between rich and poor and between town and country. In the countryside food consumption remained at more or less the prewar levels. For those deprived by poverty or geography of ready access to the black market, particularly for the poorer sections of the urban working class, life became harder and harder. By January 1943 the ration card of a worker in the Biella wool industry could enable him only to obtain food whose calorific value was an inadequate 1,000 calories a day.

Important as food shortages were in their effect on working-class morale, what really brought the war home to Italian workers in the most deadly way possible was the bombing. The impact of the bombing on the Italians cannot be measured in purely numerical terms, that is in terms of the casualties it caused. In the entire course of the Second World War 64,000 Italians were killed in bombing raids – only very slightly more than the 60,000 killed by bombs in Britain and far fewer than the number of German civilians killed in Allied bombing raids, which totalled somewhere between 600,000 and 700,000. Furthermore, of those killed in the Allied raids, only 21,000 had been killed by 8 September 1943, about half of the British total of such fatalities by that date. The crucial point is that the reaction of the Italian population to the bombing raids was very different from that of the German population to the Allied bombs, or indeed of the British population to the German bombs. In Italy bombing raids did not have the effect of unifying the population behind their own government and increasing their hostility towards the enemy, which was the majority reaction in Germany. In Italy the bulk of the anger aroused by the bombing was not directed, as the Fascist authorities had hoped, against the British and the Americans, who after all were genuinely responsible for the casualties in the most immediate, direct and physical sense; instead it was aimed against the Fascist regime and its alliance with Nazi Germany, a phenomenon that is virtually incomprehensible unless we assume the persistence of the *tradizione sovversiva* amongst significant groups within the working class. Given the extent to which the population, especially the lower classes, identified the Fascist regime with Mussolini, the remarks made about his speeches during these years give a good indication of popular morale. As early as June 1941 police informants reported Mussolini being described as 'a man in decline', by February 1942 they were saying 'he's old' and by August 1942 'he's finished'.[42] The reaction to Mussolini's broadcast of 2 December 1942, which caused panic by urging the rapid evacuation of bombed cities, was even more interesting. Police informants reported that it was widely believed that 'the voice heard on the radio is not the *Duce*'s voice'.[43] In short the myth of the *Duce* himself as all-powerful leader, a myth that permeated large sections of the working class in the course of the *ventennio* (the twenty years of Fascist dictatorship), had started to crumble, giving new heart to those workers who had never wavered in their opposition.

These subterranean currents of discontent that had expressed themselves in grumbling on the trams or slogans written on walls late at night in 1941 and 1942 rose to the surface in the spring of 1943. The outbreak of mass strikes in Turin and Milan in March and April 1943 was one of the most remarkable episodes in Italy's wartime experience, more remarkable in comparative perspective than the Resistance itself, since these strikes were directed at a native Fascist regime, not a foreign occupier. These strikes preceded the king's dismissal of Mussolini on 25 July by some months and cannot be linked in time with the disaffection of the traditional elites to which the king's action gave concrete expression. The working class acted alone, to some extent under the leadership of the clandestine Communist party, but without any support from the other social groups. The workers' action may be seen as prompting the subsequent action of the elites, who began to feel that if they did not act to remove Mussolini by conspiracy the workers would remove him by mass strikes and demonstrations, and that such events would lead not just political change but to dramatic social upheaval, sweeping aside capitalism along with Fascism. It should also be emphasised that the strikes broke out before the Allied landings in Sicily and not as a result of them – no Italian territory had been invaded in March. It is arguable that the strikes' organisers were influenced more by the course of the war in the East – by the Soviet triumph over the Nazis at Stalingrad – than by that of the war in the West – by Italy's defeats in North Africa. While by 1943 the regime was identified in the popular imagination with the increasingly hated Germans, the strikes of 1943, unlike the mass strikes of 1944, were directed against the native Fascist regime, not against German occupation.

---

[42] Nicola Gallerano, 'Gli Italiani in guerra 1940–1943: Appunti per una ricerca', in Tosi, Grassi and Legnani (eds.), *L'Italia nella seconda guerra mondiale*, p. 320.
[43] *Ibid.*

Food shortages, bombing and the military defeats in North Africa do not provide a sufficient explanation for the re-emergence of working-class militancy on this scale. The causes lay not just in the material conditions of 1943 but in the failure of Italian Fascism over two decades to win the lasting allegiance of a stubbornly recalcitrant working class, despite deploying a combination of repression, propaganda and mass organisations of a type that no previous Italian regime had had at its disposal. The strikes demonstrated the very fragile basis of Mussolini's conversion of the Italians to nationalism at the time of the victory over Abyssinia in 1936 – a conversion which some, but not MacGregor Knox, see as already reversed by June 1940.[44] And they demonstrated the enormous strength of the old subversive traditions which had out-lasted twenty years of Fascist dictatorship and which now identified themselves with the Soviet Union.[45]

---

[44] MacGregor Knox, *Mussolini Unleashed, 1939–1941. Politics and Strategy in Fascist Italy's Last War* (Cambridge, 1982), pp. 108–12.

[45] While it may seem very strange that a left-wing tradition which owed so much to Anarchism identified so heavily with Stalin and the Soviet Union, the reality of popular Stalinism has to be faced. 'Baffone viene' – 'the man with the big moustache [i.e. Stalin] – is coming' was a popular Resistance wall slogan. Enrico Mannari, 'Tradizione sovversiva e comunismo durante il regime fascista 1926–1943: Il caso di Livorno', in *La classe operaia durante il fascismo* (Milan, 1981), pp. 868–9, cites wall slogans in praise of Stalin in Livornese factories in December 1941, September 1942, November 1942 and April 1943. As Paul Ginsborg has argued recently: 'Russia's charisma in this period can not be overstressed. Tens of thousands of Italian workers looked to Russia for their model and to the Red Army for the decisive contribution to the creation of Communism in their own country. Stalin was a working-class hero, Togliatti his trusted emissary in Italy': *A History of Contemporary Italy. Society and Politics 1943–1988* (Harmondsworth, 1990), p. 54.

4

WHATEVER WAS THE ATTITUDE OF GERMAN WORKERS? REFLECTIONS ON RECENT INTERPRETATIONS

TILLA SIEGEL

For many years now, we have witnessed a protracted boom in research and debate on the question of whether or not German workers fell for Nazism – and why. For a social historian, especially for a politically minded one, this development could be gratifying were it not for the fact that the debate has become routinised and routine tends to make it seem superfluous to ask *why* a particular question should be discussed. Once the *why* seems self-evident and thus is no longer made explicit, an important point of reference for a critical reflection of the arguments put forward is lost. After all, academic discourses also reflect the changing interests or, for that matter, disinterests of researchers. Thus what, in the short perspective, might look like linear progress in the academic understanding of a particular topic in the longer perspective often turns out to be embedded in a cycle of forgetting, remembering and rephrasing that topic. This has been especially true in the case of 'workers' attitudes in Nazi Germany'. It is in order to hold up for reflection the motives for debating this topic, rather than to pretend to offer yet another answer, that this contribution begins by reviewing the fate of this theme in the cycles of academic business.

While the Nazi regime was very wary of 'its' workers and worried about reactions which might have threatened its power, contemporary critical observers, hoping for a revolution against the regime, also were deeply concerned with the attitudes of German workers. For example, in the 'Reports from Germany', which the Social Democratic Party in Exile collected and circulated from 1934 to 1940, 'the mood among workers' was a regular section dealing with the changing and diverse living conditions and attitudes of workers in Nazi Germany.[1] And for Franz Neumann, who wrote one of the first and still outstanding

---

[1] See *Deutschland-Berichte der Sozialdemokratischen Partei Deutschlands (Sopade) 1934– 1940* (reprint, Salzhausen and Frankfurt/Main, 1980).

analysis of the structure and practice of National Socialism, the question whether the Nazi theory of proletarian racism and racial imperialism had really permeated the ranks of labour was 'the decisive question, for upon the answer to it depends the fate of Europe. Upon it also depend, to a great extent, the methods of psychological warfare.' If, Neumann continued, the masses stand solidly behind the Leader and the doctrine of racial proletarian imperialism, 'then Germany's opponents can have but one war aim: to destroy Germany, divide her, and keep her enslaved. For if this is the case no attempt to drive a wedge between Hitler and the German people can be successful.'[2]

The Nazi regime had destroyed the working-class organisations and persecuted their active members. At the same time, it pretended to have ended the class struggle and promised better living conditions to the 'German' people at the expense of other 'races' – the attribute 'German' excluding from the 'German Folk Community' all Germans of 'non-Aryan' origin and those considered to be 'unfit' or 'asocial'. How difficult it was to decide what effect this double-edged policy had on the attitudes of workers is reflected in the 'Reports from Germany', in which each year evidence for workers' resistance to Nazi ideology was paralleled by signs of workers' compliance with the regime. And although Neumann agreed with other observers that by 1944 Germany had 'reached the stage where leadership and community adoration are generally considered to be what they actually are: bunk', he was not sure whether German workers had not fallen for the invitation of racial imperialism 'to join the ruling classes, to share their power, glory, and material benefits by being part of a colossal machine.'[3]

As illustrated by these two examples, contemporary critical observers, vacillating between hope and despair, had no unequivocal answer. In fact, for all their concern about workers' attitudes, they tended to concentrate on analysing the structure and the policies of the regime. However, they clearly understood the society of Nazi Germany as a class society and were intent on detecting the contradictions which might lead to a downfall of the regime.

With the defeat and division of Germany this impetus to understand society under National Socialism as one with many-layered contradictions slowly faded away and with it the knowledge produced by that impetus. In the course of the Cold War, research on National Socialism became increasingly dominated by a politico-academic blame-game between two competing camps. While the one side was intent on show-

---

[2] Franz L. Neumann, *Behemoth. The Structure and Practice of National Socialism 1933–1944* (New York, 1966), p. 190. This was first published in 1942 and as a revised edition in 1944.

[3] Neumann, *Behemoth*, p. 471 and p. 189.

ing how capitalism leads to fascism and the other side on treating the National Socialist dictatorship as an historical accident, neither side paid much attention to the history of everyday life and everyday attitudes in Nazi Germany. The question of workers' attitudes in Nazi Germany seemed to have been answered – by either one of two implicit assumptions.

The one side, usually referred to as Marxist interpretations, would insist that the Nazi regime was, after all, a dictatorship in a capitalist society and as such directed against the working class. Thus it seemed logical to see workers in their passive role as victims of the regime or, if their active role was taken into account, to restrict one's view to resistance fighters from the working-class organisations. For the other side, usually referred to as interpretations of totalitarianism, the Nazi regime was a dictatorship dominated by a totalitarian party – much like Stalinism. From this perspective, workers appeared to have been swallowed up in an amorphous National Socialist 'Folk Community' in which all class- or status-specific solidarity seemed to have disappeared. Consequently, it seemed logical to see workers as members of the fanaticised masses and thus as accomplices of the Nazi dictatorship.

This rough description of the two camps is not intended to belittle the research on other aspects of National Socialism done at the time. Furthermore, in the 1960s and up to the early 1970s the simplifying labels 'Marxist' and 'totalitarianist' had little to do with earlier and highly differentiated analyses by Marxists and/or those who used the term totalitarianism.[4] What concerns us here is that up to the early 1970s the topic 'attitudes of workers' had fallen victim to a blame-game in which it would have been easy to make a contribution. All one had to do was to fashion one's argument along one of the two established prejudices about workers in the Nazi 'Folk Community'.

A few years later, in the second half of the 1970s, it would again have been easy to make a contribution on this topic – for a very different reason. For by then *the* book had been published to which we could all refer, namely Timothy W. Mason's 'Working Class and Folk

---

[4] In this connection it is interesting to note the ambivalent treatment of Neumann's *Behemoth* in West German discussion of the 1960s and early 1970s. While the book was often highly praised and referred to as one of the early studies of totalitarianism, its contents were, then, rarely ever really discussed – which is not surprising, since it did not fit the Cold War either-or debate. In contrast to later interpretations of totalitarianism, which emphasised the monolithic aspects of the Nazi regime, Neumann had described it as an uneasy alliance of four power blocs – the party hierarchy, the ministerial bureaucracy, the armed forces, and the industrial leadership – and he openly talked of capitalism, of class rule and of class struggles. For the reception of Neumann's *Behemoth* in West German discussion, see Gerd Schäfer's epilogue to the German translation: Franz Neumann, *Behemoth. Struktur und Praxis des Nationalsozialismus 1933–1944* (Cologne and Frankfurt/Main, 1977 (!)).

Community. Documents and Materials on German Labour Policy 1936–1939'.[5] The subtitle is, indeed, a vast understatement of the work Tim Mason had presented. His documentation was combined with a comprehensive interpretation in which he discussed the continuities and discontinuities with the 1920s and early 1930s and in which he coined a new concept of resistance which went far beyond that of deliberate political opposition. Concentrating on the working class, he showed that manifold reactions and attitudes have to be taken into account if society under National Socialism is to be understood.

Tim Mason's motivation in undertaking this extensive study was not merely to colour in yet another blank in the map of German history. Lack of research in a field, he wrote, does not in itself justify doing research there – the historian not being a dentist who feels compelled to fill every hole he finds. Rather, Tim Mason was convinced that class relations are the constitutive element in the history of capitalist industrial societies. In his view, the *a priori* assumption which was implicit in so many interpretations until the early 1970s, namely that the Nazi dictatorship had produced a 'Folk Community' much like an amorphous beehive, stood in the way of understanding both the politics of the regime and the reactions and attitudes of the people it ruled. Even though the regime itself had tried to create the image of a classless 'Folk Community', it had operated in a capitalist society and as such in a class society. In fact, the regime itself was very 'class conscious' in that it always feared a recurrence of '1918', i.e. of a proletarian revolution. Numerous agencies reported regularly on the attitudes among workers, and highly differentiated social policies from outright repression to propaganda were employed to contain the working class. Thus to ask: what happened to the working class? and what were the workers' attitudes? were for Tim Mason questions central to an analysis of the structure and politics of the Nazi regime and of the impact it had on the continuities and discontinuities in German history.[6]

With his work, Tim Mason opened the doors to a genuine and hitherto unparalleled *social* history of Nazi Germany. By the same token, it is also true that the time was ripe for his work. In the course of the students' movement interest in the history of the working class had been reawakened as well as the urge to understand the political lessons of the experience with and under National Socialism. Just as Tim Mason was encouraged by the spirit of the time, the time was ripe for research such as that which he carried out. But although it is highly probable that

[5] Timothy W. Mason, *Arbeiterklasse und Volksgemeinschaft. Dokumente und Materialien zur deutschen Arbeiterpolitik 1936–1939* (Opladen, 1975).
[6] See Mason, *Arbeiterklasse*, pp. xix ff.

even without his book we would have witnessed an increasing interest in the social history of Nazi Germany, his study on the policy of the Nazi regime and on the reactions and attitudes of workers had a marked impact on later research and discussions.

In particular, four discoveries he put forward deeply influenced the ensuing research and debates. To list them briefly: one of those discoveries is that the regime was not only 'race conscious' but also 'class conscious' in the sense that its policies were not aimed in equal measure and equal form at all members of the 'Folk Community'. In another study, Mason pointed to a further aspect relevant to an understanding of Nazi policies, namely their gender-specific differentiation.[7] A second discovery is that the regime never trusted 'its' workers. A third one is that the regime had reason indeed to distrust 'its' workers: for even though it was successful in containing the working class, it did not find the 'total' approval which it tried to produce with its propaganda. And finally, the fourth discovery is that the regime was an uneasy alliance of competing power groups whose continual conflicts over spheres of influence also deeply affected the development of labour and social policies.

That fact that all four of these discoveries were basically 'rediscoveries' does not belittle Mason's achievement. Quite the contrary: by recovering and integrating into his study the impetus and analyses of contemporary observers of Nazi Germany as well as more recent analyses of the structure of the Nazi regime which had been marginalised in the blame-game dominating discussions on National Socialism up to the early 1970s,[8] Mason presented a comprehensive overview of the 'state of the art'. This he combined with hitherto unknown material and novel interpretations and thus opened avenues for a new understanding of social and political developments under Nazi rule.

One of the new perspectives which he offered and which are extremely important when discussing the attitudes of workers is what one might call the 'time factor'. Although Tim Mason restricted his analysis to the first half of Nazi rule, i.e. the period until the Second World War, he made it abundantly clear that any interpretation tends to be flawed which links the events or politics of earlier years directly with the attitudes or reactions of later years. Not only were the Nazi *movement* and

---

[7] See Tim Mason, 'Women in Nazi Germany, 1925–1940: Family, Welfare and Work', *History Workshop. A Journal of Socialist Historians,* no. 1 (Spring 1976), and no. 2 (Autumn 1976).
[8] Prior to the surge of research on working-class lives and attitudes in Nazi Germany were studies which criticised the monolithic image of the Nazi regime as it had been painted by both the 'Marxist' and the 'totalitarianist' camp. For an early overview of that discussion, see Hans Mommsen, 'National Socialism: Continuity and Change', in Walter Laqueur (ed.), *Fascism. A Reader's Guide* (Harmondsworth, 1979), pp. 151–92.

its proclamations before 1933 quite different from the Nazi *regime* and its proclamations after 1933; in addition, because of the uneasy alliance of power groups in the regime *and* because of the uneasy social and industrial peace, the politics as well as the propaganda of the regime changed drastically over time – and so did the hopes, aspirations, disappointments and reactions of the people it ruled. This is all the more true if we look at the entire period of Nazi rule, i.e. if we include the war period.

Two examples might suffice here to illustrate the argument. In the early years unemployed male workers were certainly pleased to find a job. (Many female workers might not have been so happy about being driven from the labour market.) However, it would be premature to assume that this produced stable social support for a regime that had destroyed all workers' representation and even liquidated parts of the Nazi movement itself. Furthermore, by the end of the 1930s, and even more so during the war, 'job stability' itself undermined consensus. Many workers – male and female – were clearly disgruntled about being forbidden to change their jobs for a better wage or about being conscripted to work in a factory important for armaments production and far away from their home. Or, to give another example, after the trade unions had been destroyed, the German Labour Front tried to win the favour of workers by presenting itself as the better organisation and by propagating the 'final overcoming of the class struggle' and the equality of all 'Folk Comrades' (*Volksgenossen*). According to the 'Reports from Germany' of the early years, some workers did indeed hope that the Labour Front would stand up for their interests. Yet, by the mid-1930s the Labour Front hierarchy and foremost its leader, Robert Ley, insisted that there should be 'equality' only in leisure time, not at the work place. Not much later, even that stance was given up and the purpose of the Labour Front office for the organisation of leisure-time activities, 'Kraft durch Freude' (Strength through Joy), was redefined. The task of this office was said to be no longer to create equality but to regenerate labour power so as to make war production more effective. Those workers who earlier on might have hoped for a better representation of their interests in the factory would have been blind not to see in the later years that the Labour Front officials were there to control them and to better their working conditions only if this would increase industrial efficiency.

Another new perspective offered by Tim Mason's study is what one might call the 'integration factor'. He did not spell it out explicitly, but his book showed that no society, at least no highly industrialised society, can survive if 'the people' are 'integrated' by sheer repression and nothing else. The Nazi regime most definitely could not rely on sheer repression to stay in power. On the other hand, it also could not rely on its propaganda finding whole-hearted support among the people. While Neumann wrote that people saw Nazi propaganda for what it was, 'bunk', this might not always have held true for all of the propaganda and for all workers. But it certainly held true at times for many workers and for much of the propaganda.

Tim Mason's study and an abundance of research subsequently have shown that integration into the Nazi 'Folk Community' was a complicated process. Between outright terror and political propaganda there was a wide range of measures taken in the effort to create, if not social and industrial *peace*, then at least a social and industrial *truce*. Here the conventional framework of interpretation which tries to distinguish 'typically' Nazi methods from methods 'normal' in an industrialised society can often be misleading. Labour policy, in particular, amounted to much more than direct dictatorial control and was more than a mere carrot-and-stick policy. In addition to control and material incentives, it also contained strategies to deepen hierarchies amongst workers along lines of race, gender and skill, programmes to train people in skills as well as in body and attitude, strategies to make people act according to the principle of efficiency not only in the work place but also at home. On the one hand, all these elements clearly had the function of stabilising consensus in Nazi Germany and were, indeed, propagated by the regime as being essential to a truly German 'efficiency community' (*Leistungsgemeinschaft*). But on the other, wage incentives, differentiation, selection, social engineering and the internalisation of the performance principle are also elements central to scientific management as it had developed in Germany as well as in other industrialised countries since the beginning of the twentieth century. Scientific management or, to use the more general German term, rationalisation was at the core of National Socialist labour policy – as its goal and legitimation and, at the same time, as a means of containing the working class.[9]

Mirroring the wide range of efforts to integrate workers into the 'Folk Community', there was a wide range of reactions, from wholehearted support for the regime on the one hand to outright political resistance on the other. Just as labour policy and many other aspects of social policy in Nazi Germany defy the attempt to draw a clear line between the 'typically Nazi' and 'normal' policies, in the case of the 'in between' attitudes and reactions it is also hard to draw a clear line and to define whether or not they reflected deliberate opposition to the regime.

When, for example, from the late 1930s onwards workers stayed away from work, they were violating the law and were punished accordingly –

---

[9] See Tilla Siegel, *Leistung und Lohn in der nationalsozialistischen 'Ordnung der Arbeit'* (Opladen, 1989); and Tilla Siegel and Thomas von Freyberg, *Industrielle Rationalisierung unter dem Nationalsozialismus* (Frankfurt/Main and New York, 1991).

if caught. But there is no saying whether they did this as a protest against the regime or merely in order to force their employer to let them go to a better-paid job. Or: how are we to interpret reports that employers were not very satisfied with the performance of women who were conscripted to work in armaments production? Did these women work slowly in order to be sent home, or to sabotage armaments production, or both? By the same token, the many workers – male and female – who stayed at their jobs and worked industriously might have had numerous reasons for doing so, only one of them possibly being the wish to support the regime; other, quite possible, reasons were fear of repression, the necessity to earn one's living and/or pride in performing well. And, finally, the mere fact that people, as was reported, did enjoy many of the offerings of 'Strength through Joy' or went to classes for professional training organised by the Labour Front does not necessarily indicate that they approved of the Labour Front and thus of the regime.

These are but a few examples given to illustrate, not to prove, the argument that there can be no unequivocal answer to the question of workers' attitudes in Nazi Germany. One main reason for this was the policy of the regime itself. To sum up: firstly, in its social policy the regime was race, class, and gender conscious. That implied the deliberate exclusion of those from the 'Folk Community' who were of the wrong 'race', who were considered to be 'asocial' or who had the wrong political inclination. It also implied highly differentiated policies aimed at the various groups who made up the 'Folk Community'. Secondly, not least because of the power conflicts within the regime, social policies changed drastically over time. Thirdly, when the regime legitimised its social policies, it made use not only of Nazi ideology, of 'blood and soil' or 'master race' slogans for example, but also of values accepted as normal in other political circumstances, such as 'law and order' or 'efficiency'. As for the reactions, we cannot assume that they were uniform for the 'Folk Community' as a whole and over time, nor can we assume that reactions of individuals were always consistent or that a certain reaction implied only one possible attitude.

Tim Mason did not systematically discuss the effects of the 'time factor' and the 'integration factor' – terms chosen here to underscore the argument. But by pointing to the diversity of Nazi social policies and to the diversity of reactions, his analysis and documentation have triggered a tremendous amount of research on specific aspects of Nazi social policy, on changes in the everyday life of specific groups of the population and on specific reactions and attitudes.[10] And yet, there is

[10] For a report on the state of the debate by the end of the 1980s, see Ulrich Herbert, 'Arbeiterschaft im "Dritten Reich". Zwischenbilanz und offene Fragen', *Geschichte und Gesellschaft*, vol. 15 (1989), pp. 320–60.

little room for complacency – especially if we consider how resilient discourses in other social sciences have been in the face of recent historical findings.

In political psychology, for example, it still seems acceptable to proceed from the assumption that 'the' people did fall hook, line and sinker for Nazism. How else can it be explained that a contribution to a quite influential volume on new trends in political psychology merely refers to a few juicy pieces of Nazi propaganda and then proceeds to analyse why the 'Folk Comrade' (*Volksgenosse*) fell for this propaganda?[11] With this generalised individual the author replicates, albeit unintentionally, Nazi propaganda language. He blithely ignores historical research which since the late 1970s has presented ample proof that *the* 'Folk Comrade', in the sense of an atomised, one-dimensional and uniform subject, existed only in the fantasies of that very Nazi propaganda and that the mechanisms of integration as well as reactions to them were manifold and must be analysed as such.

A peculiar immunity to historical research and the implicit return to the generalised individual can also be seen in the ongoing debate about whether women in Nazi Germany were 'victims or perpetrators'.[12] In this debate earlier women's history research is accused of depicting women solely as victims whereas, it is argued, German women who were not persecuted by the regime or who did not actively fight it should be seen as 'perpetrators'. As wardens in concentration camps and as functionaries in Nazi organisations or in positions of Nazi 'racial hygiene', it is pointed out, German women participated in the atrocities of the regime; and as wives or mothers of chauvinist German men and as beneficiaries of Nazi social policies they were at least co-perpetrators. However, this either-or argumentation not only ignores the scope and development of research on women in Nazi Germany; it also tends to distort the motives of the researchers. Although women's history initially did emphasise the sexist bias of Nazi politics and propaganda, its aim was not merely to prove that women were victims. Just as Tim Mason did by introducing the category 'class', women's history research has introduced the category 'gender' in order to dismantle the image of a uniform National Socialist 'Folk Community'. In so doing, women's history research since the late 1970s has produced highly differentiated results which go far beyond seeing women merely as victims. We now have ample evidence that in the case of women, just as in the case of workers (be they male or female), there is no collective individual and

[11] See Hermann Glaser, 'Zur Sozialpathologie des Volksgenossen', in Helmut König (ed.), *Politische Psychologie heute* (*Leviathan Sonderheft*, no. 9, 1988), pp. 171–89.
[12] See Lerke Gravenhorst and Carmen Tatschmurat (eds.), *Töchter-Fragen. NS-Frauen-Geschichte* (Freiburg, 1990).

thus no collective answer to the question whether they fell for Nazism
or not – or, in this case, whether they were victims or perpetrators.[13]

Historians cannot be content with merely deploring the fact that
social-science discourses such as the two mentioned above and, for that
matter, the more popular discourses in Germany as well, still tend to
operate with prejudices instead of trying to come to a responsible understanding of society under Nazi rule. Quite possibly, the amazing dura-
bility of such perceptions in the face of historical findings is also due to
the way historians present and discuss their work.

When Tim Mason asked what had happened to the working class and
how the behaviour of workers can be interpreted, he was very explicit
that his motive was a political one. Like many of us at the time, he
placed his hopes for a better society on the working class. It is true that
over time he rephrased his basic question. In *Arbeiterklasse und Volksgemeinschaft* the emphasis was on showing that workers did not go along
easily with the Nazi regime.[14] In his long article on the containment of
the working class, published a few years later, the emphasis was on
asking *why* German workers did not resist the regime more strongly.[15]
But, despite this pessimistic turn, the political impetus to ask what happened and why it happened remained. For a while, it was also visible
in the research done within the tradition set by Tim Mason.

We now know a great deal about how in Nazi Germany workers of
both genders, of different religious leanings, of different political incli-
nations, of different 'race', age and social status, and in different regions,
industries or enterprises fared, how they reacted and what might have
been the reasons for specific reactions. And yet, nowadays the debate
lacks a point of reference for critical reflection, since routine seems to
have made it unnecessary to discuss the motive for doing research on
the attitudes of workers towards National Socialism. The debate nowadays tends to be a truly academic one in which different parties attempt

---

[13] For a thorough discussion of the findings of women's history on Nazi Germany, see
Dagmar Reese and Carola Sachse, 'Frauenforschung zum Nationalsozialismus. Eine
Bilanz', in Gravenhorst and Tatschmurat (eds.), *Töchter-Fragen*, pp. 73–106.

[14] It is with regret that I now remember how in our first debates with Tim Mason we
attacked him harshly for using the term 'Widerstand' (resistance) so freely for many
actions which did not fit our narrow definition of deliberate political resistance. Authoritarian in our anti-authoritarian way, we hardly bothered to acknowledge what had
made him an authority: namely, the fact that he had dared to open new perspectives
by departing from ossified interpretations and definitions and that he had infused
Anglo-Saxon social-history traditions into the German debate on National Socialism,
a debate which had become rather stale by the early 1970s.

[15] Timothy W. Mason, 'Die Bändigung der Arbeiterklasse im nationalsozialistischen
Deutschland', introduction to Carola Sachse, Tilla Siegel, Hasso Spode and Wolfgang
Spohn, *Angst, Belohnung, Zucht und Ordnung. Herrschaftsmechanismen im Nationalsozial-
ismus* (Opladen, 1982), pp. 11–53.

to prove their respective points in a new version of the old either-or question: 'Did they or didn't they fall for Nazism?' And, despite all the very valuable research done in the meantime, the conclusion is equally academic: 'They did and they didn't.'

It is not the intention of this contribution to comb through the vast literature that has appeared since the mid-1970s on the question of workers' attitudes and produce a more satisfactory answer. Rather, it is argued here that the question of 'did they or didn't they?' can be a highly problematical one, even if one tries to avoid the generalised individual mentioned above. For that question implies two assumptions which remain undiscussed – and which, if they were discussed, might no longer be self-evident. One assumption is about what governs people's behaviour, and the other about what is rational and what is irrational.

To ask whether the behaviour of people indicates their approval or their rejection of the Nazi regime presupposes that people did indeed consciously act according to their attitude towards the regime, that their view of the regime governed their behaviour. Such an assumption makes it almost impossible to come to a satisfactory conclusion. This is, by the way, a problem not only for historical research; it also was a problem for the numerous agencies which tried to gauge the mood of the 'Folk Comrades'. To quote from a police report of 1934 in Aachen about mine workers' attitudes:

> The mine worker is vacillating in his criticism and far from con-
> stant. His opinion is influenced mainly by particular economic
> events. When, on the one hand, the Labour Front sees to it that
> he receives additional vacation money, he unreservedly praises the
> new State and all its institutions; but soon afterwards, when he
> comes home and his wife complains that potatoes have become
> scarce, he goes to the other extreme of being critical.[16]

It is true that the regime did relate the acts of people directly to the question whether they approved of it or not. But is the reverse equally true? Did people directly relate their acts to whether they approved of the regime or not? That this indeed was so seems to remain one of the basic assumptions in the ongoing debates on people's attitudes in Nazi Germany. For despite the highly differentiated accounts of people's lives and reactions, it seems regarded as self-evident that the pivotal question should be whether these reactions indicate an acceptance or rejection of the regime. What is rarely discussed is why this should be the pivotal

---

[16] Quoted in Bernhard Vollmer, *Volksopposition im Polizeistaat. Gestapo und Regierungsbe-richte 1934–1936* (Stuttgart, 1957), p. 58. Here this quotation has been edited slightly, since it is impossible to offer a translation which completely preserves the tortuous style of the German original and can still be understood by the English reader.

question when reconstructing and interpreting the history of people's lives and attitudes.

There is a striking difference between this and debates on other eras or, for that matter, debates on our behaviour today. Social-historical debates on, let us say, Imperial Germany or Victorian Britain are not dominated by the idea that the behaviour of people should be studied in order to find out whether they liked the Kaiser or Queen Victoria respectively. Such a question would be but one out of the many to ask in the attempt to analyse people's lives and attitudes at that time. And we know ourselves that we do not organise our lives according to whether we like Helmut Kohl or John Major. What then would justify the assumption basic to the debate on attitudes in Nazi Germany, namely that people at that time related their actions to whether they liked Hitler or not? The fact that we have every reason to condemn Hitler and his regime and the atrocities committed does indeed make for a different approach. But does it justify putting the social history of Nazi Germany into the strait-jacket of that kind of attitude research? Historians, like everybody else, have – or should have – certain moral standards by which to judge guilt and criminal behaviour. But their task goes beyond that of public prosecutors, who collect evidence to convict the guilty. Social historians who want to do their part to prevent the crimes from being committed again must contribute to an understanding of social developments.

Perhaps it is the fear that understanding equals condoning – which it does not – that stands in the way of an approach where normal people are seen as normal, even in abnormal times, rather than as monstrosities whose attitudes are totally alien to our attitudes. Let us, for example, imagine the attitudes of many people who neither wholeheartedly supported the regime nor actively resisted it. Once they admitted their rejection or criticism of the regime, if only to themselves, they faced a dire alternative. Either they acted accordingly and thus put their lives in danger; or they remained passive and thus had to live with a continual inner conflict. Dissociated thinking is one of the more usual ways of coping with such a dilemma produced by oppression. Instead of thinking coherently about one's attitude towards the regime in its totality, for many it must have seemed safer 'to praise it when there was additional vacation money and to complain when the potatoes were scarce'. Again: understanding does not equal condoning. Rather, understanding that many people tended to avoid coming to a coherent opinion about the regime, its propaganda and its abhorrent policies makes for a different 'psychological warfare' – to apply Neumann's expression today, in view of the revival of the extreme Right. Such 'warfare' would not only be directed against what is considered genuine Nazi ideology.

It would also imply a critical look at other values, norms of behaviour or social mechanisms which made people go along with Nazi politics.

The results of research on everyday life in Nazi Germany, and especially those of oral history, indicate that dissociated thinking, coupled with looking the other way, keeping one's head down, conforming with 'law and order', and concentrating on daily routines and constraints, might well have given more 'social support' to the regime than outright approval. Those and similar attitudes can be understood only imperfectly from the viewpoint of 'did they or didn't they?' In order to see and explain these attitudes it is necessary to ask in general what made people behave rather than to ask in particular what made people fall for the irrationality of Nazism.

Or, to take another perspective, if we ask what contributed to the containment of the working class, we also have to look for those elements in the ideology and politics of the regime which conventionally are considered rational. As mentioned above, one such element was the idea of rationalisation – an idea that has dominated the social norms of what is rational in the twentieth century. In the Weimar Republic rationalisation had been *the* social programme, promising progress, emancipation and welfare. Not only industrialists, but also politicians, trade unionists and reform movements of every colour were convinced that it was only rational to minimise 'waste' of time, material and labour scientifically and in a planned manner in order to achieve the utmost efficiency not only in industry but in all walks of life. Industrial rationalisation was coupled with social rationalisation, i.e. with the idea that society and social relations must be restructured and people educated according to the formal rationality of efficiency.[17]

---

[17] See Carola Sachse, *Betriebliche Sozialpolitik als Familienpolitik in der Weimarer Republik und im Nationalsozialismus* (Hamburg, 1987); Thomas von Freyberg, *Industrielle Rationalisierung in der Weimarer Republik* (Frankfurt/Main, 1989). The holistic, societal perspective of the Weimar 'Rationalisation Movement' might have been typically German. Yet what Samuel Haber writes of the more individualistic and company-minded 'efficiency craze' of the Progressive Era in the United States applies just as well for the German 'Rationalisation Movement': 'A secular Great Awakening, an outpouring of ideas and emotions in which a gospel of efficiency was preached without embarrassment to business, workers, doctors, housewives, and teachers, and yes, preached even to preachers.' The word 'efficiency' was not only used for input–output ratios of materials or of investment and revenue, but also applied to personal qualities and relationships. 'An efficient person was an effective person, and that characterisation brought with it . . . a turning toward hard work and away from feeling, toward discipline and away from sympathy, toward masculinity and away from femininity.' Between people 'efficiency meant social harmony and the leadership of the "competent"': Samuel Haber, *Efficiency and Uplift. Scientific Management in the Progressive Era 1890–1920* (Chicago and London, 1964), pp. ix f. See also Stuart Brandes, *American Welfare Capitalism 1880–1940* (Chicago and London, 1976).

As the Depression then threw a damper on the rationalisation euphoria, the Nazi regime initially proclaimed itself to be critical of rationalisation. However, it very soon turned round and propagated the 'true', the 'German' rationalisation – in contradistinction to the previous 'false' and 'un-German' one – in the truly German *Leistungsgemeinschaft*. From the mid-1930s onwards the process of industrial rationalisation along Taylorist and Fordist lines was accelerated. With it the methods employed to systematically select, train, motivate, control and appease workers were further developed – methods which pretended to scientifically and objectively justify hierarchies as well as racist and sexist discrimination. With respect to the possible effects on workers' attitudes, three aspects of these developments are particularly important. First, industrial management rationalised not *against* an 'archaic' or 'irrational' labour policy, but *with* the propagandistic and practical support by the regime and by the Labour Front. Second, the strategies of social rationalisation encompassed strategies to rationalise people and their relations in private life as well. And third, the regime and the Labour Front publicly legitimised their activities by referring to values such as efficiency, progress, and formal equality – all of them values which before, in the Weimar Republic, and even more so afterwards, in the Germany of the 'economic miracle', were considered to be very rational values.[18]

Of course, the Nazi regime was far from being as efficient as it pretended to be – a fact which after the war was triumphantly cited as proof of its irrationality. Another form of critique was that rationalisation was done under the wrong rules – namely excluding workers' representation and including racist criteria – and with the wrong goals – namely a racial imperialism which included the annihilation of millions of people. Furthermore, West German society relied on the idea of rationalisation as a safeguard against ideology,[19] saw no harm in calling itself the

[18] For the strategies to rationalise the work force and their families, see Carola Sachse, *Siemens, der Nationalsozialismus und die moderne Familie. Eine Untersuchung zur sozialen Rationalisierung in Deutschland im 20. Jahrhundert* (Hamburg, 1990). For the continuities in the development of scientific (personnel) management, see Siegel, *Leistung und Lohn*; Siegel and von Freyberg, *Industrielle Rationalisierung*, esp. Chaps. 2 and 5. For a critical discussion of the idea of social rationalisation, see also Tilla Siegel, 'Das ist nur rational. Ein Essay zur Logik der sozialen Rationalisierung', in Dagmar Reese, Eve Rosenhaft, Carola Sachse and Tilla Siegel (eds.), *Rationale Beziehungen? Geschlechterverhältnisse im Rationalisierungsprozeß* (Frankfurt/Main, 1993).

[19] At that time, little attention was paid to those who, like Horkheimer and Adorno for example, had become deeply critical of the instrumental reason inherent in the idea of rationalisation *because* of the experience of Nazi rule. 'The totalitarian order gives full rein to calculation and abides by science as such. Its canon is its own brutal efficiency': Max Horkheimer and Theodor W. Adorno, *Dialectic of Enlightenment* (translated by John Cumming, London, 1973), p. 86.

'efficiency society' (*Leistungsgesellschaft*), and smoothly incorporated into the new system of labour relations many of the methods of personnel management and industrial social policies developed and introduced during the late 1930s and early 1940s.

And yet, seeing how the Nazi regime made use of the technocratically defined concept of rationality inherent in the idea of rationalisation gives every reason to reconsider that concept itself. 'Blood and soil' and 'master race' arguments were deeply entangled – or, rather, justified – with the Darwinistic efficiency principle. And the despotic chaos of Nazi rule gave vent to the destructive dynamics of that principle which declares the optimisation of the means-and-ends relationship to be rational *per se*, without questioning the means or ends themselves. The effects are obvious when we look at the experts and technocrats who had internalised that principle and who saw to it that war production, the racist rationalisation of the nation, and even the organisation of the death camps be 'efficient'. The effects are more subtle when we look at the mechanisms of social integration. By monopolistically claiming the right to define the ends, the 'common interest', and at the same time suggesting that efficiency itself is the end, the regime fostered the attitude *not* to think beyond the limits of formal rationality. On the one hand, terror and arbitrariness made it a fatal risk to 'be different' and to 'think differently'. On the other hand, for all those who counted themselves as members of the 'German Folk Community', the efficiency principle clothed oppression in scientific, calculable rule which – within limits – seemed to give the oppressed a certain security against arbitrariness in the sense of offering an 'objective' yardstick for what may be done and what not. In addition, it offered the promise that all those who submit to that formal rationality will eventually profit from the increase in efficiency resulting from it, neglecting of course those who drop out or who were excluded from the outset.

To sketch in bold lines an historical continuity, as has been done here, can easily create the impression of inevitability. Thus, it might be opportune to point out in what respects the analytical approach suggested here differs from that of modernisation theory. The latter looks at historical developments from the perspective of a set of characteristics that define – usually rather favourably – a given model of modern society. The elements of Nazi ideology and politics can then be categorised as 'modern' or 'archaic', as accelerating or retarding the development of German society on a given path towards modernity. In contrast, the perspective suggested here neither presupposes a given model of modern society nor a given path towards it. Rather, it calls for an analysis of the dynamics of specific social values, norms and orientations which in combination or competition with each other have produced

historical developments. The outcome of these dynamics is not necessarily predetermined, since it is people whose acts give force to values,
norms and orientations. People can consciously or unconsciously carry
on or adopt them; people can be forced to adopt or to repress them;
people can use and misuse them; and people can criticise and discard
them.

The idea of rationalisation has been just one of such norms. It was
adopted, rather than invented, by the Nazi regime, and it has been
adopted not only in the sense of a conscious strategy but also as a plausible argument to justify political acts, to 'rationalise' them in the psychological sense of the word. This, and the 'time factor', have to be taken
into account when discussing the possible effects on the attitudes of
people. Historical research which concentrates on the first years of Nazi
rule has paid little attention to the importance of the idea of rationalisation in the ideology and politics of the regime and for the attitudes of
workers – and understandably so, since the regime did not and, being
an uneasy alliance of power groups, could not proceed with a uniform
strategy. Rather, it played the tune of highly contradictory social values,
norms and orientation. This also holds true for the second half of Nazi
rule, albeit in a different way. However, despite that lack of coherence
from the late 1930s onwards, especially, the regime very visibly resorted
to the idea of rationalisation – or, rather, the diverse interests, politics
and public pronouncements of the competing power groups met on that
common ground.[20]

In conclusion, it cannot be emphasised enough that the idea of rationalisation has been an increasingly dominant social norm for what is
rational throughout the twentieth century. A norm is not necessarily
equal to actual behaviour. People may adhere to it; people may – with
a bad conscience – not adhere to it; and people may use it as a justification of acts done for a quite different reason. In all three ways the
idea of rationalisation has had an important role in shaping the attitudes
of people – of the rulers and the ruled – in Nazi Germany and, for that
matter, in the excuses offered later in post-war Germany. Looking back
at the historical continuity of that idea, we have good reason to reconsider the conventional narrow definition of what is irrational, which so
often is implicitly taken for granted when discussing Nazi rule – or, vice
versa, to reconsider the rationality of the efficiency principle which today
is still put forth as an argument to justify industrial and technological

---

[20] For an extensive and highly differentiated study on the politics of the competing power
groups which made up the regime and on the situation and attitudes of workers in the
Nazi 'economic miracle', see Günter Morsch, *Arbeit und Brot. Studien zur Lage, Stim-
mung, Einstellung und Verhalten der deutschen Arbeiterschaft 1933–1936/37* (Frankfurt/
Main, 1993).

developments that destroy our environment, which drives women in eastern Germany to abortion and sterilisation so as to be fit for the free (labour) market economy, or which the New Right refers to in its propaganda for a new strong 'German' Germany – to end with but a few, randomly chosen examples.

5

WOMEN IN FASCIST ITALY

PERRY R. WILLSON

Historical study of women's experience of Italian Fascism effectively began in the 1970s. Strongly shaped by the politics of the time, many of the first publications either focused on denouncing the evil anti-feminist nature of the regime in its misogynous legislation and ideological excesses,[1] or concentrated on female contributions to the anti-Fascist cause. Even today, the topic of women and the Resistance still represents a sizeable proportion of the research published on this period. The early studies, whose aim was to highlight the hitherto neglected role that women had played in what was seen as the heroic, formative moment for Italian democracy, tended to sidestep the thornier questions. They were often hagiographic and lacking a certain critical edge, a tendency hard to avoid in the heady days of the 'seventies.

In the 'eighties the situation began to change. As part of a growing interest in women's history and social history in general there was a broadening of the historiography and a greater recognition of the complexity, diversity, and contradictory nature of the period. New research began to focus on such topics as conditions of employment, sport, the family, abortion, and Catholic efforts to mobilise women. Some of this research, largely influenced by the work of Luisa Passerini,[2] has used oral history materials to address challenging issues such as attitudes to work, female identities as workers, and the role of the family in political socialisation.

However, much remains to be studied and historical understanding of Fascism and women is still, in many respects, at an early stage. There

---

[1] See, for example, Piero Meldini, *Sposa e madre esemplare. Ideologia e politica della donna e della famiglia durante il fascismo* (Rimini and Florence, 1975).

[2] Luisa Passerini, *Fascism in Popular Memory: The Cultural Experience of the Turin Working Class* (Cambridge, 1987). On Passerini's influence on the historiography of Fascism and the working class see Alfredo Martini, 'Oral History and Italian Fascism', in *International Yearbook of Oral History and Life Stories*, vol. I, Luisa Passerini (ed.), *Memory and Totalitarianism* (Oxford, 1992).

have been few serious attempts at overviews of the subject matter. Apart from a number of articles,[3] there is only one book-length synthesis in English[4] and a handful of analogous works in Italian. Overall far more is known about middle-class[5] than working-class women, who, of course, left fewer traces of their lives in written documentation. Another big gap is the absence of any real study of the Fascist motherhood organisation (although a couple of doctoral theses have now been completed). Furthermore, what might be called the 'engendering' of the broader historiography still seems a distant prospect.[6] Studies of other aspects of Fascism have not yet really incorporated the new knowledge about women, and much of the rest of the historiography of this period remains a study of men (although not, as yet, a history of masculinity).[7]

Focusing in particular on some of the more recently published research, this essay explores three interrelated themes which lie at the heart of women's experience of Fascism. Beginning with an evaluation of the regime's attempts to mobilise women in the national cause and redefine their relationship to the state, I then go on to an examination of two case studies of key areas of Fascist policy directed specifically at the female half of the population. The final section broadens out to consider the role of some other changes in shaping women's lives in this period.

MOBILISATION, CONSENSUS AND RESISTANCE

The Italian Fascists devoted a great deal of attention to women's role in society. They tried to mobilise women both by propaganda campaigns highlighting the importance of motherhood to the nation and by the creation of women-only mass organisations. A monolithic stereotype of idealised womanhood figured *ad nauseam* in speeches, propaganda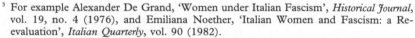

---

[3] For example Alexander De Grand, 'Women under Italian Fascism', *Historical Journal*, vol. 19, no. 4 (1976), and Emiliana Noether, 'Italian Women and Fascism: a Reevaluation', *Italian Quarterly*, vol. 90 (1982).

[4] Victoria De Grazia, *How Fascism Ruled Women: Italy, 1922–1945* (Berkeley, Los Angeles and Oxford, 1992).

[5] See Michela De Giorgio, *Le italiane dall'Unità a oggi: Modelli culturali e comportamenti sociali* (Rome and Bari, 1992), and De Grazia, *How Fascism Ruled Women*. Both of these important studies include far more information about middle-class than working-class women.

[6] Perhaps the most well-known (albeit controversial in its deconstructionist approach) discussion of the need for a gendered approach to history is Joan Wallach Scott, *Gender and the Politics of History* (New York, 1988). The publication of an Italian translation of the key article from this book led to a small flurry of theoretical articles on the issue but has as yet produced few other concrete results. (See Scott, 'Il "genere": un'utile categoria de analisi storica', *Rivista di storia contemporanea*, vol. 4 (1987).)

[7] For one attempt to look at Fascism in this way see Barbara Spackman, 'The Fascist Rhetoric of Virility', *Stanford Italian Review*, vol. 8, no. 1–2 (1990).

writings, and visual representations. This ideal woman was rounded in shape, rural, and first and foremost a mother. She was fundamentally defined and confined by her biology, which was now enrolled in the cause of the nation. Her ability to procreate conferred upon her a kind of warped citizenship in that the purpose of her maternity was to create new Italians for the Fascist state and lend muscle to its imperial strength, essentially as cannon-fodder. Thus motherhood, while still a biological act, was elevated to the status of a contribution to the nation.[8] The newly national-ised Italian woman was, however, to be primarily a domestic creature, the angel guarding the hearth as she awaitted the return of her husband from his daily toil, carrying out her national role from the confines of the home. She was to shun extra-domestic work and devote herself to maximising her output of children in order to qualify as one of the truly heroic figures of the Fascist age – the 'prolific mother'.

Such idealisation of a biologically determined domestic destiny for Italian womanhood was reinforced, but eventually also somewhat con-tradicted, by the creation of mass organisations for women. The most important of these was the *fasci femminili* founded in the 1920s.[9] Although initially neglected by the Fascist hierarchy, in the 1930s it was given encouragement as part of the general mass mobilisation drive. Its role was to channel these energies of middle-class women into caring and essentially subordinate activities, doing good works for the poor and needy, particularly mothers and children, and spreading Fascist propa-ganda. There were other organisations for women in the shape of the Massaie Rurali (Rural Housewives) founded in 1933,[10] SOLD, a special section of the *fasci femminili* for workers (including domestic servants and homeworkers),[11] and a range of organisations graded according to

[8] The pro-natalist campaign, although undoubtedly racist at heart with its emphasis on the need for 'more Italians', never descended to the terrible depths of comparable Nazi policies. Mass sterilisation, for example, was not on the agenda in Italy.

[9] See, for example, Denise Detriagache, 'Il fascismo femminile da San Sepolcro all'affare Matteotti (1919–1925)', *Storia contemporanea*, vol. 4, no. 2 (1983); Maria Fraddosio, 'La donna e la guerra. Aspetti della militanza femminile nel fascismo: dalla mobilita-zione civile alle origini del Saf nella Republica Sociale Italiana', *Storia contemporanea*, vol. 10, no. 6 (1989).

[10] The aim of the Massaie Rurali was firstly to help teach rural women how to run their homes more efficiently via domestic science, gardening, and farming courses. It also actively promoted the demographic campaign and encouraged rural craft industries particularly by helping market the goods produced. See Angela Amoroso, 'Le organiz-zazioni femminili nelle campagne durante il fascismo', *Storia in Lombardia: il fascismo in Lombardia*, vol. 1–2 (1989), pp. 305–16.

[11] SOLD (Sezione operaie e lavoranti a domicilio) had nearly a million members by the Second World War. Its primary purpose was to spread political propaganda (much of it about women's domestic mission in life) among working-class women. From 1938 it published a tedious broadsheet (tellingly entitled *Lavoro e famiglia* – Work and Family) which was distributed free to its members. Not much is known about SOLD as this organisation has never been properly studied.

age for girls and adolescents.[12] All these trod the same thin line between the provision of a certain amount of space for a public female role and an emphasis on domesticity, maternity, and self-sacrifice for a greater cause.

Such an unprecedented amount of attention to defining the female contribution to the state meant that women were brought on to the national stage for the first time. Women's role became more visible and new spaces opened up for them in the public sphere. In this respect Fascism should be considered an innovator and the interwar period a watershed in Italian women's history. The *fasci femminili* provided women with a kind of national profile, and undoubtedly gave many middle-class women a sense of importance as, dressed in their smart uniforms, they busily attended to the welfare of the poor and needy or campaigned for autarky. The girls' organisations also led to the promotion of the fit, healthy image of the 'donna sportiva' which jarred with the rotund mother ideal of the demographic campaign. This image, unlike the passive domesticity of the maternal image which merged almost seamlessly with centuries of Catholic teaching, was new.

However, such innovative and contradictory aspects were offset by the fact that the Fascists tried, at one and the same time, to mobilise women and tie them to domesticity. The more public face for women was shorn of any potentially emancipatory overtones about female citizenship and equality. Fascist ideology had replaced the women's movement's[13] assertion of 'different but equal' with 'different and subordinate'. Attention was drawn to women's role purely to emphasise their inferiority. Symptomatic of this was the fact that the *fasci femminili* had no real power whatsoever. Their leaders were excluded from policy making and reduced to simply accepting orders from above. Tellingly, the regime never had any female political figures who became important in their own right, the Fascist equivalent of Anna Kuliscioff.[14]

Energetic as the regime may have been in its efforts to mobilise women to its national and political cause, the extent of its success in consensus building is far from easy to gauge. To date there has been little serious effort to address the question of whether there existed a widespread female consensus for Fascism, in stark contrast to the heated debates about the extent of female support for Nazism and about the

---

[12] See De Grazia, *How Fascism Ruled Women*, chap. 5.

[13] In part reflecting the general weakness of the Italian middle class in the Liberal period the feminist movement was never as strong and ideologically challenging as its counterparts in some other countries such as Britain. There is a fairly copious bibliography on this in Italian. In English see, for example, Annarita Buttafuoco, 'Motherhood as a Political Strategy', in Gisela Bock and Pat Thane (eds.), *Maternity and Gender Policies. Women and the Rise of the European Welfare States, 1880s–1950s* (London, 1991).

[14] Kuliscioff was one of the leaders of the pre-Fascist Socialist Party.

attitude of the Italian working class to the regime. One rather wild attempt to tackle this question was made in 1976 by Maria Antonietta Macchiocchi in her study entitled *La donna nera*[15] in which she blithely took the bull by the horns and asserted, using a psychohistorical approach, that there was widespread consensus for the Fascist regime amongst Italian women owing to their inherent masochism. Since then the level of analysis has become more sophisticated – if far more inconclusive – and it is unlikely that many historians would today echo Simonetta Ulivieri, who wrote confidently in 1977 that 'There is no doubt that Fascism obtained a degree of consensus among the female masses, especially in rural areas . . .'[16] The issue is, of course, far more complex.

It is clear that Mussolini was successful in recruiting a number of prominent feminists to his cause. These middle- and upper-class women felt they could further their own brand of 'social feminism', now rebaptised as 'latin feminism',[17] in the new state. Some of these women were converted to Fascism after rallying to the nationalist cause during the First World War. Others lent their support once the regime was in power. Undoubtedly this seemingly startling capitulation of some of the women's movement was facilitated by the fact that the feminists themselves had failed to challenge the idea of motherhood as women's primary destiny. The reasons why other women joined must have ranged from real political commitment to the need for a party card in order to obtain employment. Many middle-class women may have got involved in order to have something to do outside the home. At the other end of the political spectrum there were a few female anti-Fascist activists, mainly Communists.

The extent of actual active support is much harder to assess. It is likely that some women had no clear personal opinions on the overall merits of different kinds of government since there was no precedent for women's views counting in the political sphere. Many women may have accepted some aspects of the regime, susceptible, for example, to the cult of Mussolini, while remaining critical of others. Large numbers of women commented in their own way by joining rival Catholic rather than Fascist organisations.[18] Class differences are crucial here. Middle-

[15] Maria Antonietta Macciocchi, *La donna nera: consenso femminile e fascismo* (Milan, 1976).
[16] Simonetta Ulivieri, 'La donna nella scuola dall'unità d'Italia a oggi: leggi, pregiudizi, lotte e prospettive. Parte II – Dalla riforma Gentile alla Resistenza', *Nuova Donna Woman Femme*, vol. 3 (1977), p. 124.
[17] See De Grazia, *How Fascism Ruled Women*, pp. 236–8.
[18] On these organisations see Paola di Cori and Michela de Giorgio, 'Politica e sentimenti: le organizzazioni femminili cattoliche dall'età giolittiana al fascismo', *Rivista di storia contemporanea* (1980).

class women had far more exposure to Fascist ideology than working-class women. They spent longer at school where propaganda was intense and were more likely to read magazines and official publications. They were also less likely to be brought up in homes with a family tradition of Socialism or Communism which might serve as a counter-weight to official propaganda.[19] Many other women, especially in rural areas, lived lives more distant from rhetoric and the intrusions of Fascist policy-makers. It seems difficult to argue that the citizenship status of such women was fundamentally recast by Fascism (although of course it is essential to emphasise that this does not mean their lives were totally unaffected by the regime).

Evidence of passive resistance might offer another 'route' to the question of attitudes to the regime. For example the persistence of abortion could be seen as a covert form of resistance to the demographic campaign and the continuing high levels of female employment as a defiant gesture. But such claims are hard to make since decisions to abort or seek a job were determined by a range of reasons, few of which could be seen as clear political statements. More open forms of resistance were rarer although at times they were fairly dramatic such as the series of violent strikes by textile workers or even, on one occasion, a pro-abortion riot.[20]

With the advent of the Second World War, of course, the lives of all Italians, even in the remotest areas, were inevitably affected. Women were recruited to take over male jobs as men were called up to fight and in the final doomed phase of the Republic of Salò a few women even donned military uniforms and joined the armed forces in non-combatant roles.[21] Others contributed to the swelling anti-Fascist Resistance movement. Here, if a mass of overly heroic literature on this subject is left aside, three main points emerge.[22] Firstly, recent research suggests that at least as many women as men were involved, and the chronology of when many got involved mirrors the chronology of the Resistance as a whole: there were tiny numbers in the 1930s and a mass movement from 1943 onwards. Secondly, Resistance roles were highly gendered. Women figured largely in what could be termed 'support' or

[19] On the role of the family in political socialisation in this period see Passerini, *Fascism in Popular Memory*; Margaret Fraser, 'Women and the Resistance in the Veneto', *ASMI Newsletter*, vol. 21 (1992).

[20] Perry R. Willson, 'The Fascist Demographic Campaign in Milan', *ASMI Newsletter*, vol. 21 (1992), p. 5.

[21] Fraddosio, 'La donna e la guerra'.

[22] The bibliography of women and the Resistance is too vast to list here, but for some recent research which raises important questions using oral history methods see Anna Bravo, 'Simboli del materno', in Bravo (ed.), *Donne e uomini nelle guerre mondiali* (Rome and Bari, 1991); Fraser, 'Women and the Resistance in the Veneto'.

'administrative' roles such as organising safe houses for fugitives, ensuring communications by acting as messengers, or supplying partisan bands with food and clothing. Few participated more directly in armed actions. Thirdly, although significant numbers of Resistance activists were female, and women's involvement – in contrast to that of most of the men – was the product of a deliberate personal choice, historians can search in vain for a really feminist theme to the activities of these militants. The Women's Defence Groups[23] ostensibly had women's emancipation as one of their aims but in practice they did little to further such an objective or to challenge male political control. There is little evidence that their opposition was in any sense a clearly formulated response to Fascism's misogyny. Women seem to have generally chosen to oppose or support anti-Fascism on other grounds. This is hardly surprising given the absence of any vocal women's movement for twenty years and the crisis situation of the war, but it argued ill for women's potential to influence the political sphere in the postwar period.

POLICY

However crude their ideology may have been, the Fascists displayed greater subtlety in legislation and recognised that blanket laws were unworkable. Policy-makers had to operate within a series of constraints and in practice they were rarely, if ever, able to implement the grand ideas outlined in rhetorical speeches. Furthermore, even where policy was ideologically motivated (it almost always was) it could backfire and have different effects from those intended. In other cases it had no real impact at all. For example, a focus on the Fascist mass leisure organisation the Dopolavoro and its policies for its female members can shed only limited light on female leisure pursuits in this period, since few women participated in it.[24] Some groups of women were more directly affected by legislation than others. Legislation could more easily target, for example, women working in the state bureaucracy in Rome than rural women in Sicily. Interwar Italy was a highly regionalised, uneven society, characterised by a very diverse economy, where state intervention had hugely differing effects according to a series of factors, par-

---

[23] These groups (the Gruppi di difesa della donna e per l'assistenza ai combattenti della libertà) were the main co-ordinators of women in the Resistance. See Angela Amoroso, 'I gruppi di difesa della donna a Milano', in Ada Gigli Marchetti and Nanda Torcellan (eds.), *Donna Lombarda 1860-1945* (Milan, 1992).

[24] On the Dopolavoro see Victoria De Grazia, *The Culture of Consent: Mass Organization of Leisure in Fascist Italy* (Cambridge, 1981). For a case study of women and the Dopolavoro see Perry R. Willson, *The Clockwork Factory: Women and Work in Fascist Italy* (Oxford, 1993), chap. 9.

ticularly geographical location and social class. Some of these problems and constraints can be illustrated by a look at two policy areas which directly targeted women – employment legislation and the demographic campaign.

To begin with employment.[25] Employment legislation towards women, was, in many ways, a typical Fascist policy, aimed at a specific ideological goal but heavily conditioned by the needs of particular interest groups. Especially important here were those lower-middle-class men who felt threatened by the feminisation of teaching and office work. Another influential group was that key group of fellow-travellers and supporters of Fascism – business interests. For them, female employment represented a cheap labour pool. Furthermore, without the costly introduction of the 'family wage' for the male breadwinner, a wholesale expulsion of women from the labour force would have had unthinkable consequences for the working classes. As a result, Fascism's emphasis on woman's place being in the home in practice added up to little more than a kind of piecemeal, contradictory campaign full of bluster and rhetorical propaganda together with a small amount of legislation, limited in scope.

Legislation to restrict female access to the labour market, although misogynous, had little discernible impact since it was class specific, heavily watered down, and dealt more in quotas than bans.[26] Its main aim was the preservation of strictly gendered work hierarchies, mainly in middle-class occupations such as office employment and teaching. Middle-class women were not to be stopped from actually working, just prevented from occupying specific work roles where they might threaten male supremacy in the labour market. Thus women were to be welcome only in subordinate positions where men did not wish to work. For working-class women legislation was limited almost entirely to protec-

---

[25] On women's employment in this period see, for example, Alessandra Pescarolo, 'I mestieri femminili. Continuità e spostamenti di confine nel corso dell'industrializzazione', *Memoria*, vol. 30 (1990). For an important attempt to make sense of the census statistics see Ornello Vitali, *Aspetti dello sviluppo economico italiano alla luce della ricostruzione della popolazione attiva* (Rome, 1970). See also the pioneering work of Franca Pieroni Bortolotti, 'Osservazioni sull'occupazione femminile durante il fascismo', in Annarita Buttafuoco (ed.), *Franca Pieroni Bortolotti. Sul movimento politico delle donne. Scritti inediti* (Rome, 1987) (the article was written in 1973).

[26] This employment legislation has been oddly interpreted by many historians, some of whom have, for example, quite wrongly presented the 1938 decree law as being a drastic piece of legislation that would, had the war not intervened, basically have spelled the end of mass female employment in Italy. For example De Grand calls it a 'draconian measure'. (See 'Women under Italian Fascism', p. 965.) Misogynous as it undoubtedly was, in fact this law, like the others, was again directed essentially at middle-class jobs and aimed at defining which jobs women could do rather than preventing them from working.

tion for the procreative capacities of those working outside the home.[27] The influence of business interests was undoubtedly important here but the generally *laissez-faire* approach was probably facilitated by the fact that in factory work men may have felt less threatened since the general trend was an increase in male rather than female labour. This occurred without the need for legislation through such changes as the crisis of the textile industry which employed many women[28] and the rise of heavy engineering bringing with it many jobs seen as 'inherently male'. In some sectors where women were employed gender hierarchies were preserved without the need for legislation by a combination of tradition and the apprenticeship system.[29]

Overall the legislation appears to have had little identifiable impact on the numbers of women working. Female employment did decline in this period, at least as far as can be discerned from the admittedly very unreliable census figures, but this was part of a long-term trend which started before Mussolini came to power and continued until the 1970s. Even middle-class women, despite being targeted by the legislation, continued to work in offices and schools. Doubtless there were some effects. Some scholars argue that there was a shift to more marginal forms of occupation for some women. Fascist rhetoric may have strengthened the position of men who wished to prevent their wives or daughters from working but since such decisions were frequently made on primarily economic grounds it is unlikely that this had a big impact. The campaign also served to reinforce the idea of women's work as somehow temporary, transitory, and subordinate. Thus it helped prevent the emergence of a middle-class 'career woman' figure or at least channelled such energies into a few areas deemed suitable (which could generally be characterised by the adjectives 'caring' or 'supportive'). Women did continue to work in white-collar jobs but the 'feminisation' of such employment was slower than in some other countries,[30] and it is not possible to know how many women would have risen up the hierarchy in offices and schools in the absence of Fascist propaganda and legislation.

[27] This ranged from 'welfare-orientated' laws such as better maternity leave to restrictions on the number of hours women could work daily. For a discussion of this 'protective legislation' see Willson, *The Clockwork Factory*, pp. 6–7.
[28] On the crisis of the textile industry see the excellent article by Bruna Bianchi, 'I tessili: lavoro, salute, conflitti', in *La classe operaia durante il fascismo* (Milan, 1981).
[29] See as a case study of this process my own book on the new light engineering sector: *The Clockwork Factory*, chap. 6.
[30] In the 1930s only about 16 per cent of Italian public employees were women, compared with, for example, 25 per cent in Germany in 1933, and 34 per cent in France in 1936 (De Grazia, *How Fascism Ruled Women*, p. 194).

In fact, for the vast majority of women, their experience of the labour market in this period was shaped more by other aspects of Fascist policy. Two good examples are labour legislation which denied a voice to the working class as a whole and facilitated abuses such as truly appalling health and safety conditions in the textile industry,[31] and the introduction of a bastardised type of Taylorism involving speed-up without the reorganisation of management methods.[32] Similarly, for middle-class women, the unbalanced nature of Fascism's version of a welfare state had a huge impact on employment prospects since most of the new caring roles for women were unpaid.

The demographic campaign had obvious relevance to women.[33] It professionalised midwives, prosecuted abortionists, taxed bachelors, saved the lives of a few illegitimate babies and preached endlessly about the virtues of motherhood, but did little else because of serious and endemic underfunding. Its primary target, the birth rate, continued to fall. The impact of the campaign did vary regionally. For example, my own study of the demographic campaign in the commercial and industrial northern city of Milan,[34] located in the province usually vaunted as the one where ONMI (the motherhood organisation) functioned at its best, shows that the Fascist measures probably had little effect on the women in this area. By contrast, the work of anthropologist Nancy Triolo, which looks particularly at western Sicily – an area marked to a degree by Muslim influences, where women still lived a semi-secluded existence in a highly gendered world – found that Fascist policies to professionalise midwives in order to curb their potential role as abortionists led to a weakening of female networks in the domestic sphere and beyond.[35]

---

[31] See Bianchi, 'I tessili'.

[32] See, for example, Giulio Sapelli, *Organizzazione, lavoro e innovazione industriale nell'Italia tra le due guerre* (Turin, 1978).

[33] On the demographic campaign see Chiara Saraceno, 'Redefining Maternity and Paternity: Gender, Pronatalism and Social Policies in Fascist Italy', in Bock and Thane (eds.), *Maternity and Gender Policies*; David V. Glass, *Population Policies and Movements in Europe* (Oxford, 1940); Lesley Caldwell, 'Reproducers of the Nation: Women and the Family in Fascist Policy', in David Forgacs (ed.), *Rethinking Italian Fascism* (London, 1986); Sergio Onger, 'Il latte e la retorica: l'Opera nazionale maternità e infanzia a Brescia (1927–1939)', *Storia in Lombardia*, vol. 1–2 (1989).

[34] See Willson, 'The Fascist Demographic Campaign'.

[35] Triolo shows how midwives in pre-Fascist Sicily served as mediators between the public and private spheres and between groups of women who lived their lives mainly secluded in the home. Thus professionalisation led to the distancing of women from their traditional support networks of female consanguinal kin. See Nancy Elizabeth Triolo, 'The Angelmakers: Fascist Pro-natalism and the Normalisation of Midwives in Sicily', Ph.D. thesis, Department of Anthropology, University of California, Berkeley, 1989.

MODERNISATION AND EMANCIPATION

In spite of ruralist rhetoric and the economic distortions caused by ill-conceived Fascist policies,[36] this period saw a gradual continuing trend towards urbanisation, commercialisation, and industrialisation. Closely intertwined with such trends were important changes in the family and demographic patterns. Although their impact was complex there is some evidence that, for certain sections of the female population, such changes led to increased emancipation[37] in this period.

Not only was the average size of the Italian family becoming smaller but changes were occurring within it with the increase in so-called companionate marriages. Despite a slight decline in the official figures, millions of women continued to work. A further noteworthy trend, stressed particularly by De Grazia, is the spread of a new commercial culture bringing with it new models of womanhood publicised through the cinema and mass circulation magazines. This new glamorous image contrasted sharply with the mythologised 'prolific mother'. Despite the fact that such models were condemned by the Fascists as the so-called *donna crisi* (the crisis woman), they were undoubtedly very appealing, particularly to the young.

Such new models of womanhood had most impact on women who were northern, urban, and middle-class. Illiteracy was much higher among those who were rural and poor, especially in the south,[38] and these too were the groups least likely to have access to the new mass cultural products such as Hollywood films. However, the rural world was far from untouched by change in this period. Urban cultural models spread as the rural–urban shift continued despite Fascist anti-migration measures,[39] and in some areas commuting to and from large cities became common. Although the number of studies of gender roles in rural areas remains low and much research remains to be done on this

---

[36] For example, the 'battle' to become self-sufficient in wheat and the 'Quota 90' campaign aimed at pegging the lira at an economically irrational exchange rate.

[37] In this essay, I am taking a broad interpretation of this term, defining it, I hope uncontroversially, as an increase in women's control over their own lives.

[38] In 1931 the national average illiteracy level was 21.6 per cent, whereas among the 'agricultural classes' it was 29.6 per cent. In the south it was 38.8 per cent rising to 53.3 per cent among 'agricultural workers' (Tullio De Mauro, *Storia Linguistica dell'Italia Unita* (Bari, 1963), p. 55). In the city of Milan in the same year it was a mere 3.0 per cent (Willson, *The Clockwork Factory*, p. 107). Illiteracy was generally higher amongst women. Of Calabrian women, 55.7 per cent were illiterate in 1931 compared with 39.1 per cent of men (Vittorio Cappelli, 'Immagine e presenza pubblica della donna in Calabria', in Paola Corti (ed.), *Le donne nelle campagne italiane del novecento. Annali Cervi, 13*, vol. II (Bologna, 1991), p. 183).

[39] On this notoriously ineffective legislation aimed at stemming the rural–urban shift see Anna Treves, *Le migrazioni interne nell'Italia fascista* (Turin, 1976).

topic, some trends are evident. For example, the importance of the peasant patriarch – the male head of the household with almost despotic power over younger members of large extended families, typical particularly in sharecropping – declined greatly in this period, largely as a result of increased interaction with the market and the labour market.[40]

A strong counterweight to such forces for change, however, was the strengthened power of the Catholic Church and the swelling of the ranks of the Catholic mass organisations. Care needs to be taken in seeing this as in some way separate from the effects of Fascism since it was, of course, the regime's reconciliation with the Church that facilitated Catholic influence. Fascism also helped open the way for the Catholic Church's powerful position in the Italian state in the postwar period which had long-lasting repercussions for women. In the interwar period Catholicism exerted a strong influence on many women's lives, for whom the spiritual world doubtless represented a haven from unpleasant realities on this earth. As such, it cannot be denied that the Church could give women strength. At the same time, however, it also hemmed them in by condemning their attempts to control their own fertility and preaching female subordination and rigid gender roles.

But, despite Catholic influence, there were significant forces for change in many women's lives in the interwar period, and little of such change was in line with Fascist ideals of womanhood, or a clear outcome of Fascist policy intentions.[41] Such changes could be grouped under the general heading of modernisation. Modernisation does not, of course, automatically mean an improved role for women. It redefines gender relations but not always in directions which increase women's ability to shape their own lives.

One excellent example of this is the new Americanised role model for women. The question does need to be asked: just how emancipating was it, in reality, for women to be able to wear make-up and revealing clothes? The new image of womanhood does, at first glance, seem a freer one, as De Grazia has suggested.[42] But in many respects the Holly-

---

[40] Both Marzio Barbagli and Paul Corner have demonstrated that these dramatic changes were occurring. See Paul Corner, 'Women in Fascist Italy. Changing Family Roles in the Transition from an Agricultural to an Industrial Society', *European History Quarterly*, vol. 23 (1993), pp. 51–68; Marzio Barbagli, *Sotto lo stesso tetto: Mutamenti della famiglia in Italia dal XV al XX secolo* (Bologna, 1984).

[41] Here I am referring to policies targeted primarily at women. It cannot be denied, of course, that the modernisation of the Italian economy was facilitated by some Fascist legislation, despite official rhetoric. See, for example, Paul Corner, 'Fascist Agrarian Policy and the Italian Economy in the Inter-war Years', in John A. Davis (ed.), *Gramsci and Italy's Passive Revolution* (London, 1979).

[42] De Grazia, 'The Nationalisation of Women Under Fascist Rule'. Paper given at conference on 'Women in Twentieth-Century Italy: History and Historiography', London, 1991.

wood starlet was just as problematic (in the sense of male-defined and essentially unrealistic) a role model for women as the heroic mother of the nation. It may be better to see such change as just that – change in women's life-style rather than improvement.

Overall, concrete evidence of female emancipation is thin on the ground. There is some evidence of what could be termed emancipatory changes in the domestic sphere for certain groups of women. For example, both the work of Chiara Saraceno[43] and my own study of light engineering workers, suggest that, amongst the urban working class, where women were employed outside the home, gender roles could become slightly blurred as men began to take on a more equal share of household tasks with the emergence of companionate marriages. How widespread all this was, however, remains unclear. Paul Corner argues that in some northern rural areas[44] the decline of the peasant patriarch spelled the advent of a new era where women's role was enhanced as female earning capacities were increasingly valued. His carefully re-searched work skilfully explores the reasons why female employment remained high in such areas despite government campaigns and legis-lation. Less convincing is his argument that the decline of the patriarchal family clearly signified greater emancipation for women.[45] The doubt remains that such changes represented a shift in the distribution of power between different generations more than between the sexes. Sig-nificantly he notes that one reason for the revaluation of extra-domestic work in this period was due to the fact that it was no longer almost exclusively a female preserve.

Other scholars interested in this question have reached different con-clusions. For example, Gloria Nemec is able to go deeper into the sig-nificance of extra-domestic female employment in rural areas by making use of oral history sources.[46] Her research, about female textile workers from peasant families in the Isonzo area, describes a world where, although widespread, female extra-domestic labour was entirely subor-dinated to the needs and life-cycle patterns of rural families. In the oral

[43] Chiara Saraceno, 'La famiglia operaia sotto il fascismo', in *La classe operaia durante il fascismo*.

[44] Corner's study ('Women in Fascist Italy') focuses on the hill areas to the north of Milan – the Alto Milanese, the Brianza and the Comasco where peasant families com-bined work on the land with rural manufacturing.

[45] It may be that Corner is confusing the patriarchal family with the broader concept of patriarchy itself. The first refers specifically to the power of the father in the family whereas the second encompasses male power in general. For a discussion of this distinc-tion and the usefulness of the study of patriarchy to women's history see the contro-versial article by Judith Bennett, 'Feminism and History', *Gender and History*, vol. 1, no. 3 (1989), pp. 251–72.

[46] Gloria Nemec, 'Identità femminile e lavoro. Le operaie tessili isontine durante il fas-cismo', *Passato e presente*, vol. 24 (1990).

testimonies of the workers themselves, employment was presented as totally unrelated to any concept of female autonomy or independence. Similarly, Barbagli's study of the Italian family based on a massive oral history sample shows – despite its almost studious avoidance of gender issues – how the sharing of domestic tasks was far from widespread in this period. Such work remained women's work.[47]

The studies I have cited, contradictory in their findings, serve to emphasise that even for those women who did work outside the home, the exact meaning of this work varied. The relationship between employment and emancipation, far too often assumed to exist, is in fact complex. A desire for independence probably figured extremely low on many women's list of reasons for working in spite of Fascist campaigns.[48] Work may not have felt particularly emancipating given the conditions of employment of many women in this period – low pay, strict gender hierarchies in the workplace, widespread homeworking etc. My own study of Sesto San Giovanni found female light engineering workers with a strong work ethic who did see work as a positive force in their lives giving them dignity. But these workers were actually part of a minority. They worked outside the home for eight–ten hours per day in bright and mostly clean conditions. Most women's experience of employment was less appealing. Many did outwork or were employed as domestic servants, and despite Italy's half-hearted industrial revolution of the end of the nineteenth century millions stilll worked in arduous jobs on the land.

Evidence of a lower birth rate can also be viewed from more than one angle. It seems undeniable that the freedom to choose a smaller family should be seen as a benefit for women. But the illegality of most forms of contraception and contraceptive information meant that for many this was won only at the terrible cost of repeated backstreet abortion.[49] Also the exact significance of keeping family size down varied according to the social and cultural context. In a northern textile town it could enable women to work outside the home but in the case of interwar Sicily Triolo argues that abortion was used by women largely

---

[47] Barbagli, *Sotto lo stesso tetto*.

[48] For example, Corner's study of rural small capitalists shows how Fascist calls for women to stop working were ignored primarily because they contradicted the plans of an emerging new small entrepreneurial class for whom female labour was deemed essential to overall family economic strategy. See Corner, 'Women in Fascist Italy'.

[49] On abortion in this period see Luisa Passerini, 'Donne operaie e aborto nella Torino fascista', *Italia contemporanea*, vol. 151–2 (1982); Passerini, *Fascism in Popular Memory*, chap. 4; Denise Detriagache, 'Un aspect de la politique démographique de l'Italie fasciste: la répression de l'avortement', *Mélanges de l'Ecole Française de Rome*, vol. 92, no. 2 (1980). On the broader question of attitudes to sexuality in this period see Bruno Wanrooij, *Storia del pudore: la questione sessuale in Italia, 1860–1940* (Venice, 1990).

as a normal part of family budget management to create the right size of family.[50] In this example family planning was not linked to expectations of a less oppressive life-style. Triolo's work, furthermore, gives pause for thought about the supposedly emancipating effects of the rise of companionate marriage. In her case study, the increase in this type of marriage, in the context of a low level of extra-domestic female employment and Muslim-influenced cultural values, resulted in even greater isolation in the home as women were cut off from some of their extended female kin networks.[51]

CONCLUSION

The work of Triolo, Nemec and Corner suggests the degree to which the female experience of the Fascist period was marked by its sheer diversity, a diversity which can be really explored only through further research of this kind. Local case studies are particularly necessary in view of just how varied a country Italy was in this period. I myself have researched women's factory work in a northern city. But what a contrast with the southern peasantry or even rural life only a few kilometres from northern urban areas! For such reasons, the history of women in interwar Italy is by no means a 'neat' subject and the impact of the regime and its policies on them was correspondingly varied.

The pattern and degree of change differed from area to area and between different social groups. The range of social, political, economic, and cultural forces affecting women's lives meant that, whilst for some groups change was slow or imperceptible, for others the interwar period constituted a significant break with the past. New public spaces opened up and the spread of mass culture brought new role models. In some areas economic change led to the erosion of traditional power relations within the patriarchal family. But even here, where there was a considerable degree of change, its impact could be seen as ambiguous and contradictory.

It is undeniable that some of these developments were a result of changes wrought by Mussolini's government. Fascist policies such as anti-migration legislation, the replacement of collective bargaining with the sham of the 'Corporate State', and the official reconciliation with the Catholic Church all had important repercussions on women's lives.

[50] Triolo, 'The Angelmakers'.
[51] Triolo, 'The Angelmakers'. Barbagli's work (*Sotto lo stesso tetto*), mainly on northern Italy, also testifies to this process. He shows how in large sharecropping units men and women tended to socialise in single-sex groups. With the decline of such large units and the increase in more isolated intimate families, women could become more separated from other women.

The Fascists also strove to reshape women's relationship to the state and in doing so created new public roles for middle-class women. However, where they tried to intervene most explicitly to mould gender roles, in their bid to stem or even reverse trends towards female emancipation through highly misogynous rhetoric and policy, they were far from successful. Although they preached, and wherever practicable, legislated for female subordination, they were doomed ultimately to fail in their declared ambition to make women into 'angels of the hearth'. There were simply too many constraints on policy-makers for legislation to have much impact, and, despite the enormous amount of attention paid to gender roles in Fascist rhetoric, it seems that the particular patterns of industrialisation, commercialisation, and urbanisation had more power to shape female experiences in this period than the crude tools of Fascist ideology and policy.

6

'THE VALUE OF MARRIAGE FOR THE *VOLKSGEMEINSCHAFT*': POLICIES TOWARDS WOMEN AND MARRIAGE UNDER NATIONAL SOCIALISM

GABRIELE CZARNOWSKI

When scholars began to take an interest in 'women in Nazi Germany', the regime's policies towards women's paid employment was one of the first things they studied and discussed.[1] The question of women's paid employment as a central issue of women's emancipation has frequently been used as a barometer of the modernity or antimodernity of Nazi policy,[2] if the regime's motherhood- and family-oriented policy towards women was not regarded *per se* as proof of anti-feminism. Tim Mason, for example, acknowledged that policies towards women were 'arguably the only new and comprehensive social policies which the regime implemented in the 1930s'. However, he considered marriage loans and child allowances as well as many 'organisational innovations' in the field of assistance for mothers and children as part of the regime's at once 'illiberal and protective' policy for women.[3] The Nazi state's investment in marriages and families was indeed greater than that of the Weimar

---

This chapter was translated by Pamela Selwyn.

[1] Cf. Jill Stephenson, *Women in Nazi Society* (London, 1975); Tim Mason, 'Women in Nazi Germany, 1925–1940: Family, Welfare and Work', parts 1 and 2, *History Workshop. A Journal of Socialist Historians*, no. 1 (Spring 1976), pp. 74–113; no. 2 (Autumn 1976), pp. 5–32; Dörte Winkler, *Frauenarbeit im 'Dritten Reich'* (Hamburg, 1977). On the politics of the *Arbeitseinsatz* (labour conscription) and the situation of foreign workers both male and female, and on foreign working mothers and children in Germany, see the later studies by Ulrich Herbert, *'Fremdarbeiter'. Politik und Praxis der 'Ausländer-Einsatzes' in der Kriegswirtschaft des Dritten Reiches* (2nd edn, Berlin and Bonn, 1986), and Raimund Reiter, *Tötungsstätten für ausländische Kinder im Zweiten Weltkrieg. Zum Spannungsverhältnis von kriegswirtschaftlichem Arbeitseinsatz und nationalsozialistischer Rassenpolitik in Niedersachsen* (Hanover, 1993).

[2] Viewed statistically, the early measures taken against employed married women produced only minor swings in the long-term trend towards regular lifelong paid work on the part of working-class wives. Up until the early 1930s, in contrast, wives and mothers had usually worked irregularly. See Rüdiger Hachtmann, 'Industriearbeiterinnen in der deutschen Kriegswirtschaft 1936 bis 1944/45', *Geschichte und Gesellschaft*, vol. 19 (1993), pp. 332–66.

[3] See Mason, 'Women in Nazi Germany', part 1, pp. 86ff.

government had been. Together with the new welfare measures, however, this cannot be seen as purely positive. What Mason, like others writing in the 1970s, did not address was the central role played in National Socialism by the racial policies that underlay all measures taken in the fields of women's, family, and social policy. It was not until ten years later when Gisela Bock published her pathbreaking study of compulsory sterilisation under National Socialism that such concerns were placed centre stage.[4]

The National Socialist 'seizure of power' installed a regime that abolished civil liberties and declared the 'national community' of 'racial equals' the highest value and objective of all politics.[5] The notion of race that shaped this politics was not one based on commonalities of language, appearance, culture or traditions. It was, rather, grounded in the scientific concept of race put forward by anthropology, biology and racial hygiene or eugenics, which defined 'race' as a procreative nexus.[6] 'Racial classification' rested upon 'blood descent'; in the case of 'hereditary diseases' the connection was self-evident. An 'improvement of the race' was possible only through selective interventions in procreation. The supervision and regulation of births, marriages and sexuality was thus an important content of National Socialist racial policy, which, during the war, arrogated to itself the power of life and death, the right to decide who should inhabit the earth and who should not. The dynamic of this process began in 1933. Cleansing the 'racial body' (*Volkskörper*) of 'inferior' individuals and those of 'alien races' became a task for the state. 'Miscegenation' was to be banished within a few generations. The ultimate aim was the 'regeneration of the racial body' (*Aufartung des Volkskörpers*) by means of hierarchically structured programmes directed at the genetic, medical, and social worth of its members (*Volksgenossen*), in conjunction with a 'war on the declining birth rate' waged on criminal-justice, administrative, and medical levels.

The National Socialist state pursued a specific policy towards women not because of its purported support for traditional motherhood, but because of women's childbearing potential. Women were of political interest, both negatively and positively, not as mothers *per se*, but rather as mothers of the 'race'. In Auschwitz pregnant Jewish women, mothers and children were murdered immediately upon arrival. In the ghettos

---

[4] Gisela Bock, *Zwangssterilisation im Nationalsozialismus. Studien zur Rassenpolitik und Frauenpolitik* (Opladen, 1986). See also Michael Burleigh and Wolfgang Wippermann, *The Racial State. Germany 1933–1945* (Cambridge, 1991).

[5] See Diemut Majer, *'Fremdvölkische' im Dritten Reich* (Boppard, 1981).

[6] See Gabriele Czarnowski, *Das kontrollierte Paar. Ehe- und Sexualpolitik im Nationalsozialismus* (Weinheim, 1991). The other side of racism, racial mythologies and ideologies, played a minor role in the administrative enforcement of racial policy.

of occupied Poland they were the first to be deported to the death camps.[7] Fascist Italy, in contrast, pursued pro-natalist rather than eugenic and racial policies. With a combination of repression, welfare measures and propaganda, the Italian government sought to 'national-ise' its female citizens and not, as was the case in Germany, to sterilise and murder many of them.[8]

NATIONAL SOCIALIST WOMEN'S AND WELFARE ORGANISATIONS: SUPPORTING WOMEN'S FAMILY WORK WITHIN THE 'RACIAL BODY'[9]

From 1934/5, there existed two National Socialist women's organis-ations, the NS-Frauenschaft (NSF) and the Deutsches Frauenwerk (DFW), both administered by the National Women's Leadership (Reichsfrauenführung) and its various sections. The DFW, the 'mass organisation' for women under National Socialism, brought together those associations of the Weimar women's movement that had not dis-banded after 1933 but had rather been 'co-ordinated' (*gleichgeschaltet*) and integrated into the Nazi structure, particularly the Housewives' Federation (Hausfrauenverband) with its large membership. In 1935, eighty-seven groups with 2.7 million members were organised in the DFW. By the end of the 1930s there were four million members. The DFW was under the 'spiritual leadership' of the NSF, the 'elite organis-ation' of National Socialist women under Gertrud Scholtz-Klink. The NSF had two million members in 1935. Based on the social background of members, both the DFW and the NSF were middle-class women's organisations. Scholtz-Klink was also nominally the head of the Women's Office of the German Labour Front (DAF) which, since all

[7] See, for example, Sybil Milton, 'Women and the Holocaust. The Case of German and German-Jewish Women', in Renate Bridenthal, Atina Grossmann and Marion Kaplan (eds.), *When Biology Became Destiny: Women in Weimar and Nazi Germany* (New York, 1984), pp. 297–333; Joan Ringelheim, 'Verschleppung, Tod und Überleben: National-sozialistische Ghettopolitik gegen jüdische Frauen und Männer im besetzten Polen', in Theresa Wobbe (ed.), *Nach Osten. Verdeckte Spuren nationalsozialistischer Verbrechen* (Frankfurt/Main, 1992), pp. 135–60.

[8] See Victoria de Grazia, *How Fascism Ruled Women: Italy, 1922–1943* (Berkeley, Los Angeles and Oxford, 1992).

[9] This section is based largely on Jill Stephenson's *The Nazi Organisation of Women* (London, 1981) and Claudia Koonz's *Mothers in the Fatherland: Women, the Family and Nazi Politics* (New York, 1986). On the National Socialist youth organisation for girls, see Dagmar Reese, *Straff, aber nicht stramm – herb, aber nicht derb. Zur Vergesell-schaftung von Mädchen durch den Bund Deutscher Mädel im soziokulturellen Vergleich zweier Milieus* (Weinheim and Basle, 1989). On women as SS members, see Gudrun Schwarz, 'Verdrängte Täterinnen. Frauen im Apparat der SS (1939–1945)', in Wobbe (ed.), *Nach Osten*, pp. 197–223.

employed people were obliged to join, had five million female members.[10]

One of the most important and popular institutions of the NSF/DFW was the Reich Mothers' Service (RMD), which was founded in 1934. In 1935 the Reich Minister of the Interior assigned it a monopoly in the field of housewives' and mothers' training; other private and particularly Church-run institutions, which had been very active in this area during the Weimar Republic, were banned, had integrated themselves, or had ceased to exist. An exception was made, however, in the case of some courses for working women and working-class wives organised by large companies and by the DAF.[11] By March of 1939 over 1.7 million women had taken part in nearly 100,000 RMD courses, 500,000 of them in 1938 alone. By 1944 five million women had attended the training courses. They included not only urban housewives, although they were in the majority, but also women in paid employment and women from the countryside.[12] The wives of self-employed men, salaried employees and civil servants dominated, while working-class women were under-represented.[13]

The cooking, sewing and domestic science courses offered by the section 'National Economy/Domestic Economy' were equally popular: 1.8 million women had already participated by the middle of 1938. The section also ran 150 consumer advice centres in consultation with the Reich Ministry of Food and Agriculture[14] and actively promoted the rationalisation of housework. It continued in a specific form the professionalisation of housework begun during the Weimar period.[15]

Mothers' and infants' classes had already been popular in the Weimar Republic, and domestic science training courses had also been offered. The new Nazi courses with explicit racial policy themes were far less popular than those with a practical focus, though the latter were not free of 'Weltanschauung' propaganda. The leadership also found it difficult even to motivate enough of those DFW members already involved

---

[10] Stephenson, Organisation, p. 148, and Koonz, Mothers, p. 183.
[11] See Carola Sachse, 'Hausarbeit im Betrieb. Betriebliche Sozialarbeit unter dem Nationalsozialismus', in Carola Sachse et al., Angst, Belohnung, Zucht und Ordnung. Herrschaftsmechanismen im Nationalsozialismus (Opladen, 1982), pp. 209–74.
[12] Stephenson, Organisation, pp. 163ff. See also Susanna Dammer, 'Nationalsozialistische Frauenpolitik und soziale Arbeit', in Hans-Uwe Otto and Heinz Sünker (eds.), Soziale Arbeit und Faschismus (Frankfurt/Main, 1989), pp. 157–75.
[13] See Sachse, 'Hausarbeit', p. 244.
[14] See Stephenson, Organisation, pp. 165f.
[15] See Barbara Orland, 'Emanzipation durch Rationalisierung? Der "rationelle Haushalt" als Konzept institutionalisierter Frauenpolitik in der Weimarer Republik', in Dagmar Reese et al. (eds.), Rationale Beziehungen? Geschlechterverhältnisse im Rationalisierungsprozeß (Frankfurt/Main, 1993), pp. 222–50.

in mothercare courses to attend the 'political' courses.[16] The extent to which the NSF was effective in convincing women of the new maxims of Nazi racial policy remains questionable.

There were close connections between the NSF and the Nazi welfare organisation Nationalsozialistische Volkswohlfahrt (NSV). With its seventeen million members, it was one of the largest welfare organisations in the world. In Nazi Germany only the DAF had more members than the NSV. The NSF/DFW and NSV depended largely on volunteer work, which in the NSV was also done mainly by women. In 'Mothers' and Children's Relief' (Hilfswerk Mutter und Kind) the NSV developed activities on a large scale, with 25,552 assistance centres in existence by 1935. Their welfare work was directed exclusively at 'valuable members of the national community'.[17]

THE PUBLIC HEALTH OFFICE AS 'BIOLOGICAL HEADQUARTERS'[18]

In 1934/5 began the successive reorganisation and expansion of the public health system into a modern tool for the enforcement of National Socialist population and racial policy. Up until this time, public health offices had existed in Germany only in large cities and some middle-sized towns, mainly in industrial regions. Prussia in particular had developed a flourishing municipal health care system during the Weimar period. Now public health offices were introduced everywhere on the lowest (local) administrative level and placed under the central authority of the Reich Ministry of the Interior (RMdI). By 1939 there were 739 public health offices. 'Untrustworthy' physicians – Jews, Communists, Socialists, including many women doctors – were dismissed. About one-half of the new public health offices were opened in rural regions.

The public health offices combined the tasks of overseeing sanitary conditions (supervising food, water, soil and air) with those of public health and preventative medicine: maternity, infant and child welfare, programmes for school children, people with tuberculosis or venereal diseases, the physically and mentally disabled, and alcoholics. 'Genetic and racial care' (*Erb- und Rassenpflege,* or racial eugenics), including counselling for engaged couples, was introduced as a specifically new National Socialist field of public health. The marriage and sex coun-

---

[16] Stephenson, *Organisation*, pp. 160f.
[17] Stephenson, *Organisation*, p. 45; Dammer, 'Frauenpolitik', p. 167. See, among others, Eckard Hansen, *Wohlfahrtspolitik im NS-Staat. Motivationen, Konflikte und Macht-strukturen im 'Sozialismus der Tat' des Dritten Reiches* (Augsburg, 1991).
[18] For a detailed discussion, see Czarnowski, *Das kontrollierte Paar.*

selling centres of the Weimar Republic,[19] which had also had a strong eugenic component, were either closed or absorbed into the public health offices.

The public health offices' administrative combination of the tasks of the 'old' social hygiene with those of the 'new' racial hygiene had a primarily strategic purpose, namely 'to assemble the documentation absolutely essential for work in the field of genetic care (*Erbpflege*)'. Every visit to the welfare office or to a client's home should 'be used to collect the material necessary to judge the individual family's genetic worth'.[20] In the large cities, where the public health system was already well developed, this facilitated free access to an existing more or less extensive body of records. All branches of the newly founded public health offices also produced a steady stream of information for eugenic selection – provided that their employees were inspired by the requisite 'spirit of race hygiene'.

The new 'genetic and racial care' counselling centres within the public health offices were sites of selection according to racial, eugenic and health criteria. Here the presiding medical officer issued the marriage approvals (*Eheeignungen*) required for marriage loans, issued prohibitions on marriage, instituted sterilisation proceedings before the Hereditary Health Court (*Erbgesundheitsgericht*) and saw to it that the operation was carried out, if necessary with police assistance. He investigated reports of miscarriages, made judgments on eligibility for settlement on suburban housing estates or farms and for naturalisation and adoption, and decided whether or not clients should receive child allowances or education grants. Even the conferring of the Mother Cross, which was introduced shortly before the war, was tied to examination by medical officers. In this way, it was possible to register groups and persons to whom the public health offices had scarcely had access before. In addition – and this could have dire consequences for those affected – the inquiries that preceded the granting of marriage loans could end not merely in the refusal of the loan, but also in a prohibition of the planned marriage or the initiation of compulsory sterilisation proceedings before the Hereditary Health Court against one or both of the engaged partners as well as their family members.

The data of all welfare offices – above all the 'genetic and racial care' counselling centres – were to be collected in an index on heredity (*erbbiologische Kartei*). In the form of a 'place of residence index' it

[19] See Cornelie Usborne, *The Politics of the Body in Weimar Germany: Women's Reproductive Rights and Duties* (Basingstoke, 1992); Atina Grossmann, *Reforming Sex: The German Movement for Birth Control and Abortion Rights, 1920 to 1950* (Oxford, 1995).
[20] Herbert Linden, 'Erb- und Rassenpflege bei den Gesundheitsämtern', *Der öffentliche Gesundheitsdient* (hereafter *ÖGD*), vol. 1 (1935), p. 3.

formed the central index of each local public health office. It was
intended to be expanded gradually, in the form of a 'place of birth
index', into a 'heredity survey' of the entire population, in order to provide an 'objective basis' for physical interventions into women's bodies,
and welfare measures. What was typical of this heredity index was that
it was not simply a record of individuals or a collection of data on particular social groups in the population. It was both and more: as a genea-
logical register (*Sippenregistratur*) it aimed to represent the kinship
relations of the public health office's clientele. Close co-operation thus
existed with the district registry office in order to check the information
clients provided about their families. The Personal Status Law of 1937
perfected this co-operation both technically and organisationally.[21]

Thus racial and genetic concerns determined not only the political
orientation and work of every branch of the public health system, but
also the organisational patterns of the bureaucracy. The implementation
of the supervision and control of marriage partners depended to a high
degree on this bureaucratic framework. Alongside the mobility of clients, its 'success rate' (from the standpoint of its authors) depended
upon the varying degrees of completion of the heredity index in the
public health offices. By 1942, some ten million people had been
'card-filed'.[22]

MARRIAGE POLICY I:

CONTROLLING AND IMPEDING MARRIAGE

The first measure relating to marriages was the introduction of marriage
loans in autumn 1933.[23] Until 1937, the receipt of such loans was contingent on the wife giving up paid employment. An important precondition for the granting of marriage loans was an official medical certificate of fitness for marriage (*Eheeignungszeugnis*). This certificate attested
to the partners' mental and physical health and their fertility and social
capability for parenthood as well as the absence of 'hereditary encum-
brances', i.e., of family members afflicted with hereditary diseases,
which were to be investigated in the case of each couple, according to
the genetic paradigm then being applied by the Nazis. The first ques-
tionnaire used had been developed for the marriage counselling centres
in Prussia by the eugenicist and social gynaecologist Max Hirsch (who
subsequently was to be persecuted as a Jew). These counselling centres
had existed since 1926 for engaged couples who were interested in

[21] *Reichsgesetzblatt* (hereafter *RGBl.*), vol. I (1937), pp. 1146–52.
[22] Bock, *Zwangssterilisation*, pp. 191f.
[23] For a detailed discussion, see Czarnowski, *Das kontrollierte Paar*.

having their eugenic suitability checked before marriage; the procedure was completely voluntary and carried with it no administrative consequences. Very few couples had visited such marriage counselling centres (unless they also offered contraceptive advice),[24] when compared to the stream of couples who were obliged to have themselves examined for a marriage loan. The requirement of 'Aryan descent' (*arische Abstammung*) was a new one. This term appeared in a legal text for the first time in April 1933 and was adopted for marriage loans. With it began the 'legal' segregation of Jewish from non-Jewish Germans. From then on 'mixed marriage' referred only to 'racially mixed marriages', and no longer, as previously, to marriages between persons of different religions.

In September and October of 1935 the 'Blood Protection Law', 'Reich Citizenship Law' and 'Marriage Health Law' were enacted.[25] From that time on freedom of marriage was abolished in Germany. The courts also began to deal with the new criminal offence of so-called 'race defilement' (*Rassenschande*), supposed or actual relationships between those classified as Germans and as Jews.[26] The 'Blood Protection Law' and 'Reich Citizenship Law' defined who was a 'Jew'. They introduced the concept of 'kindred blood' and created the categories 'mixed race of the first and second degree' (*Mischlinge ersten und zweiten Grades*). These definitions were the basis not only of regulations in matrimonial and family law, but also of all subsequent 'legal' measures depriving German Jews of their rights, including their deportation from German territory and their murder as 'stateless persons'.

The 'Blood Protection Law' contained racist bars to marriage not only between Jewish and non-Jewish Germans but also between Germans and 'other persons of alien blood' such as 'Negroes' and 'Gypsies'. The 'Marriage Health Law' set up bars to marriage on eugenic and health grounds. Partners had to provide proofs of heredity and a 'test of fitness for marriage' (*Ehetauglichkeitszeugnis*, ETZ) to demonstrate that no such obstacles applied.

Although the clause regarding these ETZ was never enacted, they were carried out from the beginning, depending on the judgment of registry officers. From 1936 on they were also required to report any impending marriage to the responsible public health office. Within the period of the publication of the banns the public health office then searched its records for any 'negative' registration of the bride, groom

---

[24] See Usborne, *Politics of the Body*, p. 144; Grossmann, *Reforming Sex*; Czarnowski, *Das kontrollierte Paar*, pp. 111ff., 226.

[25] *RGBl.*, vol. I (1935), pp. 1146, 1246ff., 1333ff., 1419ff.

[26] See Hans Robinson, *Justiz als politische Verfolgung. Die Rechtsprechung in 'Rassenschande-fällen' beim Landgericht Hamburg 1936–1943* (Stuttgart, 1977).

or family members. If such information were found, the couple was called upon to undergo an examination of their fitness for marriage. If they refused to comply, permission to marry was denied, as of course was the case if the public health officer declared the couple 'unfit for marriage'.

The most frequent reason for barring marriage under the 'Marriage Health Law' was 'mental disturbance' which, so the law reads, 'makes the marriage appear undesirable for the national community'. The other reasons for bars to marriage provided by the law were the presence of communicable diseases (particularly venereal disease and tuberculosis), legal incapacity or temporary custodianship, or an hereditary disease that might lead to compulsory sterilisation under the 'Law on the Prevention of Hereditary Diseases' (feeblemindedness, schizophrenia, epilepsy, manic depression, Huntington's chorea, congenital blindness and deafness, severe physical deformities and severe alcoholism). People classified as 'hereditarily diseased' were, however, allowed to marry if 'the other partner in the engagement' was infertile. Whether this was a result of compulsory sterilisation or some other cause was unimportant. The main thing was that the marriage could produce no 'undesirable issue'. The medical certificate of infertility required in such cases was waived only if the woman was over the age of forty-five.

During the war, control over a large number of marriages was subject to military marriage regulations, which were changed several times.[27] These required an additional medical examination of the bride by the public health officer. By 1942, men eligible for military service were declared fit for marriage without any further medical examination. The following bars to marriage were instituted over the course of the war for soldiers: marriage to foreign women (except those of 'kindred blood', i.e. Dutch and Scandinavian women), to prostitutes, or to 'unworthy and hereditarily diseased women'.[28]

Beginning in 1941, all people desiring to marry were required to present a so-called 'Marriage Clearance Certificate' (*Eheunbedenklichkeitsbescheinigung*) at the registry office.[29] Since men 'in active military service' were exempted, this directive particularly targeted women. Indeed, the primary intention was to prevent a 'fraudulent contraction of marriage' by 'women whose offspring are undesirable'.[30] If previously the question of fitness for marriage had been answered behind the engaged

---

[27] See Czarnowski, *Das kontrollierte Paar*, pp. 175ff.
[28] See Czarnowski, *Das kontrollierte Paar*, pp. 178, 228; Institut für Zeitgeschichte (IfZ), MA-470.
[29] *RGBl.*, vol. I (1941), pp. 650f.
[30] Linden, 'Die Eheunbedenklichkeitsbescheinigung', *ÖGD*, vol. 8 (1942), pp. 139f.

couples' backs, they were now required to appear at the public health office in person in order to obtain a certificate. Staff shortages and time pressures meant that medical examinations to determine fitness for marriage were to be undertaken only if one of the partners or their family members was 'negatively' registered at the public health office. A 1941 police decree stipulated that cohabitations resulting from a bar to marriage under the Marriage Health Law should be separated by interning the 'guilty' party – when in doubt, the man – in a concentration camp if a warning by the police was unsuccessful. Such cohabitation was considered 'asocial'.[31]

In 1943, the Reich Ministry of the Interior tried to extend the obstacles to marriage under the 'Marriage Health Law' to include the grounds of 'age difference' and 'infertility', grounds that had long been sufficient for the refusal of marriage loans.[32] At this period the RMdI used arguments related to the war. It demanded that 'in light of the existing shortage of men, men capable of procreation only marry fertile healthy women', and that this be anchored in the 'Marriage Health Law' as a 'flexible regulation', to be decided in each case by the medical officer's evaluation of the individual couple. The RMdI was not, however, able to overcome the persistent rejection of its desired amendments by the Reich Ministry of Justice (RMJ). The RMJ criticised the vagueness of bars to marriage, and proposed a bar to marriages between women over forty-five and men under fifty-five years of age, alongside an improvement within matrimonial law of the position of the wives with many children. The RMdI stood by its 'flexible regulations' here, arguing that the RMJ draft forced the legal establishment of a 'defensible' age difference, and this was scarcely feasible.

These debates reflected not simply a conflict between two ministries over competencies, but also different notions of marriage. On the basis of bars to marriage on racial policy, health, and eugenic grounds, for the 'remaining' majority of society the RMJ upheld a pro-natalist concept that foresaw a subordinate but secure position for wives and thus bound husbands to unwanted unions. On the same basis, the RMdI, in contrast, upheld what amounted to a promotion of the husband's sexual and familial irresponsibility – supposedly his 'nature' – a notion similar to the gender concepts of (present-day) sociobiology. This was particularly apparent in discussions surrounding the reform of laws on divorce.

[31] Bundesarchiv Koblenz (BAK), Slg. Schumacher, Nr. 271: Reichssicherheitshauptamt, Decree of 25 Oct. 1941.
[32] On the following, see BAK, R 43 II, Nr. 722; Bundesarchiv Potsdam (BAP) 30.01, 10118.

MARRIAGE POLICY II: FACILITATING DIVORCE

Whereas the National Socialist state, particularly the RMdI, began early to exercise a decisive and increasing influence on marriage, it was not until the Marriage Law of 1938 that it undertook a reform of divorce law. This reform was preceded by protracted debates on how a new, National Socialist marriage law might look. In the end, the law was only a compromise and gave rise to repeated attempted interventions and amendments until the end of the war.[33]

The Marriage Law completed the 'nationalisation' of marriage with a new divorce law. The impeding, control and selective promotion of marriage was now supplemented by a facilitation of divorce. In contrast to the legal bars to marriage, which abolished the freedom to choose a marriage partner, the new divorce law did not express a legal obligation to terminate a marriage, unless one of the partners petitioned for divorce.[34] The Marriage Law of 1938 changed the legal framework for a possible separation and offered partners petitioning for divorce new grounds upon which to do so. At the same time, it set political targets. Social and political pressures aside, marriages the state considered 'undesirable' were generally upheld, if the partners were agreed. Thus for example a Sicherheitsdienst (SD) report of 1943 pointed out that there were still many German-Jewish 'mixed marriages'.[35]

Nevertheless by the end of 1933 German courts had already begun to recognise 'racial error' as a ground for contesting marriage, and had dissolved marriages between Jewish and non-Jewish Germans before a single law had been changed.[36] The rise in the divorce rate in 1934 and 1935 may be attributed primarily to this practice. The 'Blood Protection' and 'Marriage Health Laws' of 1935 legalised the contesting of 'mixed marriages' and of 'marriage to a partner with an hereditary disease'.[37]

---

[33] On the history of the drafting and effects of the Marriage Law of 1938, see Dirk Blasius, *Ehescheidung in Deutschland im 19. und 20. Jahrhundert* (Frankfurt/Main, 1992), pp. 188–223. My account here is based in part on his book. See also Stephenson, *Women in Nazi Society*, pp. 42ff.; Anka Schaefer, 'Zur Stellung der Frau im nationalsozialistischen Eherecht', in Lerke Gravenhorst and Carmen Tatschmurat (eds.), *Töchter-Fragen. NS-Frauen-Geschichte* (Freiburg., 1990), pp. 183–92.

[34] Marriages contracted through 'deceit' (i.e., concealment of an impediment to marriage) could, however, be annulled on application to the courts from the Director of Public Prosecutions.

[35] BAP, 30.01, 10118, f. 173: Chief of the Sicherheitspolizei (SiPo) and SD to RMJ (personal), 18 June 1943.

[36] Hans Wrobel, 'Die Anfechtung der Rassenmischehe. Diskriminierung und Entrechtung der Juden in den Jahren 1933 bis 1935', *Kritische Justiz*, vol. 16 (1983), pp. 349–74.

[37] See the official commentary on the *Blutschutz- und Ehegesundheitsgesetz . . . Dargestellt, medizinisch und juristisch erläutert von Arthur Gütt, Herbert Linden, Franz Maßfeller* (Munich, 1936), pp. 102–6, 208–10.

The Marriage Law of 1938 upheld these grounds for annulment, adopted 'mental illness' as a ground for divorce from the old matrimonial law in the Civil Code (Bürgerliches Gesetzbuch, BGB) and added two new 'non-guilty' grounds for divorce: 'mental disturbance' and 'contagious or loathsome disease'. With this, divorce was now fully connected to the system of marriage bars on racial policy, eugenic and health grounds.

The new Marriage Law also facilitated the dissolution of existing marriages for reasons of population policy. To this end, three new grounds for divorce were introduced. First, in addition to the old blame paragraphs of the BGB (adultery and serious matrimonial offences), a new offence was included, the 'refusal to procreate'. The justification was that the primary purpose of marriages was the preservation and increase of the 'race'. The 'use of illicit means to prevent birth' also fell under this offence. Second, divorce 'without blame' – which in the BGB had been possible only in exceptional cases of mental illness – was now possible not only on the above-mentioned eugenic and health grounds, but also for reasons of 'premature infertility', 'because the most important objective of marriage can no longer be fulfilled'.[38] In all cases of eugenic and health-related grounds for divorce without personal blame what was decisive was not the will of the defendants, but the medical verdict on the case. Third, the most important, in practical terms, and the most controversial of the innovations over the BGB's old law of obligations was, however, the introduction of the principle of broken marriage (*Zerrüttungsprinzip*), which provided for divorce without guilt after a three-year 'dissolution of the joint household'.[39]

Thus the impetus to facilitate divorce did not rest on 'liberalistic ideas', but rather on 'the value of marriage for the national community (*Volksgemeinschaft*)'. This is demonstrated not least by the fact that there was no provision for divorce by mutual agreement. Only the judge could decide whether, 'objectively', an 'irretrievable breakdown' had occurred. The aim was to facilitate the dissolution of marriages that had become 'worthless for the national community': 'dead marriages' were to be 'liquidated'. According to the National Socialist interpretation, these

---

[38] See Cosima König, *Die Frau im Recht des Nationalsozialismus. Eine Analyse ihrer familien-, erb- und arbeitsrechtliche Stellung* (Frankfurt/Main, Berne, New York and Paris, 1988).

[39] It is quite interesting to note that during the Weimar Republic, marriage reforms intended to introduce this principle had failed because of the resistance of the Catholic Centre Party. In the 1920s, however, the background to reform efforts had been a liberal view of marriage and privacy rights. National Socialism firmly rejected this position, viewing marriage not as a 'liberalistic institution' or a 'relationship contracted for the realisation of individual interests', but as an institution that should serve the purposes of the state. See 'Begründung des Ehegesetzes 1938', IfZ, Fa 195/4, vol. III.

were marriages that would produce no more genetically healthy, 'racially German' children. The complete replacement of the principle of guilt with that of irretrievable breakdown, which the RMdI and Himmler had favoured for reasons of population policy, could not be pushed through because the RMJ, as well as Hess (Party Chancellery), insisted on the maintenance of the traditional notion of 'negligent matrimonial offences' (*schuldhafte Eheverfehlungen*). In this case, the Minister of Justice had Hitler on his side.

The intentions of the new paragraph on irretrievable breakdown, which primarily involved population policy, were not clear from its wording. It was formulated as a blanket clause and provided for divorce when 'the restoration of a community of life that corresponds to the essence of marriage cannot be expected'.[40] One partner's objection to the other's petition for divorce should be taken seriously. In practice, then, it was often a matter of the judge's interpretation of the 'essence of marriage'.

The rulings of the Supreme Court of the Reich followed the lines of population policy and were thus in contradiction to the RMJ. It regularly ignored the objections of wives and granted the divorces husbands asked for because no further offspring could be expected of a marriage that had broken down irretrievably. The judges of the high court were especially divorce-happy when it came to helping plaintiff husbands transform their adulterous relationships into 'racially valuable' second marriages. They regarded the broken marriage as an obstacle to the contracting of a new marriage that would be 'valuable to the national community' to the extent that children could be expected. If, however, the new marriage envisaged by the husband appeared less promising in population policy terms, or for other reasons less 'desirable', wives had greater chances of success with their refusal to consent.[41]

Initially, the trial courts were slow to follow the rulings of the Supreme Court of the Reich.[42] According to the President of the Division for Civil Matters at a conference of divorce-court judges in the summer of 1944, a period of 'intense hostility to divorces' on the ground of irretrievable breakdown in the years immediately following the reform of matrimonial law (which the Supreme Court of the Reich had to 'com-

[40] *RGBl.*, vol. I (1938), p. 813.
[41] Bernd Rüthers, *Die unbegrenzte Auslegung. Zum Wandel der Privatrechtsordnung im Nationalsozialismus* (Kronberg, 1975), pp. 400–20, 409f. Most recently, in her legal study, *Die Frau im Recht des Nationalsozialismus* (pp. 75–107), Cosima König has analysed the published rulings of the Supreme Court of the Reich and selected District Courts and their significance for wives.
[42] See Blasius, *Ehescheidung*, pp. 213ff. Interestingly, younger judges tended to rule more in favour of husbands, and older judges more in favour of wives. There was no uniform attitude. Women were barred from the judiciary during the Nazi period.

bat' with its rulings) had apparently been followed by a 'stronger' shift in the desired direction 'than even the Supreme Court of the Reich itself' had intended.[43] Thus at this time the Supreme Court was getting closer to the position of the RMJ, which had been trying unsuccessfully since 1943 to achieve a partial reform of matrimonial law, among other things in order to achieve a partial withdrawal of the irretrievable breakdown paragraph for wives with three or more children. The main topic of the conference was 'divorce without guilt'. At stake was the attempt to convince judges of the lower courts to scrutinise more closely than previously the objections of wives with numerous children and the remarriage plans of plaintiff husbands.

The statistics published up until 1941 allow us to document only the early phase.[44] The number of divorces rose in 1939, with about 20 per cent being cases of irretrievable breakdown, a proportion that fell however in 1940 and 1941.[45] Even after the reform, by far the most common ground for divorce remained a 'serious negligent matrimonial offence against marriage' (schuldhafte schwere Eheverfehlung). Unlike in the case of divorces out of anti-Jewish motives, here the majority of judges ruled according to the traditional conservative view of marriage. From 1938/9 to 1941, 94,882 divorces were granted in which the husband was the guilty party, and 62,740 in which the wife was the guilty party. Adultery was the second most frequent ground. From 1938/9 to 1941, 20,960 men and 19,715 women were divorced for adultery. In third place was irretrievable breakdown as a ground for divorce. Here too, though, about half of cases ended with blame being apportioned, in 14,278 cases to the husband, in 850 cases to the wife and in 566 to both. This leaves 15,173 'true' divorces without guilt on the grounds of irretrievable breakdown for the period from 1938/9 to 1941.[46]

The number of petitions for divorce on the ground of irretrievable breakdown filed by husbands far exceeded those filed by wives. In the period between 1938/9 and 1941, 21,293 men and 6,648 women petitioned for divorce on this ground. In only 1,503 cases were proceedings initiated by both parties together. Apparently it was also only husbands who had the energy (and the money) to pursue their cases of irretrievable breakdown – against their non-consenting spouses – to the highest

---

[43] BAP, 30.01, 10121, f. 109: Senatspräsident Dr Jonas, Anlage 5.
[44] The following figures are from *Wirtschaft und Statistik*, vol. 19 (1939), pp. 755–8; vol. 22 (1942), pp. 21–6; and vol. 23 (1943), pp. 87–9. These compile the divorce figures for 1938, 1939, 1940 and 1941. They add up to more than the absolute number of divorces, because in some cases more than one ground was named for the divorce.
[45] Stephenson, *Women in Nazi Society*, p. 43.
[46] Of these in 8,724 cases it was the man, in 5,503 cases the woman, and in 946 both who had petitioned for divorce.

court, the Supreme Court of the Reich.[47] Women, like men, nevertheless produced a 'deluge of petitions' to the RMJ which, according to
a ministerial official, could be very easily classified 'according to the
petitioner's sex', depending upon their content and objectives: 'The
man has petitioned for divorce and complains that his petition had been
denied, while the wife complains about the court's ruling granting a
divorce on the basis of §55, but also enquires fearfully whether a divorce
is possible without her consent or any guilt on her part'[48] – which it
frequently was when the judge ignored her objections. He noted further:
'It is striking how well men integrated National Socialist ideas into their
arguments, claiming them as rights.' As a result, husbands desirous of
obtaining a divorce were very successful in making the underlying 'significance' of the Marriage Law conform to their individual interests:
'men in particular recognised that they could bolster their divorce suits
with National Socialist arguments that corresponded to interpretations
of the term irretrievable breakdown'.[49] The minuscule numbers of men
who petitioned for divorce on the grounds of 'refusal to procreate' or
'premature infertility' make clear that there was no sudden outbreak of
'reproductive drives' or of unfulfilled desires for (renewed) fatherhood.
From 1938/9 to 1941, 260 marriages were dissolved because of the
wife's 'premature infertility', and 123 because of the husband's. During
the same period 894 women and 877 men were divorced as the guilty
party because of their 'refusal to procreate'.

The numbers therefore tell us less about relations between married
people than about the different meanings marriage had for men and
women at this period. To contemporaries it was clear: women clung to
marriage more because of their economic dependency. Of socio-
historical interest is the fact that the greatest number of couples divorc-
ing on the grounds of irretrievable breakdown came 'from the lower
middle classes, particularly the less well-situated civil service'. 'Marital
conflicts between economically better-off people' could be 'settled much
more easily' than those 'in the narrowness of lower middle-class circumstances'. In 'quite primitive – let us say, proletarian, circumstances'
(according to the President of the Division for Civil Matters) – 'all these
questions were also much simpler'.[50]

The Marriage Law's new regulation of alimony payments also contributed to the 'far greater impact of divorce on the woman'. Despite
the (possibly non-consenting) divorced wife's right to alimony, the judge

---

[47] This at least is what emerges from the existing literature. Thus far there has been no
study of Supreme Court cases using trial records.
[48] BAP, 30.01, 10121, f. 124: Dr Hinrichs, 'Scheidung ohne Verschulden'.
[49] Schaefer, 'Zur Stellung der Frau', p. 191.
[50] BAP, 30.01, 10121, f. 115: Jonas.

could decide to free the husband of his obligations, or to reduce the payments, if the man planned to start a new family. The divorced wife could be expected to earn her own money, regardless of what had been 'usual in the circumstances in which the couple had lived while married'. This was practically 'revolutionary'. In this question even the RMJ no longer oriented itself towards marriage as a separate 'estate' with different duties and rights for the two sexes, but rather towards the economy and 'national community': because of the 'position of the employed woman in contemporary economic life, and in the social web of the nation' and 'the present-day attitude towards the value of work as an obligation to the national community', the divorced woman could be expected to 'earn money through her own labour', especially when the husband acquired new family obligations.[51] The RMJ's arguments, as expressed in the legislative history of the Marriage Law, were 'modern' here.

For the NSF, the new regulation of alimony 'logically presupposed that every woman had the right to train for an occupation'. Every father with daughters should be obliged to provide for their training so that they could support themselves in case of divorce. Not least in response to these developments the NSF proposed 'a dual educational objective': the preparation of girls for family work *and* for paid employment. Vocational training and its 'application on the job' should also prepare girls for 'women's function in the family'.[52]

From the beginning, the new divorce law was regarded by many as a law that favoured husbands. In 1943, the SD reported from various cities that 'there has been frequent disgruntlement over the fact that on the one hand we promote large families and award the Mother's Cross to mothers of many children, and that on the other divorce law leaves these women without adequate protection'.[53] Herbert Linden, a high-ranking official at the RMdI, one of the authors of the official commentary on the 'Blood Protection and Marriage Health Law', and co-organiser of the murder of patients in sanatoriums, believed that, in the long run, the Marriage Law would have negative effects on population development. In contrast to his colleagues, who were fixated on men's pure 'procreative drives', Linden believed, realistically enough, that 'the woman's attitude is decisive in determining how many children are born in a marriage. For this reason the National Socialist state [must] pay particular heed to woman's position in marriage.' The new Marriage Law, however, had weakened this very position. Any female factory

---

[51] IfZ, Fa 195/4, vol. IV. See Stephenson, *Women in Nazi Society*, pp. 43f. Here, too, an analysis of trial records would be useful for gender history.
[52] BAP, 30.01, 10121, f. 152f.: Dr Else Vorwerck, 'Familienpolitik im Kriege'.
[53] BAP, 30.01, 10118, f. 179.

worker or salaried employee had more security for the future than a wife. He thus feared that 'If we do not grant the woman more security, she will think twice before taking upon herself the sacrifice of giving birth and raising children.'[54] He recommended that, in cases where the mother of many children was involved, irretrievable breakdown be abolished as a ground for divorce and the courts return to the principle of guilt. He also argued for the principle of 'community property accumulated during marriage' – a reform that had already been discussed during the Weimar Republic – to replace the man's sole control over the couple's finances as intended by the BGB's property regime that was still in force under National Socialism.[55]

Let us look, finally, at the figures for divorces on eugenic and health grounds in the years between 1938/9 and 1941. The number of marriages dissolved because of the husband's 'mental disturbance' was 579 and, because of the wife's 'mental disturbance', 669. The figures are somewhat higher for 'mental illness': here 1,528 husbands and 2,565 wives were divorced without guilt. The number of women and men filing for divorce on the ground of a 'contagious or loathsome disease' was 191 and 99 respectively. There are no separate statistics for marriages annulled under the Blood Protection Law and Marriage Health Law. The total number of contested marriages (including those on grounds such as formal defects, bigamy etc. that were taken over from the BGB) was very small after the reform. While there were 982 in 1938 (under old and new matrimonial law combined), the numbers declined to 57 in 1939, rising again only slightly to 76 in 1940 and 97 in 1941.

THE SUBVERSIVE EFFECTS OF TRADITIONAL MATRIMONIAL LAW

Racial policy's grip on the right to marry – and thus on controlled sexuality and reproduction – was still not total in the German Reich at the end of the Second World War. Under conditions of the racial state, which was still bound to some international legal relationships, racially discriminated women actually benefited somewhat from the private law institution of marriage precisely because they were not equal to their husbands under marriage law.

'Undesirable marriages between eastern female labourers (*Ostarbeiterinnen*) and foreign men' were the subject of a letter from the

---

[54] BAP, 30.01, 10118, f. 18–27: 'Bevölkerungspolitisches Programm nach dem Kriege'. This confidential memorandum was a pro-natalist programme for raising birth rates on a eugenic and racial policy basis.
[55] See König, *Die Frau im Recht*, pp. 31f.

Gauamtsleiter of the Office of Racial Policy in Graz to the Gestapo in the summer of 1944.[56] In this letter he called on the police to 'find a practicable way to prevent the marriages between eastern female labourers and foreign citizens, which have been increasing of late'. Through marriage, these women exchanged their absence of rights as 'protected dependants (*Schutzangehörige*) of the German Reich' for the legal protection of their husbands' citizenship. One of the women, for example, married a stateless Russian immigrant, whereupon 'she was released from the eastern labourers' camp . . . [and] received normal rations. Naturally she never wore her eastern insignia [*Ostabzeichen*] again after she married.' Another married a Greek. In this way, the women managed to escape the miserable conditions the Nazi state prescribed for 'eastern labourers' (hence the racial policy functionary's indignation), which included:

> the prohibition on visiting public hairdressing salons, churches, cinemas and restaurants, the stipulation that eastern labourers may only wear special or old clothing and shoes, that they will receive only short or inferior rations, that they may only leave the area with the permission of the responsible local police authorities, that they receive low wages and not use public transport.

He saw the 'danger' that 'ever more eastern female labourers', through their individual emergence from the 'labelled' and ghettoised 'mass' in the camps, would no longer be recognisable as what they were, although marriage would not change them 'racially and biologically'. He was primarily alarmed by the notion that these 'free foreign marriages' would produce children who, legally equal to Germans, would attend German schools and grow up in Germany. 'The differences in national characteristics become blurred or are, after a short while, no longer present.' Thus such marriages would become 'a constant danger to the racial value of our nation'. Whether, and how, the Graz Gestapo intervened is not known. In light of the over two million mainly young female forced labourers from the Soviet Union in the 'Greater German Reich' these marriages were, however, occurrences of some social significance.

CONCLUSION

National Socialism pronounced marriage and the family the 'basic unit of the state' or the '*völkisch* community', and accorded its 'special protection' to marriages it considered healthy, genetically sound, racially pure and fruitful. Consequently it restricted freedom of marriage

---

[56] IfZ, NO-1796.

according to racial, medical and eugenic criteria, and facilitated divorce on the same grounds. The biologisation and medicalisation of marriage in combination with bureaucratic access to the body created the preconditions for a basically unlimited scientific and administrative restriction of individual liberties, not only for minorities, but also for the majority, not only for women, but also for men – albeit with extremely divergent consequences.

To promote the 'full-time housewife and mother', that is, a private status, did not represent National Socialist policy towards the majority of German women. This policy should rather be regarded more as a functional strengthening of and control over women's efficiency as housewives and mothers while at the same time undermining their traditional legal status in marriage and family. This is demonstrated by the examination methods and criteria used by doctors to determine 'fitness for marriage', in the judgments handed down in the cases of most female victims of compulsory sterilisation, and by the massive expansion of the public health system and the extensive apparatus for training housewives and mothers on the one hand, and by the tendencies in politics and divorce jurisdiction that measured wives' value solely by the number of children they had and that supported the disappearance of husbands and fathers from the family on the other. The Nazi policy of promoting the sexual and social irresponsibility of men as fathers led to a development which threatened the aim of National Socialist population politics themselves. The desired results in respect of the *Volksgemeinschaft* were not achieved.

7

EXPANSIONIST ZEAL, FIGHTING POWER, AND
STAYING POWER IN THE ITALIAN AND GERMAN
DICTATORSHIPS[1]

MacGREGOR KNOX

The leaders of Fascist Italy and Nazi Germany claimed a common origin and destiny for their two regimes. Yet Fascist Italy's last war collapsed within six months of its beginning in June 1940; Greeks and British inflicted staggering defeats in Albania, the Mediterranean, and North Africa. The Fascist regime itself then dissolved mutely in July 1943 in the bloodless royal and military *coup d'état* provoked by the Anglo-American landings in Sicily. Mussolini's fitful resurrection in the Salò republic from autumn 1943 onward was far from bloodless, but rested solely on German power, not his own strength. By contrast the frenetic outward thrusts of Hitler's dictatorship between 1938 and 1942 subjugated Europe from the North Cape to the Pyrenees and from Finisterre to the Don steppes. Then Germany bitterly resisted over three years of concentric ground and air attack by three world powers, and only disintegrated as Hitler's suicide released the German people from their allegiance.

That immense disparity in performance provoked naive witticisms about Italy from the victors, but little systematic explanation, despite the profusion of *ad hoc* comparisons between the two regimes and the existence of noteworthy comparative studies of their structures and of particular sectors within them.[2] Nor has comparative analysis of their dynamics – the mechanisms and forces that propelled them and the

[1] My thanks to the John Simon Guggenheim Foundation, Woodrow Wilson International Center for Scholars, Institute for Advanced Study, and German Marshall Fund of the United States for supporting much of the research for the ongoing comparative history of the two regimes from which this essay derives.
[2] See especially Wolfgang Schieder, 'Das Deutschland Hitlers und das Italien Mussolinis: Zum Problem faschistischer Regimebildung', in Gerhard Schulz, (ed.), *Die Grosse Krise der dreissiger Jahre* (Göttingen, 1985); Gustavo Corni, 'La politica agraria del fascismo: un confronto fra Italia e Germania', *Studi Storici*, vol. 28 (1987), pp. 385–421; Charles S. Maier, 'The Economics of Fascism and Nazism', in his *In Search of Stability: Explorations in Historical Political Economy* (Cambridge, 1987), pp. 70–120.

goals toward which they moved – attracted scholars to any great extent.[3] Intentionalists and functionalists have debated whether the Führer's vision or blind bureaucratic rivalries propelled the German regime. Marxists and non-Marxists have clashed over whether capitalism was the driver or merely the motor of either or both dictatorships. No satisfactory framework uniting the two and explaining their similarities and differences has yet emerged.[4]

One major feature that unites the two regimes is nevertheless clear. Both rested on compromises between revolutionary movements aiming at total power (not 'bourgeois restoration') and Establishments shaken in their commanding positions by the impact of mass politics and the storms of the First World War.[5] Those founding compromises and their root cause – the survival despite war, inflation, and depression of functioning civil societies in both Italy and Germany – thwarted the revolutionaries thereafter. Unlike Lenin and Stalin, who could write upon a political and social *tabula rasa*,[6] Mussolini and Hitler could not at first simply decree the liquidation of entire groups. Their road to total power was, and had to be, indirect. It led through war, and not merely because both leaders and movements celebrated the right of the stronger and hailed war as father of all things, highest expression of the individual and of the *stirpe* or *Volk*. War was an instrument as well as a goal; an instrument not merely for external conquest but for the barbarisation of Italian and German society and the final taming or destruction of all institutions, from churches to officer corps to the Italian monarchy, that blocked the regimes' paths at home. Fascist and Nazi expansion was the polar opposite of 'social imperialism', the preservation or restoration of the political and social order at home through success abroad. The wars of Fascism and Nazism, far from aiming to avert revolution, were designed to make it.[7]

---

[3] Henry A. Turner, Jr., 'Fascism and Modernization', in Turner (ed.), *Reappraisals of Fascism* (New York, 1975), pp. 117–39, is a notable exception to this rule.

[4] The literature on 'fascism' (lower case) is too vast for summary here; Gerhard Hirschfeld and Lothar Kettenacker (eds.), *Der 'Führerstaat': Mythos und Realität. Studien zur Struktur und Politik des Dritten Reiches* (Stuttgart, 1981) still offers the best introduction to the intentionalist–functionalist debate; Tim Mason, 'The Primacy of Politics. Politics and Economics in National Socialist Germany', in Stuart J. Woolf (ed.), *The Nature of Fascism* (London, 1968), pp. 165–95, offers a telling critique of the most common Marxist approach.

[5] Less likely artificers of 'bourgeois restoration' than Mussolini and Hitler can scarcely be imagined; on the latter, see particularly Rainer Zitelmann, *Hitler: Selbstverständis eines Revolutionärs* (Hamburg, Leamington Spa and New York, 1987); for the early NSDAP as one component of the German nationalist revolt against the very *idea* of class, see Harold J. Gordon, Jr., *Hitler and the Beer Hall Putsch* (Princeton, 1972), pp. 13–21.

[6] See Martin Malia, *Comprendre la Révolution russe* (Paris, 1980).

[7] For more on this thesis, MacGregor Knox, 'Conquest, Foreign and Domestic, in Fascist Italy and Nazi Germany', *Journal of Modern History*, vol. 56 (1984), pp. 1–57, and Tim Mason's suggestion that '... National Socialism appears as a *radically new* variant

That thesis, if sustained, helps to explain the two regimes' thirst for high-risk foreign-policy gambles and marks them off from the third great interwar dictatorship, that of Stalin, which scarcely disdained expansion but was not driven to it by internal stalemate. It can also explain the dialectical interaction of foreign and domestic policy visible in both regimes and the steadily intensifying radicalisation of their policies. What it does not account for is the wide disparity, even before those defeats, in willingness to pay the price for conquest and in man-for-man and unit-for-unit military performance. Nor does it throw much light on why the German armed forces and population fought with such determination in an increasingly hopeless cause after 1941–2.

Exploring the two regimes' differences in expansionist zeal, fighting power, and staying power requires an analysis centred less on the dictators than on their surroundings. It requires an attempt, necessarily crude and conjectural given the present state of knowledge, to separate the chronological and causative layers that affected the result. The most important factors appear to fall into three categories: underlying or inherited structures and forces, structures and forces connected with the regimes themselves, and events and their sequence.

I

The regimes inherited from their respective national pasts wide differences in socio-economic conditions and structures, political institutions, military–economic potential, military expertise and traditions, and ideological climate. Italy was – in the aggregate – thirty to fifty years behind Germany in becoming an industrial society. Literacy in 1931 was roughly 90 per cent of those of six years of age or over in the north, 79 per cent in the centre, and 61 per cent in the south and islands, whereas illiteracy in Germany had virtually vanished by 1900.[8] By the late 1930s slightly less than a third of Italy's work force was industrial, and about half agricultural; the corresponding German figures were 42 per cent for industry and 26 for agriculture (1939). Northern Italy was markedly closer to Germany in structure, at 36 per cent of the work force in industry and 42 per cent in agriculture. But only Italy's Ruhr, the Milan–Turin–Genoa triangle, came close to the aggregate level of industrialisation of Germany as a whole.[9] At the level of elites, that disparity

of the social imperialism of Bismarck and Wilhelm II . . . successful foreign expansion would legitimize not an inherited political and social system but *an entirely new one*' ('The Legacy of 1918 for National Socialism', in A. J. Nicholls and E. Matthias (eds.), *German Democracy and the Triumph of Hitler* (London, 1971), p. 218 (my emphasis)).

[8] Italy: SVIMEZ, *Un secolo di statistiche italiane. Nord e Sud 1861–1961* (Rome, 1961), p. 795.

[9] Data: *Ibid.*, pp. 51–2; B. R. Mitchell, *European Historical Statistics, 1750–1975* (2nd rev. edn, New York, 1981), pp. 164, 166.

meant that Italy's pool of technological and military talent was far smaller in proportion to the demands of world war than that of Germany.[10] At the level of the masses, it meant that a gulf far deeper than any existing in Germany separated over half the population of Italy, including the immense majority of those living south of Rome, from the modern world and the national community. That gulf was far deeper than the already deep fractures that separated Italy's Catholic and Socialist subcultures from the Liberal state. It also had direct effects on military effectiveness, for universal conscription and the assignment of most peasants to the infantry reproduced it within the army's combat units.

Germany's deepest cleavages were of an entirely different character. Deep regional economic disparities and socio-cultural divides existed – East Elbia was in some respects a far more literate Italian south. Religion and political religion divided the Catholic and Socialist subcultures from the dominant Protestant Prussian culture. But regional and confessional divides were ultimately of less consequence than the rigid horizontal segmentation inherited from the *ancien régime*, the divisions between estates or *Stände*. Despite industrialisation and the lifting in 1918 of the last laws that enshrined social distinctions, the divisions between *Stände* – especially those frozen into the educational system – retained much of their force. Horizontal barriers to social ascent were more rigid in Germany than in northern Italy – and because of Germany's higher level of industrialisation and literacy, they were also more galling to those they held down. The collapse of the monarchy in November 1918 largely failed to throw open new paths of social ascent, and the ensuing economic roller-coaster ride through inflation, uneven and uneasy prosperity, and deepening slump after 1927–8 further constricted opportunity.

One of the deepest and most galling of Germany's social cleavages was that imposed by the Prussian military state. Until the Prussian army reforms of 1807–14, the lower boundary of the *Offizierstand* had coincided roughly, except in the technical branches of the army, with the line in society between noble and commoner. But thereafter the officer corps accepted non-noble officers equipped with 'knowledge and *Bildung* in peacetime . . . and in war outstanding bravery and military judgement.'[11] What the reformers did was to divide Prussia's already

---

[10] See Ernesto Ragionieri, *Storia d'Italia*, vol. IV.3, *Dall'Unità a oggi* (Turin, 1976), pp. 2005–6, on Italy's difficulties in finding suitable junior officers in the First World War; on the overproduction of lawyers and doctors and the dearth of scientists and engineers, Massimo Barbagli, *Disoccupazione intellettuale e sistema scolastico in Italia (1859–1973)* (Bologna, 1974), especially p. 62.

[11] For the decree of 1808, see Ernst Rudolf Huber, *Deutsche Verfassungsgeschichte seit 1789* (Stuttgart, 1957–), vol. I, pp. 232–8.

fragmented society of *Stände* into two great blocs rigidly defined by *military* function: those capable of becoming officers, the nobility and the highly educated upper middle classes, and those fated to serve only in the ranks of Prussia's new universal service army. Knowledge and *Bildung* cost money, and officer or reserve officer status in the new Prussia–Germany of 1871 thus remained the prerogative of narrow elites well into the age of mass literacy. The result, given the military-mindedness that pervaded Prussian society and soon permeated south Germany as well, was a powerful head of steam of frustrated ambition that had no counterpart in Italy.

The political structures that the Fascist and Nazi regimes inherited were almost equally disparate. Liberal Italy was not quite as unlike Imperial Germany as often thought: foreign and military policy formed a preserve of royal and ministerial quasi-absolutism. Parliaments in both countries before 1918/19 were either unrepresentative of the electorate and/or could block but not initiate policy. But Italy's ruling groups, bound together by Masonry and Catholicism as well as by monarchism, nevertheless formed a far more cohesive whole than Germany's.[12] Even before November 1918, Germany's Establishment had shown a tendency toward fragmentation, thanks to the greater depth and number of horizontal social cleavages than in northern Italy, to Germany's federal structure, and to the ramshackle organisation of its executive, which after Bismarck's departure degenerated into a 'polycratic but uncoordinated authoritarianism' under the increasingly theoretical overlordship of Kaiser Wilhelm II.[13]

The Great War, bitterly lost or barely won, ended some crucial similarities. War and its after-effects did paralyse and destroy parliamentary institutions in both countries: almost immediately in the Italian case and in the German case by delayed action. But the Italian monarchy and its officer corps nevertheless survived the war and the postwar crisis. And the social conservatism of the Vatican and the deep roots of the Italian Church made them tenacious forces against change that were lacking north of the Alps. In Germany the war, with its interminable quarrels between generals and civilians, interest groups and bureaucrats, industry and labour, further intensified the polycratic character of the state. Defeat and the 1918 revolution left a vacuum at the top that Weimar, even after Hindenburg became its president, could not fill. The army and navy, cut loose from the monarchy, were now answerable to no one but themselves. And religion, far more than in Italy, was a source

---

[12] The best description of Italy's pre-1915 political elite of lawyers and professionals is Paolo Farneti, *Sistema politico e società civile* (Turin, 1971), pp. 178–83.

[13] For the phrase, Hans-Ulrich Wehler, *The German Empire 1871–1918* (Leamington Spa, 1985), pp. 62ff.

of conflict rather than of cohesion within the Establishment. The Nazi movement faced far less tenacious Establishment opposition after 1933 than did its Italian counterpart after 1922; Germany's pre-existing 'polycracy' contributed mightily to Hitler's success.

The Nazi movement also inherited a military–economic potential that by 1938 was well over four times that of Italy, although the ratio between the two populations was only 5:3. Germany had coal in abundance, while 85 per cent of Italy's coal supply was imported. German steel production in 1938–9 was ten times Italy's.[14] And in most areas of military and production technology, Germany's scientists, engineers, and industrialists were level with or ahead of Britain and the United States – whereas Italy, despite isolated and poorly exploited successes such as the early development of radar, produced armoured vehicles, motors, and aircraft increasingly inferior to those of its ally and of its enemies.[15]

The two nations' disparity in military traditions and expertise was almost equally great. Conscription, and the training in national loyalty, sense of duty, obedience, punctuality, and precision that went with it, dated from the early eighteenth century for Prussia's agricultural population; in theory military service had become universal in 1814, in practice from the 1860s onward. In Italy universal service had taken hold only in the 1870s. Nor did the Piedmontese–Italian Regio Esercito ever enjoy anything remotely resembling the social distinction conferred by Prussia's long if not unbroken run of victories from 1740 to 1866/71. After 1871, the Prussian lieutenant 'made his way through the world as a young god and the civilian reserve lieutenant at least as a demigod'.[16] And the Prusso-German army also had a genuine mass following utterly without counterpart in Italy. The *Kriegervereine* ('warrior clubs') of army veterans formed Imperial Germany's largest mass organisation, the Kyffhäuser League, encompassing in 1913 some 2.8 million members, or better than one in every seven adult male Germans.[17]

---

[14] 'Total industrial potential' as a percentage of Britain in 1900: Italy, 1938, 46 per cent; Germany, 214 per cent: Paul Bairoch, 'International Industrialization Levels from 1750 to 1980', *Journal of European Economic History*, vol. II, no. 2 (1982), p. 299. For steel, Mitchell, *European Historical Statistics*, p. 421; coal imports and production (1938-9), Benedetto Barberi, *I consumi nel primo secolo dell'Unità d'Italia 1861-1960* (Milan, 1961), p. 245.

[15] For careful analysis of the inadequacies of Italian armaments, see Lucio Ceva, 'L'evoluzione dei materiali bellici in Italia', in Ennio di Nolfo *et al.* (eds.), *L'Italia e la politica di potenza in Europa (1938-1940)* (Milan, 1985), pp. 343–90 and Ceva and Andrea Curami, *La meccanizzazione dell'esercito italiano dalle origini al 1943*, 2 vols. (Rome, 1989).

[16] Friedrich Meinecke, *The German Catastrophe* (Boston, 1950), p.12.

[17] See Hansjoachim Henning, 'Kriegervereine in den deutschen Westprovinzen', *Rheinische Vierteljahrsblätter*, vol. 32 (1963), pp. 430–58 and Klaus Saul, 'Der "Deutsche Kriegerbund". Zur innenpolitischen Funktion eines "nationalen" Verbandes in kaiserlichen Deutschland', *Militärgeschichtliche Mitteilungen*, vol. 6 (1969), pp. 95–130 (2,837,944

As a result, the German army could take its pick of a large pool of eager well-trained talent. The upper middle classes actively sought careers as officers, and the NCO corps could easily recruit highly talented individuals confined by the barriers of *Stand* to subordinate roles, but fully capable of leading troops in combat.[18] The Italian army had no such good fortune. Italy's pool of suitable talent was smaller, and the army's low reputation meant – in the perhaps excessively harsh words of Giovanni Giolitti, who dominated Italian politics in the decade before 1914 – that Italy's First World War generals were products of an age in which 'they sent into the army the stupidest son of the family'.[19] The war of 1915–18, despite its victorious conclusion for Italy, did not markedly raise the armed forces' social status or prospects for recruiting talent at any level.

The two armies' leadership traditions – corresponding in part to their differences in success in recruiting talent – were sharply different. The Prussian officer corps learned from catastrophic defeat at Napoleon's hands in 1806–7; the rigid drill and 'corpse-obedience' of the army of Frederick the Great gave way to a peculiarly Prussian cult of individual tactical and operational freedom. Clausewitz, whose writings summed up the military legacy of Prussia's reformers, described war as the realm 'of the play of chance and probability within which the creative spirit is free to roam'. Especially after the early 1860s, the army sought to harness that creativity within a doctrinal framework shared by leaders at all levels and rehearsed through relentless training. Subordinates were not merely permitted but were increasingly expected to improvise on their own responsibility, within the limits imposed by the intent of their commander and the tasks allotted to their own and to neighbouring units. And the chilling isolation of the modern battlefield led the twentieth-century German armies to extend the privilege and duty of creativity in combat to every one of their infantrymen – whereas Italy's military leadership style remained tied to the Piedmontese old-regime barrack-square tradition.

The consequence of all these disparities was a staggering contrast in performance between the military instruments which the Fascist and Nazi regimes inherited. At the tactical and operational levels the German army was the most expert and innovative of all contenders in

members, against the 2,483,661 members of the SPD trade unions); Gerd Hohorst *et al.*, *Sozialgeschichtliches Arbeitsbuch II. Materialen zur Statistik des Kaiserreiches 1870–1914* (Munich, 1975), p. 23, gives the male population 20 or older as 17,757,000 (1911).

[18] Ceva, 'Riflessione e notizie sui sottufficiali', *Nuova Antologia*, no. 2181 (April–June 1992), pp. 331–53, offers a highly instructive comparison between the German and Italian NCO corps.

[19] Olindo Malagodi, *Conversazioni della guerra (1914–1919)* (Milan, 1960), p. 58 (May, 1915); likewise p. 200 (November, 1917).

the Great War, and despite the obstacles of Versailles it further improved its performance in the interwar period. The Regio Esercito's officer corps by contrast learned industrial warfare in 1915–18 no more swiftly than the French and British.[20] Italy's one major clash with German forces, at Caporetto in October 1917, was a disaster of immense magnitude redeemed only by a successful holding action at the very end, just short of Venice. Italian units, outflanked or taken in the rear by the swift-moving Germans, had disintegrated along the Regio Esercito's principal social fault line, that between city-dwellers and peasants, north and south, officers and men; the Germans had taken 294,000 prisoners of whom only 4,170 were wounded. After 1919 Italy's victorious generals and admirals then imposed a military–technical, tactical, and operational conservatism even more deadening than that of their French counterparts. Until it was too late, the army neglected medium tanks; the navy disdained radar; and the air force opposed the all-metal monoplane fighter. Inadequate training, doctrinal lethargy, administrative disorganisation and the active discouragement of individual creativity produced – in the belated self-criticism of the army's own leaders – a junior officer corps with 'insufficient capacity for command' and non-commissioned officers with an 'almost total absence of initiative'. Nor did the officer corps take kindly to volunteers, or accept the regional recruitment or the long-service combat NCO corps that were among the German army's greatest strengths.[21]

Last but not least, the ideological climates which the two regimes inherited were markedly different. By 1915 Italy's narrow urban intelligentsia had elaborated a panoply of national myths that included the claim that post-Risorgimento Italy was incomplete both internally and externally, and that genuine national integration and European great power status could only come through a great war. Domestically, liberal disorientation in the age of mass politics also led to a yearning, con-

---

[20] See (among much other evidence) Giorgio Rochat, 'La preparazione dell'esercito italiano nell'inverno 1914-15 in relazione alle informazioni disponibili sulla guerra di posizione', *Il Risorgimento*, vol. 13 (Feburary 1961), pp. 10–32, and the detailed comparison between Italian and German doctrine and training in 1914–17 in Mario Silvestri, *Caporetto* (Milan, 1984), pp. 38–111.

[21] Quotations: Roatta circular of 15 March 1941 in Knox, 'The Italian Armed Forces, 1940-3', in Allan R. Millett and Williamson Murray (eds.), *Military Effectiveness*, vol. III, *The Second World War* (Boston, 1988), p. 165; on armaments, doctrine and training, leadership traditions, and 'national' recruitment, see especially Ceva, 'L'evoluzione dei materiali bellici in Italia' and his 'Riflessione e notizie sui sottufficiali'; Ferruccio Botti and Virgilio Ilari, *Il pensiero militare italiano dal primo al secondo dopoguerra (1919–1949)* (Rome, 1985), Chap. 3; and Rochat and Giulio Massobrio, *Breve storia dell'esercito italiano dal 1861 al 1943* (Turin, 1968), pp. 90–6. For the sharp contrast between the army's organisational and administrative failings and German practice, see Dorello Ferrari, 'La mobilitazione dell'esercito nella seconda guerra mondiale', *Storia Contemporanea*, vol. 18, no. 6 (1992), pp. 1001–46.

spicuously unfulfilled by the Italy of Giolitti, for a 'new state' dominated by a new elite less corrupt and possibly more authoritarian than the existing parliamentary one. But the traditions upon which to erect the dictatorship of an individual were weak. Rome, despite its often immoderate celebration in post-Risorgimento oratory and schoolbooks, was both too distant and too ambiguous to serve well; Roman authority rested as much on law as on charisma. Rome also meant the authority of the papacy, a force by its very nature opposed to total claims by secular rulers and possessing a charismatic leader of its own. And after Garibaldi, who had had the good sense to retire to Caprera, only the hated, feared, and revered commander of the army until 1917, Luigi Cadorna, and the warrior–aesthete Gabriele D'Annunzio offered models for a national *duce*.[22]

German myths were of sterner stuff, and thanks to near-universal literacy and the relative absence of countervailing forces had a far deeper grip on the population than their Italian counterparts. The Protestant upper middle class – the *Bildungsbürgertum* – had evolved by 1914 a national mythology that combined four essential elements. First came the cult of the national leader, from the myth of Frederick Barbarossa waiting under the Kyffhäuser for a call to save Germany, through Luther and Frederick the Great to Bismarck. Friedrich Meinecke well described the force of that cult in a commemorative speech of 1913: 'we long for a Führer for the nation, a Führer for whom we can march through fire'.[23] Second came Germany's leading mission in the world, which corresponded to the mission of the coming Führer in Germany and derived ever-heightened plausibility from Germany's growing economic prowess and military victories. Third came the primacy of *Geist* over matter and the teleological notions of historical development derived from Hegel and transmuted, by the coincidence of the victories of Bismarck and Moltke with the coming of Darwin to Germany, into pseudo-biological theories of history that cast Germany's mission as one of racist world redemption.[24] Those theories intersected with middle-class and peasant economic discontents to create from the 1890s onward a broad spectrum of nationalist–racist groups and minor parties. A final ingredient in Germany's national mythology was the Protestant apocalyptic tradition, for which the wars against Napoleon in 1813–14, against

[22] See especially John A. Thayer, *Italy and the Great War* (Madison, 1964); Mario Isnenghi, *Il mito della grande guerra da Marinetti a Malaparte* (Bari 1970), pp. 7–168; Emilio Gentile, *Il mito dello Stato nuovo dall'antigiolittismo al fascismo* (Bari, 1982).

[23] Quoted in Elizabeth Fehrenbach, *Wandlungen des deutschen Kaisergedankens 1871–1918* (Munich, 1969), p. 91.

[24] See especially Karl-Georg Faber, 'Realpolitik als Ideologie. Die Bedeutung des Jahres 1866 für das politische Denken in Deutschland', *Historische Zeitschrift*, vol. 203 (1966), pp. 1–45; the literature on the origins of *völkisch* thought is too vast for summary here.

France in 1870–1, and against a 'world of enemies' in 1914–18 were
the Last Judgment, *Das Weltgericht*, to be enforced upon God's enemies
by the German people in arms.[25]

The apocalypse of the Great War reinforced and further spread the
most radical elements in Germany's national myths, but had if anything
a chastening effect on Italy. The legend of defensive war and the 'August
days' of 1914 gave Germans an unforgettable taste of national unity as
a militant egalitarian *Volksgemeinschaft*. War poems such as Ernst Lis-
sauer's 'Hymn of Hate against England' and fanatical Protestant–
Hegelian war sermons enjoyed a huge popular audience well into
1916.[26] In Italy's 'radiant May' of 1915, by contrast, king, ministers,
and a pugnacious urban minority forced a terrorised parliament, a hostile socialist movement, and passive rural masses into war in an atmosphere that a contemporary accurately described as one of civil war. The
Italian Church – even before Benedict XV described the war as a 'useless massacre' in his August 1917 peace note – in general enjoined
obedience to duly constituted authority and a resigned acceptance of
duty rather than the holy war favoured by Germany's Protestant pastors
and by many of their Catholic counterparts. And the brief Turin
working-class revolt of August 1917 was only the most extreme
expression of the urban and rural masses' hostility or indifference to this
'war of the *signori*'.

The German experience was different. The enthusiasm of 1914 gave
way to a grimmer myth of sacrifice and embittered endurance. The
western front's 'storm of steel' transformed Germany's infantrymen into
Frontkämpfer, faces shadowed after autumn 1916 by their medieval–
modern 'Siegfried-helmets', prototypes for the 'political soldiers' of the
postwar and Nazi eras.[27] Italy's closest counterpart to that myth was far
more exclusive; the epic of the *Arditi*, the picked assault units, a myth
for and in part about the supermen or urban, literate, literary Italy,
rather than the whole nation.[28] And the war was also the hour of Germany's anti-Semites, who had no Italian counterparts; in a society

[25] See especially Klaus Vondung, 'Geschichte als Weltgericht: Genesis und Degradation
einer Symbolik', in Vondung (ed.), *Kriegserlebnis* (Göttingen, 1980), pp. 62–84, and
his *Die Apokalypse in Deutschland* (Munich, 1988), Chaps. 5–11.
[26] See Vondung, 'Geschichte als Weltgericht', pp. 63–4 and notes.
[27] For the origins of the myth in summer–autumn 1916, see Gerd Krumeich, 'Le Soldat
allemand sur la Somme', in Jean-Jacques Becker and Stéphane Audoin-Rouzeau (eds.),
Les Sociétés européennes et la guerre de 1914–1918 (Nanterre, 1990), pp. 367–74; for its
later development, Volker R. Berghahn, *Der Stahlhelm. Bund der Frontsoldaten 1918–
1935* (Düsseldorf, 1966), pp. 91–101 (but see also Ernst Jünger, *In Stahlgewittern*
(Berlin, 1920).
[28] See Giorgio Rochat, *Gli arditi della grande guerra: origini, battaglie e miti* (2nd rev. edn,
Gorizia, 1990).

besieged by what it perceived as a ring of demonic enemies their theories swiftly gained ever-wider acceptance.[29]

Finally, the German and Italian myths of war's end were unequal in their virulence and appeal. In Germany the stab-in-the-back legend emerged effortlessly from the officer corps' hatred for civilians in general and Socialists and Jews in particular, from the agitations of the anti-Semites, from Protestant war theology (since God could not have failed the German people, the German home front must have failed God), and from the way in which the *Bildungsbürgertum* had cast the war as a struggle between spirit and matter in which matter was doomed to defeat – unless dark forces first blunted the edge of German *Geist*.[30] The legend's Italian counterpart was the myth of the 'mutilated victory' (D'Annunzio's phrase), the thwarting of Italy's far-reaching war aims in 1918–19. Traumatic defeat at Caporetto had allegedly been the work of Socialists and of other representatives of the 'cowardly, ignorant, and corrupt little Italy that stabbed us in the back as we fought'.[31] Then the 'internal enemy' had combined with Italy's faithless allies to undo the final victory it had failed to prevent. But that myth, although a powerful force in middle-class opinion, failed to command the widespread assent that many elements of the *Dolchstosslegende* enjoyed in Germany. To the level-headed upon mature reflection, Austria-Hungary's disintegration in 1918 and the achievement of Italy's natural frontiers were already immense victories – whereas even moderate Germans utterly rejected the Reich's territorial mutilation in favour of the hated and despised Poles.

II

The two regimes built upon their inheritances edifices of markedly different shapes and sizes, despite their common character as dictatorships of an individual resting upon a militant mass party born of 1914–18. The principal factors within the regimes that affected their expansionist

[29] See in general Werner Jochmann, 'Die Ausbreitung des Antisemitismus', in Werner E. Mosse (ed.), *Deutsches Judentum in Krieg und Revolution 1916–1923* (Tübingen, 1971) and Uwe Lohalm, *Die Geschichte des Deutschvölkischen Schutz- und Trutz-Bundes 1919–1923* (Hamburg, 1970), pp. 46–76.

[30] For the last two points, see Arlie J. Hoover, 'God and Germany in the Great War: The View of Protestant Pastors', *Canadian Review of Studies in Nationalism*, vol. 14, no. 1 (1987), pp. 65–81.

[31] Piero Jahier (a democratic *interventista* and later opponent of Fascism), in September 1919 (' . . . quella Italiuccia vigliacca, ignorante e corrotta che ci pugnalava alle spalle mentre combattevamo'), in Mario Isnenghi, *I vinti di Caporetto nella letteratura di guerra* (Padua, 1967), pp. 258–9; similarly Benito Mussolini, *Opera omnia* (Florence and Rome, 1951–80), vol. XI, p. 402.

zeal, fighting power, and staying power were three. First came their
depth of ideological conviction, then the scope they gave to individual
initiative and the extent to which they rewarded that initiative with
'careers open to talent', and finally their ability and willingness to use
terror.

Depth of conviction was in part a function of the convictions and
personal qualities of the leaders themselves. Mussolini's ideology indeed
celebrated force: 'machine guns are adorable devices, especially when
they serve an idea'.[32] But Fascism, unlike Nazism or Marxism, lacked a
teleological mechanism that rooted the dictator's geopolitical and
internal goals in the historical process. The 'Fascist idea' also had to
compete with the monarchy, the focus of loyalties for the officer corps
and the pre-Fascist notables. From the Church it faced – under a façade
of astute collaboration with the regime – a hostility to Mussolini's neo-
paganism and total claims that markedly increased as the Fascist regime
drew closer to its even more neo-pagan and totalitarian German
counterpart after 1935. The 'Fascist faith' failed to inspire the working
classes of north Italy, and scarcely reached the peasantry of the south
and islands. And Mussolini himself, while ever more impressed with
German power, regarded his German partner as a doctrinaire and something of a freak – testimony to his own more sceptical nature.

Hitler by contrast genuinely believed that history was biology and that
the Germans, given proper leadership, were bound for world mastery.
His own force of conviction and the comparative clarity and consistency
of his ideology was a major source of the tighter grip of his personal
cult and of the 'National Socialist idea' upon the German people.[33] His
ideology derived from and resonated with the ideas of nationalist–racist
movement that had taken off in the 1890s and achieved a mass following
in 1914–23. His cult of the will, of the primacy of spirit over matter,
had even older and deeper roots. His promise to reverse the internal and
external verdict of 1918 – peacefully or otherwise – evoked widespread
enthusiasm. And thanks to the decapitation of the state in November
1918 and the mutual rivalry and weakness of the German churches, he
faced far less competition for popular loyalties than did Mussolini.

At least as important as ideology in propelling the regimes' expansion
was the scope that they gave, or could afford to give, to individual initiative and the extent to which they could reward their followers with
careers and booty. Mussolini – unfortunately for his prospects but fortu-

---

[32] Mussolini, *Opera omnia*, vol. XXIV, p. 125.
[33] For the cult's remarkable strength even in adversity, see especially Ian Kershaw, *The
'Hitler Myth': Image and Reality in the Third Reich* (Oxford, 1987), Chaps. 7 and 8; for
its Italian counterpart, see (with caution) Piero Melograni, 'The Cult of the Duce in
Mussolini's Italy', *Journal of Contemporary History*, vol. 11 (1976), pp. 221–37.

nately for Italy – took power *after* Socialist ineptitude, the recession of 1920–1, and the bludgeons of his movement had ended Italy's two 'red years' of strikes and Socialist agitation. The indispensability of Fascist violence and disorder was no longer apparent to his conservative allies. And Mussolini's perpetual scepticism about his sometimes rebellious party subordinates' abilities and loyalties, the myth of the 'new state' which Fascism and its nationalist and bureaucratic allies claimed to incarnate, and the watchfulness of the monarchy, its military, and those same allies led him to demand subordination and order rather than decentralisation and movement. Not for nothing did the regime's ideological journal bear the title *Gerarchia* – hierarchy. Inconvenient subordinates and potential rivals he curbed by sudden and repeated 'changes of the guard' among his ministers. His aim was not the primacy of the Partito Nazionale Fascista over the state but a gradual fusion of the two that would stealthily unseat both his party rivals and his conservative allies.

In the short term, Mussolini demanded the party's subordination to the state, confident that meant subordination to himself. In 1926–8 he publicly placed the PNF under the authority of the prefects at the periphery and of the determined and loyal Augusto Turati at the centre. The party provided candidates for leadership positions in the state and eventually pressed party cards on the civil service. But the static and inefficient state bureaucracy, whether in the traditional ministries or in the quasi-governmental organisations that sprouted like mushrooms in the 1920s and 1930s, ultimately owed its loyalty to Mussolini only as chief of government, a position the king had given and the king might yet take away.[34] The party retained freedom for bureaucratic expansion; by 1939 it was about the same size in relative terms as its German counterpart, encompassing roughly 8 per cent of Italy's population to the NSDAP's 7 per cent of the Germans in prewar 'Greater Germany'. But the expansion of the PNF was a tightly controlled top-down exercise aimed less at power in the present than at gaining commanding positions for the inevitable succession struggle.[35]

The PNF and its offshoots provided static jobs – *il posto* or *la sistemazione* – not the intensifying careers in domination and violence of their German counterparts. Even the Fascist Militia – the regime's 'armed guard of the revolution', its SA and SS – failed to take wing. In 1924

---

[34] For the bureaucracies and the regime, see especially Mariuccia Salvati, *Il Regime e gli impiegati. La nazionalizzazione piccolo-borghese nel ventennio fascista* (Bari, 1992).

[35] Numbers and PNF policy: Emilio Gentile, 'Le Rôle du parti dans le laboratoire totalitaire italien', *Annales ESC*, vol. 43, no. 3 (1988), pp. 567–91; for the NSDAP (5.3 milliion members in 1939), Michael Kater, *The Nazi Party: A Social Profile of Members and Leaders, 1919–1945* (Cambridge, 1983), Figure 1.

Mussolini's allies forced upon it an oath to the king, and officers from the rank of major upward drawn from the army. Its ostensibly voluntary recruitment and its residue of old *squadristi* was not enough, under those circumstances, to make its members fanatical 'political soldiers'. Despite Mussolini's care to give it prominent combat roles in Libya, Ethiopia, and Spain, it remained a black-shirted and subordinate copy of the army, whose level of fighting power it shared.[36] Nor did the army itself offer scope for initiative. Its doctrine remained determinedly top-down; senior officers did not merely prescribe what subordinates were to do but also how they were to do it, often in crippling detail. And its wars lacked the sustained combat needed to force renewal upon the officer corps. Promotion by seniority remained the rule; with the exception of the generals killed or captured in North Africa, East Africa, and Russia in 1940–3, the vast majority of the over-age figures of doubtful leadership qualities with whom Fascist Italy had begun its last war remained firmly rooted in place.[37]

Germany was very different. Hitler became chancellor in an atmosphere of apocalyptic crisis. The deepest depression yet to strike industrial societies, the paralysis of the hated parliamentary state, the apparent Communist threat, and their own thirst for revenge upon the Left made his conservative allies willing to overlook until too late the violence and disorder of his *Machtergreifung*. Germany's pre-existing polycratic structure and the decapitation of the state in 1918 helped create the weaknesses and divisions among the conservatives that Hitler exploited. And on top of their rivalries he imposed, even before Hindenburg's death in 1934, his own social Darwinist style. Whereas Mussolini merely preserved his authority by 'changes of the guard' that devoured the PNF's leaders, Hitler fostered a war of all against all for missions, authority, and booty that encompassed both Nazi party and state, and progressively increased both his own power and his subordinates' loyalty to him personally. The winners were not merely the fittest, but the fittest as defined by Hitler, those whose aims and deeds coincided most closely with the Führer's wish.[38] This 'political free enterprise', as Ronald Smelser has aptly called it, was the political mainspring of the regime,

---

[36] Ceva, 'Fascismo e ufficiali di professione', in Giuseppe Caforio and Piero Del Negro (eds.), *Ufficiali e società. Interpretazioni e modelli* (Milan, 1988), pp. 387–95.

[37] See Cava, *Le forze armate* (Turin, 1981), pp. 356–8, and the comparison between the army's divisional commanders in June 1940 (pp. 492–5) and those of June 1941 (pp. 501–5); for a scathing contemporary judgment on the divisional and corps commanders in Albania in 1940–1, see Stato Maggiore dell'Esercito, Ufficio Storico, *La campagna di Grecia* (Rome, 1980), vol. I, pp. 905–6.

[38] For a good description of the technique, and Himmler's imitation of it, see Shlomo Aronson, *Reinhard Heydrich und die Frühgeschichte von Gestapo und SD* (Stuttgart, 1971), p. 112.

the complement from below of the Führer's foreign and internal policy programme above. It was also closely connected with the regime's social mainspring and chief legacy to its successors: the career open to talent in bureaucratic piracy, warfare, and mass murder.[39]

The far greater relative strength of Hitler and his movement compared to their conservative allies and – paradoxically – the efforts of the victors to disarm Germany after 1918 combined to offer immense opportunities for ambition. Hitler repeatedly proclaimed from on high that each *Volksgenosse* carried his baton in his knapsack, without regard for distinctions of background, property, *Bildung*, or *Stand*. Rearmament bought virtual full employment by 1938 and innumerable chances to rise. The expanding party organisations, especially the SS and its ever-larger military formations, offered astonishing careers to figures such as Reinhard Heydrich or Theodor Eicke, who rose – respectively – from disgraced ex-naval officer and police informer to 'Himmler's Himmler' and highly decorated Waffen-SS division commander. But the regular armed forces offered most of all: the 115,000-man Versailles Treaty armed forces of 1932 multiplied fifty times by June 1940.[40]

By doctrine, German officers had long enjoyed wide autonomy within the general framework of missions assigned from on high. And now promotions, although formally still by the time-honoured principle of seniority, opened up even in peacetime in a way that had, and could have had, no Italian counterpart. Then the immense strains and losses of winter 1941–2 forced a generational change at the division commander level and the introduction of accelerated promotion based exclusively on *Leistung* – achievement and efficiency. By the Stalingrad crisis in winter 1942–3, the army hierarchy had lost control of pro-

[39] See Ronald Smelser, 'Nazi Dynamics, German Foreign Policy, and Appeasement', in Wolfgang J. Mommsen and Lothar Kettenacker (eds.), *The Fascist Challenge and the Policy of Appeasement* (London, 1983), pp. 31–47; Martin Broszat, 'Soziale Motivation und Führerbindung des Nationalsozialismus', *Vierteljahrshefte für Zeitgeschichte*, vol. 18, no. 4 (1970), pp. 392–409; and, for a bold and influential statement of the long-term impact of Nazi careerism on German society, Ralf Dahrendorf, *Society and Democracy in Germany* (New York, 1967), especially Chap. 25.

[40] For this and what follows, see Jürgen Förster, 'Vom Führerheer der Republik zur nationalsozialistischen Volksarmee. Zum Strukturwandel der Wehrmacht 1935-1945', in Jost Dülffer, Bernd Martin and Günter Wollstein (eds.), *Deutschland in Europa: Kontinuität und Bruch* (Frankfurt/Main, 1990), pp. 311–28; Bernhard R. Kroener, 'Strukturelle Veränderungen in der militärischen Gesellschaft des Dritten Reiches', in Michael Prinz and Rainer Zitelmann (eds.), *Nationalsozialismus und Modernisierung* (Darmstadt, 1991), pp. 267–96 and 'Auf dem Weg zu einer "nationalsozialistischen Volksarmee". Die soziale Öffnung des Heeresoffizierkorps im Zweiten Weltkrieg', in Martin Broszat, Klaus Dietmar Henke and Hans Woller (eds.), *Von Stalingrad zur Währungsreform. Zur Sozialgeschichte des Umbruchs in Deutschland* (Munich, 1988), pp. 651–82; Reinhardt Stumpf, *Die Wehrmacht-Elite. Rang- und Herkunftsstruktur der deutschen Generale und Admirale 1933-1945* (Boppard, 1982); Bernd Wegner, *The Waffen-SS. Organization, Ideology and Function* (Oxford, 1988).

motions and regimental officers ceased to meet as a corporate body to choose their junior colleagues, as tradition had decreed. By 1944, even before Himmler became commander-in-chief of the home army, the insatiable demands of total war and Nazi policy had between them destroyed the officer corps. The Prusso-German *Offizier* gave way to the German military *Führer*-personality, in whose selection, as Hitler insisted in a key order of January 1943, only combat effectiveness – *Leistung* – counted: 'All other circumstances, such as age, seniority, background, educational qualifications and the like, are utterly unimportant . . .'[41] Of the army officers commissioned after 1942 fewer than half had their university entrance qualification, the badge of *Bildung* required of non-nobles joining the *Offizierstand*. Waffen-SS officer recruitment was even more egalitarian; by July 1944 over a fifth of Waffen-SS officers of major and above had only elementary schooling.[42]

Last but decidedly not least of the features of the regimes that contributed to fighting power and staying power came the use of terror. Thanks to the circumstances under which he took power and the continuing resistance of the monarchy, of the officer corps, of upper-middle-class opinion, and of the Church, Mussolini's dictatorship was unable to wield it either in peace or war. His clumsy attempts to crush opposition nearly destroyed the regime in 1924; Italian opinion reacted with such horror to the murder of Giacomo Matteotti that Mussolini recognised thenceforth the existence of a line that the Establishment would not let him cross. A series of attempts on his own life gave him the pretext for instituting a 'Special Tribunal for the Defence of the State' in 1926, but it put to death only nine men in peacetime, and twenty-two, mostly Slavs from the eastern borderlands, in war. The Italian army apparently condemned to death only 92 men in the course of 1940–4 – a record that contrasted sharply with the over 4,000 death sentences, 750 executions, and numerous shootings without trial with which Cadorna and his successor had held Italy's peasant infantrymen in line in 1915–18.[43]

---

[41] Führer directive, 19 January 1943, printed in Gerhard Papke *et al.*, *Untersuchungen zur Geschichte des Offizierkorps. Anciennität und Beförderung nach Leistung* (Stuttgart, 1962), p. 276.

[42] Kroener, 'Strukturelle Veränderungen', p. 295; Wegner, *The Waffen-SS*, p. 248. These figures undermine the apparent suggestion of David Schoenbaum, *Hitler's Social Revolution* (New York, 1966), pp. 285–6 that the Nazi revolution existed primarily in '*interpreted* social reality' (my emphasis); for more evidence on the issue, see William Jannen, Jr., 'National Socialists and Social Mobility', *Journal of Social History*, vol. 9 (1976), pp. 339–66.

[43] Special tribunal: Alberto Aquarone, *L'organizzazione dello Stato totalitario* (Turin, 1965), p. 103 and note; military death sentences 1940–3 (data on how many were actually carried out is lacking): Giorgio Rochat, 'La giustizia militare nella guerra italiana 1940–3). Primi dati e spunti di analisi', *Rivista di Storia Contemporanea*, vol. 4

Here again, the German record was utterly different. Hitler, his party, and the leaders of Germany's armed forces were determined to repair what they took to be the criminal weakness of Germany's rulers in 1917–18. And although the circumstances of Hitler's seizure of power and the greater relative strength of his movement did not allow him to dispense entirely with legal procedures, SA and above all SS and Gestapo terror[was outside or above the law from the beginning. The judiciary itself, despite Hitler's frequent private attacks on its alleged 'other-worldliness' and lack of 'healthy *Volk*-consciousness', followed suit. By August 1944 the civilian courts alone had condemned to death at least 12,000 Germans and inhabitants of areas annexed to Germany. The Wehrmacht, not to be outdone, made up for the Imperial German Army's execution of a mere 48 men in 1914–18. By 1945 Wehrmacht courts had condemned at least 35,000 military personnel to death and had executed up to 22,000 of them for offences ranging from desertion or theft to newly minted ideological crimes such as *Wehrkraftzersetzung*, 'subversion of the will to fight'.[44]

III

Finally, events and their sequence had striking effects on the two regimes' fighting power and staying power. Mussolini's Italy began its greatest military test, the war of 1940–3, with a string of catastrophic failures. Defeats inflicted not merely by the British but also by the unwisely despised Greeks destroyed for good the prestige of dictator and regime.[45] Italians thenceforth might fight for Italy, though with an enthusiasm sapped by the sensation that Italy's real enemy was its overmighty Nazi ally and by the likelihood of good treatment on surrender by British and Americans. But willingness to die for the *Duce* sharply diminished, while war and blockade demoralised the home front, cutting food consumption by a quarter or more between 1939 and 1943. Hitler by contrast became Führer indeed – for his generals, his junior officers, his troops, and his people – by defeating France in 1940 where Wilhelm II had failed. Victory seized the food, goods, and slave and

(1991), pp. 536–7. For 1915–18, see Enzo Forcella and Alberto Monticone, *Plotone d'esecuzione. I processi della prima guerra mondiale* (Bari, 1968), especially pp. 433–512.

[44] Civilian death sentences (1938 to August 1944): Martin Broszat, *The Hitler State* (London, 1981), pp. 340–1; military death sentences: Manfred Messerschmidt and Fritz Wüllner, *Die Wehrmachtjustiz im Dienst des Nationalsozialismus* (Baden-Baden, 1987), p. 87 (my thanks to Dr Messerschmidt for confirming that these figures remain the best available estimate).

[45] See MacGregor Knox, *Mussolini Unleashed, 1939–1941* (Cambridge, 1982), pp. 260–72, and Renzo De Felice, *Mussolini l'alleato, 1940–1945* (Turin, 1990), vol. I, Part 2, pp. 728ff.

conscript labour that kept the German people from feeling the full weight of the war until 1944. And with the launching of his racial–ideological war of annihilation in the east, Hitler locked in loyalty through forced complicity. The immensity of German crimes against POWs and civilians left the Soviet peoples little alternative but to fight for Stalin; those same crimes also left the Germans little alternative but to fight for Hitler.

CONCLUSION

Between 1922 and 1943, and 1933 and 1945, these three layers of factors and forces combined to produce the wide difference in lust for expansion and in *Leistung* that distinguished the two regimes. The Fascist regime lacked the ideological coherence and conviction needed to generate fanaticism. It lacked the courage to delegate authority and the political freedom of action to exploit the population's thirst for careers open to talent. Italy's lower levels of literacy, economic development, and national integration, its less virulent national mythology, and the pervasive influence of the Church also meant a shortage of talent for many such careers, a lowered receptiveness to Fascist appeals, and a wide gulf in most Italian units between officers and men. In Germany, racist fanaticism, 'political free enterprise', and careers for masses eager to trample flat the remaining barriers of *Stand* drove Nazism forward against both internal and external foes. Germany's traditional military and economic prowess gave assurance of success. Young Germans responded with enthusiasm: in 1938–9 one fifth of the students receiving their university entrance qualification sought careers in the Wehrmacht, a figure unthinkable in Italy.[46] The dictator took the key decisions in foreign policy and war, but the pace and success of expansion also depended on the enthusiasm, ambition, and initiative of his subordinates at all levels.

In war the disparities in equipment, doctrine, training, and leadership between the two armies became immediately obvious. The patriotism and monarchical loyalty of the Italian officer corps and the resignation of Italy's peasant soldiers were no substitute for fanaticism. Ever-growing dismay at the inadequacy of the military preparations made by army and regime undermined what fanaticism existed. Victory rarely came, and when it did, rarely brought accelerated promotion; defeat or dereliction of duty little punishment. In North Africa, Italy's longest cam-

---

[46] Memorandum of the Reich education ministry, September 1939, in Herbert Michaelis and Ernst Schraepler (eds.), *Ursachen und Folgen* (Berlin, 1958-64), vol. XIII, p. 654.

paign, only a few picked units emerged as equals to the Germans after making allowance for disparities in equipment: the youthful volunteers of the Giovani Fascisti, the paratroops of the Folgore division, and the Ariete armoured division. The case of the Giovani Fascisti is particularly instructive as an example of the regime's failure or inability to mobilise the fighting power of its strongest potential supporters. The unit originated in 1940 in a sort of conspiracy – against the army hierarchy – by enterprising junior officers and enthusiastic Fascist youth volunteers. Its members secured passage to North Africa in mid-1941 by luck and influence, and achieved divisional status and an enviable combat record with little encouragement from the regime. Only after 1943, in the Italian Social Republic, did a Fascist regime shorn of most of its conservative allies override the continuing opposition of the military professionals and acquire, with German help, volunteer forces glued together by ideology.[47]

The German case, especially after 1942, was the epic of the Giovani Fascisti writ very large indeed. The perpetual emergency, appalling conditions, and immense casualties of the eastern front demanded in fullest measure the initiative from below that German tactical traditions had long encouraged. Ideological indoctrination – which troops in the east themselves eagerly and repeatedly demanded – taught that final victory was certain and surrender to the 'Judaeo-Bolshevik subhumans' unthinkable.[48] The career open to talent *in killing* in the 'National Socialist people's army' and the Waffen-SS indeed brought talent to the fore and fostered deep commitment born of gratitude to the regime. And terror of the regime's drumhead courtsmartial and of Stalin's tender mercies concentrated the minds of all concerned on resistance to the last cartridge. Even in the west, against enemies who threatened their prisoners with Canada and Arizona rather than Siberia, the Germans fought with dogged inspiration. It was no accident that the unit that gave the Allies the greatest difficulty in the Normandy campaign was the 12th SS Panzerdivision 'Hitler Jugend', formed from young enthusiasts under the leadership of eastern front veterans. So powerful was the force of belief that wounded 'Hitler Jugend' prisoners refused medical care, preferring to 'die for the Führer' until quelled by the threat

[47] On the origins of the Giovani Fascisti, see particularly Alpheo Pagin, *Mussolini's Boys. La battaglia di Bir el Gobi* (Milan, 1976); on the RSI, Virgilio Ilari, 'Il ruolo istituzionale delle forze armate della RSI e il problema della loro "apoliticità",' in Ilari and Antonio Sema, *Marte in orbace. Guerra, Esercito e Milizia nella concezione fascista della nazione* (Ancona, 1988), pp. 415–54.

[48] See the pioneering works of Omer Bartov, *Hitler's Army: Soldiers, Nazis, and War in the Third Reich* (Oxford, 1991) and *The Eastern Front, 1941–1945. German Troops and the Barbarization of Warfare* (London, 1985).

of transfusions with Jewish blood.[49] Nor did the end come easily in 1945; German forces were so reluctant to give in – even to the Americans – that they killed 9,373 US ground troops and aircrew in April 1945, only slightly below the monthly average for the entire US advance from Normandy to the Elbe.[50]

The home fronts showed much the same pattern. In Italy, thanks to early defeats, the public turned – 'in the name of the best kind of Italian nationalism' – *against* the regime that had brought Italy so low.[51] The Church's semi-public rejection of the regime's efforts to instil hatred of the enemy, the regime's own inner lack of conviction, the growing inefficiency, corruption, and disloyalty of its organisations and leaders, the steady decline in rations and living standards, and the impossibility of using terror meant swift and bloodless collapse once the king at last determined on Mussolini's removal.[52] The Fascist regime's foremost legacy to its successor was a tradition of bureaucratic elephantiasis, inept or corrupt intervention in the economy, and static mass-party patronage machines.

The German regime after 1938 was by contrast irreversible from within short of a successful assassination of Hitler. The German home front held on thanks to memory of the benefits the regime had brought, to the relatively high standard of living enjoyed until 1944, to the satisfactions of dominating the Reich's millions of foreign and slave labourers, to conviction of racial superiority and devotion to Hitler, to fear both of Himmler and of Stalin, and to anger and thirst for vengeance through the new V-weapons.[53] Only in the last months, and then above all in the west, did the loyalty of key subordinates, of some combat units, and of the population crumble under intolerable strain. The Nazi

---

[49] John Colville, *The Fringes of Power: 10 Downing Street Diaries, 1939–1945* (New York, 1985), pp. 497–8; for 12th SS *Panzerdivision* military performance, see Max Hastings, *Overlord: D-Day and the Battle for Normandy* (New York, 1984), pp. 127–8, 317.

[50] US Army battle dead, European Theatre: June 1944: 10,539; December 1944: 14,675; March 1945: 12,077; April 1945: 9,373; monthly average, June 1944–April 1945, 10,972 (data: Department of the Army, *Army Battle Casualties and Non-Battle Deaths in World War II: Final Report, 7 December 1941–31 December 1946* (Washington, D.C., n.d.), p. 106).

[51] See Knox, *Mussolini Unleashed*, pp. 268–72, 289 (quotation: *Questore* of Venice to Senise, 11 February 1941).

[52] For Church opposition at all levels to Mussolini's repeated exhortations to hate the enemy, see Franco Malgeri, *La chiesa italiana e la guerra (1940–1945)* (Rome, 1985), especially pp. 34–40; on corruption and disorganisation, De Felice, *Mussolini l'alleato*, vol. I, Part 2, Chap. 5.

[53] On German workers, slave labour, and the war, see John Gillingham, 'Ruhr Coal Miners and Hitler's War', *Journal of Social History* (summer 1982), pp. 637–53 and Alf Lüdtke, 'The Appeal of Exterminating "Others": German Workers and the Limits of Resistance', *Journal of Modern History*, vol. 64 (supplement) (1992); on the V-weapons, Gerald Kirwin, 'Waiting for Retaliation: A Study in Nazi Propaganda Behaviour and German Civilian Morale', *Journal of Contemporary History*, vol. 16 (1981), pp. 565–83.

regime, although hardly in the way it had intended, made good its promise that Germany would never suffer another November 1918. And along with the ruins it bequeathed to its successor, the shining new steel-and-glass *Leistungsgesellschaft* of the postwar era, came a society levelled and fierce individual expectations raised through the National Socialist career open to talent in war and mass murder.[54]

[54] See in general the works cited in notes 40 and 42 above, and especially Dahrendorf, *Society and Democracy*.

8

RESTORATIVE ELITES, GERMAN SOCIETY AND THE NAZI PURSUIT OF WAR

MICHAEL GEYER

Nazi Germany prepared, planned, and initiated war deliberately and unilaterally. German political and military elites escalated local wars in central Europe to intercontinental wars – not simply wars across immense spaces but self-consciously wars of global geopolitics. At the same time, they radicalised violence to stretch from the limited conduct of intra-European land-war to genocidal destruction – the latter encompassing not simply 'total' or 'mass' destruction but the deliberate, violent remaking of the European body politic. The Third Reich extended the pursuit of war into unprecedented dimensions.

These wars drew in the whole world. They set in motion a global realignment of forces that left behind the old European order of things. It is true, the independent war course of Japan suggests that the hemispheric division between a European–Atlantic and an East-Asian–Pacific world remained intact with the 'third world' of the Indian Ocean forming yet another hemispheric arena. But the realignment that came with the German onslaught not only transformed Europe, but changed the world. The remaking of the European order in the violent convulsions of the 1940s dovetails with decolonisation as one of the most important outcomes of the war and a distinct globalisation of the international order. German aggression had unpremeditated consequences which reshaped the twentieth-century world.[1]

The rapid expansion and intensification of violence occurred within merely three years, between 1938 and 1941. In this explosive process, the gravitational pull of the German wars superseded other European wars: the unrest in the Balkans and in Greece, the civil war in Spain, the Italian war of conquest in Ethiopia, the wars of Soviet aggrandisement in Poland, the Baltic and in Finland. These violent conflagrations were

---

[1] Gerhard L. Weinberg, *A World at Arms: A Global History of World War II* (Cambridge and New York, 1994).

folded into the grand European war launched by the Third Reich and, if one looks carefully enough, the Second World War is shot through with traces of these localised confrontations. The Second World War is a composite conflict that is forced together by the German pursuit of war. In 1941, we find a single, continent-wide, European theatre of war, dominated by a new kind of warfare – genocidal war.

The explosive compression of Europe as a result of German aggression is utterly astounding. A mere three years of an excessive outburst of violence form the pivot around which European history in the twentieth century turns. Between 1938 and 1941 a whole civilisation was dislodged by the German pursuit of war. What kinds of arguments can historians marshal in order to explain this extraordinary moment?

THE LEGACY OF 'CONTEMPORARY HISTORY'

Zeitgeschichte, or contemporary history, made its initial mark as the rigorous critique of sources and as an antidote to apologetic memories. Thus, Martin Broszat developed his 'structuralist' interpretation of the social dynamics of the Third Reich mainly by using Hitler's so-called 'second book'. He explored this text, because it seemed to provide an 'expanded source base for explaining the remarkable correspondence between theory and practice in regard to the foreign and war politics of Hitler'.[2] Tim Mason, the Marxist critic, insisted in turn that 'the inadequate treatment of German foreign policy' resulted not the least from 'the limited nature of the source material selected, and the way in which this material is used'.[3] Andreas Hillgruber, the leading representative of the intentionalist school and conservative historian *par excellence*, formulated the task of 'contemporary history' paradigmatically for all three postwar positions. He insisted that only the most stringent, philological critique of sources could overcome the incongruencies in the history of the Third Reich, which resulted in part from 'the situations themselves and in part developed out of the situation of the critic who has experienced the most recent past, perhaps shaped it to a small degree or – often – suffered through it'.[4] Contemporary history set out to transform the incongruities of Nazi politics into a verifiable and coherent narrative of the foreign and war politics of the Third Reich.

[2] Martin Broszat, 'Betrachtungen zu "Hitlers Zweitem Buch" ', *Vierteljahrshefte für Zeitgeschichte*, vol. 9 (1961), pp. 417–29, 426.
[3] Timothy Mason, 'Some Origins of the Second World War' (orig. publ. 1964), in Timothy Mason, *Nazism, Fascism and the Working Class*, ed. Jane Caplan (Cambridge and New York, 1995), pp. 33–52, here p. 38.
[4] Andreas Hillgruber, 'Quellen und Quellenkritik zur Vorgeschichte des zweiten Weltkrieges', (1964) in Gottfried Niedhart (ed.), *Kriegsbeginn 1939: Entfesselung oder Ausbruch des Zweiten Weltkrieges* (Darmstadt, 1976), p. 370.

The postwar historians succeeded in one respect. Despite a continuous stream of apologetic arguments which insinuated if not the innocence then the reactive nature of the Third Reich's decision to pursue war, the very fact of German aggression is not controversial.[5] There is no question about war guilt – the Third Reich having deliberately initiated every single campaign and having escalated the Second World War onto its intercontinental and genocidal plane. However, the factual truth about the aggressive nature of the Third Reich and the effort to shape the evidence into an argument about the nature of Nazi aggression proved to be two quite different challenges. In fact, the more historians have learnt about the preparation and the conduct of the German wars, the more difficult it has become to explain them.

With so little to argue about the 'origins of the Second World War', why is there so much disagreement about the aggressive politics of the Third Reich? A first answer takes historians over familiar ground.[6] Taking their cues from theories of 'totalitarianism' there are those who insist that the origins of the Second World War must be sought in Hitler's dogmatically held and fanatically pursued will either for world dominion or for a geopolitically and racially motivated hegemony of the Third Reich over Russia. These historians maintain that Hitler was able to assert his agenda thanks to his dictatorial control over foreign political and military decision-making. More or less explicit in this argument is a presumption about the primacy of foreign policy, one no longer rooted in the nature of the modern state but in Hitler's dictatorial powers. If anything, these historians and in their wake a 'realist' group of political scientists consider the changing international balance of power as the element that pushed and pulled Hitler's otherwise unequivocally aggressive goals in unpredictable directions – and, if managed differently, could possibly have forestalled his policy of conquest.[7] This argument is commonly labelled 'intentionalist'.

The main counter-argument focuses on the internal structures of the Nazi state and is commonly associated with theories of 'fascism'. Historians in this interpretative tradition emphasise the way in which

---

[5] This situation has not changed despite a latest round of revisions which points to a much more aggressive stance of the Soviet Union. See, for example, Werner Maser, *Der Wortbruch. Hitler, Stalin und der Zweite Weltkrieg* (Munich, 1994). It can be expected that our assessment of the Soviet Union will change quite considerably, but it is a reflection of the single-minded and autistic pursuit of war in the Third Reich that Soviet plans and intentions had no noticeable impact on what the German side did.

[6] Gerhard Hirschfeld and Lothar Kettenacker (eds.), *Der 'Führerstaat': Mythos und Realität. Studien zur Struktur und Politik des Dritten Reiches* (Stuttgart, 1981); Ian Kershaw, *The Nazi Dictatorship. Problems and Perspectives of Interpretation* (3rd edn, London, 1993).

[7] See, for example, Barry Posen, *The Sources of Military Doctrine: France, Britain and Germany between the World Wars* (Ithaca and London, 1984).

foreign and military policy decisions got entangled in the domestic agendas of competing institutions or 'power blocs' (Franz Neumann) whose competition radicalised and escalated German policy toward utopian ends and hurtled Hitler into a war which he fanatically desired but did not make of his own volition. Accordingly, the definition of war aims and the 'realisation of [an ideological] utopia' are commonly seen as a product of domestic social and political tensions in a system of governance in which each part preyed on others and all of them together depended on plundering Europe.[8]

Both interpretations are stumped by the contradictory realities of policy-making in the Third Reich which attest, time and again, to the deliberate nature of German aggression but do not allow for an unequivocal identification of the causes of war in either ideology or the structural dynamics of the regime. Recent, more eclectic approaches have tried to make a virtue out of this deficiency, insisting that all we want to know is the factual order of the events.[9] Suffice it to say that, while these approaches establish with unsurpassed precision what happened, they are at a loss when it comes to evaluating and assessing the place of this crucial moment in the European past. They succeed as chronicles but fail as history.

In this they fall behind insights already achieved by political thought on totalitarianism and fascism.[10] To be sure, a return to this initial thought – and the concepts of 'totalitarianism' and 'fascism' are significant only in their initial, mimetic reaction to an overwhelming reality of destruction – is not warranted as a blueprint for an accurate study of the origins and the conduct of the Second World War. However, this thought may serve as a reminder of the initial shock whereby the unprecedented quality of interwar tyrannical regimes and their wars remains imprinted. Thus, the main claim of Fascists in Italy and Nazis in Germany had always been that they were able to mobilise people beyond the boundaries of class, gender, and region. And this they proceeded to do in an unprecedented fashion, even if the process and the outcome had little to do with what they intended, the constitution of a homogeneous society. The most perceptive critics of fascism recognised and reflected on this fact. But such knowledge was quickly eviscerated by outlandish arguments about the petit-bourgeois nature of fascist

---

[8] Hans Mommsen, 'The Realization of the Unthinkable', in Gerhard Hirschfeld (ed.), *The Politics of Genocide* (London, 1986), pp. 97–144.

[9] Christopher Browning, *The Path to Genocide: Essays on the Launching of the Final Solution* (Cambridge and New York, 1992).

[10] Abbott Gleason, *Totalitarianism: The Inner History of the Cold War* (New York, 1995) shows the mutual imbrication of theories of fascism and totalitarianism very well. Roger Griffin, *The Nature of Fascism* (London, 1993) is an effort to kick-start a debate on fascism which was entirely lost in political sectarianism.

movements or the failure of the Nazis to live up to their propaganda. These endeavours desperately tried to unmake in theory what had happened in actual fact.[11] The real question is how and why Fascists and Nazis got as far as they did.

The other main boast of Fascists and National Socialists had always been that they would use their control of the state in order to wage war – not just any war, but a war of unheard-of geopolitical proportions and of mythical, genocidal violence that would regenerate their nations. This kind of rhetoric was difficult to believe for the majority of Europeans who, despite the First World War, still trusted the inherent constraints of state power. The 'total' remaking of society in genocidal violence shook the very foundations of contemporary life in Europe. But this knowledge of unprecedented terror as a social and political force also withered away in efforts to theorise 'totalitarianism'. Postwar theorists relentlessly normalised terror into a dependent variable, a particularly vicious form of state surveillance, or they abandoned the notion of terror altogether.[12] Nonetheless, 'terror' as the violent remaking of the European body politic remains the enduring challenge of thought on totalitarianism. Without assessing the role of terror in these interwar regimes, any effort to write a history of the Second World War will fall short of coming to terms with the magnitude of the challenge.

In this topsy-turvy situation in which the 'right' theories point in the wrong direction, we cannot go wrong picking up on what are, in the light of recent research, false starts which, however, point in the right direction. Tim Mason, for one, had long been puzzled by the making and un-making of class and gender identities in fascist regimes and by the central role of solidarity or its absence in this process. He despaired over the dissolution of the bonds of mutuality in Germany in the face of war and terror.[13] Detlev Peukert, for another, came to distrust the progressive veneer of modernity and saw underneath it the impulse of social engineers to customise societies.[14] Although promising in a

[11] Nicos Poulantzas, *Fascisme et dictature* (Paris, 1970) and *Pouvoir et classes sociales de l'état capitaliste* (Paris, 1982) is among the most interesting theorists of this kind. See Jane Caplan, 'Theories of fascism: Nicos Poulantzas as Historian', *History Workshop. A Journal of Socialist and Feminist Historians*, vol. 3 (Spring 1977), pp. 83–100.

[12] Juan Linz, 'Some Notes Toward a Comparative Study of Fascism in Sociological and Historical Perspective', in Walter Laqueur (ed.), *Fascism. A Reader's Guide* (Harmondsworth, 1979), pp. 13–78.

[13] Tim Mason, 'Women in Nazi Germany, 1925–1940: Family, Welfare and Work', parts 1 and 2, *History Workshop. A Journal of Socialist Historians*, no. 1 (Spring 1976), pp. 74–113; no. 2 (Autumn 1976), pp. 5–32, as well as his 'The Workers' Opposition in Nazi Germany', *History Workshop. A Journal of Socialist and Feminist Historians*, vol. 11 (Spring 1981), pp. 120–37.

[14] Detlev J. K. Peukert, 'The Genesis of the "Final Solution" from the Spirit of Science', in Thomas Childers and Jane Caplan, (eds.) *Reevaluating the Third Reich* (New York and London, 1993), pp. 234–52.

renewed concern with fascism and totalitarianism, these arguments suffered from the fact that the two foremost historians of their generation
invoked the transformatory role of terror in shaping interwar European
societies but never seriously approached the actual pursuit of war – not
because they underestimated its centrality, but because they were both
too deeply disturbed by the realities of a violent, genocidal society and
distrusted the ways in which the notion of war and genocidal violence
were framed in the prevailing academic discourse. In the prevailing historiography, contemporary history, war and terror either remained over-
determined – i.e. were reduced to a mere function of structural imbal-
ances and asymmetries and thus turned into 'ultimately' derivative
phenomena – or they were underdetermined in that they were read as
the outcome of the sheer volition of Hitler and thus removed into the
realm of historical chance.

These approaches effaced what troubled Mason and Peukert most
deeply: violence which mercilessly cut into any hope for the good life
as a project of modernity. Hannah Arendt, the refugee scholar from
Germany, had faced the same quandary. She reasoned in the face of
terror that the ultimate object of totalitarianism was human spontaneity
as the ever-renewable source of democracy. She also reasoned that one
would have to destroy all of humanity before one could destroy this
perennial well-spring of human rebirth and political renewal.[15] Nothing
less than the destruction of humanity is what totalitarianism intended
(and she did not hesitate to list both Bolshevism and nuclear omnicide,
together with National Socialism, as totalitarian threats). But she upheld
that the human spirit could not be cowed. In Arendt's tightly packed
philosophical argument I see the chance for a history of war and genocide in twentieth-century Europe that recognises Mason's and Peukert's
despair and yet points beyond it – to the source of the good life then
and now, the ever-regenerated spontaneity of democratic thought and
action. I take this to be a promising point of departure which entails
rethinking the moment of German aggression in the late 1930s as a
struggle against the democratic constitution of European society.

THE CRISIS OF RESTORATIVE POLITICS

At the end of the 1930s the Third Reich faced not an ordinary con-
vulsion or blockage which had accompanied the Nazi rise and the seizure of power from the very beginning, but a 'crisis of social reproduction'.[16] This provocative judgment by Tim Mason and Jane Caplan

---

[15] Hannah Arendt, *The Origins of Totalitarianism* (New York, 1973; 1st edn, 1951).
[16] Tim Mason, 'Intention and Explanation: A Current Controversy about the Interpretation of National Socialism', in Hirschfeld and Kettenacker (eds.), *Der 'Führerstaat'*,
pp. 23–42.

was instantly appropriate for arguments about the nature and the extent of working-class discontent in 1938, of which there was little, and a presumed dead-end of armaments politics, for which there is little proof and none that would actually link it to the decision for war.[17] The 'system' was not breaking down in 1938.[18] But it was not business as usual either. Neither the notion of a shrewdly calculating dictatorship which overcame German infrastructural limitations nor the alternative argument about a wasteful but persistent preparation for total war capture this moment. Mason and Caplan grasped the extreme tension of the situation in the late 1930s but could not quite instantiate their insight in the diffuse and contradictory politics after 1938. They were puzzled by the quickening of the pace and by the quite stunning reversals of domestic and international politics and were right in highlighting this key characteristic of the middle years of the Third Reich. But the meaning of this acceleration of time, of the fury of rapid German decisions in favour of war with global implications – what this all meant, exactly, escaped them.[19]

This much seems evident. The Third Reich faced ubiquitous problems of rearranging internal power alignments as the nation emerged from the economic slump and left behind the last remnants of the Weimar state and its internationally sanctioned limitations on military power. These turbulences in which the power alignments of 1933 were remade are most evident in Hitler taking control of the military leadership and the jettisoning of Hjalmar Schacht and his export-oriented industrial policy in favour of an accelerated course of armaments production in 1937/8. What followed was a massive rearrangement not

---

[17] Timothy W. Mason, 'Innere Krise und Angriffskrieg 1938/1939', in Friedrich Forstmeier and Hans-Erich Volkmann (eds.), *Wirtschaft und Rüstung am Vorabend des Zweiten Weltkrieges* (Düsseldorf, 1975), pp. 158–88 and Hans-Erich Volkmann, 'Die NS-Wirtschaft in Vorbereitung des Krieges', in Wilhelm Deist *et al.*, *Ursachen und Voraussetzungen der deutschen Kriegspolitik* (= *Das Deutsche Reich und der Zweite Weltkrieg*, vol. I) (Stuttgart, 1979), pp. 211ff.

[18] This has been the subject of considerable debate. See Ludolf Herbst, 'Die Krise des nationalsozialistischen Regimes am Vorabend des Zweiten Weltkrieges und die forcierte Aufrüstung', *Vierteljahrshefte für Zeitgeschichte*, vol. 26 (1978), pp. 347–92 as well as R. J. Overy, 'Germany, "Domestic Crisis" and War in 1939', *Past and Present*, no. 116 (1987), pp. 138–68; 'Debate: Germany, "Domestic Crisis" and War in 1939', with comments by D. Kaiser and T. W. Mason and a reply by R. J. Overy, *Past and Present*, no. 122 (1989), pp. 200–40.

[19] On the acceleration of politics, Gerhard L. Weinberg, *The Foreign Policy of Hitler's Germany: Starting World War II, 1937–1939* (Chicago, 1980). Jost Dülffer, 'Der Beginn des Krieges 1939: Hitler, die innere Krise und das Mächtesystem', *Geschichte und Gesellschaft*, vol. 2 (1976), pp. 443–70, gave the crisis argument a foreign-political slant. While the argument of the current essay is strictly 'domestic', I have used it to explain the transformation of the international realm; see my 'Crisis of Military Leadership', *Journal of Strategic Studies*, vol. 14 (December 1991), pp. 448–62. Neither domestic nor international crisis, however, explain the 'origins' of the Second World War.

simply of national politics on a ministerial level but also of the micro-management of the everyday organisation of power. The assertion of Hitler's supremacy in 1938 cut so deep because it was propelled forward both by shifts in political alignments between relatively autonomous and only loosely interacting institutions of power (redefining who gets what) and, equally important but more difficult to grasp, by the reworking of the micro-politics (who implements what to which end) within institutions like 'the military' and 'industry'.

The downfall of military autocracy and the assertion of Hitler's control over the armed forces was the most visible event in this process. Tensions between the military, especially the army, and the Nazi Party were a recurrent feature of the Third Reich, but they should not deceive us as to the mutually beneficial arrangement between the two contending powers.[20] In 1933, the military had extricated itself from the political and fiscal constraints of constitutional governance in order to pursue its own single-minded course of war preparations. The new military leadership, especially the army, insisted that only military autonomy would guarantee the timely rebuilding the armed forces. The leading officers thought of this course of action as a restoration of its previous stature over and against the diminution of its powers under parliamentary government. Notwithstanding persistent protests, the military leadership got what it wanted – and what it could not get (absolute priority of military matters in society and economy) was beyond the powers of the Nazi leadership to give. Obviously, the Nazi politicians, Hitler included, were shrewd enough to capitalise on what they did for the military (securing the process of rearmament domestically and internationally), but there is no indication that they were holding back. Military autocracy was not done in by dirty tricks even in 1938, when the Nazis instigated a smear campaign against key officers.[21] Rather, the military leadership stumbled when the armed forces could not and would not deliver what they set out to do – to get Germany ready for war.

In the context of an escalating controversy, in late 1937, over the policy of the Third Reich – within the military, between the military and industry, between the military, industry and Hitler – it began to dawn on some officers that their plans might as well be a pipe dream. Five years of rearmament, the introduction of conscription, and 'total-war' preparations of the economy and society did not suffice to make Germany ready for war in the foreseeable future. The military estimates

[20] Klaus-Jürgen Müller, *The Army, Politics and Society in Germany, 1933–1945* (Manchester, 1987).
[21] Karl-Heinz Janssen and Fritz Tobias, *Der Sturz der Generale: Hitler und die Blomberg-Fritsch Krise 1938* (Munich, 1994).

were unequivocal. The German armed forces were unprepared to wage
(two-front) war in central Europe – and a two-front war seemed the
only reasonable strategic assessment of the situation in 1938. Moreover,
there were growing doubts whether the armed forces were ever going
to be ready for a European war. For at the point at which the military
preparations were going to be well enough advanced (1942–6), the
window of opportunity due to a slow start of French and British rearmament would probably be closed again as a result of the preparations
by the western allies. General Ludwig Beck, the Chief of General Staff
of the Army, was most explicit about this issue in a series of memoranda
in 1938 and resigned over what he considered the unwarranted hazard
of war in central Europe. His successor, General Halder, much as his
conservative colleagues in the Foreign Office, was less consistent when
facing the same dilemma in 1939/40, in planning the attack on France.
According to their expertise Germany was not ready, yet they proceeded
to wage war. Their wholesale abandonment of military and diplomatic
orthodoxy was compensated by a mixture of indecision, bouts of protest
and fear, and, mostly, opportunism which filtered into the decision-
making process and the daily routines of these leading professionals.
Professionally, they no longer had any ground to stand on.[22]

The impasse of 1938/9 cost the military leadership its autonomy, but
the military continued to expand by leaps and bounds. More importantly, it dazzled itself and the nation with extraordinary victories. In the
wake of the triumph over France, the military leadership regained its
self-confidence – but this renewed sense of self-esteem was quite different from the military outlook of old. The military now came to believe
that what they had done in France, *Blitzkrieg*, was indeed what they
had always set out to do. They had found the new formula for success.
The attack against the Soviet Union was the first and only operation in
the Second World War that was deliberately designed to fit the image
of *Blitzkrieg*. 'Image' should be taken quite literally, because the officers
got their ideas about the new 'strategy' where everybody else got them
as well. They saw themselves in the newsreels and in the movies doing
the right thing. Obviously, *Blitzkrieg* was based on a series of innovative
tactics to exploit massed fire-power and movement, linked through
improved communications, which dated back to the 1910s and 1920s.
But as an operational design it was a make-believe spectacle that was
put together in hindsight for public consumption.[23]

[22] Michael Geyer, *Aufrüstung oder Sicherheit. Die Reichswehr in der Krise der Machtpolitik
1924–1936* (Wiesbaden, 1980), and Christian Hartmann, *Halder, Generalstabschef Hitlers 1938–1942* (Paderborn, 1991).

[23] On some of the origins see James Corum, *The Roots of Blitzkreg: Hans von Seeckt and
German Military Reform* (Lawrence, Kan., 1992) as well as Geyer, *Aufrüstung oder*

The invention of *Blitzkrieg* masked a far-reaching transformation of the officer corps. First, the crisis of military orthodoxy came at a propitious moment in the sociological remaking of the officer corps. It catapulted the so-called *Frontkämpfer* generation of the First World War into leading positions – a process which had been under way for some time and finally took hold with the fall of France.[24] Second, this sociological transition was accompanied by a novel micro-management of power. The issue is somewhat clouded by the fact that the German army had always given a great deal of independence to its commanding officers in the pursuit of their tasks (the so-called *Auftragstaktik*), but this freedom of action was circumscribed by similarity of outlook and the prerogatives of hierarchy. In the situation of utter indecision over war against France, a new element of competition was inserted into operational planning by happenstance when von Manstein, supported by the commanding officer of his army group who wanted a bigger piece of the action, pushed an operational idea which was quite beyond his sphere of activity – to Halder, to Hitler and anyone who could further the cause – and won out. The *Sichelschnitt* operation was a brilliant idea, to be sure, but above all it threw operational planning open to a much wider range of officers. By the same token, Guderian went way beyond his orders during the operation so as to capture a strategic advantage – and again succeeded.[25] Both von Manstein's and Guderian's actions had their precedents in the German army, but they exhibited a novel activism, irrespective of rank and position, that knew but the fullest possible exploitation of a momentary situation by all available means. This kind of situational efficiency- and action-oriented behaviour, which undercut

Sicherheit. On France see Hans Umbreit, 'Der Kampf um die Vormachtstellung in Westeuropa', in Klaus A. Maier *et al.*, *Die Errichtung der Hegemonie auf dem europäischen Kontinent* (= *Das Deutsche Reich und der Zweite Weltkrieg*, vol. II) (Stuttgart, 1979). On Russia, Horst Boog *et al.*, *Der Angriff auf die Sowjetunion* (= *Das Deutsche Reich und der Zweite Weltkrieg*, vol. IV) (Stuttgart, 1983), pp. 3ff., 190ff., 430ff. For films and newsreels I rely on a preliminary survey of the German *Wochenschau*, especially in the wake of the victory against France. (Poland provided something of a first exploration of the possibilities of presenting war on newsreels.) A detailed analysis of these immensely popular newsreels and the pseudo-documentary film production which it spawned would be highly welcome. The literature on *Blitzkrieg* is vast. It generally reproduces the process of 'discovery' that the German army went through in 1940/1, with always the same surprise effect.

24 Bernhard R. Kroener, 'Strukturelle Veränderungen in der militärischen Gesellschaft des Dritten Reiches', in Michael Prinz and Rainer Zitelmann (eds.), *Nationalsozialismus und Modernisierung* (Darmstadt, 1991), pp. 267–96, and his 'Auf dem Weg zu einer "nationalsozialistischen Volksarmee"'. Die soziale Öffnung des Heeresoffizierkorps im Zweiten Weltkrieg', in Martin Broszat, Klaus Dietmar Henke and Hans Woller (eds.), *Von Stalingrad zur Währungsreform. Zur Sozialgeschichte des Umbruchs in Deutschland* (Munich, 1988), pp. 651–82.

25 See the self-advertising memoirs of Erich von Manstein, *Lost Victories* (Novato, Calif., 1994; 1st edn, 1958), and Heinz Guderian, *Panzer Leader* (4th edn, London, 1977).

systemic or orthodox military planning, befitted a generation of exceedingly ambitious officers who were set free by a regime that honoured nothing more than success in the pursuit of conquest. This competitive quest for success, rationalised as the search for optimal performance and eventually as the 'heroism' of the front-line officers, transformed the officer corps from a corporate body of professionals into a society of military achievers whose performance was a matter of public acclaim. The popular adulation for the most dashing officers like Rommel, which continued into the postwar literature (and films), is a case in point.[26]

Simultaneously, Hitler, in his new capacity of Commander in Chief of the armed forces, ridiculed military 'bean counting', cracking open the claustrophobic world of orthodox military deployment planning and substituting the 'laws' of race for those of power politics. Whereas the military counted and compared war potentials of nations, Hitler insisted that the willingness to fight and to endure was the only thing that mattered. He displaced prevailing professional notions of military readiness, shifting the focus of strategy from military considerations to an appraisal of the potentials of each 'people' and 'race'. He intuited a strategy which required a leap of faith, initiation rather than schooling and training, from his followers. As was the case in operational planning, the only measure of this 'strategy' was success, for it was nothing more than the expectation of fortuitous circumstances which allowed the military to fight war against all odds. Strategy thus degenerated into a matter of cunning – but this is exactly the ground on which Hitler met the emergent society of officers.[27]

The preparation and conduct of the war against the Soviet Union showed the consequences of the fusion of technocracy and ideology. Much has been made of the ideological conditioning for this campaign. Certainly, Hitler and the military shared a deep hatred of Bolshevism which was laced with a virulent anti-Semitism. But equally important is the remarkably exuberant planning in which all parties tried to outbid each other with dazzling ideas and expected instant rewards. The military hoped to find an unlimited field of display for its skills in decisive warfare and looked forward to tangible returns in terms of prestige, promotion and remuneration. Hitler considered the Soviet Union his true object of conquest, the capstone of his effort to establish the Third Reich

[26] In passing one might note that English popular military history and the American film industry picked up on these mass-produced images at a point when the Germans began to grow out of their infatuation with military heroes. This subject is worth further study.
[27] The proximity of Nazi ideology and technocratic strategy seems rather difficult to accept for military historians; see Michael Geyer, 'German Strategy in the Age of Machine Warfare, 1914–1945', in Peter Paret et al. (eds.), *Makers of Modern Strategy* (Princeton, 1986), pp. 527–97.

as a racial Empire. These expectations fuelled the universal eagerness to have a hand in the defeat of the Soviet Union that overwrote any hesitation and caution. In 1941, the German military was ready to take on the world. What had been a professional impasse in 1938 ended three years later in the confluence of a hyper-competitive officer elite and Hitler's ideological ambitions which set Europe ablaze.[28]

If the crisis of military elites had come to pass in 1938, the crisis of economic preparations for war reached a head only in 1941/2. It was resolved with Albert Speer's installation as Minister of Armaments and Munitions in February 1942 in the wake of the military disaster of that winter. At the centre of this twisted story is the growing imbalance between the military–economic preparations for 'total war' and actual weapons production between 1938 and 1941. It led to a situation in which ever more resources were mobilised for the military–industrial sector, but the armed forces were notoriously undersupplied with weapons and material. The discrepancy is remarkable. The Third Reich was *de facto* on a 'total war' footing since 1938, but the yield from the investments in actual military hardware was pitiful.[29] In order to make sense of this disparity, we need to put three activities into perspective – 'total war' preparations organised within the framework of Göring's Four-Year Plan, the preparation for 'total mobilisation' by the *Wehrwirtschaftsstab*, and the procurement planning of the armed services. All three open a window for the exploration of the economy and the transformation of industry in these three years. They suggest that a restorative industrial policy was going for broke.

First, historians have doubted if the Third Reich ever prepared for 'total war' as Hitler had said the Nazi leadership would in his famous 1936 memorandum which kicked off the Four-Year Plan under Göring's leadership. But the fact is that the Four-Year Plan (with its subsequent modifications) achieved exactly what it was supposed to do. Even if Göring proved to be incapable of masterminding the project, the Plan prepared Germany for a long war by 'hardening' Germany against an Atlantic blockade.[30] The problem is that these activities,

[28] Bernd Wegner (ed.), *Zwei Wege nach Moskau. Vom Hitler–Stalin-Pakt zum 'Unternehmen Barbarossa'* (Munich, 1991), and Gerd Rolf Ueberschar and Wolfram Wette (eds.), *Unternehmen Barbarossa* (Paderborn, 1984).

[29] This is the key insight of R. J. Overy, *War and Economy in the Third Reich* (Oxford, 1994); see esp. 'Hitler's War and the German Economy: A Reinterpretation', pp. 233–56.

[30] Rolf-Dieter Müller, 'Die Mobilisierung der deutschen Wirtschaft für Hitlers Kriegsführung', in Bernhard R. Kroener et al., *Organisation und Mobilisierung des deutschen Machtbereiches* (= *Das Deutsche Reich und der Zweite Weltkrieg*, vol. V/1), pp. 349ff. Despite recent studies, the whole issue of the Four-Year Plan is up for revision because of the availability of new source materials among the 'captured documents' in Moscow.

which made up a good part of German military preparations, did next to nothing to prepare the Third Reich for the wars which it actually fought. Second, while the military efforts to put German economy and society on a war footing – 'mobilisation' – were altogether less success-ful, they were of consequence nonetheless. The military planners in the *Wehrwirtschaftsstab* were never able to put together a unified and central-ised system of mobilising the German nation as they had hoped. But their stop-and-go activities were preparing the ground for full-scale armaments production under Speer by shifting capital, labour, and resources into the military sector in a piecemeal fashion.[31] However, they did not commensurately increase the output for military hardware. Third, the procurement of weapons revolved around target plans which were designed for the pursuit of fictitious all-European (and even inter-continental) wars. Whether we take the expansion and mechanis-ation plans of the army, the naval 'Z-Plan' or the four-fold increase of the Luftwaffe – all these were meant to be achieved in a distant future with some weapons yet fully to be developed. The massive conflicts over priorities between the military services ever since 1937/8 were about negotiating immediate needs in light of what might be achieved ten years hence. What was available for actual war-fighting in 1939–41 was scraped together from otherwise futuristic plans.[32]

Between 1936 and 1941 the Third Reich built up a huge machinery for the logistical preparation for a future European war – preparations that would have won the First World War for certain. The resource requirements for these preparations ran down the balance of payments of the Third Reich in 1938 and amassed foreign currency debts. Steeply rising armaments expenditures had a distinct inflationary effect. More-over, they surpassed by far the resources and the capacities of the Third Reich, which has led some historians to argue that the sources of the 'domestic crisis' in 1938 must be sought in these endeavours. The fact of the matter is that the sum total of war preparations resulted in a huge, lumbering bureaucratic bulge, sustained jointly by the Party and by the military, which was undercut in the face of actual war. The pecul-iarity of this system was that a good deal of German energy and expendi-ture was sunk into planning for the repetition of a European war that did not materialise and into industries that only indirectly contributed

[31] Overy, *War and Economy*, pp. 259ff.
[32] Wilhelm Deist, 'Die Aufrüstung der Wehrmacht', in Wilhelm Deist *et al.*, *Ursachen und Voraussetzungen*; Jost Dülffer, *Weimar, Hitler und die Marine. Reichspolitik und Flottenbau 1920–1939* (Düsseldorf, 1973); Dietrich Eichholtz, *Geschichte der deutschen Kriegswirt-schaft 1939–1945*, vol. I, *1939–1941* (Berlin, 1969).

to the war effort. Only when this system came crashing down in 1941/2 did armaments production actually take off.[33]

'Inefficiency' is not a good explanation for this extraordinary bonanza. Indeed, if we want to grasp what happened it pays to think of the development up to the war as a failed restoration which was undone in a hurry in 1940/1. The world economic crisis had brought to the fore some of the most conservative groupings within the economy and had re-established something of a hegemony for basic industries whose politics had faced a challenge to their dominance during the twenties rather similar to the one faced by the orthodox military.[34] The industrial elites confronted their own 'crisis' of confidence after the collapse of the short-term recovery of the world market in 1936/7. Hermann Göring and his politics of creating a nationalised industrial conglomerate was unquestionably one source of the problem. But he was so serious a threat because the industrialists could not help themselves despite the favourable circumstances which came with the Nazi seizure of power.[35] They were still not competitive on international markets despite the destruction of organised labour and despite the suppression of wage negotiations. The German recovery, moreover, favoured capital goods, electrical engineering and even consumer goods, but not the traditionally most powerful sectors of basic industry. Also, if industrial politics in the Third Reich started out as the reassertion of entrepreneurial authority in the factory and in the market place, it ended up in a tedious web of regulations that stymied initiative and reduced flexibility. Industry, rather than being set free, was tied down. Internationally, German industry had neither the right product mix nor the financial muscle to break open and control the system of international corporate relations. The presumption of 1934 that one could outflank the international capitalist system through state-sponsored industrial politics had all but collapsed by 1938.

[33] Albert Speer, *Inside the Third Reich* (New York, 1970) claimed many things in his second life after Hitler, but he is right on this point.

[34] 'Inefficiency', of course, provides a very sensible measure for the analysis of actual production, as is shown in one of the few studies of an armaments manufacturer: Gustav-Hermann Seebold, *Ein Stahlkonzern im Dritten Reich: Der Bochumer Verein 1927–1945* (Wuppertal, 1981). The general situation is complicated by Göring's massive intrusion into the economy which finds its military equivalent in the build-up of the SS. See Overy, *War and Economy*, pp. 93ff., and the more comprehensive study by Gerhard Mollin, *Montankonzerne und 'Drittes Reich': Der Gegensatz zwischen Monopolindustrie und Befehlswirtschaft in der deutschen Rüstung und Expansion 1936–1944* (Göttingen, 1988). But see also Peter Hayes, *Industry and Ideology: I.G. Farben in the Nazi Era* (New York and Cambridge, 1987) with a careful assessment of the imbrication of industry and national industrial politics.

[35] Arthur Schweitzer, *Big Business in the Third Reich* (Bloomington, Ind., 1964), is outdated but still unsurpassed on this issue.

The way out of this situation is confusing. First, in order to achieve a full-scale conversion to armaments production as it occurred in 1941/2, the Four-Year Plan preparations for German autarky had to be undone in favour of up-front investment in the rationalisation of production which generally favoured the capital-goods sector rather than heavy or chemical industry.[36] Second, the conversion of industry was removed from the bureaucratic, state-sponsored military–industrial mobilisation project and organised in a system of industrial self-government which was initiated by Todt and institutionalised by Speer. This system was increasingly micro-managed by a new breed of engineers and middle managers who became the backbone of German armaments production.[37] Third, the procurement bureaucracy of the services (and their ideals of a high-quality, dispersed armaments production) was abandoned in favour of a politics of producer-oriented (instead of a military consumer-oriented) armaments. The favourites of the military bureaucracy, speciality manufacturers of armaments, were replaced by large conglomerates and their rapidly expanding system of subcontractors.[38] The end result of this tormented process of interminable policy battles, turf-wars and stop-and-go activities was not simply a mobilised industry, but a transformed regime of industrial alignments which left behind the power arrangements of 1933.

The turn of German industry to armaments production as the capstone of this transformation came only slowly and hesitantly, if we leave aside the armaments sector proper. But it eventually did come in the context of and as a result of the occupation of western Europe in the winter of 1940/1. This is an exceedingly puzzling moment, because as the actual conversion of industry was going into high gear, pressures for a demobilisation mounted at the same time. Much has been made of this in order to show the war-weariness of German industry. But in fact this contrary development makes sense only if we keep in mind that 'demobilisation' meant the curtailment of state-military control in favour of self-government. To simplify somewhat: what was effectively demobilised was Göring's bulge so as to allow the armaments industry to manage itself without constraints. The occupation of Europe had strengthened industry to a point where it could and did challenge the state- and military-led industrial policies of recovery during the 1930s.

[36] Michael Geyer, *Deutsche Rüstungspolitik, 1860–1980* (Frankfurt/Main, 1984).
[37] Alan Milward, 'Fritz Todt als Minister für Bewaffnung und Munition', *Vierteljahrshefte für Zeitgeschichte*, vol. 14 (1966), pp. 40–58 and Karl-Heinz Ludwig, *Technik und Ingenieure im Dritten Reich* (Düsseldorf, 1974).
[38] Lutz Budraß, 'Unternehmer im Nationalsozialismus: Der Sonderbevollmächtigte des Generalfeldmarschalls Göring für die Herstellung der Ju 38' (unpublished MS) and Michael Geyer, 'Der Einfluß der nationalsozialistischen Rüstungspolitik auf das Ruhrgebiet', *Rheinische Vierteljahresblätter*, vol. 45 (1981), pp. 201–64.

The turn to armaments production in the context of industrial self-government came about within the framework of German corporate control over Europe which entailed a new economics of space, *Groß-raumwirtschaft*, and new economies of scale. It was not plunder, as Tim Mason suggested, but hegemony over European markets which got German industry out of its rut and into full-scale armaments production.[39]

The occupation of Europe completed a twisted course of rebuilding the might of German industry and the military in an unforeseen and unexpected way. This process began with the revolt of industry and military (as well as the ministerial bureaucracy) against the pluralism of interests in the Weimar Republic. The military and industrial elites, with very few exceptions, insisted that the curtailment of political partici-pation and the autonomy of their institutions from politics would regen-erate their efficiency and facilitate a more rational governance. In this they were supported by an intellectual elite which considered the pro-ceduralism of parliamentary democracy a sham and pleaded for a government of experts that they saw exemplified in the Prussian tra-dition. But these restorative projects proved to be pipe dreams. Govern-ance set free from parliamentary constraints was instantly engulfed in rampant competition, cut-throat fights over petty advantages, excessive regulations and plain corruption. The Brüning and Papen presidential regimes had set in motion what the Third Reich exacerbated. The delib-erate destruction of constitutional governance led to the unmediated collision of interests that generated, at one and the same time, predatory competition and the search for protection which shaped the whole decade. The latter goes a long way to explain the peculiar rise of a privatised, person-to-person politics, based on a crude mixture of deals and loyalties, which stunned political observers schooled in the tradition of Max Weber and puzzled German social and political scientists. Yet, there it was, and it continued to produce results – six years of unpre-cedented war.

Restoration did not yield the results which the majority of officers and industrialists had expected in the wake of *their* seizures of power in conjunction with the National Socialist occupation of public politics. In fact, they achieved none of their goals, and not simply because the Nazis would not let them. It is true, the National Socialist leadership was wary in its relations with what they perceived as 'old elites' and attempted to cut them down whenever possible. But the Nazis only succeeded when these 'old elites' began to slip on their own. If there was a 'domestic crisis', this was it. It was the crisis of the piecemeal rearrangement of

---

[39] Alan Milward, *War, Economy and Society 1939–1945* (London, 1977).

power alignments which came to a head in 1938 when the future of the military institution and of industrial politics was up for grabs. The result was neither a breakdown of the regime nor an end to the powers of industry and the military, but a rearrangement of governance and a remarkable acceleration of the pace of events. Unable to bring restoration to a successful conclusion, the elite arrangements of 1933 gave way, piece by piece, to new ones which were now facilitated by upstart functional elites. These elites could be found in the NSDAP as much as in industry and the military. An emergent elite of ideological, industrial, and military technocrats began to set upon a frantic course of growth and expansion after 1938, leaving behind depression-period politics and entering what seemed to them an age of unlimited opportunity. War was not the first and surely not the only choice of these groups – and that includes the military. But war was accepted inasmuch as it came as a surgical means to break open international power arrangements. Industry and the military dramatically expanded and accelerated in this process. The military's technocratic core remade itself in the National Socialist image as an efficiency-oriented, publicity-conscious European elite.[40]

TERROR AND IDENTITY

The destruction of representative government is also the proper starting point for discussing the social dynamics of the National Socialist pursuit of war. How could the will of the nation be represented in a regime that declared itself to be the sole representative of the German people? This is to ask how popular assent was gained once government became unaccountable, party-political competition was outlawed, and alternative political opinions were repressed. The studies on this subject point unequivocally to the central role of the 'militarisation of the masses' as a substitute for politics.[41] They rely on a long tradition of theorisation which conceives of 'militarisation' as an act of 'social imperialism', that is, the deflection of the real wants and desires of people into artificial and pathological ones.[42] But this assessment does not quite fit a critical evaluation of the evidence.

[40] This argument is advanced convincingly by John Gillingham in *Industry and Politics in the Third Reich: Ruhr Coal, Hitler and Europe* (Stuttgart, 1985), and *Coal, Steel and the Rebirth of Europe 1945–1955: The Germans and French from Ruhr Conflict to Economic Community* (New York and Cambridge, 1991).
[41] The first to advance this point was George Mosse, *The Nationalization of the Masses: Political Symbolism and Mass Movements in Germany from the Napoleonic War through the Third Reich* (rev. edn, Ithaca and London, 1991).
[42] Wolfram Wette, *Militarismus und Pazifismus. Auseinandersetzung mit den deutschen Kriegen* (Bonn, 1991).

In the simplest terms militarisation meant that the Nazi propaganda machine cranked out masses of military images and that the young in particular were inundated with military rhetoric.[43] The nation came to be identified in not very subtle ways with men in uniform. Militarisation further entailed the censorship and repression of opinions which in the view of the Nazis and the military jeopardised the preparation for war. And it encompassed the violent persecution of any opposition against the military and against war. Some of these policies began to be put into action as early as 1928/9. The legal provision of high treason (*Landesverrat*) was extensively used in order to gain control over anti-militarist publics, but legality, while stretched to the limits, was by and large maintained. After 1933 the extra-legal physical violence of the SA and, subsequently, the systematic surveillance and persecution of the political police/Gestapo accompanied the remaking of Germany in the military image. The mixture of propaganda and state terror suggests the desire of the ruling elites to win over the 'people' but also their profound distrust concerning the popular readiness for war. In particular class and class division, apparently more so than gender, were considered to militate against war-readiness. The lingering memory of the revolution of 1918 and the uneasy attention of military officers and Nazis to the potential recurrence of this past are abundantly in evidence.[44]

If the German war course had been up to the military and the more old-fashioned Nazis like Hermann Göring, 'militarisation' might well have been realised by organising 'the people' for war. Their top-down militarisation started from the recognition, elaborated during the First World War, that society at large was necessary to fight modern war, and propaganda and surveillance were the means to assure the proper working of the national machine. Göring represented this view succinctly in November 1938 when he spoke to the issue of 'human economies':

> Every German, man or woman, between 14 and 65 must have his mobilisation order in his pocket, must know where to go. In a future war we can dispense with neither the fourteen-year-old nor the sixty-five-year old; we must be able to give some task to everyone.

---

[43] Jutta Sywottek, *Mobilmachung für den totalen Krieg: Die propagandistische Vorbereitung der deutschen Bevölkerung für den Zweiten Weltkrieg* (Opladen, 1976); Wolfram Wette, 'Ideologien, Propaganda und Innenpolitik als Voraussetzung der Kriegspolitik des Dritten Reiches', in Deist *et al.*, *Ursachen und Voraussetzungen*, pp. 25ff.; Franz-Werner Kersting, *Militär und Jugend im NS Staat. Rüstungs- und Schulpolitik der Wehrmacht* (Wiesbaden, 1989).

[44] Tim Mason, 'The Legacy of 1918 for National Socialism', in Anthony Nicholls and Erich Matthias (eds.), *German Democracy and the Triumph of Hitler* (London, 1971), pp. 215–39.

> We must register everyone and we must distribute everyone pre-
> cisely in order to know – this one will go to the military, this one
> will go to the factory, this one will stay in the factory and this one
> will be called up and passes on his job to his wife.[45]

The state appears in this scheme as a totalising machine that puts everyone into 'his' place according to what 'we' decree necessary in order to
wage war. The object of militarisation are men who may be substituted
by women and children. The purpose of the enterprise is to put every
man to work in a war-related capacity. The whole apparatus is to be
guided by the overarching rationality of a plan which is quite commonly
represented as an anthropomorphic machine. The idea of a totality of
mobilised people in which every man is in 'his' place, works for the
common end and follows the inexorable logic of nature or history (or of
a madman like Caligari) is probably the most pervasive interwar political
fantasy – and not just of the Right. It is most commonly associated with
Fritz Lang's *Metropolis* or Ernst Jünger's essay on 'Total Mobilisation'.
In all its vulgar racist and sexist presuppositions it is rather more fully
sketched by Erich Ludendorff.[46] Ludendorff also retains the crazy edge
of this kind of thinking, the manic compulsion it takes to want that
anything and everything strive purposefully for the final goal: destruction. In this world of totalised (inter)dependence, representation (as the
work of mediation and imagination) was unnecessary and, surely,
unwelcome, because everyone was already accounted for, registered,
and put in his place. For a portion of German society – and no small
one at that – this state of affairs seemed attractive, because it promised
order and predictability when disorder and turbulence were the overwhelming realities of the day.

The violence of this scheme is evident. The state of total mobilisation
does not recognise self-representation but only the subordination of
the individual to what 'we' – the state and its functionaries – dictate.
Total mobilisation, moreover, rejects any corporate forms of
(self)-organisation which might intrude into the 'human economies' of
the state. It may even come to reject family bonds, although support
for the latter distinguished a younger breed of techno-fascists from an
older group of bureaucratic totalitarians. This kind of rabid func-
tionalism in politics and social life was found most commonly among
a variety of social-engineering professions (prominently architects,
demographers) who had claimed, ever since the turn of the century, to

[45] Quoted in Timothy W. Mason, *Arbeiterklasse und Volksgemeinschaft. Dokumente und Materialien zur deutschen Arbeiterpolitik 1936–1939* (Opladen, 1975), p. 928.
[46] Ernst Jünger, 'Die totale Mobilmachung', in *Werke*, Part 2, *Essays*, vol. I (Stuttgart, 1982); Erich Ludendorff, *Der totale Krieg* (Munich, 1935); *Metropolis*, dir. by Fritz Lang (1926).

possess the solution to all social and political ills in the perfection of the mechanics of the nation's body.[47]

This system of total mobilisation did find a place in the German machinery of war, but not quite where one might expect it. The system of surveillance and terror was crucial to the regime of forced labour and in this capacity formed an ever-growing part of the Nazi war effort. In this regime we can plainly see the elements that total mobilisation theorists had mapped as the prerequisite for modern war. The anonymisation and atomisation of individuals and their assessment entirely in terms of use-value, the violence of a merely functional distribution of human resources as well as the surplus of terror which came as an intrinsic element with this kind of total war mobilisation – all this encapsulates in practice what total war theorists had sketched out in their planning fantasies. What I call the surplus of terror, the persistent and common mistreatment of foreign labourers, needs some emphasis. For terror was not an extrinsic, 'ideological' element in this system – as if it could be taken away and 'total mobilisation' would still work. This is what many Germans may have wanted to believe during and after the war.[48] But slave labour and good intentions do not go together. It takes excessive violence to keep the system of total mobilisation in place. It is not by chance that this system produced exactly what veteran planners had feared most ever since the First World War – a persistent and pervasive effort to escape and an extraordinary readiness to resist. In fact, the kind of everyday resistance that some historians have sought and occasionally uncovered among Germans is far more frequently found among the victims of the total mobilisation regime than among the Germans.[49]

Notwithstanding pervasive surveillance and persecution, this regime did not apply to the majority of Germans. It is difficult to say what is more surprising – the degree to which a great number of officers, Nazis and intellectuals fantasised about this machinery of omniscient and totalising control as the most efficient way of preparing war, or the degree to which historians have repeated this fascination by taking it for the reality of social mobilisation for war in the Third Reich. No doubt, this is what the military and Göring had in mind and what became partial

[47] Michael Burleigh, *Death and Deliverance: 'Euthanasia' in Germany 1900–1945* (New York and Cambridge, 1994); Daniel Pick, *War Machine: the Rationalization of Slaughter in the Modern Age* (New Haven and London, 1993); Götz Aly, *Endlösung. Völkerverschiebung und der Mord an den europäischen Juden* (Frankfurt/Main, 1995).

[48] Hayes, *Industry and Ideology*, shows this point convincingly, because he takes the cognitive dissonance of Germans (in this case: I.G. Farben managers) for real rather than as a deceit. Of course, this reality of not-seeing when seeing remains to be studied beyond attesting the fact of it.

[49] Ulrich Herbert, *'Fremdarbeiter'. Politik und Praxis des 'Ausländer-Einsatzes' in der Kriegswirtschaft des Dritten Reiches* (Bonn, 1985), pp. 288ff.

reality as, for example, in the registration of each and every person and the repression of all forms of self-organisation. However, as far-reaching as these efforts were, it is also evident that this scheme fell short *in its totalitarian aspirations* for the Germans. Schemes of total surveillance and mobilisation never advanced quite as far as social engineers imagined them – because there were ideological proclivities and there were concerns for regime stability and because it proved to be impossible to run a nation, as opposed to slave labour, like a machine. It was not necessary either, because of the self-mobilisation of German society for war as a substitute for political participation. At the centre of this nascent National Socialist pursuit of war was not the totalising state but the mobilisation of individual ambitions and their representation as acts of national self-determination. This became the German pursuit of identity through terror in the crucial mid-years of the Third Reich.[50]

The German pursuit of war was deliberate and self-willed, even if not without hesitation. It was far more the result of individual initiative than the product of state pressure. Propaganda did everything to massage this individual initiative. To be sure, compulsion was a crucial part of the system, but it was a compulsion – as for example military conscription – that put individual initiative at the centre. Such initiative, while compelled by the ever-present recourse to persecution, was reinforced by appeals to responsibility, honour, courage, virility.[51] It was not forthcoming enthusiastically, but even groups such as Communist workers or traditionalist Catholics who had opposed the Nazis and had themselves been victims of Nazi violence ultimately joined in and participated in the mobilisation for war. In the transitional middle years of the Third Reich between 1938 and 1942 this participation became rather more attractive than it had been during the first years. This is, at least, what the reports from and about Germany recounted with increasing frequency. The appeal to individual initiative within the context of an overarching responsibility to the *Volk* – and always against the background of the Gestapo as an ever-present deterrent for opposing attitudes and actions – did work. All opinion surveys point to the active participation of the Germans and to the importance of individual initiative in the

---

[50] Alf Lüdtke, 'The Appeal of Exterminating "Others": German Workers and the Limits of Resistance', in Michael Geyer and John W. Boyer (eds.) *Resistance against the Third Reich, 1933–1990* (Chicago and London, 1994), pp. 53–74.

[51] Wolfram Wette (ed.), *Der Krieg des kleinen Mannes. Eine Militärgeschichte von unten.* (Munich, 1992); H. J. Schröder, *Kasernenzeit. Arbeiter erzählen von der Militärausbildung im Dritten Reich* (Frankfurt/Main, 1985); more generally, Ulrich Herbert, 'Arbeiterschaft im "Dritten Reich". Zwischenbilanz und offene Fragen', *Geschichte und Gesellschaft*, vol. 15 (1989), pp. 320–60.

preparation and the pursuit of war[52] – in other words not at all to what many historians would like to see as (and what many contemporary officers feared to be) the prevailing sentiment in which war becomes a monstrous imposition on the real wants and desires of the people.

This is not to say that when it came to fighting people were reckless. They were cautious. Their memories of the First World War did not entice them to enter war easily. The fact that there were no jubilant parades in 1939 is by now as much a cliché as the reference to the prevalence of such enthusiasm in 1914.[53] In both cases reality was actually more mixed. What Germans feared in 1939/40 was not war as such but a repetition of the First World War. The memory of mass death, hunger, and privation formed a strong deterrent against war. Hence every foreign-policy initiative of the Third Reich was accompanied by a jolt of fear. Most of all, popular opinion responded vigorously when it came to wage cuts, the reduction of rations, the curtailment of allowances which it read as indications that old privations would return.

The weariness persistently fuelled resentments against the old elites rather than against the Nazis. The zenith of this development came in 1944 when the overwhelming majority of German soldiers denounced the coup against Hitler vigorously as the presumption of privilege and wealth in the face of what most soldiers considered the common predicament of all Germans.[54] Military service was taken quite literally as an instantiation of equality and of the Nazi community ideology. This particularly striking instance is a reflection of a far more general tendency which associated military service with 'normalcy' and gave it a distinctly egalitarian ring.[55] The politics of *Wiederwehrhaftmachung* (the

---

[52] Take as a concrete example Heinz Boberach (ed.), *Meldungen aus dem Reich. Die geheimen Lageberichte des Sicherheitsdienstes der SS 1938–1945*, 17 vols. (Herrsching, 1984), esp. vol. IV, p. 1,305; or more generally the *Deutschlandberichte der Sozialdemokratischen Partei Deutschlands (Sopade) 1934–1940*, 7 vols. (Frankfurt/Main, 1980), esp. vol. VII (1940), and Bernd Stöver, *Volksgemeinschaft im Dritten Reich. Konsensbereitschaft der Deutschen aus der Sicht sozialistischer Exilberichte* (Düsseldorf, 1993), pp. 173ff., 204ff.

[53] Wolfgang Benz, 'Freude am Krieg oder widerwillige Loyalität. Die Stimmungslage der Deutschen bei Beginn des Zweiten Weltkrieges', in Wolfgang Benz, *Herrschaft und Gesellschaft im nationalsozialistischen Staat. Studien zur Struktur- und Mentalitätsgeschichte* (Frankfurt/Main, 1990), pp. 63–71; Ian Kershaw, *The 'Hitler Myth': Image and Reality in the Third Reich* (Oxford, 1987).

[54] The primary evidence of summary censorship reports from all fronts for August and September 1944 (the only reports of this kind surviving) is rather more impressive than the historiography on resistance makes it out to be – although there is general agreement on the rejection of the coup by the vast majority of soldiers. See Bundesarchiv-Militärarchiv, RH 13/47 and 48.

[55] Jürgen Förster, 'Vom Führerheer der Republik zur nationalsozialistischen Volksarmee. Zum Strukturwandel der Wehrmacht 1935–1945', in Jost Dülffer *et al.* (eds.), *Deutschland in Europa: Kontinuität und Bruch* (Frankfurt/Main, 1990), pp. 311–28, and gener-

fortification of the body politic) was widely welcomed. While the military expected a massive revulsion against military service, there was little protest and that protest was quickly located, because it came from isolated groups of pacifists and conscientious objectors. The reintroduction of military service was quite commonly understood as the long-overdue instantiation of the national community (*Volksgemeinschaft*) which suggested a male world of honest work, skill and pride in national achievement. Such labours linked the individual to the nation, however much anyone might have grumbled about the years lost to the state. The military became a powerful male bonding agent – it seems far more so than any other National Socialist institution. If the national community proved to be less of a reality than the recruits would have liked, this rather enhanced resentment; that is, the *vox populi* leaned rather to the Right, decrying the reality and appearance of privilege, clamouring for the inclusion of everyone in the war effort and demanding severe punishment, indeed, persecution of real and presumed shirkers. Historians have observed this reaction quite extensively in the backlash against Nazi bosses, but this disenchantment was predicated on very National Socialist presumptions. It thrived on the populist egalitarianism of the regime and rehearsed National Socialist ideologies even where it rejected the Nazi Party. 'The people' had their own version of total mobilisation which was radically populist in the assumption that 'my war had better be your war as well'. A radical egalitarianism linked to war became the mainstay of the German pursuit of war which a majority sentiment saw as a mechanism of radical levelling and came to identify with National Socialism – even as they rejected the Nazi party as selling out and the military as a distant power elite.[56]

There is yet another aspect of the fear of war in 1939 which is easily overlooked. It is the fear of defeat – of exertion and suffering that leads to naught. This sentiment is evident in a relentless war literature after the First World War which fought a lost war to a fictitious victory after all.[57] The turning of the tables in the forest of Compiègne as the tri-

ally on this issue Frank Trommler, 'Between Normality and Resistance: Catastrophic Gradualism in Nazi Germany', in Geyer and Boyer (eds.), *Resistance against the Third Reich*, pp. 119–38.

[56] See, for example, Horst Fuchs Richardson (ed.), *Sieg Heil: War Letters of Tank Gunner Karl Fuchs 1937–1941* (Hamden, Conn., 1987) or Guy Sajer, *The Forgotten Soldier* (2nd edn, London, 1977). With a somewhat different emphasis, Ian Kershaw, *Popular Opinion and Political Dissent in the Third Reich: Bavaria 1933–1945* (Oxford, 1983).

[57] Scott Denham, *Visions of War: Ideologies and Images of War in German Literature before and after the Great War* (Berne and New York, 1992). For the Second World War see Frank Trommler, ' "Deutschlands Sieg oder Untergang". Perspektiven aus dem Dritten Reich auf Nachkriegsdeutschland', in Thomas Koebner, Gert Sautermeister and Sigrid Schneider (eds.), *Deutschland nach Hitler: Zukunftspläne im Exil und aus der Besatzungszeit 1939–1945* (Opladen, 1987), pp. 214–28.

umphal vindication of 1918 symbolised this sentiment very well. The common apprehension of 1939 pertained also to the possibility of defeat – in a war that was perceived as a people's war and, hence, entailed not just the potential defeat of the state but of every individual who fought it. Like egalitarian populism, the resentment of defeat proved to be a persistent and ever more pronounced element of the German war effort. The refusal to give in kept Germans fighting long after the war was effectively lost.[58] As much as anxiety rose at the beginning of war, the hope for victory ultimately did not die until 1945. For each seeming reversal was accompanied by sighs of relief and the expectation that defeat still could be averted.[59] The contrast between 1918 and 1945 is illustrative in this respect. If the First World War ended in revolution, the Second World War ground to a halt only after Germany was occupied and its armed forces were destroyed. The nation that engaged in war so reluctantly fought it doggedly to the very end – and fighting continued long after a discernible ideological commitment to the regime had collapsed.

Fear of defeat and resistance to 'total mobilisation' were balanced by a willingness to show the world who is best – ordinary ambitions to be sure, but of extraordinary consequence for the German pursuit of war once the initial blockage was overcome. *Blitzkrieg* squared the circle and resolved the tensions between the contrary sentiments. We have already seen that *Blitzkrieg* was not a strategic design. It was instead what the military elites, the Nazis and the masses jointly saw themselves doing and came to like. This spectacular war they were eager to fight – and in the violent spectacle of the newsreels found themselves represented as a nation. This war emerged from the cutting room and was accepted as national representation. The irony is that the 'people' much like a discordant military elite came to believe that what appeared in the movies was in fact what they were doing of their own free will.

The cutting-room collage of war presented the nation with an image of self-mobilisation[60] – and, hence, was quite the opposite of the numb-

---

[58] This is the subtext for Andreas Hillgruber's much criticised essay (which I quote in its original version), *Der Zusammenbruch im Osten 1944/45 als Problem der deutschen Nationalgeschichte und der europäischen Geschichte* (Opladen, 1985). Hillgruber suggests, however, that fear of Soviet revenge explains the refusal to give in. This is undoubtedly much too narrow an interpretation.

[59] The basic study on popular opinion during the war, apart from Kershaw, is Marlis G. Steinert, *Hitler's War and the Germans* (Athens, Ohio, 1977). My own conclusions are based on preliminary studies about the public reaction to the Battle of the Bulge (Ardennen-Offensive); see also Michael Geyer, 'Civitella in Val Chiana: June 1944–June 1994', in Klaus Naumann and Hannes Heer (eds.), *Vernichtungskrieg. Wehrmacht und NS-Verbrechen* (Hamburg, 1995).

[60] Unfortunately, there is little historiography on German war-reporting; see, generally, K. R. M. Short, *Film & Radio Propaganda in World War II* (London, 1983).

ing mobilisation schemes of a Göring or a *Wehrwirtschaftsstab*. The majority of Germans were captivated by success made visible on the screen and identified it with the National Socialist ethos of success which said that, if you disciplined body and mind and fanatically pursued your goal, success would indeed come. War as the gambit of a people on the rebound from depression, and the spoils of war as the right of all those who risked their lives for success – this was by far the best preparation for and representation of war. Leni Riefenstahl's *Triumph of the Will* and *Olympiad* were far more indicative of the nature of militarisation in Germany than the total mobilisation fantasies of Göring and the military caste.[61] The sense of achievement and, with the first victories, the feeling of collective invincibility laid the foundations for a relentless pursuit of war. A sense of superiority (instilled by propaganda but eagerly picked up by the masses) permeated all aspects of German war making. It came initially as the image and sense of superiority of German technology against the European enemies (Stuka bombers diving on enemy positions) and continued in the belief in miracle weapons to the end of the war. It also came as the presumption of cultural and racial superiority in the campaigns in Poland, the Balkans, Greece and the Soviet Union; and it persisted as the insistence on the superiority of German fighting skills (endurance, courage, and cunning) against an overwhelmingly superior Allied war machine. It was this tangible sense of superiority, mirrored in public spectacle, that got Germans into the war and kept them in it.

They also believed that they would reap the rewards of their superiority. Nazi planning for the welfare of the Germans on the one hand, and for representational architecture on the other, are commonly read as the main indication of the sense of privilege (and commonly discussed as a 'modern' feature of the Third Reich).[62] While this is appropriate, superiority was much more bluntly stated and brutally realised. If the welfare of the Germans was the subject of extensive blueprints of Nazi and state agencies, plunder was the currency of everyday life – both on a grand institutional and on a petty individual scale.[63] If architectural planning revealed the megalomania of the Nazi vision for a postwar order, this same sentiment was picked up and reverberated in the yearning for

---

[61] Martin Loiperdinger, *Der Parteitagsfilm 'Triumph des Willens' von Leni Riefenstahl. Rituale der Mobilmachung* (Opladen, 1987).

[62] Prinz and Zitelmann (eds.), *Nationalsozialismus und Modernisierung*.

[63] Theresa Wobbe (ed.), *Nach Osten. Verdeckte Spuren nationalsozialistischer Verbrechen* (Frankfurt/Main, 1992) reflects on the controversial role of German women in the system of plunder.

'respect' by the common soldier.[64] 'Honour', previously the privilege of officers, gained popular currency in the Nazi pursuit of war. It was a key to the identity of the German soldiers and a feature of German identity that Nazi propaganda never failed to emphasise. Deference was maintained by retribution, ultimately the willingness to kill. It should therefore not surprise that massacres – few on the scale of Oradour in France or Marzabotto in Italy but many small acts of violence everywhere – became ever more frequent and were no longer 'racially' motivated towards the end of the war. In fact, the system of retribution was carried back into Germany as the armies retreated.

This Social Darwinism of everyday life moved Germans into war and had them go on fighting long after the war was lost and, indeed, long after they were defeated.[65] For if the First World War was fought for a way of life which a good part of German society had come to reject, the Second World War was fought for the construction of a better life which a good part of German society strove very hard to achieve. This is the space where identity and terror could merge.

This German pursuit of war dovetailed with a process of social rearrangement quite similar to the one which I have outlined for the military and industrial elites. This process is easily misperceived, because the Nazi regime had so much at stake in selling it as a 'social revolution' toward the vaunted *Volksgemeinschaft*. There was no such thing. And yet, social boundaries did give way and worlds of new possibilities – quite literally – opened to allow for an escape from the constraints of a highly stratified and hierarchical society. War (like rearmament before) proved to be a potent arena in this respect both in the sense that war opened new opportunities and that its pursuit was reflected as national achievement. This was a 'crisis of social reproduction' in that older norms and older bonds no longer quite held and new ones were being forged through war and terror. It was not a crisis, though, in which the regime ran up against insurmountable obstacles, be it class barriers, gender hierarchies, foreign exchange shortages, or resource limits. Even as these limits were evident and became subject to conflictual debate, a sense of limits does not encapsulate the reality of the years between 1938 and 1942. In those years the sky was the limit and everything seemed possible. The sense of war as achievement is difficult to fathom in more civilian times, but it was so frequent and so persistent among contemporaries that it cannot be discounted. It is

[64] Mark Mazower, 'Military Violence and National Socialist Values: The Wehrmacht in Greece, 1941–1944', *Past and Present*, no. 134 (February 1992), pp. 129–58.
[65] Rolf Schörken, *Jugend 1945. Politisches Denken und Lebensgeschichte* (Opladen, 1990).

anchored in the fusion of individual labours and myths of collective or national regeneration rather more firmly than in the First World War vision of soldiers as prosthetic gods.[66] This sense of achievement is, in any case, the bottom line of a 1940s mentality which long outlived National Socialist ideology.

This observation allows us to rethink the initial question of how popular assent was gained once government became unaccountable. The simple answer to this question is tyrannical rule – a combination of surveillance and terror. While this answer reflects a central tenet of the Third Reich, it does not account for the reality of the years between 1938 and 1941/2. These years form the high point of an arrangement between the Nazi regime and the German people. This arrangement was not a contract among believers. If the war had had to be fought by committed Nazis, it would have been a puny affair. But the regime activated large segments of society and crucial elements into self-sustaining participation. The peculiarity of the Nazi pursuit of war consisted in the ability to release individual ambition from constraints of profession, class, religion and gender – from the constraints of old society – and at the same time to represent this ambition as the will of the nation, embodied in the *Führer*.

In this respect, National Socialism was far closer to the liberal pursuit of happiness than to fascism, which tended to stymie individual initiative in favour of one or the other form of incorporation into self-restricting, hierarchical social bodies. The decisive difference, though, was the absence of politics – of 'men' gathering, as it were, to deliberate their fate, because deliberation may indeed have raised second thoughts whereas the unmediated pursuit of ambitions and untrammelled action postponed thinking until after the killing was done. The destruction of a political public proved to be fatal. It is the origin of the German pursuit of war.

NATIONAL SOCIALIST REALISM

German society came out of depression with a vengeance and was poised to take on the world. 'Take on the world' is above all a metaphor. In the years between 1938 and 1942 we find this metaphor expressed in everyday life as increased mobility and the search for new opportunity. We find it in the challenges to the moral universe of traditionalist society which had little room for an assertive youth. We find it in the expansion of local worlds into national and, indeed, global audio-visual spaces as radio and newsreels became popular. Despite the rise of a mass political conscious-

---

[66] Klaus Theweleit, *Männerphantasien* (2 vols., Frankfurt/Main, 1977–8) (English version: *Male Fantasies* (2 vols., Cambridge, 1987–9), has done a great deal to advance a 'cultural' interpretation of war, but has also narrowed the focus to a very peculiar kind of soldierly personality.

ness dating back to the 1890s, it could well be argued that this was the first
time when a majority of Germans experienced their Germanness. Individual assertiveness and the widening of local horizons accompanied and
intertwined with military expansion. We can observe this same expression
of daring in the heroism of National Socialist art, allegories of (male)
strength, ambition and courage to be vindicated by (female) tranquillity
and harmony after the storms had passed, and of an architecture that was
to serve as the encasement of monumental achievements yet to come.
Much can be said about this world of National Socialist metaphor which
grew explosively in these years.[67] But the troubling truth of the matter is
that the National Socialist regime did not limit itself to metaphors. The
singularity of National Socialist rule – as opposed to their fascist contemporaries – consisted, as Broszat has rightly argued, in its utter realism
(*Realitätsrigorismus*).[68] The National Socialist regime surprised even its
most ardent followers with the compulsive implementation of what otherwise were collective (although not universally shared) imaginings – for the
beliefs of a Hitler or a Goebbels were not so uncommon after all. But their
actual realisation was. The National Socialist regime moved relentlessly
from the virtual realities of images and metaphors to the actual reality of
fighting war and organising annihilation.

  Why should the Nazi regime engulf the whole world in war and, in the
end, pursue a course of self-destruction rather than desist from fighting
and killing? Elite dispositions and popular proclivities suggest that war
became a self-sustaining, national enterprise once it was started. But why
was it started in the first place when elite resistance and popular fear still
held the balance? The compulsion to wage war was due, in part, to the
fanaticism of the leading National Socialists and most of all of Hitler. It is
strange how this element of utter and blind fanaticism, the 'mad-dog'
politics above all of Hitler, is downplayed.[69] The 'gentrification' of Hitler,
particularly among those who see Hitler as a moderniser, is one of the
main reasons for not understanding the decision for war. Hitler bet his life
on undoing the trauma of war and defeat – and once in power, he was not
going to be denied short of being deposed.[70] To reduce this element of

[67] Much, in fact, has been said. See, for example, Neue Gesellschaft für bildende Kunst
    (ed.), *Inszenierung der Macht. Ästhetische Faszination im Faschismus* (Berlin, 1987) or
    Richard J. Golsan (ed.), *Fascism, Aesthetics, and Culture* (Hanover, N.H., and London,
    1992).
[68] Broszat, 'Betrachtungen zu "Hitlers Zweitem Buch" '.
[69] I take the notion of 'mad-dog' politics from Gaines Post, *Dilemmas of Appeasement:
    British Deterrence and Defense, 1934–1937* (Ithaca and London, 1993).
[70] Gerhard Weinberg (*The Foreign Policy of Hitler's Germany*) has convincingly made this
    point, which is argued in a much more arcane fashion by psychohistorians such as
    Rudolph Binion, *Hitler among the Germans* (New York, 1976).

compulsive fanaticism misrepresents the essence of National Socialist leadership.

But fanaticism was not simply a mentality which reflected some general tenets of German sensibilities. This it did. But, more importantly, fanaticism became an institution and the dynamics of these institutions have much more to do with the decision to initiate war than historians have commonly assumed. The rapid expansion of National Socialist ideological apparatuses, in particular of the SS, and their enduring cut-throat competition for leverage is a much neglected factor in the decision for war. This Nazi sphere of power expanded dramatically after 1938 and formed a powerful, expansive and elaborate network which began to move and shape ideological politics in its own right. It is in the actions of the newly emerging apparatuses like the SS that we can discern the substantiation of National Socialist visions in a pervasive practice. This process was aided and abetted by a scientific establishment of therapeutic intellectuals which took it upon themselves to map out the future of Europe.[71] They also took on the remaking of the German and, indeed, the European body politic as the main goal of the pursuit of war.[72] It seems to me that we must place the actual decision for war into this context. It is the spark that kept the deliberate transformation of German society going. As restorative policy initiatives unravelled one after the other between 1938 and 1942, governance was rewound around the pursuit of war – but the pursuit of war was now ever more driven by and imbricated in the effort to forge the German nation as the superior race.[73] As we have seen, this war aim had considerable popular appeal.

It would take a separate essay to explicate the link between the expansion of the racial state, the 'cleansing' of the German body politic, and its resettlement in an imperial space which became the cornerstone of the fusion of ideology and institutional power. I have suggested the permeability of ideological politics, social engineering, and military and economic efficiency. For the moment it may suffice to point out that historians have gathered sufficient, if dispersed evidence to make plausible

[71] Götz Aly and Susanne Heim, *Vordenker der Vernichtung. Auschwitz und die deutschen Pläne für eine neue europäische Ordnung* (Hamburg, 1991), but see also the critique of Dan Diner, 'Nationalsozialismus und Stalinismus: über Gedächtnis, Willkür, Arbeit und Tod', in Dan Diner, *Kreisläufe. Nationalsozialismus und Gedächtnis* (Berlin, 1995), pp. 47–75.
[72] Michael Geyer, 'Krieg als Gesellschaftspolitik. Anmerkungen zu neueren Arbeiten über das Dritte Reich im Zweiten Weltkrieg', *Archiv für Sozialgeschichte*, vol. 20 (1986), pp. 557–601.
[73] This is not to argue for another 'domestic origins' of war. However, to work on the international crisis of the late 1930s would mean to start the same analysis from the opposite end. The best combination of the two approaches is MacGregor Knox, 'Conquest, Foreign and Domestic, in Fascist Italy and Nazi Germany', *Journal of Modern History*, vol. 56 (March 1984), pp. 1–57.

the connection between the domestic initiatives to purify the German body politic, the pursuit of colonial expansion in genocidal wars in eastern Europe and the Soviet Union, and a deliberate and pre-meditated politics of annihilation which single-mindedly focused on the Jewish population of Europe. Rather than seeing them apart as distinct, even competing facets of a regime, it is now possible to trace the growth of their destructive synergy in the years between 1938 and 1942.

National Socialist war was no foregone conclusion, even after the initial decision for war was made on 30 May 1938.[74] This decision is so commonly overlooked, because it initiated preparations for war which in the end did not take place in quite the way it was mapped out – a war against Czechoslovakia as a means to unhinge the interwar order of Europe. What remained of this decision was neither political nor military calculation (which changed repeatedly in the frantic pace of events after 1938) but the unequivocal intent to wage war. War became the only point of reference that the Third Reich had as it set out to organise the diverse interests of the nation without recourse to governance, and to present the nation to the people as geopolitical, and racial destiny as substitute for political self-determination. The decision for war served, over time, as an 'attractor' for the ambitions not only of the elites but of large segments of German society. It served as a perfect substitute for politics. It is therefore utterly misleading to speak of a relative autonomy of politics in the pursuit of war. To be sure, this argument once had its uses in countering the notion of war as a conspiracy of the most reactionary forces of capitalism and militarism and of the National Socialist elites as mere puppets.[75] But the basic thrust of the argument misses the very core of the National Socialist pursuit of war which consisted in the destruction of politics and its displacement by a regime of violent opportunity. Here again, the contrast with other fascist movements becomes evident. The Nazis implemented their visions of national regeneration and, more perniciously, let ordinary people take part in the process as well – ordinary people who thought of it as their purchase into the dream of the good life which in their mind would surely come once the killing was done.[76]

Historians will continue to wrestle with so unequivocal a fact as the German decision to wage and escalate war, culminating in the ferocious war for the destruction of the Soviet Union and a European-wide politics

---

[74] Michael Geyer, 'Rüstungsbeschleunigung und Inflation. Zur Inflationsdenkschrift des OKW vom November 1938', *Militärgeschichtliche Mitteilungen*, vol. 2 (1981), pp. 121–86.

[75] T. W. Mason, 'The Primacy of Politics. Politics and Economics in National Socialist Germany', in S. J. Woolf (ed.), *The Nature of Fascism* (New York, 1969).

[76] This is my reading of Walter Kempowski, *Das Echolot: ein kollektives Tagebuch Januar–Februar 1943* (4 vols., Munich, 1993).

of ethnic cleansing, which crystallised in the deliberate annihilation of the European Jewry. I have suggested that the goal of National Socialist war consisted in establishing an exclusive 'space' for the relentless pursuit of opportunity. Efforts to that end came to fruition only with the collapse of restorative politics, domestically and also internationally, which had destroyed the national and European constitutionalism of the interwar years. The new rule was predicated on terror, but it was a popular rule all the same. It was a system of governance that was held in place by professionals and technocrats. It was counter-revolutionary violence in a quite literal sense and in that respect coincided with the ambitions of European fascism. For the rationale of 'fascism' was the extirpation of the two grand revolutionary traditions of the nineteenth century: the constitution of the identity of the nation and its citizens through participation in politics and the mutually assured self-determination of nations in an European community of nation-states.

9

~~~~~~

FROM FASCISM TO 'POST-FASCISTS': ITALIAN
ROADS TO MODERNITY

CARL LEVY

In the last decade of his life, Tim Mason lived in Italy and made several significant contributions to debates in Italian historiography. He addressed central themes in contemporary Italian history including the degree to which Fascism modernised Italian society and the related issue of an Italian revisionist account of Fascism. Many of the points Mason raised in his insightful and acerbic review of the Great Industry Show, held in Rome in 1984[1] – an exhibition which uncritically celebrated the achievements of Italian industry during a period (1919–39) spanning much of the Fascist *ventennio* – would become important political issues in 1993–4. For with the collapse of the old political certainties of the 'First Republic' and the incorporation of the neo-Fascist Movimento Sociale Italiano/Alleanza Nazionale within Silvio Berlusconi's short-lived coalition government, the revisionist historiography of Fascism and the Resistance has been directly linked to the 'normalisation' of the neo-Fascist or, as they call themselves, 'post-Fascist' Right. The young leader of the MSI, Gianfranco Fini, has tried to differentiate Mussolini's regime between a pre-1938 period when Fascism, he argues, achieved admirable reforms that assisted in the long-term social and economic modernisation of Italy, and the post-1938 disastrous alliance with the Nazi regime.[2] Even earlier in 1987, Renzo De Felice, the moderate lay

---

In writing this chapter I was unable to take into account Philip Morgan, *Italian Fascism 1919–1945* (Basingstoke, 1995).

[1] Tim Mason, 'The Great Economic History Show', *History Workshop. A Journal of Socialist Historians*, no. 21 (1986), pp. 3–35.

[2] For a recent interview with Fini see Robert Graham, 'Game Player of the Right', *Financial Times*, 2 Dec. 1994, p. 14. For the continuity of MSI policy before and after the foundation of the Alleanza Nazionale see Pietro Ignazi, 'Alleanza nazionale', in Ilvo Diamanti and Renato Mannheimer (eds.), *Milano a Roma. Guida all'Italia elettorale del 1994* (Rome, 1994), and Chiara Valentini, 'Alleanza Nazionale: la componente "storica" del Polo della libertà', in Paul Ginsborg (ed.), *Stato dell'Italia* (Milan, 1994), pp. 677–81.

biographer of Mussolini, had argued for a post-Fascist approach to the study of the regime that would take a critical stance against post-1945 historiography inspired by the exaggerated and misplaced moralism of the Resistance tradition.[3] He raised a storm when he asked for the lifting of the constitutional ban on the reconstitution of the Fascist party. But seven years later the extreme Right was incorporated into a right-of-centre government for the first time since 1945. The normalisation of the extreme Right was even accepted by many intellectuals on the Left. However, the 'post-Communists' (PDS, Partito Democratico della Sinistra) were still affected by the *conventio ad excludendum* which has functioned since 1948, and still functioned in the minds of a significant section of the Italian electorate in the spring of 1994. Even five years after the fall of the Berlin Wall, Berlusconi never tired of explaining how the victory of the most right-wing government in Italian history since 1945 prevented a left-wing minority from seizing power.[4] The one constant in modern Italian history remains that the major left-wing party has never led a national government. As of 1994, Italians had never experienced a real alternation of government at the national level. To that extent modern Italian political history has been dominated by varieties of the Right: from pre-1922 Liberal and Conservative notables, to Mussolini's dictatorship, to Christian Democracy and its odd successor amalgam of neo-liberals, neo-Fascists and northern populist federalists. The results of the 1994 elections point to another theme of this chapter, the historiographical debate over continuities or discontinuities present in the histories of Liberal, Fascist and Republican Italy.[5]

This chapter is split into two parts. The first part reviews and assesses the historiographical debate concerning the role of modernisation during the Fascist regime and assesses the extent to which a distinctively Fascist form of modernisation laid the framework for the politics and political economy of Republican Italy. The second part of this chapter addresses the issue of how far the Fascist legacy and neo-Fascism impinged upon the administrative, legal and party systems of Republican Italy. While both West German and Italian postwar politics were

[3] For a recent summary of De Felice's position and the ensuing controversy see Massimo Legnani, 'Sistema di potere fascista, blocco dominante, alleanze sociali. Contributi ad una discussione', *Italia Contemporanea*, vol. 194 (1994), pp. 31–52, and R. J. B. Bosworth, *Explaining Auschwitz and Hiroshima* (London, 1993), pp. 138–40.
[4] For a general summary of the results of the general election of 1994 see Diamanti and Mannheimer (eds.), *Milano*.
[5] For the debate about the historical continuities between the Liberal, Fascist and Republican eras of modern Italian history see John A. Davis's 'Remapping Italy's Path to the Twentieth Century', *Journal of Modern History*, vol. 66 (1994), pp. 291–320. The persistence of the Right has recently been discussed by Luigi Bobbio in 'Dalla destra alla destra, una strana alternanza', in Ginsborg (ed.), *Stato*, pp. 654–60.

dominated by a centrist Christian Democratic 'catch-all' party, Italy was different owing to the persistence of a small but significant neo-Fascist party in its party system, the extent of extreme Right street violence and terrorism, and the persistent and serious attempts of subversion of the democratic order by the extreme and conservative Right within the very institutions of government. Modernisation theorists in the postwar era found the 'Italian model' a particularly happy hunting ground precisely because it appeared to present a more problematic picture of the process of modernisation during the great postwar economic boom and its after-math than did the Federal Republic of Germany. And as Tim Mason noted in an insightful article, the Italian educated middle classes were besotted by the magic of modernisation.[6] This chapter will offer a modest dose of sober disenchantment.

VARIETIES OF MODERNISATION IN FASCIST ITALY

Since the term modernisation has been used in such a broad and indis-criminate fashion by historians and social scientists, there is no sensible way to test the reality of a Fascist modernisation of Italy during the *ventennio* if the process intended to be explained is not more clearly defined. If the process of modernisation has any purchase, it must be more closely identified with certain measurable changes in Italian his-tory between 1922 and 1943 (or 1945). Historians of the *ventennio* have used the term modernisation to explain changes in the Italian state and civil society. Before I turn to civil society I would like to address the issue of the modernisation of the Italian state under Fascism and conti-nuities in the post-Fascist era.

Although both Fascists in Italy and Nazis in Germany relied on con-servative and moderate support to hoist them into power, once there the degree to which the older structures were swept away varied signifi-cantly. Italy retained a constitutionally separate and unmodernised army, a monarchy and a Senate, which eventually helped unseat Musso-lini in 1943. If the Italian army was subservient to Mussolini, it resisted any fascistisation and the party militia and the Fascist party itself were quickly assimilated into the state apparatus.[7] The Lateran Accords of 1929 and the sometimes grudging allowance for the independence of action of widespread activities of Catholic Action meant that a Catholic

---

[6] Tim Mason, 'Italy and Modernization: A Montage', *History Workshop. A Journal of Socialist and Feminist Historians*, vol. 25 (1988), pp. 127–47.

[7] For a recent overview of the process see Doug Thompson, *State Control in Fascist Italy* (Manchester, 1991). The classic studies are Alberto Aquarone, *L'organizzazione dello Stato totalitario* (Turin, 1965) and Guido Quazza (ed.), *Fascismo e società italiana* (Turin, 1973).

subculture, although not unhappy with Mussolini's crusades against heretic Christian Ethiopia or the atheistic Spanish Republic, kept its own political elite alive and separate from the Fascist state.[8] In Germany, Hitler achieved control of the army by 1938–9 and his party militia, the SS, created a state within the state. Indeed Himmler drew the comparative lessons when he privately warned the *Duce* that his regime's Achilles' heel was precisely his failure to create an independent source of power and terror separate from the traditional forces of law and order.[9]

Fascist Italy can never be equated with the two monstrous industrialised death regimes in Nazi Germany and the Stalinist Soviet Union. Indeed it has been argued by MacGregor Knox elsewhere that although Mussolini's decision to enter the war in 1940 was motivated partially by his fear of an overly dominant Germany and partially by his jealousy of Hitler's stunning victories, it had also to do with his desire to use the dialectic of war to radicalise his regime.[10] Since his acceptance of the Nuremberg Laws and his pact with Hitler, the Italian people in general and the conservative establishment in particular had turned away from their enthusiasm for the *Duce* which had been noticeable in the wake of the Ethiopian War. War would settle Mussolini's accounts with the conservatives and the Church just as Hitler's war Nazified the Wehrmacht and to a certain extent the German private economy. As MacGregor Knox notes, on the broader European stage, if Stalin followed a conservative foreign policy in order to consolidate his personal dictatorship in the late 1930s, Hitler and Mussolini carried out a revolution in the European balance of power as a way to accelerate their revolutionary aims at home. But it was precisely the weak hold that Mussolini had on his own state bureaucracy and army, as MacGregor Knox shows in his contribution to this volume, which prevented Mussolini turning his ideological plans into reality.

In this regard, Mack Smith's portrait of Mussolini as a ruthless but ridiculously incompetent dictator (whom an earlier foreign commentator called the 'Sawdust Caesar') is an exaggeration and De Felice's appreciation of Mussolini's totalitarian potential closer to the mark.[11]

[8] John Pollard, *The Vatican and Italian Fascism, 1929–1932* (Cambridge, 1985). Also see Richard Webster, *The Cross and the Fasces: Christian Democracy and Fascism in Italy* (Stanford, 1960).

[9] Carl Levy, 'A Comparative Overview of Fascism after the First World War', in Klaus Funken and Wolfgang Deckers (eds.), *The Revival of Right-Wing Movements in Europe* (London, 1993), p. 12. For a detailed account of the constitutional position of the dictatorship within the context of the Italian monarchy see Paolo Pombeni, *Demagogia e Tirannide. Uno studio sulla forma-partito del fascismo* (Bologna, 1984).

[10] MacGregor Knox, 'Conquest, Foreign and Domestic, in Fascist Italy and Nazi Germany', *Journal of Modern History*, vol. 56 (1984), pp. 1–57.

[11] Denis Mack Smith, *Mussolini* (London, 1981); George Seldes, *Sawdust Caesar: The Untold History of Mussolini and Fascism* (London, 1936); Renzo De Felice, *Mussolini il*

But potential is the word to be stressed, because although Muss
outlawed the opposition after 1926 and replaced a parliamentary reg
with his ramshackle corporative regime in the years that followed,
forms of repression had many continuities with Liberal Italy's. Industrial
mobilisation during the First World War, the state of siege in much of
northern Italy during 1917 and 1918, the use of internal detention for
'subversives' during the First World War and the political role of the
all-powerful prefects by the Liberal and Fascist regimes alike are continuous rather than discontinuous themes in the first half the twentieth
century.[12] Indeed, since Adrian Lyttelton's pathbreaking account of the
origins of the Fascist regime, and Emilio Gentile's more recent history
of the Partito Nazionale Fascista (PNF), it is accepted that if one of
Mussolini's main aims was to seize power, the method by which he did
it was determined by the unpredicted rapid rise of the Fascist squads
in the Po Valley in 1921.[13] For the next five years Mussolini's aim was
to use this militia to help him carve out a place in the Italian political
elite but he was also partially forced to create his new state precisely to
incorporate and normalise the maverick provincial *Ras*. The older and
authoritarian structures of the Liberal state were employed to tame the
unpredictable behaviour of his very power base, while the more traditionalist if authoritarian ideologues from the Nationalists (Alfredo
Rocco) created the legal regime of the Fascist state. Once the PNF was
changed from party militia to adjutant of the Fascist state its role
became of secondary importance. And when Mussolini grew impatient
in the late 1930s with the compromises of this state, he was too constrained by its political conservatism and bureaucratic incompetence to
carry out a 'second wave' revolution through war.

One of the most notable changes in the Italian state in the 1930s was
the rapid expansion of the bureaucracy and the qualitative change in its
structure which would affect the post-1946 Republic. In a pioneering
work on the Fascist bureaucracy, Mariuccia Salvati has shown how
the traditional administrative, legal and educational components of
Liberal civil service were joined by state and para-state industrial

---

Duce, vol. II, *Lo Stato totalitario, 1936–1940* (Turin, 1981); *Mussolini l'alleato 1940–
1945*, vol. I, *L'Italia in guerra 1940–1943* (Turin, 1990).

[12] Nicola Tranfaglia, *Dallo Stato liberale al regime fascista* (Milan, 1973); Roberto Vivarelli,
Il fallimento del liberalismo. Studi sulle origini del fascismo (Bologna, 1981); Giovanna
Procacci, *Stato e classe operaia in Italia durante la prima guerra mondiale* (Milan, 1983);
John A. Davis, *Conflict and Control: Law and Order in Nineteenth-Century Italy*
(Basingstoke, 1988).

[13] Adrian Lyttelton, *The Seizure of Power: Fascism in Italy 1919–1929* (2nd edn, London
and Princeton, 1988); Emilio Gentile, *Storia del Partito Fascista 1919–1922: Movimento
e Milizia* (Rome and Bari, 1989).

bureaucracies.[14] The two cultures of these different bureaucracies varied. Whereas the traditional civil service tended to be dominated by southerners, new northern managers were present in state/para-state empires. The judicial formalism of the former and the modernising impulses of the latter laid the foundations for the peculiarly eccentric bureaucratic culture of the postwar Republic. Whereas activist managers like a Mattei could fashion ENI (Ente Nazionale Idrocarburi, National Agency for Hydrocarbons) into a world-class petroleum company in the 1950s, the bureaucratic incompetence and excessive legal formalism of the older state structures left Republican Italy with very uncertain fiscal collection and service delivery systems.[15] Furthermore, major reforms of the Fascist or Republican civil services were always halted by the close connection between the interests of the civil service and the ruling party. Fascist support in 1921 reflected an alliance of northern urban educated middle-class and middle- and upper-class agrarian activists, and a mass base of smallholders and agricultural workers largely located in the Po Valley; however, after the seizure of power, and following the institutionalisation of the party from 1923 to 1926, the PNF was colonised by middle-class public employees.[16] Similarly the Christian Democrats in the postwar era found a major source of support in this expanding constituency.[17]

Two themes concerning the modernisation of the economy and the modernisation of civil society have dominated the discussion. The first theme is the argument that Mussolini's regime intentionally created one of Europe's first mixed economies and pioneered welfare reforms usually associated with post-1945 democratic welfare states. The other theme deals with the 'nationalisation of the masses'. This debate centres on the degree to which the Fascist regime during the 1930s manufactured a form of popular consent.

The most consistent and perhaps extreme proponent of the economic modernisation thesis is Gregor, who argued that Mussolini's regime was a prototype for the Third World developmental dictatorships of the 1950s and 1960s.[18] Gregor believed that Mussolini's economic policies

[14] Mariuccia Salvati, *Il Regime e gli impiegati. La nazionalizzazione piccolo-borghese nel ventennio fascista* (Bari, 1992).
[15] Sabino Cassese and Claudio Franchini (eds.), *L'Amministrazione pubblica italiana. Un profilo* (Bologna, 1994).
[16] Marco Revelli, 'Italy', in Detlef Mühlberger (ed.), *The Social Basis of European Fascist Movements* (London, New York and Sydney, 1987), pp. 9–19.
[17] Robert Leonardi and Douglas A. Wertman, *Italian Christian Democracy: The Politics of Dominance* (London, 1989).
[18] A. James Gregor, *Italian Fascism and Developmental Dictatorship* (Princeton, 1979). Other interesting interventions about the degree to which Fascism modernised Italy are: Roland Sarti, 'Fascist Modernization in Italy: Traditional or Revolutionary?', *American Historical Review*, vol. 75, no. 4 (1970), pp. 1029–45; Valerio Castronovo, 'Il potere

were a coherent package which sought to create a modern mixed economy to allow 'proletarian' Italy to share in the world's economy dominated by 'plutocratic' bourgeois nation-states. He argued that Mussolini's monetarist and *liberista* policies of the middle and late 1920s, and his state interventionism of the 1930s, were all cut from the same cloth. The aim was to foster a stronger economic base at home firstly through a monetarist-inspired discipline and then through the use of state interventionist autarky in the 1930s to help stimulate the growth of modern chemical, electrical and metallurgical industries. Furthermore, Mussolini's 'Battle for Wheat' and his land reclamation projects helped create a modernised agricultural base. However, not much of this picture can be accepted if we look at the work of economic historians and economists of the past fifteen years.

It is probably best to start with agriculture since Italy remained a fundamentally peasant nation until the 1950s. The works of Corner, Corni and Zamagni demonstrate rather conclusively that land reclamation may have eliminated the incidence of malaria in certain districts but funds set aside for these projects were never used in a systematic fashion.[19] Furthermore, the 'Battle for Wheat' resulted in the expansion of wheatlands in agriculturally inappropriate parts of the mainland south and Sicily. The citrus industry, which earned Italy hard currency, was damaged. The 'Battle for Wheat', Maier argues, was used to save Italy's precious foreign exchange without helping the peasant population who suffered a decline in living standards during the *ventennio*.[20] Even the stimulation of a smallholder class was unsuccessful, as Corner demonstrates.[21] In the interwar conditions, many new smallholders of the postwar era were transformed into leaseholders whose conditions were not very different from those of the landless labourers of the 'red' unions whom the Fascists smashed in 1921–2.

The weakness of Fascist agricultural modernisation is best revealed in the two contending schools of Fascist thought in the 1930s: ruralism

economico e fascismo', in Quazza (ed.), *Fascismo*, pp. 47–88; Henry A. Turner, Jr., 'Fascism and Modernization', in Henry A. Turner (ed.), *Reappraisals of Fascism* (New York, 1975), pp. 117–39; Gino Germani, *Autoritarismo, fascismo e classi sociali* (Bologna, 1975); Mason, 'Italy'; Jon S. Cohen, 'Was Italian Fascism a Developmental Dictatorship? Some Evidence to the Contrary', *Economic History Review*, 2nd series, vol. 41, no. 1 (1988), pp. 95–113.

[19] Paul Corner, 'Fascist Agrarian Policy and the Italian Economy in the Inter-War Years', in John A. Davis (ed.), *Gramsci and Italy's Passive Revolution* (London, 1979), pp. 239–74; Gustavo Corni, 'La politica agraria del fascismo: un confronto fra Italia e Germania', *Studi Storici*, vol. 28 (1987), pp. 385–421; Vera Zamagni, *The Economic History of Italy 1860–1990. Recovery after Decline* (English edition of *Dalla periferia al centro* (Bologna, 1990)) (Oxford, 1993), pp. 261–4.

[20] Charles S. Maier, 'The Economics of Fascism and Nazism', in Charles S. Maier, *In Search of Stability: Explorations in Historical Political Economy* (Cambridge, 1987), p. 92.

[21] Corner, 'Fascist Agrarian Policy', pp. 244–54.

and urbanism. Whatever the aesthetic and intellectual merits of either school, from the point of view of the economy Fascist laws against urbanisation prevented the migration of an underemployed rural population into cities. The Fascist regime encountered the same problem of excess rural population which both Liberal and Republican Italy had at least partially solved through internal and foreign migration but which, in the economic circumstances of the interwar years, led the regime to restrict the movement of the rural underemployed and unemployed.[22]

When we turn to Mussolini's financial and industrial policies, continuities between the Liberal and Fascist regimes are evident. The Q-90 policy of the late 1920s (90 Lire to the Pound Sterling) may have been partly motivated by Mussolini's nationalism, but this deflationary policy is not very different from policies carried out by the democratic and 'plutocratic' governments of France, Germany and Britain during the 1920s.[23] Indeed a similar constituency of conservative small savers was a not inconsiderable motivation in all four cases. The monetary policies of Mussolini were largely conditioned by the experiences and legacies of the Liberal era. In a recent book, Forsyth demonstrates that Italian dependence on American loans meant that whereas Mussolini's predecessors were neither prepared nor strong enough to exercise the monetarist discipline of eliminating the bread subsidy, privatising various state industries and cutting public employment on the railways and elsewhere, Mussolini had the will and the coercive means to do so.[24] The net result was that American capital flowed into Italy in the late 1920s and increased the prestige of the regime. However, with the Great Crash, this source of funds dried up and exposed the rickety private financial and industrial system and the Bank of Italy to a very serious crisis. The result was the transformation of Mussolini *liberista* to Mussolini state interventionist. Through the creation of state and para-state holding companies the Italian economy was rescued from collapse but this was not a thought-out master plan, rather improvisation on a grand scale which developed into long-term policy when the IRI (Istituto per la Ricostruzione Industriale, Institute for Industrial Reconstruction) and the IMI (Istituto Mobiliare Italiano, Italian Credit Institute) were given permanent legal status.[25] And just as monetary policy was linked to the

---

[22] Corner, 'Fascist Agrarian Policy', p. 265.
[23] Cohen, 'Was Italian', p. 101. Also see Jon S. Cohen, 'La rivalutazione della lira del 1927. Uno studio sulla politica economica fascista', in Gianni Tonioli (ed.), *Lo sviluppo economico italiano 1861–1940* (Bari, 1973).
[24] Douglas J. Forsyth, *The Crisis of Liberal Italy. Monetary and Financial Policy 1914–1922* (Cambridge, 1993). Also see Paolo Frasciani, *Politica economica e finanza pubblica in Italia nel primo dopoguerra (1918–1922)* (Naples, 1975).
[25] Cohen, 'Was Italian', pp. 106–9. Also see Gianni Toniolo, *L'economia dell'Italia fascista* (Bari, 1980), p. 247.

problems of pre-1922 Liberal Italy so too was the *modus operandi* of this crisis plan.

From before 1914 the Italian state was determined to protect strategic industries by either direct intervention or using a close relationship with mixed banks sitting on the boards of these key industries. The war and postwar era saw the spectacular growth and bust of several trusts – the steel-shipbuilding-financial empire of Ansaldo and the iron and steel combine, ILVA. The mixed banking system of the early twentieth century was further compromised by the Great Crash of 1929 because its long-term liquidity was locked into illiquid industrial assets while its paper assets lost value as security markets nose-dived. Therefore, just as in the immediate postwar era, so too in the early 1930s, industrialists looked to the state to bail them out of difficulties.[26] By the middle of the 1930s Italy had the highest percentage of state-owned enterprise outside of the Soviet Union.[27] But the managers and former owners of these nationalised assets were allowed to run them as if nothing had changed. Beneduce and the other managers of IRI and IMI were encouraged by Mussolini to develop modern iron and steel plants, and other state-owned firms began prospecting for gas and oil reserves which would become such a valuable ingredient of the postwar economic miracle. Mussolini sought the mobilisation of resources for world war. However, the actual outcomes only resulted in the Italian economy achieving little more than mediocre growth. With few natural resources and a surplus population, costly experiments in autarky were no help in a world of trading preference blocs and universal protectionism.[28] Nor did the mighty German industrial ally after 1938 fill in the gap. Indeed Zamagni has argued that Italy did far worse in its industrial mobilisation in the Second compared to the First World War because Germany could never replace the resources and capital of the USA and the British Empire.[29] State-owned industry therefore did not improve or modernise the Italian economy because, as a trading nation locked into a protectionist alliance and with depressed domestic demand caused by the poverty of its rural population, the resulting margins for real growth were tight indeed.

It has also been argued that the Fascist conception of *competenza* spurred Mussolini's regime to engage in the spread of Taylorisation of industrial techniques in the northern industrial triangle. As Mark

[26] Forsyth, *The Crisis*, pp. 21–60, 247–60; Richard Webster, *Industrial Imperialism in Italy, 1908–1915* (Berkeley, 1975).
[27] Rosario Romeo, *Breve storia della grande industria in Italia* (Rocca San Casciano, 1963), p. 171.
[28] Maier, 'The Economics', pp. 88–104; Cohen, 'Was Italian', pp. 105–12.
[29] Zamagni, *The Economic History*, p. 271.

Roseman and MacGregor Knox show in their respective chapters in this volume, the mobilisation of the German economy after 1942 may have laid the basis for the Americanisation of German industry after the war, but it would be difficult to argue a similar case for Italy. While Bigazzi has shown how there were some advances in production in the early 1940s,[30] the broader picture over the entire *ventennio* is rather different. Taylorisation remained largely restricted to discussion in magazines. Perry Willson demonstrates in her recent monograph there were very few plants in Italy which could use the full panoply of Taylorist or Fordist methods until the 1950s.[31]

The net effect of the policy of state intervention of the 1930s deepened the promiscuous relationship between certain large, usually family-controlled industrial empires, state owned industries and capital and politicians. To this extent the origins of the state capitalists (*razza padrone*) of Christian Democratic Italy[32] are indeed found in the Fascist regime but the promiscuous use of state and private interests carries on a tradition already firmly established in the Liberal era. The assets of the IRI and IMI and other para-state enterprises were there to be used by another political ruling class in the 1950s but they were used not to wage war, rather to integrate the Italian economy into the EEC and the free-trade internationalist capitalist system championed by the Marshall Plan. Economic assets developed during the Fascist period were used in the profoundly different international, political, and macro-economic context of the Republic to help fuel the Italian economic miracle of the late 1950s and early 1960s.[33]

The degree to which one might consider Fascist Italy to have been a modern welfare state can be quickly dismissed. Ferrera and others have demonstrated that the peculiar mixed welfare state of the post-1945 era

---

[30] D. Bigazzi, 'Organizzazione del lavoro e razionalizzazione nella crisi del fascismo', *Studi Storici*, vol. 2 (1978).

[31] Perry R. Willson, *The Clockwork Factory: Women and Work in Fascist Italy* (Oxford, 1993), pp. 35–62.

[32] Eugenio Scalfari and Giuseppe Turani, *Razza padrona: storia della borghesia di stato* (Milan, 1974); Alessandra Nannei, *La nuovissima classe* (Milan, 1978); A. Mutti, 'Elementi per un'analisi della borghesia di stato', *Quaderni di Sociologia*, vol. 33 (1979), pp. 84–95. On the role of managers in the state sector from the 1930s to the 1950s, see Marco Maraffi, *Politica ed economia in Italia. Le vicende dell'impresa pubblica dagli anni trenta agli anni cinquanta* (Bologna, 1990). And for the long-term characteristics of Italian finance see Paul Furlong, 'State, Finance and Industry in Italy', in Andrew W. Cox (ed.), *The State, Finance and Industry* (Brighton, 1986), pp. 142–71.

[33] Zamagni, *The Economic History*, pp. 279, 291, 321, 347; F. Bonelli (ed.), *Acciaio per l'industrializzazione* (Turin, 1982); Mariuccia Salvati, *Stato e industria nella ricostruzione: alle origini del potere democristiano 1944/1949* (Milan, 1982); David Ellwood, 'Il piano Marshall e il processo di modernizzazione in Italia', in Elena Aga-Rossi (ed.), *Il piano Marshall e l'Europa* (Rome, 1983), pp. 149–62; Paul Furlong, *Modern Italy. Representation and Reform* (London, 1994), pp. 47–8.

can be located in developments during the Fascist era, but it is precisely the archaic and ramshackle nature of this structure which exercised the minds of social scientists and policymakers from the 1960s onwards.[34] A rudimentary form of state insurance had been created by the Liberal Prime Minister Giolitti in the immediate postwar era. However, many of its functions were given back to the private insurance firms during Mussolini's initial *liberista* phase. Fascist violence and law destroyed a good deal of the mutual-aid institutions of the Socialist and Catholic subcultures. Some of these functions were adopted by the Fascist unions of the 1920s but in the 1930s a system of social insurance and health funds was created by the Fascist state. These elephantine institutions did not create a universal welfare state but separate plans for different occupational categories. Universal health care only arrived in Italy in 1978.

There were several weaknesses in this vast empire of systems. First of all it was administered by Fascist party officials and therefore was discriminatory. Secondly, these systems were ineffective outside urban areas: peasant Italy was still little affected except to the point that peripatetic doctors started to control disease in the countryside more effectively.[35] And even they (the *medici condotti*) were a product of the Giolittian age. Perhaps one of the greatest legacies of the Fascist welfare state was the use of occupational pension funds by the state for other projects. So, just as Mussolini raided these funds to help finance his campaigns in Ethiopia and elsewhere, the Christian Democratic state in the 1960s would use the excess liquidity of the manual workers' funds to top up the undercapitalised funds set aside for artisans and small shopkeepers.[36] Another legacy was the party political rather than formal bureaucratic control of this welfare system. If Fascist party officials helped administer these funds in the 1930s, in the postwar era Christian Democrat, and later even Socialist or Communist political gatekeepers exercised a wide degree of discretion in determining who received that disguised form of long-term unemployment insurance known as the invalidity pension. This continuity is truly a profound and long-lasting one. Much Christian Democratic power in the Mezzogiorno during the postwar era was founded on the use of these funds backed up by Treasury guarantees to advance block grants to cover deficits. The passage from a clientelism

---

[34] Maurizio Ferrera, *Il Welfare State in Italia. Sviluppo e crisi in prospettiva comparativa* (Bologna, 1984), pp. 28–37; Mariuccia Salvati, 'Da piccola borghesia a ceti medi. Fascismo e ceti medi nelle interpretazioni dei contemporanei e degli storici', *Italia Contemporanea*, vol. 194 (1994), pp. 78–81.

[35] Domenico Preti, *La modernizzazione corporativa. Economia, salute pubblica, istituzioni e professioni sanitarie* (Milan, 1987); Zamagni, *The Economic History*, pp. 315–17.

[36] Carl Levy, 'Italian Trade Unionism in the 1990s: The Persistence of Corporatism?', *Journal of Area Studies*, vol. 5 (1994), pp. 74–6.

of large landowners to Christian Democratic notables was eased through the use of public monies such as social insurance funds, which the party hierarchy controlled. But the fiscal crisis of the Italian state in 1994 can be traced through fifty years of clientelistic Keynesian spending which characterised the post-1945 Italian welfare state. Although the Fascist welfare system was far less universal and even more openly party political, the *modus operandi* was not so very different.[37]

The partial welfare state certainly engineered a degree of compliance and consensus in the urban population of Italy in the 1930s. How far this consensus extended has stimulated major historiographical controversy. It seems to be generally agreed that the apogee of consensus was in the period 1935–6 during the Ethiopian War and in reaction to the League of Nations' sanctions against Italy.[38] However, since the 1920s Mussolini had attempted to build a broad coalition of Nationalist, Conservative and Liberal opinion around his regime.[39] He was fairly successful to the extent that he clipped the claws of the PNF and subsumed it under an authoritarian but still vaguely familiar form of state. He also wooed Catholic opinion by signing the Lateran Accords and agreeing to allow Catholic Action a relatively free hand. Although newspapers were Fascistised and anti-Fascist newspapers banned after 1926, Mussolini, as Forgacs has recently shown, did not really interfere with the culture industry. Indeed, there seem to be some continuities with the Republican period in as much as the state did protect the Italian film industry and the so-called Resistance genre of neo-realism was already apparent in the early 1940s.[40] Universities were largely untouched until the racial laws of 1938. Although professors had to swear allegiance to the regime, it did little to reorganise the universities along Fascist lines. And the net effect of the Gentile educational reforms of 1923 was to re-emphasise the traditional humanistic vocation of higher education, restrict the growth of student populations (at least temporarily) and ghettoise modern technical and vocational education.[41]

---

[37] Ferrera, *Welfare*; Emilio Reyneri, 'The Italian Labour Market: Between State Control and Social Regulation', in Peter Lange and Mario Regini (eds.), *State, Market, and Social Regulation. New Perspectives on Italy* (Cambridge, 1989), pp. 130–45; Felice Roberto Pizzuti and Guido M. Rey (eds.), *Il sistema pensionistico. Un riesame* (Bologna, 1990); Gloria Regonini, 'Le pensioni in balia degli equilibri politici', in Ginsborg (ed.), *Stato*, pp. 451–3.

[38] Renzo De Felice, *Mussolini il Duce*, vol. I, *Gli anni del consenso 1929–1936* (Turin, 1974).

[39] Thompson, *State*, pp. 1–62.

[40] David Forgacs, *Italian Culture in the Industrial Era 1880–1980. Cultural Industries, Politics and the Public* (Manchester, 1990), pp. 57, 67–82.

[41] See the telling remarks by Edward R. Tannenbaum, *The Fascist Experience: Italian Society and Culture 1922–1945* (New York, 1972), pp. 169–72, and, in general, see Marzio Barbagli, *Educating for Unemployment: Politics, Labor Markets, and the School*

All of the examples shown so far stress Mussolini's attempts at soothing well-entrenched elements of the urban middle classes. But to what extent did the Fascist state use its organs of power to nationalise the masses? And did Fascism succeed in creating younger generations of Fascists?

Much recent work has been done on the institutions of mass leisure, education and indoctrination. What is probably not in dispute is that the syndical and corporative institutions of the state were largely ineffectual. Although Mussolini used Fascist-organised strikes in 1925 to cow the industrialists, Sarti and others have shown that through much of the history of the regime the syndical and corporative institutions were a sham.[42] The question of the degree of working-class consensus is dealt with by Tobias Abse in this volume. However, I would like to approach the effectiveness of the nationalisation of the masses by measuring to what extent the urban working and middle classes were converted to Fascism by the state-controlled forms of mass society. There are several problems with assessing these effects from testimony and recollections, as oral historians such as Passerini have shown.[43] It is hard to gauge how far compliance is due to generally apolitical apathy, opportunism or fear. But the striking difference with Germany must surely be the fact that the peasants of the south, and even of the mountainous parts of the north, seemed little affected by the wider ideological message. They confronted this regime as all others: with caution and suspicion. In the urban centres the net result of Fascist indoctrination was not very impressive, if we consider De Felice's conclusion that the regime was beginning to be undermined in the late 1930s by the widespread perception that the first generation of Fascist leaders were either corrupt or bureaucratic ciphers. Fascism was being challenged not because the anti-Fascist opposition had a significant foothold within Italy, but

System: Italy 1859–1973 (trans. R. Ross) (New York, 1982), pp. 142–210. Elsewhere I have criticised Barbagli's methodology which exaggerates the degree of intellectual unemployment in Italy and its effects on politics; see Carl Levy and Chris Rootes, 'Disoccupazione intellettuale e mobilitazione politica', *Biblioteca della Libertà*, vol. 97 (1987), pp. 139–69.

[42] Roland Sarti, *Fascism and the Industrial Leadership in Italy (1922–1943). A Study in the Expansion of Private Power under Fascism* (Berkeley, 1971); Piero Melograni, *Gli industriali e Mussolini* (Milan, 1972). But even if these institutions were a sham, Mussolini used the corporative experiment to good effect on international public opinion. See Marco Palla, *Fascismo e stato corporativo. Un'inchiesta della diplomazia britannica* (Milan, 1991). A recent excellent survey of the relationship of the working class to the Fascist regime can be found in Paul Corner, 'Italy', in Stephen Salter and John Stevenson (eds.), *The Working Class and Politics in Europe and America 1929–1945* (London and New York, 1990), pp. 154–71.

[43] Luisa Passerini, *Fascism in Popular Memory: The Cultural Experience of the Turin Working Class* (Cambridge, 1987).

through the failure of the regime to create a new ruling class from the next generation.[44]

If we examine in turn the chief mass organisations of leisure and indoctrination, their effects on creating a new Fascist culture are limited. The most important, the Dopolavoro, studied in detail by De Grazia, was firstly male-dominated, secondly conditioned by the particular employer and factory culture present and, thirdly, successful to the extent that it offered value-free cheap forms of entertainment and recreation.[45] The youth and university organisations failed because rather than indoctrinating a new generation of Fascists they exposed the weaknesses and hypocrisies of the older generation.[46] As Willson shows in her chapter in this book, the 'nationalisation of Italian women' had mixed results too. For most peasant and working-class women the double burden of paid work and housework precluded direct participation in the mass organisations of socialisation. Fascist encouragement of larger families through pro-natal programmes was as ineffective at increasing population growth as similar if less authoritarian attempts in pre-1940 France or social-democratic Sweden.[47]

To sum up: if in both Italy and Germany apathy and antipathy towards the Fascist and Nazi parties grew through the years, the crucial difference between the two cases was that whereas there existed a cult of Mussolini, it was only in Germany that the cult of the leader became a direct and powerful link between the regime and the younger generation. However, it might be argued that a weaker version of the De Felice consensus thesis could be advanced. Open opposition to the regime only occurred when the Fascist state failed comprehensively in battle and exposed Italy itself to Allied carpet-bombing. The form of consensus that the regime engendered might be more usefully compared with the Franco regime in the postwar period or the *modus operandi* of certain eastern European states from the 1950s to the 1980s, not the

---

[44] Renzo De Felice, *Intervista sul fascismo* (ed. Michael A. Ledeen) (Bari, 1975), p. 25: 'il fallimento del fascismo fu nella incapacità di dar vita ad una nuova classe dirigente'. Also see Bruno Wanrooij, 'The Rise and Fall of Italian Fascism as a Generational Revolt', *Journal of Contemporary History*, vol. 22, no. 3 (1987), pp. 401–18.

[45] Victoria De Grazia, *The Culture of Consent: Mass Organization of Leisure in Fascist Italy* (Cambridge, 1981).

[46] Tracy H. Koon, *Believe, Obey, Fight. Political Socialization of Youth in Fascist Italy, 1922–1943* (Chapel Hill and London, 1985).

[47] Also see Victoria De Grazia, *How Fascism Ruled Women: Italy, 1922–1945* (Berkeley, Los Angeles and Oxford, 1992), pp. 42–52; Chiara Saraceno, 'Redefining Maternity and Paternity: Gender, Protonatalism and Social Policies in Fascist Italy', in Gisela Bock and Pat Thane (eds.), *Maternity and Gender Policies. Women and the Rise of the European Welfare States, 1880s–1950s* (London, 1991) pp. 196–212.

mobilisation of the German population engineered by the Nazi state.[48]

Even if we can place rather tight limits on the effects of Fascist consensus building during the *ventennio*, there are still certain important continuities in political socialisation and consensus formation evident in the Fascist regime and the postwar Republic. I would like to cite two of them.

The first has received little research, but with the recent transformation of Communist states into multi-party systems it might have great interest. Although there has been much work on the origins and development of the intellectual and cadre elites of the DC (Democrazia Cristiana) and the PCI (Partito Comunista Italiano), we still have few social and longitudinal histories of the mass membership of these two parties.[49] Both parties grew rapidly into mass parties with memberships of millions. Both parties depended on the pre-Fascist red and white subcultures for their core memberships. The DC obviously used the networks of the Church and Catholic Action, while both the Christian Democrats and Communists were also beneficiaries of the mobilisation of partisans in the north. However, it should be borne in mind that the Resistance was very much a minority pursuit: it was only at the very end that it became a mass movement. It could also be argued that working-class discontent ushering in the mass strikes of 1943 reveals a vast underground of organised potential for the Left. However, Mason argued that the first strikes were largely spontaneous.[50] If there were political opportunities for organisation, it was within the Fascist trade

---

[48] James Kurth, 'A Tale of Four Countries: Parallel Politics in Southern Europe, 1815–1990' and 'A Tale of Two Peripheries: Southern Europe and Eastern Europe', in James Kurth and James Petras, with Diarmuid Maguire and Ronald Chilcote, *Mediterranean Paradoxes. The Politics and Social Structure of Southern Europe* (Oxford, 1993) pp. 27–66, 225–42; Paul Ginsborg, 'L'Italia, l'Europa, il Mediterraneo', in Ginsborg (ed.), *Stato*, pp. 643–8. Renzo De Felice sums up the nature, limits and legacy of Fascist consensus in *Mussolini l'alleato*, vol. I, p. 81. Also see Enzo Collotti, 'Fascismo', in Ginsborg (ed.), *Stato*, pp. 99–102.

[49] For standard accounts of the origins of the cadres and intellectuals of the DC and the PCI see Gianni Baget-Bozzo, *Il partito cristiano al potere. La DC di De Gasperi e di Dossetti, 1945–54* (2 vols., Florence, 1974); Giorgio Galli, *Storia della Democrazia Cristiana* (Bari, 1978); Renato Moro, *La formazione della classe dirigente cattolica (1929–37)* (Bologna, 1979); Paolo Spriano, *Storia del Partito Comunista Italiana* (5 vols., Turin, 1967–75); Donald Sassoon, *Togliatti e la via italiana al socialismo* (Turin, 1980); Grant Aymot, *The Italian Communist Party* (London, 1981). A new interest in the origins of the mass party can be found in the following recent works: Paolo Pombeni, *Introduzione alla storia dei partiti politici* (Bologna, 1985); Gaetano Quagliariello (ed.), *Il partito politico nella Belle Epoque. Il dibattito sulla forma-partito in Italia tra '800 e '900* (Milan, 1990); Maurizio Ridolfi, *Il PSI e la nascita del partito di massa 1892–1922* (Bari, 1992).

[50] Tim Mason, 'Gli scioperi di Torino del marzo 1943', in Francesca Ferratini Tosi *et al.* (eds.), *L'Italia nella seconda guerra mondiale e nella Resistenza* (Milan, 1988), pp. 385–408.

unions and the Fascist version of the factory works committee. Indeed, Contini has shown how the *fiduciari* in the 1930s more than occasionally won concessions on piece work and other grievances.[51] It must be admitted that many individuals within the mass membership of the two great parties were socialised within the Fascist party and its collateral organisations. Membership may have been entered into for purely pragmatic reasons, but this does not mean that a habit of working within a mass party organisation would not then be transferred into the party system of Republican Italy. The experience of membership in the PNF was in some ways unique, because before 1922, except for a few frenetic years during the *biennio rosso* (1919–20), party and trade union membership in Liberal Italy had always been quite low. The big research question must surely be: how was the habit of taking part in politics through the Fascist party and its collateral organisations transformed when Italy recovered its democratic political life?[52]

The second approach is beginning to be researched. This returns us to the question of the degree of consensus found towards the regime. There has been a considerable amount of discussion, if not that much empirical work, on the related questions of who supported the Fascists, who voted for them in the early 1920s, and how party membership changed over time. It is generally agreed that voter support and membership comprised a significantly heterogeneous population from elements in the working class, the *ceti medi* and business, professional and aristocratic elites. It is probably not only the status-threatened old middle class nor the status-hungry new middle classes who provide the answer.[53] It is certainly true that the *squadristi* were disproportionately composed of young men who had experienced the Great War or were just too young to have participated.[54] Young men with military experience provided the muscle but they certainly did not supply all the votes or all the cadres and members when Fascism transformed itself from

[51] Giovanni Contini, 'Politics, Law and Shop Floor Bargaining in Postwar Italy', in Steven Tolliday and Jonathan Zeitlin (eds.), *Shop-Floor Bargaining and the State. Historical and Comparative Perspectives* (Cambridge, 1985), p. 196.
[52] Paolo Farneti, *Sistema politico e società civile. Saggi di teoria e ricerca politica* (Turin, 1971). For a first polemical attempt to trace the authoritarian origins of the Italian Republic's *partitocrazia*, see Luciano Cafagna, *C'era una volta . . . Riflessioni sul comunismo italiano* (Venice, 1991), and Ernesto Galli della Loggia, *La democrazia immaginaria. L'azionismo e l' 'ideologia italiana'* (Bologna, 1993).
[53] For a discussion of this, see Revelli, 'Italy'; Gino Germani, 'Fascism and Class', in Stuart Woolf (ed.), *The Nature of Fascism* (London, 1968), pp. 65–96; Renzo De Felice, 'Italian Fascism and the Middle Classes', in Stein Ugelvik Larsen et al. (eds.), *Who Were the Fascists: Social Roots of European Fascism* (Oslo, 1980), pp. 312–17; David D. Roberts, 'Petty Bourgeois Fascism in Italy: Form and Content', in Larsen, *Who?*, pp. 337–47.
[54] Gentile, *Storia*, pp. 48, 60–162.

movement to party. In any case, what is of interest to us in the context of this discussion is how the PNF and the regime shaped the social landscape to create their own constituencies.

Mussolini used the Fascist movement and the party as a vehicle for his own private agenda, and when he created the regime the PNF was used by him and the elite to create a power base. The most recent and exciting work on the relationship between Fascism and social classes is investigating how political action, indeed a form of social engineering, created the Fascist regime's own power base and form of consensus. Both Salvati and Berezin have recently investigated how the policies of the regime in the 1930s called forth a new type of *ceti medi*.[55] Through the expansion of the older state bureaucracy, the creation of para-state and state industries and the leisure and cultural arms of the regime, vast new areas of employment for the urban *ceti medi* came into being. Furthermore, the regime was solicitous to the needs of the artisan and small trader populations. Laws regulating and protecting smaller retail businesses, and the destruction of Socialist and Catholic co-operatives, helped the commercial *petite bourgeoisie*. These policies are not very different from the DC's form of social engineering in Republican Italy. Starting from the first premises of Catholic political doctrine, in the postwar period DC politicians and policy-makers sought to create a large class of property owners. Through land reform, soft loans and licensing laws the DC stimulated the growth of the commercial, entrepreneurial and artisanal *ceti medi*.[56]

Furthermore, in Republican Italy the DC, as the Fascist regime previously, found the large state industrial sector and the traditional civil service as key sources of support. Neither Fascist nor Republican Italy ever enacted a consistent system of reform of the selection procedures and training of state bureaucrats. Italy never created a civil-service college; neither did its system of recruitment become rationalised.[57] Selection continued to be made through outmoded *concorsi* and the *raccomendazione*. If the PNF card was essential for employment during the *ventennio*, the DC and other party cards were almost as essential in Republican Italy. Finally, the independent role of university professors

---

[55] Salvati, *Il Regime*; Salvati, 'Da piccola borghesia'; Mabel Berezin, 'Created Constituencies: The Italian Middle Classes and Fascism', in Rudy Koshar (ed.), *Splintered Classes: Politics and the Lower Middle Classes in Interwar Europe* (New York, 1990) pp. 142–63.

[56] Alessandro Pizzorno, 'I ceti medi nel meccanismo del consenso', in Alessandro Pizzorno, *I soggetti del pluralismo* (Bologna, 1980), pp. 67–98; Linda Weiss, *Creating Capitalism. The State and Small Business since 1945* (Oxford, 1988); Massimo Paci, *Il mutamento della struttura sociale in Italia* (Bologna, 1992).

[57] David Hine, *Governing Italy. The Politics of Bargained Pluralism* (Oxford, 1993), pp. 225–56.

as gatekeepers to the cultural and bureaucratic worlds of employment was fundamentally unchanged. If there was a challenge to their hegemony it does not come in 1943 or 1945 but temporarily in the late 1960s and later, through the cumulative effects of a post-industrial globalised economy, only in the last few years.[58] In short, the DC and its allies inherited and embellished the regime's mechanism of consensus.

NEO-FASCISM, REPUBLICAN ITALY AND MODERNISATION

In his famous book written in the 1960s, Ralf Dahrendorf argued that the failed coup against Hitler in 1944 and the comprehensive destruction of the Third Reich meant that not only had the Nazi regime been utterly discredited but, equally, the pre-1933 anti-democratic aristocratic and military elites had been destroyed.[59] The unintended consequences of Hitler's extremism, and the failure of his conservative opposition, meant that threats from the Right to the Federal Republic's democracy in the postwar era were neutralised. Mark Roseman has argued in his chapter that Dahrendorf's thesis is exaggerated; that many of the political and economic effects of the Third Reich affected the formation of the Federal Republic. Furthermore, other political scientists and historians have noted that Adenauer and the Christian Democrats had everything to play for in the late 1940s and early 1950s. The party system and the famous stability of the Federal Republic's democracy were not established until the 1950s or even perhaps only with the accession of the Social Democrats into national government in the 1960s. It is not without reason that this is sometimes described as the 'second founding of the Republic', because it was only then that alternation in national government happened.[60] Whatever the strengths and weaknesses of the Dahrendorf thesis, it a useful device for measuring the evolution of another post-fascist society after 1945.

As I have already noted, the first noticeable difference between Hitler's Germany and Mussolini's Italy was that in the latter key institutions of the pre-Fascist past retained real or latent powers during the *ventennio* (army, monarchy, Senate and Church). Mussolini's regime was always constrained and influenced far more profoundly by the pre-Fascist elites

---

[58] Carl Levy, 'The Politics of the Higher Educated in Italy since 1945' (forthcoming). Also see Burton R. Clark, *Academic Power in Italy: Bureaucracy and Oligarchy in a National University System* (Chicago, 1977); Roberto Moscati, *Università: fine o trasformazione del mito?* (Bologna, 1983). On the relationship between various professions and Fascism, see Nanda Torcellan (ed.), *Cultura e società negli anni del fascismo* (Milan, 1982).

[59] Ralf Dahrendorf, *Society and Democracy in Germany* (London, 1968).

[60] For a good example of this approach, see Gordon Smith, *Democracy in Western Germany* (London, 1986).

than Hitler's. Furthermore, the collapse of Mussolini's regime and post-Fascist reconstruction occurred in a profoundly different manner from in Nazi Germany.

It is therefore worthwhile examining three events that are the founding myths of the Italian Republic: the Resistance, 1943–5; the referendum for the abolition of the monarchy in 1946; and the Constitution of 1948.

In the past ten years the historiography of the Resistance has been under sustained attack. It has long been acknowledged that the disasters which followed the coup in Rome in 1943 resulted in the political culture of the Resistance being limited to the north. As Federico Chabod noted in a lecture at the Sorbonne in 1950, the vagaries of war created three Italies: the Monarchist south occupied by the Allies from 1943 onwards, the area between the Gustav and Gothic lines which suffered the intense battles fought between the winters of 1943 and 1944, and the area north of the Gothic line where the Resistance mounted its insurrections in the spring of 1945.[61] Anti-Fascism and Republicanism were therefore northern rather than southern experiences. This means that an ideological and psychological break with the past was far more prevalent in the north than in the south, but this should not be over-stressed. The most recent histories of the Resistance have undermined the older more romanticised accounts. Claudio Pavone has insisted on describing the Resistance as a civil war.[62] His work generated controversy because it seemed to relativise the violence of the Salò Republic with that of the Resistance.[63] But what is important to recognise is that a substantial proportion of the population in the north either openly or passively accepted the Nazi-supported regime of Mussolini. Furthermore, the Resistance itself was by no means united: the tensions between left-wing partisans and Christian Democratic units were real and persistent.

Another interpretation of the Resistance is perhaps even more challenging than Pavone's. The works of Absalom and Lamb demonstrate that much of the peasantry of the north were either fearful of, or ambivalent to, all sides in the Resistance.[64] Not all armed bands in the

[61] Cited in Pietro Scoppola, *La repubblica dei partiti. Profilo storico della democrazia in Italia (1945–1990)* (Bologna, 1992), p. 81.
[62] Claudio Pavone, *Una guerra civile* (Turin, 1991). Also see Massino Legnani and Ferruccio Vendramini (eds.), *Guerra, guerra di liberazione, guerra civile* (Milan, 1990).
[63] Gabriele Ranzato, 'Alcune considerazioni su Resistenza e guerra civile', *Italia Contemporanea*, vol. 193 (1994), pp. 315–31; Stefano Battilossi, 'Oltre la normalizzazione. Per una storiografia critica (e un nuovo senso comune democratico)', *Italia Contemporanea*, vol. 195 (1994), pp. 419–35.
[64] Roger Absalom, 'A Resistance to the Resistance: The Italian Peasant in History', in Judith Bryce and Doug Thompson (eds.), *Moving in Measure: Essays in Honour of Brian*

Resistance were under the strictest of political discipline and some
resorted to plain banditry. With the disintegration of the pre-1943
regime, vast areas of the countryside were traversed by deserters from
the Italian army and Allied prisoners of war. Thus if the Resistance has
been presented as a form of radical social and democratic catharsis for
the populations of the north, in fact a significant portion of the population in the countryside and in the urban centres was either ambivalent
towards, cautious about or hostile to its message.

The referendum on the monarchy demonstrated a neat division
between Republican north and Monarchist south. Finally, the Constitution of 1948 reflected the extent to which the legacies of 1943–8 were
contested. By then the Cold War had firmly divided the country into
red and white subcultures, with the lay and Republican resisters of the
Partito d'Azione split down the middle and marginalised by the two
major 'red' and 'white' blocs in Italian politics. The Constitution, Pietro
Scoppola has argued, reflected the fact that attempts by the intellectuals
of this radical third way had been defeated.[65] The attempt to create a
decentralised industrial and civic democracy fostering the development
of non-party political associational life was buried. The Constitution of
1948, with its low-threshold-based proportional representation and
strong parliament, strengthened the role of the mass parties and their
collateral organisations. And although under the emergency conditions
of the Cold War De Gasperi was as strong an executive as Chancellor
Adenauer of the Federal Republic of Germany, by the 1950s the *partitocrazia* was firmly in place.

So far in this chapter I have measured the extent to which the Fascist
ventennio left its mark on the politics and political economy of Republican Italy. We have just discussed the extent to which the collapse of
the Fascist regime and the transition to the Republic in Italy left a set
of different legacies from those found in Germany after 1945. In any
case, as I have mentioned, the establishment of post-fascist regimes in
Italy and the Federal Republic of Germany was neither entirely dependent upon the legacies of the previous fascist eras nor on the type of
transition from dictatorship to democracy that Italy and West Germany
experienced. However, it remains the case that Italy offered much more
political and social space for neo-Fascism to flourish. I will examine the
role of the extreme Right in the apparatuses of the Republic and the
party system to illustrate this point.

The extreme and neo-Fascist Right played an important and, at times,
sinister role within the institutions of the Republican state which far

Moloney (Hull, 1989), pp. 169–79; Roger Absalom, *A Strange Alliance* (Florence,
1991); Richard Lamb, *War in Italy 1943–1945* (London, 1992).
[65] Scoppola, *La repubblica*, pp. 177, 198–9.

outweighed its performance at the ballot box. Pavone has demonstrated the continuity of the judiciary, police, army and prefects from the Mussolini regime to the Republic.[66] The purge of Fascists from the state apparatus was a half-hearted affair and Communist party leader Togliatti's support for a general amnesty after the Republican outcome of the 1946 Referendum closed the season of governmental cleansing.[67] The Cold War meant that both the American and Italian governments protected and recruited senior police and espionage personnel from the former Salò Republic. Indeed, the only substantial purges of the armed forces were of Resistance recruits integrated at the end of the war. The net effect of all that was that even in the late 1960s the higher civil service of the Italian Republic was still far to the right of the entire population.[68] Fascist law remained the basis of much Republican jurisprudence. Until the Constitutional Court began functioning in 1959, and even afterwards, large parts of the Rocco Code were still enforced. Labour law, for instance, remained a legal 'no-man's-land', and the Fascist law against 'urbanism' meant that migrants from the south lived a semi-legal existence in many northern towns and cities until 1960.[69] Laws concerning abortion, divorce and others circumscribing the right of women to live autonomous lives were only amended under the pressure of the women's movement in the late 1960s and 1970s.[70]

The most difficult area in which to gauge the extent of the neo-Fascist presence in the Republic is what is sometimes called the 'second state' or the 'invisible government'. Social scientists and historians have approached this theme with some caution. But we now have enough empirical evidence to demonstrate the persistence of shadowy organisations linking the Carabinieri, the military, the Masonic Lodge P2, and the American-sponsored stay-at-home Gladio paramilitaries who were supposed to fight a guerrilla war against a Soviet occupation force.[71]

---

[66] Claudio Pavone, 'La continuità dello Stato. Istituzioni e uomini', in Claudio Pavone, *Italia 1945–48. Le origini della Repubblica* (Turin, 1974), pp. 137–289.

[67] The most detailed and recent account of the purges can be found in Roy Palmer Domenico, *Italian Fascists on Trial 1943–1948* (Chapel Hill, 1991).

[68] Robert Putnam, 'The Political Attitudes of Senior Civil Servants in Britain, Germany and Italy', in M. Dogan (ed.), *The Mandarins of Western Europe* (New York, 1975), pp. 86–126.

[69] For labour law see Contini, 'Politics', pp. 199–204. A more general account is found in Gian Carlo Jocteau, *La magistratura e i conflitti di lavoro durante il fascismo* (Milan, 1978).

[70] This has been studied in depth by Judith Adler Hellman, *Journeys Among Women* (Oxford, 1987); Lesley Caldwell, *Italian Family Matters. Women, Politics and Legal Reform* (Basingstoke, 1991).

[71] In Italian see Giovanni De Lutiis, *Storia dei servizi segreti in Italia* (Rome, 1991); Gianni Flamini, *Il partito del golpe* (4 vols., Bologna, 1980–4); Giorgio Galli, *L'Italia sotterranea* (Bari, 1983). In English see (but with great caution) Philip Willan, *Puppetmasters: The Political Use of Terrorism in Italy* (London, 1991). A more measured and prudent

Not only is the influence of the neo-Fascists documented in all these organisations, they also created their own paramilitary and terrorist organisations by the late 1940s, succeeded by the more persistent Ordine Nuovo and Avanguardia Nazionale in the 1950s and 1960s and second-generation offshoots in the 1970s and 1980s. Many of the leading lights behind neo-Fascist terrorism had documented links with the MSI and connections with the Salò Republic.

From the late 1950s onwards plots against the Republic were brewing, although Carabiniere General De Lorenzo's Piano Solo in 1964, intended to prevent the functioning of a Centre–Left government under Aldo Moro was the most serious. De Lorenzo never carried out his coup.[72] However, the message did not go unheeded: reforms ground to a halt and this in no small measure created the social explosions of the student revolt of 1968 and the 'Hot Autumn' of labour in 1969. Between 1969 and 1974 a strategy of tension carried out by this 'second state' appeared in earnest. A bloody bombing in Milan in 1969 was attributed to anarchists but proven to have been planted by neo-Fascists with direct links to the secret service. In 1970 the neo-Fascist and Salò veteran, Prince Valerio Borghese, attempted a coup in Rome and in 1974 various plots by military officers – the most famous the Rosa dei Venti conspiracy – seemed aimed to carry out a neo-Gaullist putsch. In the same years bombs exploded in Brescia and on a passenger train near Bologna. The aim of all these efforts was to rally the various larger organisations of the 'silent majority' mobilised in opposition to the student and worker unrest to demand an authoritarian government. In fact these provocations were largely unsuccessful: the PCI achieved its best results ever on local, regional and national levels in 1975 and 1976. But just as the De Lorenzo plot made the Socialists cautious in 1964, so too did these events and the recent examples of military intervention in Greece and Chile make the Communists behave very carefully.[73]

The question of the extent to which this 'second state' undermined the attempted 'historic compromise' of the 1976–9 period must be approached with great caution. The attempts started by Aldo Moro were cut short once he was kidnapped and murdered by the Red Brigades in 1978. While there are still unsubstantiated and, one must admit, fairly wild theories, claiming that the extreme Right and elements of the

approach is adopted by Franco Ferraresi, 'The Radical Right in Italy', *Politics and Society*, vol. 16, no. 1 (1988), pp. 74–119; 'A Secret Structure Codenamed Gladio', in Stephen Hellman and Gianfranco Pasquino (eds.), *Italian Politics: A Review* (London, 1992), pp. 29–48.

[72] The fullest account is found in Richard Collin, *The De Lorenzo Gambit* (London, 1976).

[73] See the comments of Paul Ginsborg in his magnificent *A History of Contemporary Italy. Society and Politics 1943–1988* (Harmondsworth, 1990), pp. 348–405.

state were involved in this assassination, there is solid proof that Prime Minister Andreotti's American advisers strongly suggested that no deal be struck with the terrorists. This contrasts very sharply with deals struck a few years later to free a kidnapped Neapolitan DC politician.[74] It has similarly been argued that the red terrorism of the period 1974–81 was at least partially accelerated by suspiciously lax law enforcement and the alleged police infiltration of certain left-wing terrorist groups, which suggest some ties with the strategy of tension.[75] All of this is still highly controversial. What is clear is that the inability of the PCI to reward their working-class base with anything more than austerity, and to offer erstwhile middle-class voters anything more than chaos, undermined their 'historic compromise'.

Besides the huge Bologna railway bomb of August 1980, and several other incidents in the mid-1980s, bombs began to explode once again in the summer of 1993 as the old regime collapsed and the Cosa Nostra appeared to be on the run. At the moment of writing Silvio Berlusconi has resigned and has been replaced by a government of technocrats.

The contexts of these forms of terror are important. They take on a more sinister tone once one recalls that the extreme Right had a much more significant role to play within the party system of the Italian Republic than its counterparts in the Federal Republic of Germany. It is therefore worthwhile summarising the unique position of the extreme Right in post-1945 Italian politics.

As is well known, the political history of the Italian Republic until 1992 was characterised by Christian Democratic dominance through centrist coalitions in the 1950s and early 1960s, mainly Centre–Left coalitions with the PSI (Partito Socialista Italiano) from the mid-1960s to the early 1970s, Communist parliamentary support for the Christian Democrat governments of National Solidarity from 1976 to 1979 and finally either four- or five-party Christian-Democrat-led coalitions or governments formally led by Republican or Socialist Prime Ministers but in which the Christian Democrats still kept key cabinet positions.[76] There never was a German-style second founding of the Republic: the Christian Democrats either transformed the Socialists into placemen, bureaucrats and criminals or neutralised the Communists through the immobility of the governments of National Solidarity. In short, the Christian Democrats perfected the ancient art of *trasformismo* and to a

[74] See the remarks by Silvio Lanaro in his *Storia dell'Italia Repubblicana. Dalla fine della grande guerra agli anno novanta* (Venice, 1992), p. 441.
[75] See Willan, *Puppetmasters*.
[76] For excellent overviews of the Italian Republic's political system see Hine, *Governing*, and Furlong, *Modern*.

certain extent continued a way of taking part in politics which stretched from the Liberal through the Fascist eras.[77]

However, it should not be implied that politics for the DC were a simple process of manipulation. The space to the right of the DC remained contested territory. Indeed, in the late 1940s and early 1950s it was far from certain that the DC would be able to act as the bulwark of moderate and conservative Italian politics. The mixed results of both the Resistance and the referendum on the monarchy left Italy with a potentially large constituency for an extreme conservative or neo-Fascist party. Although the revival of the PNF was made illegal, a direct successor composed of veterans of the Salò Republic founded the Movimento Sociale Italiano by the end of 1946. The millions of Italians who supported the populist Qualunquisti (the Everyman Party), the Monarchists and the MSI in the years immediately after the war underlined this potential.[78] In the long run, however, the MSI and the extreme Right never succeeded in graduating from being the fourth largest party in the Republic. Their electoral fortunes averaged 5 to 6 per cent, reaching a high point of nearly 8.7 per cent in 1972 and exceeding this only in the 1994 elections (with 13.5 per cent).[79]

But the relative marginalisation of the neo-Fascists in the political history of the Republic should not be exaggerated. Traditionally, historians have stressed the struggle during the immediate postwar period between the alliance of Christian Democratic-led moderates and the Communist/Socialist Popular Front being decided with the impressive victory of the Centre–Right in 1948. Although the Cold-War struggle between Christian Democrat- and Communist-dominated blocs were central to the early history of the Republic, more recently historians have also stressed the other struggle over who would control this anti-Communist alliance.[80] De Gasperi at certain times seemed to have been equally preoccupied by his competitors to the Right rather than his Communist adversaries. Indeed, the absolute dominance of the DC

[77] On the history of the concept of *trasformismo*, see the excellent overview of the literature by Nicola Tranfaglia, 'Trasformismo', in Ginsborg (ed.), *Stato*, pp. 96–8.

[78] For the situation in the south see Nicola Gallerano, *L'altro dopoguerra. Roma e il sud 1943–1945* (Milan, 1985).

[79] For a review of the electoral fortunes of the extreme Right in post-1945 Italy see Piero Ignazi, *Il polo escluso: profilo del Movimento sociale italiano* (Bologna, 1989). In English see Ferraresi, 'The Radical'; Roberto Chiarini, 'The Movimento Sociale Italiano: A Historical Profile', in Luciano Cheles (ed.), *Neo-Fascism in Europe* (London, 1991), pp. 19–42; Paul Furlong, 'The Extreme Right in Italy: Old Actors and Dangerous Novelties', *Parliamentary Affairs*, vol. 45, no. 3 (1992), pp. 345–56. For the 1994 general election see Ignazi, 'Alleanza'. In English, see Hilary Partridge, 'The Italian General Election: Something New or More of the Same Thing?', *Politics*, vol. 14, no. 3 (1994), pp. 121–3.

[80] See the interesting comments by Pietro Scoppola in *La repubblica*, pp. 112, 143.

over the Monarchist and neo-Fascist Right was far from certain until the middle of the 1950s. De Gasperi's policy of 'no enemies to the Right' caused the DC to take a cautious line during the referendum of 1946, even if the northern wing of the party voted against the king. The persistent local strength in the south of the neo-Fascists and the Monarchists in the 1950s meant that the DC formed municipal coalitions with the extreme Right throughout this period. And although the so-called *legge truffa* ('the swindle law') of 1953, an electoral reform which would have allowed the party winning 50 per cent of the vote and being awarded 65 per cent of the seats in parliament, has been traditionally seen as a way to marginalise the Left, in fact it now appears that much of its intent was motivated by De Gasperi's desire to be free of the potential or real dependence on the parliamentary votes of the extreme Right.[81]

The failure of the *legge truffa* meant that the DC was increasingly forced to look for a partner to its Left. From the 1950s to the 1980s the political space allotted or afforded to the MSI and the extreme Right can be measured in direct proportion to the health of the relationship between the DC and the PSI.[82] The PSI did not enter a *centro-sinistra* government until December 1963. After Khrushchev's revelations of Stalin's crimes and the suppression of the Hungarian Revolution in 1956, the PSI widened an already incipient split with its Communist partner. But the formation of a coalition government with the DC took years to bring to fruition and only occurred after the DC attempted an opening to the Right in 1960, when Tambroni sought support from the MSI in a DC-led government.[83] This sparked widespread civil unrest in the north and the deaths of ten demonstrators. Although the DC governments of the early 1970s leaned towards the MSI in the wake of the conservative backlash unleashed by the students' and workers' revolts of 1968 and 1969, the DC never again tried to bring the MSI into national government. Ironically, it was left to the new-style Socialist Bettino Craxi, during his tenure as Prime Minister between 1983 and

[81] Scoppola, *La repubblica*, pp. 112, 143, 170–1, 239–70. And for a deeper analysis of De Gasperi's politics, see Scoppola's *La proposta politica di De Gasperi* (Bologna, 1977).

[82] For an overview of the history of the PSI see David Hine's work: 'Social Democracy in Italy', in William E. Paterson and Alastair H. Thomas (eds.), *Social Democratic Parties in Western Europe* (London, 1977), pp. 67–85; 'The Italian Socialist Party', in Tom Gallagher and Allan M. Williams (eds.), *Southern European Socialism: Parties, Elections and the Challenge of Government* (Manchester, 1989), pp. 108–32; 'The Italian Socialist Party and the 1992 General Election', in Gianfranco Pasquino and Patrick McCarthy (eds.), *The End of Post-War Politics in Italy. The Landmark 1992 Elections* (Boulder, 1993), pp. 50–62. Also see Spencer M. Di Scala, *Renewing Italian Socialism: Nenni to Craxi* (New York, 1988).

[83] A good account is found in Ginsborg, *A History*, pp. 255–8.

1987, to attempt to bring the MSI back into the constitutional fold.[84] Not only did he consult the leader of the MSI when he formed his government with the DC, his drive to turn the PSI into the party of the modern *ceti medi emergenti* was accompanied by both a re-emphasis on Italian nationalism and the encouragement of debate over constitutional reform that stressed the replacement of the existing political system with a strongly presidential regime.

As political scientists have noted, Craxi's premiership is important for the gradual normalisation of the MSI. First of all, the MSI took a major role in the debate over constitutional reform; secondly, Craxi broke the taboo about the MSI established after the riots of July 1960; and finally, ironically, the quantum leap in corruption in Italian life during the Craxi years was accompanied by the rise of Silvio Berlusconi to media monopolist assisted by his patron Craxi.[85] It is not fanciful to see the direct connection between the rise of Berlusconi as politician in 1994 and his heavy dependence upon the old Socialist party electorate of the 1980s, and equally to see the fulfilment by Berlusconi of Craxi's strategy of using the MSI vote to create an alternative moderate power bloc once the Christian Democrats and the Socialists splintered in the wake of the political upheavals of 1989, Mafia revelations and the Tangentopoli scandals.

In retrospect it can be seen that the Christian Democrat policy of 'no enemies to the Right' was never completely successful. A neo-Fascist or extreme conservative alternative always awaited its chance throughout the history of the Republic. But its success was dependent on the collapse of the Christian Democratic mechanism of consensus I mentioned above. As we have seen, the DC employed the state apparatus and some of the policies shaped during the *ventennio* to create and nurture its electorate. Visceral anti-communism was always important and easier to employ in a state with the largest Communist party in western Europe. However, the strategy of De Gasperi and his successors also relied upon the support of the progressive pre-Fascist white associational culture of the industrial districts and the urban centres of the north, and the establishment of a strong Christian Democrat base in the virgin territories of the south and the islands.

The development of the south was linked intellectually to American Cold-War political science, sociology and economics. The authoritarianism, criminality and lack of a civic culture in the south detected by a legion of American social scientists in the 1950s and 1960s could,

---

[84] Tim Mason had some sharp words to say on this manoeuvre in 'The Great Economic History Show', pp. 20–5, 28–35.
[85] On Craxi's approach to the MSI, see Furlong, 'The Extreme', pp. 345–51. On Berlusconi as Fini's patron see Valentini, 'Alleanza Nazionale', pp. 680–1.

it was argued, be overcome by Keynesian-style DC policies.[86] To what extent the ills of southern political culture were linked to the *ventennio* or to processes going back much further in time was unclear in the minds of Italian and American experts in the 1950s, even if in the post-1989 era the sins of southern political culture were traced back by the American political scientist Putnam to the lack in the south of a communal city-state era (1000–1300 CE) similar to that experienced in parts of the centre and north![87]

From the 1950s onwards development of the south was used by the DC and its closest allies to prevent the extreme Right from making further advances. Land reform in the late 1940s and 1950s undermined pre-Fascist landlord notables and created a Christian Democratic clientele; para-state and state industries were encouraged to industrialise the south, the social-welfare system's invalidity pensions hid unemployment and the excess rural population was allowed and encouraged to migrate to the north and abroad to Europe.[88]

But the establishment and maintenance of the DC system of political exchange was not without its difficult moments. In the middle and late 1940s the initial phases of the project were gravely compromised by the Sicilian independence movement.[89] Supported by the great landlords, the Cosa Nostra, some elements of the urban middle class, and the Americans when they still feared a Communist victory on the mainland, the extreme Right equally fished in these troubled waters. The granting

---

[86] A good survey of Christian Democratic developmental policies is found in Ginsborg, *A History*, pp. 229–33. For a general survey of the arguments of the academics see Paul Ginsborg, 'Familismo', in Ginsborg (ed.), *Stato*, pp. 78–82 and Alberto De Bernardi, 'Clientelismo', in Ginsborg (ed.), *Stato*, pp. 83–6. Also see Tranfaglia, 'Trasformismo'. For organised crime, see Diego Gambetta, *The Sicilian Mafia* (Cambridge, Mass., 1993); Salvatore Lupo, *Storia della mafia dalle origini ai giorni nostri* (Rome, 1993). A general survey of the developmental literature from the perspective of the 1990s can be found in Antonio Mutti's 'Sociologia dello sviluppo e questione meridionale di oggi', *Rivista Italiana di Sociologia*, vol. 32, no. 2 (1991), pp. 153–76.

[87] Robert Putnam, *Making Democracy Work. Civic Traditions in Modern Italy* (Princeton, 1993). Also see Carlo Trigilia, *Sviluppo senza autonomia* (Bologna, 1992). The theme of Italy's missed modernisation has also seen a revival in Italy. One of the main themes of Lanaro's history of Republican Italy is the failure of modernisation through a failure to integrate Italians into the Italian nation-state: see his *Storia* and his *L'Italia nuova. Identità e sviluppo 1861–1988* (Venice, 1992). On the other hand, Giulio Sapelli has pointed to the failure of industrial citizenship which reflects on the failure of modernisation in Italy. See his *L'Italia inafferrabile. Conflitti, sviluppo, dissociazione dagli anni cinquanta a oggi* (Venice, 1989).

[88] For the creation of a southern DC clientele see Percy Allum, *Politics and Society in Post-War Naples* (Cambridge, 1973); Luigi Graziano, *Clientelismo e sistema politica. Il caso dell'Italia* (Milan, 1979); Judith Chubb, *Patronage, Power and Poverty in Southern Italy* (Cambridge, 1982).

[89] On the Sicilian independence movement see R. Mangiameli, 'La regione in guerra (1943–50)', in Maurice Aymard and Giuseppe Giarrizzo (eds.), *La Sicilia* (Turin, 1987).

of regional government and the emergence of a Christian Democrat/ Mafia alliance within the politics of the island and factions of the DC associated with Sicilian politicians helped marginalise the extreme Right. Twenty years later, when Rome refused to choose Reggio Calabria as the capital of the newly constituted region of Calabria, the famous revolt occurred (1970–1) and the MSI scored impressive electoral victories after local Socialist and Christian Democratic notables were discredited.[90] Here, too, developmental programmes introduced to meet this threat from the Right were jointly administered by local organised crime and DC/PSI politicians.

Linking these developments to the possible effects of Fascist modernisation leads one to very ironic conclusions. The southern electoral base of the MSI probably for the most part saw the local extreme Right opposition as a bargaining tool when Rome forgot its specific needs. The south had never been the heartland of historic Fascism and, as Lyttelton and others have demonstrated, local Nationalist and Liberal notables were incorporated into the regime after Mussolini took power not without some friction.[91] Furthermore, recent histories of the Cosa Nostra have demonstrated how Mussolini used considerable coercion to incorporate or suppress Sicilian elites associated with organised crime.[92] In the postwar era the extreme Right probably inherited more of a traditionally authoritarian bureaucratic clientele rather than one which had been actively Fascist from the beginning. Several ambiguities stand out: between the Monarchists and those neo-Fascists who treasured the corporative and *republican* experience of Salò, and between the resentment of Mussolini's treatment of the Cosa Nostra during the *ventennio* and the undeniable links between organised crime and elements of the terrorist extreme Right. Nevertheless, once DC rule was undermined, the MSI was present in the south to collect its clientele and curiously, because it had been shut out of so much of the mainstream of politics of the previous forty years, to claim to be the party of good government.

While attempts to modernise the south were not completely mired in criminality and corruption, and, as John Davis has recently noted, the south, or at least significant sections of it, have been the beneficiaries of a process best characterised as 'modernisation without growth', the net effect of the postwar era was a region with a standard of living and

[90] James Walston, *The Mafia and Clientelismo: Roads to Rome in Postwar Calabria* (London, 1988).
[91] Lyttelton, *The Seizure*, pp. 118–20; 180–201; Gentile, *Storia*, pp. 314–86; Alexander De Grand, *The Italian Nationalist Association and the Rise of Fascism in Italy* (Lincoln, 1978).
[92] Christopher Duggan, *Fascism and the Mafia* (New Haven, 1989).

way of life profoundly different from that of 1945.[93] But this still could not disguise the fact that the difference between the relative performance of Sicily, Calabria, Campania, Apulia, Basilicata and Molise and that of the north had not narrowed by the 1990s.

The 'historic compromise' between the northern and southern wings of the DC ultimately failed because the contradictions at its very heart alienated supporters throughout Italy. In the south a series of brave judicial investigations and a few seasons of mass mobilisation against the Cosa Nostra and the Camorra discredited the DC and in the north the rise of a populist federalist and anti-southern movement of the Northern League severely undermined the very white heartland of small-town Lombardy and the Veneto.[94] But the impetus behind what Paul Ginsborg has called the virtuous minorities could not last for ever.[95] So long as the 'clean hands' investigation judges of the early 1990s centred on the local and national elite of politicians and businessmen they were applauded, none more so than by the MSI. Once their investigations began to threaten the very mechanism of consensus from which a significant proportion of the population benefited economically, a revolt against the anti-corruption campaign itself and a visceral fear of a victory for the Left pushed Berlusconi to power. The extreme Right adopted an ambiguous but successful strategy. The MSI/ Alleanza Nazionale were one of the chief inheritors of the DC's mainland southern clientele, while Berlusconi inherited its votes in Sicily. The extreme Right seemed to embrace its corporative past but was also pleased to be associated with Berlusconi's neo-liberalism. It was awarded the votes of disgruntled and frightened DC clients but also posed as the party of clean government. Ultimately, the continuity of the extreme Right in the south allowed it to occupy a political space left vacant by its discredited DC rivals. In short, once the regional bases of the Christian Democratic party began to implode, the strategy of 'no enemies to the Right' successfully followed for most of the history of the Republic saw these 'non-enemies' return with a vengeance in the 1990s.[96]

CONCLUSION

The modernisation of Italy has been an obsessive theme for Italian intellectuals and foreign students of Italian society and history. In the first

---

[93] Davis, 'Remapping'.
[94] For an up-to-date account see Stephen Gundle and Simon Parker (eds.), *The New Italian Republic. From the Fall of Communism to the Rise of Berlusconi* (London, 1995).
[95] In a talk at the Italian Cultural Institute, London, May 1994.
[96] See Ignazi, 'Alleanza'; Bobbio, 'Dalla destra'.

half of this chapter I showed the weaknesses in attempting to make a direct correlation between Fascism and the modernisation of Italy. In the second half of this chapter I suggested ways in which the legacy of the Fascist regime has distorted civic life under the Republic, and showed in which ways neo-Fascism remained a political actor within the state and the party system. The paradoxical conclusion drawn from this chapter is that whereas Fascist modernisation under the Fascist regime had mixed results and relied heavily on legacies and events located either in the Liberal era or in broader changes in the world capitalist economy, neo-Fascism retained a clearer profile in the Italian Republic than neo-Nazism did in the Federal Republic of Germany. The persistence and relative strength of right-wing extremism in Italy may at least partially be attributed to the presence of the largest and most dynamic Communist party in western Europe. In the Federal Republic of Germany the Communist 'other' was safely placed in another state. Of course this did not prevent the backlash against the student revolt of the 1960s or the peace movement of the 1980s – or for that matter Chancellor Kohl's accusation that the Sozialdemokratische Partei Deutschlands (SPD) had become untrustworthy once it attempted to form coalition governments with the Partei des demokratischen Sozialismus (PDS) in the *Länder* of the former German Democratic Republic. But Adenauer's strategy of 'no enemies to the Right' was far more successful than De Gasperi's. The West German extreme Right of the immediate postwar era was either neutralised or incorporated into the Christlich-Demokratische Union/Christlich-Soziale Union (CDU/CSU). The anti-immigrant racist policies of the Nationaldemokratische Partei Deutschlands (NPD) in the 1960s and of the Republikaner and the Deutsche Volks-Union (DVU) in the 1980s and early 1990s never translated into a presence in the Bundestag. A higher threshold in Germany's proportional representational system cannot be the answer, because if the Italians had adopted a similar system the MSI would have still been represented in parliament.

But another reason for the persistence of the extreme Right in Italian politics was the ambiguous effects of modernisation. We have seen how these effects in the south allowed for neo-Fascism to be an important local player in an area whose historical linkages to an authoritarian Liberal or Nationalist heritage were always stronger than their linkages to Fascism as a movement. The southern supporter of the MSI harked back to the *ventennio* not as the Fascist revolution but as a conservative restoration.

The end of the Cold War and reunification of Germany may have led to new challenges to the Christian Democratic leadership of the Federal Republic of Germany, but the Centre–Right coalition survived

and won two national elections, and recently seemed to have marginalised the extreme Right. In Italy the end of the Cold War and the
pressures of the Maastricht Treaty caused a collapse of DC leadership.
The older mechanism of consensus could no longer be operated by the
DC because of the catastrophic Italian budget deficit. Privatisation of
state industry, reform of the pension system and the fiscal revolt of
northern middle-class taxpayers angered by spending in the south *and*
a more effective collection of their own taxes undermined DC power.
The corruption scandals in both north and south did the rest. The
emergence of the MSI/Alleanza Nazionale as a partner in government
can be attributed to two causes. First of all the current leadership of
the MSI has sought to distance itself from the corporative and more
radically Fascist policies of the minority within the party. This has been
a contradictory process since, as I mentioned at the beginning of the
chapter, Fini still admired the pre-1938 Mussolini. But, secondly, in
terms of electoral support, although the MSI/Alleanza Nazionale
achieved good showings in border ethnic regions of the north such as
Friuli–Venezia Giulia and Trentino–Alto Adige, its core support is in
the mainland south amongst the clientele and Rome civil servants of
the 'First Republic'.

But the extreme Right and Berlusconi's movement could play another
card–a generalised cynicism towards reformist politics found widely just
below the skin of the Italian voter.[97] Much of Tim Mason's politics had
been shaped by the universal imperatives of the great changes thrust
upon the western world in the 1960s and early 1970s. In Italy, the
changes associated with the New Social Movements left very ambiguous
results. Although alternation of government did not occur in the 1960s
and 1970s, with reforms came the emergence of institutions of industrial
democracy, regional government, a national health system and local
school and neighbourhood councils. The radicals of 1968 and 1969
envisaged these institutions as ways to threaten and overturn the *partitocrazia*. It has been argued by Sidney Tarrow that these social movements deepened Italy's formal democracy.[98] But the slogan of the New
Left that politics were everywhere was turned around to mean that political parties should share out the institutions of the state and civil
society. The parties of the 'constitutional arc' colonised the grassroots
of civil society and divided up broadcasting and state and para-state

---

[97] See Ilvo Diamanti, 'Forza Italia: il mercato elettorale dell' "imprenditore politico" ',
in Ginsborg (ed.), *Stato*, pp. 665–7; Marco Revelli, 'Forza Italia: l'anomalia italiana
non è finita', in Ginsborg (ed.), *Stato*, pp. 667–70.

[98] Sidney Tarrow, *Democracy and Disorder. Protest and Politics in Italy 1965–1975* (Oxford,
1989). Also see Robert Lumley, *States of Emergency: Cultures of Revolt in Italy from 1968
to 1978* (London, 1990).

industry.[99] By the early 1990s outsiders such as the Northern League, the MSI and even, oddly, Berlusconi could claim to be the real revolutionaries questioning the first premises of the 'First Republic'.

By the 1990s Italy had the fifth or sixth largest industrial economy in the capitalist world, but it was the only western European state which had allowed neo-Fascists into national government. Italy had successfully integrated herself into the European Union and the international free-trade capitalism of the post-1945 era. Italian democracy had survived and changed under the great social movements of the 1960s and 1970s, under the threats of terrorism and organised criminality, as well as under the rapid economic modernisation of much of the country. And yet, somehow the formula of 'modernisation without growth' still haunted Italian politics and its civic culture.

[99] See Luisa Passerini, *Autoritratto di gruppo* (Florence, 1988).

10

NATIONAL SOCIALISM AND MODERNISATION

MARK ROSEMAN

> Da sind mittelalterliche Gassen wieder, Veitstanz, totgeschlagene
> Juden, Brunnenvergiftung und Pest, Gesichter und Gebärden wie
> auf der Verspottung Christi und anderen gotischen Tafeln.[1]

> Don't worry, the poison is only crushed laurel leaves, a very old
> way, nothing modern from IG Farben.[2]

Over the last few years, a spate of books and articles has appeared seeking to establish the 'modernity' of National Socialism or to demonstrate
the Nazis' commitment to modernisation. This recent literature builds
on work undertaken in the 1960s and 1970s, when a number of scholars
used modernisation theory to produce highly influential explanations of
the Third Reich's origins and impact. The aim of the present piece is to
compare and evaluate these two waves in the historiography of National
Socialism.

Whereas the earlier trend treated National Socialism as a reaction
against modernity, evolving from an imperfectly modernised society, the
recent literature views National Socialism both as a product of and as
warmly embracing the modern world. What is fascinating about juxtaposing the two interpretations is that we find ourselves torn in both
directions. We sense in Nazism the triumph of Bloch's 'medieval streets,
St Vitus' Dance, Jews beaten to death, poisoned wells and plague' over

I would like to thank my colleagues at Keele Ian Bell, Colin Richmond, Richard Sparks
and Charles Townshend for helping me to think through many of the issues involved
here and David Laven and Joan Roseman for their many stylistic improvements.
[1] Ernst Bloch, 'Amusement Co., Grauen, Drittes Reich' (1930), in Ernst Bloch, *Erbschaft
dieser Zeit. Gesamtausgabe*, vol. IV (first published 1935, this edn. Frankfurt/Main,
1977), pp. 61–9, here p. 62.
[2] Oberleutnant Frick in Eric Newby, *Love and War in the Apennines* (this edition London,
1983), p. 133.

the forces of modern civilisation. But then we look again and wonder whether the true story of Nazism and the Holocaust was not, in the final analysis, a combination of science, selective social engineering and negative eugenics, revealing the full menace of something 'modern from IG Farben'. It is clear, either way, that untangling the relationship between the barbaric and the modern lies at the very heart of understanding National Socialism.

Where the two waves of historiography differ, then, we find much that is plausible in both assessments. But where they agree, namely in the view that the concepts 'modernity' and 'modernisation' represent clearly defined social phenomena which can be used to evaluate or explain National Socialism, we may be more sceptical. Our scepticism arises not from an aversion to big theory as such,[3] rather because unlike, say, capitalism (another global phenomenon in which theorists have located the origins and character of National Socialism) it is not clear that 'modernisation' and 'modernity' really exist, except as glosses on a number of disparate and only loosely interrelated phenomena. The very fact that an advanced society could descend to National Socialism has reinforced our suspicion that 'modernity' is simply an illusion. And even if there *is* some recognisable 'syndrome' of modernisation, some broad evolutionary process which all societies go through, is this process fine-grained enough to account for a phenomenon as specific and short-lived as National Socialism? Is it not more suited to exploring long-range transitions over centuries as pre-modern become modern societies?

In response to these questions, sections I and II survey the older and newer literatures of modernisation respectively. Section III evaluates their ability to capture the reality of National Socialism while section IV considers the issue of whether the National Socialists could be said to have modernised German society. The final section draws some conclusions about the impact of National Socialism on our understanding of modernity.

I

Under the general heading of modernisation theory the 1950s and '60s saw the emergence of a number of highly influential (and largely American) accounts of the development of modern societies.[4] The pro-

---

[3] Notwithstanding Heinz Bude's witty characterisation of the historian in *Bilanz der Nachfolge. Die Bundesrepublik und der Nationalsozialismus* (Frankfurt/Main, 1992), pp. 17–22.

[4] Marion J. Levy, *Modernisation and the Structure of Societies* (Princeton, 1966); S. N. Eisenstadt, *Modernisation, Protest and Change* (Englewood Cliffs, N.J., 1966); Talcott Parsons, *The Evolution of Societies* (Englewood Cliffs, N.J., 1966).

liferation of definitions of modernisation was 'such', as one observer noted wryly, 'that the ratio of those using the term to [those using] alternative definitions would appear to approach unity'.[5] But broadly speaking, modernisation theories were conceived as an answer to Marxist models of capitalist development. They employed much of Marx's materialist societal analysis but attempted to explain the success, stability and liberality of capitalist democracies rather than predict their downfall. Instead of dividing societal development primarily into stages of capitalist development, modernisation theories began with a binary opposition between traditional and modern societies. Modernisation, the process whereby the traditional became the modern, was conceptualised as a non-revolutionary, incremental and self-stabilising process, involving a series of functionally interrelated mechanisms which together led to modern (i.e. western) society.[6] Modernity was understood as comprising individualism, democratic structures, dynamic capitalist economic systems, high levels of social mobility and communications, growing influence of scientific thinking and practice, the steady subjection of inherited values, goals and legitimacies to increasingly rationally defined goals and the development of a state apparatus able to perform ever greater feats of social organisation and control.

Against this background American and German historians in the 1960s revived and gave new depth to the view, first articulated in 1915 by Thorstein Veblen, that German society had acquired a peculiar character in the course of the nineteenth century because it had modernised so unevenly.[7] During the 1960s it rapidly became part of 'social theorists' basic field kit'[8] to believe that, whilst Germany had industrialised at a tremendous pace in the late nineteenth century, its political structure and value system had failed to keep in step. Feudal elites continued to control the system and were able to disseminate their values throughout society. The 'feudalisation' of the bourgeoisie and the ostracising of the Socialists inhibited the development of structures and prac-

---

[5] Dean C. Tipps, 'Modernization Theory and the Comparative Study of Societies: a Critical Perspective', *Comparative Studies in Society and History*, vol. 15 (1972), pp. 199–226.

[6] Parsons, *Evolution*; Jeffrey Alexander, 'Modern, Anti, Post, and Neo: How Social Theories Have Tried to Understand the "New World" of "Our Time"', *Zeitschrift für Soziologie*, vol. 23, no. 3 (1994), pp. 165–97, here p. 168.

[7] The idea has a long pedigree. As well as Thorstein Veblen, *Imperial Germany and the Industrial Revolution* (orig. 1915; this edn. New York, 1954), see Ernst Bloch, *Erbschaft*. See also Pierre Ayçoberry, *The Nazi Question* (London, 1981), pp. 200ff.

[8] Hans-Peter Schwarz, 'Modernisierung oder Restauration? Einige Vorfragen zur künftigen Sozialgeschichtsforschung über die Ära Adenauer', in Kurt Düwell and Wolfgang Köllmann (eds.), *Rheinland-Westfalen im Industriezeitalter*, vol. III, *Vom Ende der Weimarer Republik bis zum Land Nordrhein-Westfalen* (Wuppertal, 1984), pp. 278–93, here p. 285.

tices for the rational regulation of conflict. The population remained divided by innumerable rigid subdivisions and failed to become a political nation. After 1918 the weak development of liberal values meant that there was little love for Weimar's democracy; the lack of central political integration and the failure of capital and labour to create institutions of conflict regulation meant that democracy was simply overwhelmed by the challenges of modernisation. The resulting crisis of control and confidence produced a massive reaction among all those groups which had failed psychologically and socially to adjust to modernisation: the outcome was National Socialism with its incoherent bundle of anti-modernist resentments.

Thus modernisation theory provided a long-term societal explanation for National Socialism, locating its origins in Germany's uniquely uneven development. In contrast to the Marxist emphasis on the relationship between fascism and capitalism, one virtue of this approach was that it could easily explain why big business support for Nazism before 1933 was comparatively limited.[9] Instead, it drew attention to the role of feudal elites, the aristocracy and the generals in aiding and abetting the Nazi rise to power; to the significance of electoral support from small businessmen and farmers (the two groups which lost most or gained least from modernisation),[10] and to the many vague and contradictory promises of restoration which Nazi ideology contained.[11] Finally, other scholars argued that to the extent that German capitalists *had* played a negative role, namely by engendering a crisis of confidence through their rejection of Weimar's social and industrial relations system, it was because their feudal patriarchal outlook had rendered them unable to work within a modern and functional system of wealth redistribution and dispute arbitration.[12]

Within this paradigm, the National Socialists themselves appeared as reactionaries, blindly opposing the march of progress. They were hostile to any form of political pluralism and reversed many of the new rights and freedoms which Weimar had established. They destroyed the bargaining rights of organised labour and restored in the factories conditions which Social Democrat observers in exile saw as reminiscent of the early stages of industrialisation.[13] They sought to reverse female emancipation, returning women to the home. This hostility to freedom

[9] Henry Ashby Turner, *German Big Business and the Rise of Hitler* (Oxford, 1985).
[10] Seymour Martin Lipset, *Political Man. The Social Bases of Politics* (New York, 1960).
[11] Heinrich A. Winkler, 'Hitler, German Society and the Illusion of Restoration', *Journal of Contemporary History*, vol. 11, no. 1 (1976), pp. 1ff.
[12] Bernd Weisbrod, *Schwerindustrie in der Weimarer Republik – Interessenpolitik zwischen Stabilisierung und Krise* (Wuppertal, 1978).
[13] Michael Prinz, 'Die soziale Funktion moderner Elemente in der Gesellschaftspolitik des Nationalsozialismus', in Michael Prinz and Rainer Zitelmann (eds.), *Nationalsozialismus und Modernisierung* (Darmstadt, 1991), pp. 297–327, here p. 300.

NATIONAL SOCIALISM AND MODERNISATION

and emancipation was portrayed as going hand in hand with a more generally romanticised restorative vision in which the farmer and the small businessman were extolled at the expense of the modern business world.

Of course, those who argued that National Socialism was fundamentally opposed to modernisation had to contend with the fact that the Nazis successfully mastered national economic recovery and prepared Germany for a major war. In the course of the 1930s industry expanded, agricultural revival was restrained to keep down industry's costs and preparation for war became a more and more central priority. These developments not only appeared to contradict the idea that the Nazis genuinely wanted to reverse the process of social change but also challenged the notion that only a pluralist political system could cope with the challenges of modernisation. But Henry Ashby Turner and David Schoenbaum among others were able to provide a plausible reason for the apparent contradiction between the Nazis' goals and the policies they adopted.[14] The Nazis' ultimate aim was to create an agrarian-based, ethnically pure community, restoring an idealised picture of medieval Germany. To achieve this, however, and in particular to secure the territorial gains which they believed necessary for the new Reich to work, they needed the modern means of the twentieth century. Thus the atavistic Nazis were forced to deploy modern technologies.[15]

Other authors devoted themselves to confirming the Nazis' incapacity to provide sustained, coherent management of the system. Tim Mason, arguing more from a Marxist perspective, believed the Nazis were precipitated into declaring war in 1939 because of their incapacity simultaneously to maintain their armament programme and make the material concessions necessary for industrial peace.[16] The destruction of trade unions had, by robbing the regime of means to gauge labour opinion, proved seriously dysfunctional.[17] Matzerath and Volkmann took a similar line, arguing that the system's dysfunctionality was evinced by its incapacity to maintain ordered and regulated government or accommodate and deal with social conflict.[18] Within a few years of its creation,

---

[14] H. A. Turner, 'Faschismus und Anti-Modernismus', in Turner, *Faschismus und Kapitalismus in Deutschland. Studien zum Verhältnis zwischen Nationalsozialismus und Wirtschaft* (second edn., Göttingen, 1980), pp. 157–82; David Schoenbaum, *Hitler's Social Revolution* (orig. 1966; here New York, 1980).

[15] *Ibid.*, and see Ayçoberry, *Nazi Question*, p. 205.

[16] Tim Mason, *Social Policy in the Third Reich. The Working Class and the 'National Community'* (Providence and Oxford, 1993).

[17] Tim Mason, 'The Workers' Opposition in Nazi Germany', *History Workshop Journal*, vol. 11 (1981), pp. 120–37.

[18] Horst Matzerath and Heinrich Volkmann, 'Modernisierungstheorie und Nationalsozialismus' in Jürgen Kocka (ed.), *Theorien in der Praxis des Historikers. Geschichte und Gesellschaft* (henceforth *GG*), Sonderheft 3 (Göttingen, 1977), pp. 86–102 (with discussion of the piece by other historians, pp. 102–16).

the whole system of command began to break down as more and more
special plenipotentiaries and 'Führer commands' replaced the practice
of ordered government. Against this background, war and racism appear
as instruments of social integration in a system that had no internal
mechanisms for regulating conflict. The system's growing internal disintegration and extremism thus appeared to vindicate the view that change
in modern societies can be achieved only through open, pluralist
structures.

Those who accepted the modernisation paradigm tended also to
believe that West Germany had finally joined the 'normal' path and
become a thoroughly modern nation. Relatively few authors, however,
asked whether National Socialism itself had, in some way, been responsible for this change. Ralf Dahrendorf's innovative, eloquent and witty
study *Society and Democracy in Germany* was the only real attempt to
pose this question.[19] Dahrendorf's argument was that the 'totalitarian'
destructiveness of National Socialism, though anti-modern in intent,
had in fact sufficed to destroy the feudal elements in the German tradition. The political aristocracy had been wiped out after the failed
bomb plot of 1944, their role in army and foreign service neutralised
long before. The particularistic loyalties and political subcultures which
had so divided the German nation had been eroded and then destroyed
in the process of *Gleichschaltung*. Nazism had, in a word, destroyed its
own authoritarian roots and thus created the foundations for a modern,
liberal postwar order. David Schoenbaum's study *Hitler's Social Revolution* is more ambiguous in its conclusions about the Führer's enduring
legacy, not least because the study stops in 1939. But it seems that
Schoenbaum too believed that the combination of a revolution of values
and perceptions coupled with what he called a 'revolution of destruction' permanently transformed what had been an 'arrested bourgeois–
industrial society'.[20]

Though both these studies were widely admired it should be noted
that the idea that the Third Reich brought about a 'revolutionary thrust
in to the modern' never enjoyed the same broad acceptance as the idea
that the regime originated in the uneven modernisation of German
society. Perhaps because the social history of the Third Reich itself was
only beginning to be written, perhaps for psychological and political
reasons,[21] few historians ventured across the dividing line of 1945 to
look at the regime's lasting impact. And, as we will see below, those

[19] Ralf Dahrendorf, *Society and Democracy in Germany* (London, 1968). Page references
are to the German edition *Gesellschaft und Demokratie in Deutschland* (Munich, 1965).
[20] Schoenbaum, *Hitler's Social Revolution*, p. 287.
[21] This is the surmise of Tim Mason in his *Social Policy in the Third Reich*, p. 282.

who did often concluded that the Nazis had in fact effected little endur-ing change to German society.[22]

II

In the late 1960s and early 1970s western social scientists grew increas-ingly critical of modernisation theory. The assumption that there is one standard modernisation path in which western-style democracy emerges quasi-automatically as the handmaiden of continued industrialisation came to seem increasingly unlikely.[23] Modernisation theory appeared both ethnocentric and also overly materialist in its approach to political change. It became clear, to take one example, that the evolution of eighteenth- and nineteenth-century political liberalism in Britain and in the US was as much the result of contingent factors as of some iron law of modernisation.[24] As well as prescribing an over-rigid connection between industrialisation and political change, modernisation theory also came to be seen as a prisoner of structural–functional thinking in which social stability was reified as the norm and conflict side-lined as the exceptional case.[25] Instead, Marxist paradigms of fundamental and enduring social conflict seemed to many observers a more convincing explanation of social development. As a result, historians became increasingly unhappy with the modernisation paradigm and Matzerath's and Volkmann's 'Modernisierungstheorie und Nationalsozialismus' (1977)[26] was probably the last attempt to apply it explicitly to the study of National Socialism.

Yet just five years later, Detlev Peukert's *Volksgenossen und Gemein-schaftsfremde* (1982)[27] and then his *Die Weimarer Republik. Krisenjahre der klassischen Moderne* (1987)[28] signalled the return of the concepts of 'modernity' and 'modernisation' to the analysis of National Socialism. However, as even a cursory glance makes clear, this new literature con-

---

[22] See H. A. Winkler, 'Vom Mythos der Volksgemeinschaft', *Archiv für Sozialgeschichte* (henceforth *AfS*), vol. 17 (1977), pp. 488–520 and Winkler's comments in Insititut für Zeitgeschichte (ed.), *Alltagsgeschichte der NS-Zeit. Neue Perspektive oder Trivialisierung* (Munich, 1984), p. 45.

[23] Hans-Ulrich Wehler, *Modernisierungstheorie und Geschichte* (Göttingen, 1975), pp. 18ff.

[24] A similar point is made by Rainer Zitelmann, 'Die totalitäre Seite der Moderne', in Prinz and Zitelmann (eds.), *Nationalsozialismus und Modernisierung*, pp. 1–20, here p. 5.

[25] *Ibid.*, pp. 23–4.

[26] See note 18.

[27] Detlev Peukert, *Volksgenossen und Gemeinschaftsfremde. Anpassung, Ausmerze und Aufbegehren unter dem Nationalsozialismus* (Cologne, 1982), translated as *Inside Nazi Germany. Conformity, Opposition and Racism in Everyday Life* (Harmondsworth, 1989). Page references are to the German edition.

[28] Detlev Peukert, *Die Weimarer Republik. Krisenjahre der klassischen Moderne* (Frankfurt, 1987), translated as *The Weimar Republic* (London, 1991). Page references are to the German edition.

ceptualises modernity in a radically new way. In a somewhat ironic twist, the word 'modern' has come, in some recent texts, to be as loaded with sinister meaning as ever it was on the lips of Prussia's most repressive Junker.

What had happened was that new movements in the social and political sciences and in literary thought had begun to spread to the historians. As is well known, in the late 1970s former 'new Left' political and social scientists, whilst retaining their disaffection from modern industrial capitalism, were growing increasingly disillusioned not just with Marxism but more generally with broad evolutionary theories and the knowledge claims they represented. Out of the intellectual 'crisis of the Left' emerged a range of critical perspectives on modernity which have been somewhat loosely grouped under the heading of 'postmodernism'.[29] Not only the diversity of approaches but also the self-conscious disavowal of the 'grand narrative' means that the paradigm of modernity which the historians of National Socialism have borrowed from this new theoretical literature is far less well defined than was classical modernisation theory. What we can say is it incorporates a shift of both mood and emphasis. The mood is far more sombre. Some elements of older modernisation theory – industrialisation, rationalisation, secularisation – remain. But gone is the confidence in the benign outcome of the belief in pluralism as the quintessentially modern political form. Instead, influenced by the work of Foucault,[30] by the revival of interest in both the Frankfurt school[31] and, in the German case particularly, in Weberian critiques of rationalisation,[32] there is far greater awareness of the strait-jacketing effects of professionalisation, rationalisation and state intervention and of a modern world in which, as Michel Foucault tells us, 'prisons resemble factories, schools, barracks, hospitals, which all resemble prisons'.[33] What is emerging, then, is less a coherent theory of social evolution (modernisation) than a broad con-

[29] See Jean-François Lyotard, 'Answering the Question: What is Postmodernism?', which appears in translation as an appendix to Lyotard, *The Postmodern Condition: a Report on Knowledge* (Manchester, 1984), pp. 71–82; see also Barry Smart, *Post-modernity* (London, 1993). I have not explored the conflict between avowed postmodernists such as Lyotard and 'radical modernists' such as Habermas since it is less the precise positions than the broadly critical reappraisal of the modern, which both share, which has influenced the historiography of National Socialism. See Emilia Steuerman, 'Habermas vs Lyotard. Modernity vs Postmodernity?', in Andrew Benjamin (ed.), *Judging Lyotard* (London, 1992), pp. 99–118.

[30] On Michel Foucault see Herbert L. Dreyfus and Paul Robinow (eds.), *Michel Foucault: Beyond Structuralism and Hermeneutics* (second edn., Chicago, 1983).

[31] See Max Horkheimer and Theodor Adorno, *Dialektik der Aufklärung: Philosophische Fragmente*, published in Adorno, *Gesammelte Schriften*, vol. III (Frankfurt/Main, 1981).

[32] See for example Detlev Peukert, *Max Webers Diagnose der Moderne* (Göttingen, 1989).

[33] Michel Foucault, *Discipline and Punish. The Birth of the Prison* (orig. French edn., 1975, this edn. Harmondsworth, 1979), p. 228.

ceptualisation of modernity at the core of which lies danger: the search for dominance and control, be it against colonial peoples abroad or the population at home.

The new paradigm has absorbed many strands of the Marxist criticism of capitalist society, rather than defusing it, as the older modernisation paradigm sought to do. It accepts Marx's criticism of the bourgeois enlightenment that the advance of reason was ever harnessed to the assertion of particular interests. But it neither expects heroic redemption from any agency (the proletariat) nor sees the relations of production as the only source of contradiction and struggle. Instead, in line with the work of Foucault and others, a number of agencies – the state, professional elites, the search for knowledge and the power inherent in language itself – figure, with varying degrees of emphasis, as essential forces in a struggle for domination and control that is intrinsic to the modern.

While this paradigm was evolving in the social sciences, work was under way on the history of pre-Nazi Germany challenging many key assumptions of the earlier uneven modernisation approach. David Blackbourn and Geoff Eley showed for the German Kaiserreich that the bourgeoisie, far from being held back by feudal elites and losing sight of its own identity, was well able to assert its interests in a non-democratic framework – indeed in some ways better able, because the autocratic state protected it from having to share power with a growing Socialist movement.[34]

Confirmation that the illiberal values on which the Nazis were able to draw did not necessarily imply a resistance to modernisation is provided by analysis of the social roots of Nazism. The computer-aided studies of the last fifteen years or so have proven that a great many of the Nazis' followers could not in any sense be seen as 'losers' in the modernisation process, much as they may have felt unsettled or hard hit by the more short-lived phenomenon of the Slump.[35] And a glance at Nazi ideology and Nazi self-presentation shows that alongside the language of restoration there were also a great many promises of a brave new world, of jobs, dynamism and industrial–military renaissance. Moreover, recent work on the collapse of the vote for the established centre parties has revealed voter behaviour that ill accords with the Dahrendorfian model of the 'unmodern' individual unwilling to take on the role of the citizen; instead, German political life was characterised by an increasingly active electorate which, whilst rejecting conventional *party*

---

[34] David Blackbourn and Geoff Ely, *The Peculiarities of German History* (Oxford, 1984).
[35] Jürgen Falter, *Hitlers Wähler* (Munich, 1991); Thomas Childers, *The Nazi Voter. The Social Foundations of Fascism in Germany, 1919–1933* (Chapel Hill, 1983).

politics, used the political process to assert its interests – initially through the medium of interest groups and splinter parties and eventually by voting for National Socialism.[36] If ever there was a society where respect for the old notables had broken down it was Germany in the 1920s.

Recent work has also made clear that the elites backing an authoritarian alternative to Weimar could not lightly be dismissed as 'feudal' or 'anti-modern'. It was not just in Germany in the interwar years that many members of the intelligentsia and scientific professions believed that the technocracy of the future was incompatible with democracy. It was time for rule by the experts.[37] In addition, the crucial contribution of the military in toppling Weimar and backing Hitler was led not by the nostalgic supporters of the old monarchy but by the new 'technocrats' of total war who understood the challenges which preparation for total war placed on society and believed Weimar incapable of shouldering the burden.[38]

Drawing on these theoretical and empirical literatures, then, a new discourse of modernity found its way into studies of National Socialism. In fact, we can almost speak of two discourses or at least two emphases, one of which tends to restrict itself to the term 'modernity', the other of which retains the less static concept of 'modernisation'.[39] Historians of National Socialism who use the concept of 'modernity' (of whom Detlev Peukert is perhaps the most prominent example) tend to want to show that the negative aspects of National Socialism, particularly its racial policy, bore the unmistakable stamp of the modern. For Peukert, National Socialist ideology and practice was born not of a protest against industrial society but of a thoroughly modern crisis in a thor-

[36] Peter Fritzche, *Rehearsals for Fascism. Populism and Political Mobilization in Weimar Germany* (New York and Oxford, 1990); Rudy Koshar, *Social Life, Local Politics and Nazism. Marburg 1880–1935* (Chapel Hill and London, 1986); Peukert, *Weimarer Republik*, p. 228.

[37] Monika Renneberg and Mark Walker, 'Scientists, Engineers and National Socialism', in Renneberg and Walker (eds.), *Science, Technology and National Socialism* (Cambridge, 1994), pp. 1–29.

[38] Michael Geyer, 'Professionals and Junkers: German Rearmament and Politics in the Weimar Republic', in Richard Bessel and E. J. Feuchtwanger (eds.), *Social Change and Political Development in Weimar Germany* (London, 1981), pp. 77–133.

[39] Norbert Frei is, as far as I know, the only other author to draw attention, though in somewhat different form, to this division within recent interpretations of National Socialism. See Norbert Frei, 'Wie modern war der Nationalsozialismus?', *GG*, vol. 19, no. 3 (1993), pp. 367–87. The weakness of Frei's (excellent) piece is that because he wants to isolate the most radical versions of the new approaches (i.e. Zitelmann and Roth/Aly) from other work he ends up grouping Peukert in the same camp as the earlier approaches of the 1970s – see page 378 and note 40 – and thus rather misses the underlying paradigm change.

oughly modern society.[40] Weimar, so the argument runs, was the first capitalist democracy to legitimate itself as a welfare state. The growing economic crisis at the end of the 1920s subjected it to pressures and strains which over-stretched the welfare system (and would have done so even without the Wall Street crash). This produced bitterness and disorientation amongst those who expected a safety net when they fell and fear of revolution among those unnerved at the possible reaction of the dispossessed. The economic crisis caused many of the elites administering the social service system to jettison the idea of welfare for all and, in keeping with the growing momentum enjoyed by racist and eugenic ideas, to advocate a society which excluded those it could not provide for so that it could afford to care properly for the productive remainder. Nazi ideology, then, was at its core a totalitarian and racial reaction to a crisis of welfare-state capitalism, backed by modern elites who believed that democracy did not work.

Peukert deployed the concept of a 'crisis of modernity' to distance himself not just from older theories of relative under-development but also from the notion of a crisis of capitalism; the state apparatus and key professional elites played a crucial role and the strategy of response was shaped as much by this wider sense of rescuing the legitimacy of the system as by simply saving the capitalist enterprise. Whereas Marxists simply had to discount Nazi racist ideology as irrational pandering to a petty-bourgeois following, Peukert has been able to discern an inner logic to that ideology in relation to the crisis. Racism was not just a ragbag of resentments but a systematically applied, detailed and – within its own terms – rational strategy of social regeneration. It drew on patterns of policy and thought which had been evolving as a result of modernisation and it was carried to its logical extreme with the assistance and energy of a wide range of modern elites.

A large body of literature has emerged developing and expanding these ideas (though by no means all the contributors would fully accept Peukert's theoretical framework). In her path-breaking study on Nazi sterilisation policy, for example, Gisela Bock has shown the scientific self-image and methods of advocates of racism, many of whom believed that sterilisation was a policy of modern 'Kulturstaaten'.[41] The long

---

[40] For the following, see Peukert, *Volksgenossen und Gemeinschaftsfremde*, esp. pp. 289–96; also Peukert, *Weimarer Republik*; Peukert, *Grenzen der Sozialdisziplinierung. Aufstieg und Krise der deutschen Jugendfürsorge 1878 bis 1932* (Cologne, 1986); and Peukert, 'Zur Erforschung der Sozialpolitik im Dritten Reich', in Hans-Uwe Otto and Heinz Sünker, *Soziale Arbeit und Faschismus* (Frankfurt/Main, 1989), pp. 36–46.

[41] Gisela Bock, *Zwangssterilisation im Nationalsozialismus. Studien zur Rassenpolitik und Frauenpolitik* (Opladen, 1986), here p. 8, p. 366.

intellectual pedigree of policies of sterilisation, euthanasia and racially based killing has also been widely acknowledged.[42] Many authors have made clear how much support racial policy enjoyed from doctors, social workers and psychologists.[43] The head of the Reich health office of Weimar, Franz Bumm, was, as Cornelie Usborne tells us, in favour of sterilisation of the mentally inferior because it reduced 'useless and good-for-nothing elements'.[44] 'Eugenic laws after 1933 codified the demand voiced, albeit often only implicitly, during the Weimar years that individual birth control should be subordinated to population control.'[45]

Others have shown how carefully the Nazis tried to ensure that racial policy did not collide with the needs of industrial society. Whereas the earlier literature saw an illogical Nazi drive to end female employment finally jettisoned because of the demands of the war effort, recent work portrays Nazi policy towards women as being based on a coherent and comprehensive racial ideology and designed so as not to conflict with the needs of industrial society.[46] Women, it is now clear, were forced out of jobs only in a very limited way – far more limited than in the US in the 1930s.[47] A similar revision of assessment can be found in treatments of Nazi labour policy.

Many advocates of this approach have difficulty fitting the Holocaust into their interpretation but some have laid claim to the modernity of the Final Solution. 'We suspect (even if we refuse to admit it)', writes Zygmunt Bauman, 'that the Holocaust could merely have uncovered another face of the same modern society whose other, more familiar, face we so admire'.[48] Bauman's argument is that the separation of the use of violence from immediate moral calculus and the detachment of the desirability of rational decision from ethical criteria, characteristic of the modern, mean that the institutions of the modern state are ill equipped to prevent a Holocaust. The Holocaust, in other words, was

[42] Kurt Nowak, *Euthanasie und Sterilisierung im Dritten Reich. Die Konfrontation der evangelischen und katholischen Kirche mit dem 'Gesetz zur Verhütung erbkranken Nachwuchses' und der 'Euthanasie'-Aktion* (Göttingen, 1978); Ernst Klee, *'Euthanasie' im NS-Staat. Die 'Vernichtung lebensunwerten Lebens'* (Frankfurt/Main, 1983).
[43] Paul Weindling, *Health, Race and German Politics between National Unification and Nazism 1870-1945* (Cambridge, 1989); Robert N. Proctor, *Racial Hygiene: Medicine under the Nazis* (Cambridge, Mass., 1988).
[44] Cornelie Usborne, *The Politics of the Body in Weimar Germany: Women's Reproductive Rights and Duties* (Basingstoke, 1992), p. 152.
[45] *Ibid.*, p. 205.
[46] Carola Sachse, *Siemens, der Nationalsozialismus und die moderne Familie. Eine Untersuchung zur sozialen Rationalisierung in Deutschland im 20. Jahrhundert* (Hamburg, 1990).
[47] Gisela Bock, 'Gleichheit und Differenz in der nationalsozialistischen Rassenpolitik', in *GG*, vol. 19, no. 3 (1993), pp. 277–310; A. Kessler-Harris, 'Gender Ideology in Historical Reconstruction: a Case Study from the 1930s', in *Gender and History*, vol. 1 (1989), pp. 31–49.
[48] Zygmunt Bauman, *Modernity and the Holocaust* (Cambridge, 1991), p. 7.

not *caused* by the modern world but features of the modern world facilitated it. A small number of German historians have gone further than this and have explicitly attributed the Holocaust to the drive for the disburdening of the welfare state and the desire for economic exploitation of the occupied territories.[49] Racial policy was, in the words of Götz Aly, simply the 'final solution of the social question'.[50]

The thrust of this writing is to acknowledge, indeed re-emphasise, the distinctiveness of Nazi racial policy, yet to see that policy as the product of the modern world. Alongside and partly overlapping with this approach a body of literature has emerged which does not seek to prove the 'modernity of the Nazis' differentness' but instead argues that Hitler and other policy-makers in the Third Reich sought to modernise German society, i.e. to implement social changes which either paralleled or anticipated visions and practices adopted elsewhere in the industrialised world. The criteria of modernisation are rarely spelled out very precisely, but they include rationalisation; mobilisation; extension of participation, social opportunity and access to goods and services; removal of inherited status barriers and distinctions; transformation of status elites to functional elites and so on. Such approaches differ crucially from interpretations based on classical modernisation theories in that, first, there is no longer an assumption that modernisation is benign or automatically leads to political pluralism and, second, the Nazis are seen as enthusiastic and deliberate rather than inadvertent modernisers.

Rainer Zitelmann has been the most prominent and controversial exponent of this line. Zitelmann shows how far Hitler's own societal vision was from the rambling, archaic–romantic *Weltanschauung* conventionally attributed to him.[51] He welcomed and accepted industrial society. It was only Nazis on the periphery who seriously wanted to turn the clock back and create an agrarian idyll. Hitler was a strong advocate of modern technology and also of the growing dispersion of consumer durables; he hoped that Germany would soon surpass the USA in this respect.[52] His vision of a *Volksgemeinschaft* incorporated a strong aware-

---

[49] See Götz Aly *et al.*, *Sozialpolitik und Judenvernichtung. Gibt es eine Ökonomie der Endlösung?* (Berlin, 1987).

[50] 'Editorial', in Götz Aly, Angelika Ebbinghaus, Matthias Hamann, Friedemann Pfäfflin and Gerd Preissler, *Aussonderung und Tod. Die klinische Hinrichtung der Unbrauchbaren. Beiträge zur nationalsozialistischen Gesundheits- und Sozialpolitik*, vol. 1 (Berlin, 1985), pp. 7–8.

[51] Rainer Zitelmann, *Hitler: Selbstverständnis eines Revolutionärs* (Hamburg, Leamington Spa and New York, 1987), p. 320 and the concluding section, pp. 495ff.

[52] See Zitelmann, *Hitler*, pp. 318f. and also Rainer Zitelmann, 'Die totalitäre Seite der Moderne', in Prinz and Zitelmann, *Nationalsozialismus und Modernisierung*, pp. 1–20, here p. 15; see also Jeffrey Herf on Goebbels' 'stählerner Romantik' in *Reactionary Modernism: Technology, Culture and Politics in Weimar and the Third Reich* (Cambridge and New York, 1984), pp. 195f.

ness both of the American challenge and of Soviet achievements and
aimed to create a mobile, open consumer society.[53] In Zitelmann's
interpretation, the adoption of terror and the pursuit of *Lebensraum*
should not be seen as reflecting a permanent commitment to struggle
and terror. Rather they were the necessary means, based on Hitler's
sophisticated understanding of Germany's economic position in the
1920s, of attaining the kind of prosperity achieved by the United
States.[54] If Hitler was ultimately wrong in his lack of faith in world
markets, he was, as Albrecht Ritschi has observed, in very good
company.[55]

Many other authors (who by no means share all Zitelmann's views)
have complemented this work by identifying the many areas of Nazi
economic and social policy in which modernisation was consciously and
deliberately pursued. In their fiscal policy the Nazis proved themselves
to be 'Keynesians before Keynes'.[56] Under the heading of *Volksgemeinschaft*, Nazi policy-makers attacked all kinds of inherited status barriers,
most notably those isolating the manual working class from the rest of
the community. In terms of wages, social policy, informal gratification,
and collective organisation the differences between manual and white-
collar workers were being eroded on all sides.[57] The DAF promoted
the modernisation of leisure, introducing mass tourism for the working
class.[58] Indeed, the DAF, once dismissed as an ungainly self-serving
body, forced to feign proto-unionism to serve its scrabble for power and
influence, is now assigned a crucial role in this interpretation of National
Socialist social policy.[59] Its modernising vision was most clearly

[53] Zitelmann, *Hitler*, p. 322.
[54] Zitelmann, *Hitler*, p. 342.
[55] See Albrecht Ritschi, 'Zum Verhältnis von Markt und Staat in Hitlers Weltbild. Überlegungen zu einer Forschungskontroverse', in Uwe Backes, Erhard Jess and Rainer Zitelmann (eds.), *Die Schatten der Vergangenheit. Impulse zur Historisierung des Nationalsozialismus* (Frankfurt/Main and Berlin, 1990), pp. 243–65, esp. p. 248.
[56] Werner Abelshauser and Anselm Faust, *Wirtschafts-und Sozialpolitik. Eine Nationalsozialistische Sozialrevolution?* (Nationalsozialismus im Unterricht, Studieneinheit 4,
Deutsches Institut für Fernstudien an der Universität Tübingen, Tübingen, 1983), p.
116.
[57] Michael Prinz, *Vom neuen Mittelstand zum Volksgenossen* (Munich, 1986); Wolfgang
Zöllitsch, *Arbeiter zwischen Weltwirtschaftskrise und Nationalsozialismus* (Göttingen,
1990), p. 175; Rüdiger Hachtmann, *Industriearbeit im 'Dritten Reich'. Untersuchungen
zu den Lohn- und Arbeitsbedingungen in Deutschland 1933–1945* (Göttingen, 1989); and
see the comments in Michael Schneider, 'Nationalsozialistische Durchdringung von
Staat, Wirtschaft und Gesellschaft. Zur Sozialgeschichte des "Dritten Reichs"', *AfS*,
vol. 31 (1993), pp. 514–57.
[58] Carola Sachse, 'Freizeit zwischen Betrieb und Volksgemeinschaft. Betriebliche Freizeit-
politik im Nationalsozialismus', *AfS*, vol. 33 (1993), pp. 305–28, here p. 326.
[59] Tilla Siegel, 'Rationalisierung statt Klassenkampf. Zur Rolle der Deutschen
Arbeitsfront in der nationalsozialistischen Ordnung der Arbeit', in Hans Mommsen
(ed.), *Herrschaftsalltag im Dritten Reich. Studien und Texte* (Düsseldorf, 1988), pp. 97–

expressed during the war when the DAF Labour Science Institute produced a blueprint for a comprehensive Beveridge-style welfare and housing system to be implemented after eventual victory.[60]

The DAF's aspirations were, as indicated, aimed not just at social harmony but also at greater efficiency, and this brings us to the second major modernising goal of Nazi policy-makers – the *Leistungsgemeinschaft*.[61] A growing literature has highlighted the breadth and intensity of measures aiming at social and technical rationalisation.[62] The replacement of status by performance wage categories and the growth of universal wage norms is one such area.[63] The approach to labour relations in the factory, it is now clear, was less a return to feudal conditions than a National Socialist variant of the human relations approach being adopted in the USA.[64] As Wolfgang Spohn has shown, the labour lawyers involved in commenting on and interpreting the Law for the Ordering of National Labour of 20 January 1934 were able, without any great ideological modification of their position, to play a leading role in labour law after 1945.[65] In relation to women, too, a number of recent authors have identified the continuation of social rationalisation.[66]

If modernisation is to mean more than just a series of developments that are more or less *accidentally* to be found in contemporary societies, then some kind of syndrome or set of forces must be involved which gives these processes their universal character. There must, in other words, be a pressure or momentum or balance of forces which ensures that under normal conditions modernisation takes place and will continue to take place. This raises the question of how that modernisation pressure exerted itself on National Socialism. The older modernisation literature, of course, argued that the Nazis were a product of *resistance*

143; Prinz, 'Soziale Funktion moderner Elemente', p. 302; Sachse, *Siemens, der Nationalsozialismus und die moderne Familie*.

[60] Marie Luise Recker, *Nationalsozialistische Sozialpolitik im Zweiten Weltkrieg* (Munich, 1985), pp. 82ff.; Prinz, 'Soziale Funktion moderner Elemente', p. 319.

[61] On the DAF and rationalisation, see Tilla Siegel and Thomas von Freyberg, *Industrielle Rationalisierung unter dem Nationalsozialismus* (Frankfurt/Main and New York, 1991).

[62] For a good recent statement on the Nazis and technical rationalisation see Richard Overy, *War and Economy in the Third Reich* (Oxford, 1994), pp. 343–75.

[63] Tilla Siegel, 'Lohnpolitik im Nationalsozialistischen Deutschland', in Carola Sachse, Tilla Siegel, Hasso Spode and Wolfgang Spohn, *Angst, Belohnung, Zucht und Ordnung. Herrschaftsmechanismen im Nationalsozialismus* (Opladen, 1982), pp. 54–139; Hachtmann, *Industriearbeit im 'Dritten Reich'*, pp. 302–3.

[64] Matthias Frese, *Betriebspolitik im 'Dritten Reich'. Deutsche Arbeitsfront, Unternehmer und Staatsbürokratie in der westdeutschen Großindustrie 1933–1939* (Paderborn, 1991), p. 450.

[65] Wolfgang Spohn, 'Betriebsgemeinschaft und innerbetriebliche Herrschaft', in Sachse et al., *Angst, Belohnung, Zucht und Ordnung*, pp. 140–208, here p. 141, note 7.

[66] Sachse, *Siemens, der Nationalsozialismus und die moderne Familie*; Dagmar Reese, Eve Rosenhaft, Carola Sachse and Tilla Siegel (eds.), *Rationale Beziehungen? Geschlechterverhältnisse im Rationalisierungsprozeß* (Frankfurt/Main, 1993).

to modernisation and opposed it, but that their need to compete with other nations in the modern world effectively forced them to modernise against their will. The Zitelmann tendency rejects this since it regards the Nazis as consciously pursuing modernisation. But if they were consciously pursuing modernisation – why? To what extent was National Socialist ideology a product of the need to modernise? Was National Socialism indeed *necessary* for modernisation?

Neither Zitelmann nor any other historian has offered a fully fledged theory on this, though one can see in the work of Michael Prinz, among others, overtones of an interpretation. Prinz's argument is twofold. In the first place, National Socialist ideology and Hitler's own thinking represent 'the attempt to re-enact the First World War but with a thoroughly revised script, and one in particular that corrected the mistakes of domestic and social policy' that had undermined the war effort the first time.[67] In undertaking this project, the Nazis were, in fact, paralleling in many respects the efforts in other countries to 'recast bourgeois Europe' and taking on the role of state involvement in stabilising the system so central to modernisation theory. Secondly, once the Nazis came to power their goals – *Volksgemeinschaft* and *Leistungsgemeinschaft* – were sufficiently vague to accommodate energetic middle-class groups who sought to achieve a more efficient and egalitarian social order. Thus, instead of the older model of archaic Nazis forced by circumstance and the rationality of established elites to abandon some of their more crazy romanticism, we see a process whereby the party's own vague ideology was given new precision and purpose by the reforming energies the regime was able to absorb and attract. This is of course far from arguing that the Nazis were *necessary* for modernisation, though Avraham Barkai has argued that a dictatorship *was* necessary to solve Germany's economic problems.[68] Zitelmann might also argue that at the time it was extremely plausible that *Lebensraum* was necessary for prosperity. Once the logic of *Lebensraum* had been accepted this, in turn, required if not genocide than at the least some tough treatment of the indigenous populations.

We thus have two overlapping approaches linking National Socialism to the modern world. One seeks to establish that the abhorrent character of National Socialism, above all its racial and genocidal policies, was a product of modernity. The other aims to show that National Socialism sought the same kinds of social change and societal goals as other modern states. Are these two approaches two sides of the same coin or are they incompatible?

---

[67] Prinz, 'Soziale Funktion moderner Elemente', pp. 323–4, my translation.
[68] Avraham Barkai, *Das Wirtschaftssystem des Nationalsozialismus. Der historische und ideologische Hintergrund* (Cologne, 1977), p. 177.

Both clearly reflect on the part of the historian the more critical attitude towards modernity and progress we have already described. They differ in that Peukert's approach uses 'modernity' essentially as a static concept comprising certain enduring features or potentialities inherent in the modern. Those who have revived the notion of modern*isation*, by contrast, retain the classical theory's sense of *process*. The universal standard is not the enduring character of the 'modern' but the recognisably common path of modernisation.

In terms of the underlying theory of modernity, these two approaches are not necessarily irreconcilable. It could be argued, for example, that there is an ongoing process of development but that, whilst this brings changes, it does not affect certain enduring features of the modern world. Those enduring features of the modern mean that, occasionally, some kind of crisis takes place which interrupts modernisation and produces a different 'pathological' development. This seems to be the way in which Peukert uses the terms. There is nevertheless at least a tension between 'modernity's' implication of a modern world which may develop in many different ways but retains certain underlying characteristics or potentialities and 'modernisation's' connotation of evolving characteristics and a common developmental path.

As far as the conceptualisation of National Socialism is concerned, this tension finds expression in the degree of emphasis placed on the distinctiveness of Nazi racial doctrine.[69] For Peukert, the Nazis' policy branches out in a new direction, one which he would have difficulty categorising as modern*ising*, but which bears the mark of the modern world; for Zitelmann, the Nazis are pursuing the kinds of social goal and social change which one can easily fit under the general rubric of modernisation. We will consider below which if either of these conceptualisations is the more appropriate.

First, though, what has the recent literature made of Dahrendorf's claim that German society was radically, if inadvertently, modernised by the Third Reich? For those authors concerned with modern*ity* rather than modern*isation* the Dahrendorf thesis has become almost irrelevant to their interests. The genesis and character of National Socialism are the main issue. Moreover, if Weimar is no longer seen as having been particularly backward there is little room for Dahrendorf's revolutionary transformation in the Third Reich.

Even those recent writers who *have* written about modernisation in the context of the Third Reich have had relatively little to say about the

---

[69] Though, as Norbert Frei points out, in the radical version of the Peukertian view advanced by Götz Aly and colleagues this distinction is less clear cut because the latter argue that a similar degree of racism is inherent in the practice of other industrial nations.

Nazi legacy for the postwar world. They too have been far more interested in what the Third Reich's policies tell us about the Nazis' social
vision. In addition, Dahrendorf's belief in the link between social modernity and democratic stability allowed him to give a sharp political
focus to the modernisation question. Germany's postwar democratic
stability was the evidence of its modernity. In the more recent literature,
where the notion that there is any characteristic 'modern' political form
has been discarded, there has been no clear-cut way of describing the
overall level of modernisation.

There is, it is true, a limited but nevertheless very important literature
on the Nazis' social impact and we will return to this below. However,
it bears in two senses only a tenuous relationship to the new modernisation paradigm of Zitelmann or Prinz. In the first place, the best work
on these lines – for example from Lutz Niethammer and his associates[70]
or Martin Broszat's team at the Institut für Zeitgeschichte – rarely pays
more than lip service to the language of modernisation.[71] Secondly,
where such studies *have* talked more earnestly about modernisation the
long-term changes they describe are often clearly *not* what the Nazis
wished or intended, as, for example, in Dagmar Reese's impressive work
on the emancipatory impact of the Bund deutscher Mädel.[72] Here, Dahrendorf's thesis of unintentional modernisation has sneaked in through
the back door.

                                        III

Looking at the two generations of modernisation theorists, the suspicion
arises that quite a lot of the debate is merely about attaching different
labels to the same phenomena. For example, classical modernisation
theorists would not have had much difficulty in accepting some of the
modernity claims in recent work. It was never in dispute that totalitarianism or 'plan rationality' were products of the modern world or that
they would have been unthinkable or unrealisable in earlier periods.[73] In

---

[70] Lutz Niethammer (ed.), *'Die Jahre weiß man nicht, wo man die heute hinsetzen soll.'
Faschismuserfahrungen im Ruhrgebiet* (Berlin and Bonn, 1983); Lutz Niethammer (ed.),
*'Hinterher merkt man, daß es richtig war, daß es schiefgegangen ist.' Nachkriegserfahrungen
im Ruhrgebiet* (Berlin and Bonn, 1983); Lutz Niethammer and Alexander von Plato
(eds.), *'Wir kriegen jetzt andere Zeiten.' Auf der Suche nach der Erfahrung des Volkes in
nachfaschistischen Ländern* (Berlin and Bonn, 1985).

[71] See Martin Broszat, Klaus Dietmar Henke and Hans Woller (eds.), *Von Stalingrad zur
Währungsreform. Zur Sozialgeschichte des Umbruchs in Deutschland* (Munich, 1988).

[72] Dagmar Reese, 'The BDM Generation. A Female Generation in Transition from Dictatorship to Democracy', in Mark Roseman (ed.), *Generations in Conflict. Youth Revolt
and Generation Formation in Germany 1770–1968* (Cambridge, 1995), pp. 227–46.

[73] Talcott Parsons, for example, saw Communism as a 'modern' choice. Karl Muller,
' "Modernising" Eastern Europe: Theoretical Problems and Political Dilemmas', *European Journal of Sociology*, vol. 33 (1992), pp. 109–50, here p. 118.

that sense, the 'modernity' of totalitarian anti-democracy was never in doubt.

Moreover, it is clear that whilst recent writers might justifiably describe older definitions of modernisation as being too prescriptive, their own weakness is that they are too vague.[74] The terms 'modern' and 'modernisation' are now being used so loosely as to make it hard to imagine any policy or approach that could *not* be subsumed under one or other heading. When Rainer Zitelmann talks, for example, about 'ecological modernisation',[75] we are puzzled, not because we see ecological policy as necessarily incompatible with modernity, but because it is no longer clear what distinguishes modernisation from any other kind of policy or process. Similarly, Michael Prinz, looking at the Nazis' attempts to reverse the bureaucratisation of the welfare state and reintroduce older forms of charity, argues that this exemplified not anti-modernity but rather the cyclicity of the modern.[76] The problem here is not that Prinz is wrong in seeing modern policy developments as characteristically moving in cyclical fashion; the problem, rather, is that acknowledgement of the cyclicity lays open the question whether, at the level of particular social and economic policies, the notions of 'modernity' and modernisation provide any sort of criterion for distinguishing between one policy and another. Similarly, the admittedly more precise notion of 'social rationalisation' also easily falls into the trap of tautology; every coherent social policy has some clearly defined end view and is, to that extent, designed to create a more rational society. In part, then, the new work simply involves putting new – and not always particularly helpful – labels on already known phenomena.

One area where the classical modernisation paradigm did clearly differ from recent work is in the former's assumption that *under normal conditions* modernisation is accompanied by increasing pluralism and democracy. This was accompanied by the claim (which has enjoyed a new boost from the recent collapse of Communist regimes) that successful management of rapid social change *requires* open pluralist structures. Perhaps fortunately, the Third Reich's life was too short to allow us to test the hypothesis. In the short term Nazi social policy did *not* prove dysfunctional. To that extent the classical modernisation approach is misleading. But on the other hand, as Matzerath or Volkmann would no doubt be quick to point out, this does not tell us how the Nazis would have survived in the medium to longer term. They might well

[74] Abdoloreza Scheybani commented recently that modernisation theories tend either to be over-prescriptive or to mean nothing more than 'social change'. See 'Soziale Ungleichheit, Betriebsstruktur und Staatsinterventionismus in der säkularen Modernisierung', *AfS*, vol. 31 (1991), pp. 481–92.
[75] Zitelmann, 'Totalitäre Seite der Moderne', p. 10.
[76] Prinz, 'Soziale Funktion moderner Elemente', p. 305.

argue that if 'modernity' is meant to imply some capacity to survive in the modern world, one should not rush to describe so short-lived a regime as modern.

The real meat of the controversy and the real value of recent work is that it has irrevocably demonstrated that the Nazis subjectively and objectively operated on the terrain of industrial society. Agrarian pipe-dreams existed only on the peripheries of Nazi thought. Nazi social policy often embodied innovative responses to problems of industrial society, responses that sometimes paralleled, sometimes preceded anal-ogous efforts in other advanced industrial nations and which in any case often proved themselves consistent with the smooth functioning of that society. Nazi societal policy was not dysfunctional. Even though the Nazi system of government gradually disintegrated, this was because of the nature of Hitler's personal style of government, not the incompati-bility of Nazi policy with society's needs. Recent work suggests that the Nazis were astonishingly successful at integrating very heterogeneous social groups into the *Volksgemeinschaft*.[77] Thus they were, for example, not forced to go to war in 1939 because of growing internal opposition; to quieten discontent all they would have had to do was slow down the pace of rearmament a notch.[78] Finally, it is also clear that Nazi racial policy was by no means just the atavistic irrational fantasy that the ear-lier wave of historians assumed. These are all powerful, troubling and instructive conclusions of the recent historiography.

The question is whether it is possible to go further than this: can we assent to Peukert's hypothesis of the essential modernity of the Nazis' racial policy, or to the Zitelmann claim that Hitler's vision was essen-tially a modernising one?

The latter approach is, in my view, the more obviously flawed. Zitel-mann has undoubtedly surprised us with the degree to which Hitler was a child of the modern age and Michael Prinz's sophisticated work on modernisation has raised some profound questions about the Third Reich. But it is equally clear that Nazi goals cannot be seen as largely analogous with those of other western nations. Quite apart from the moral repugnance of an approach which consigns the Holocaust to the footnotes of history the better to focus on Hitler's speeches about the Volkswagen, it is flawed even if we take the Nazis on their own terms. Applying the simple criterion that where an idea is repeated often it must be important, it is clear that racial struggle and conquest enjoyed a centrality to Hitler's thought that precludes their being viewed as

---

[77] Amongst other studies, see Norbert Frei, 'Wie Modern' and Gunther Mai, ' "Warum steht der deutsche Arbeiter zu Hitler?" Zur Rolle der Deutschen Arbeitsfront im Herrschaftssystem des Dritten Reichs', *GG*, vol. 12 (1986), pp. 212–34.

[78] Overy, *War and Economy*, pp. 219–21.

merely the means to a social vision of prosperity and opportunity.[79] The central image of the *Volksgemeinschaft*, with its racial foundation, broke with fundamental principles of western industrial societies, most notably the relationship of the individual to the collective. Indeed, if, as Ute Daniel has argued recently,[80] the changing relationship between individual and society should be regarded as one of the fundamental elements of the evolution of modern society, this radical break from the process of individualisation needs closer attention. Examination even of organisations such as the DAF reveals how firmly tied they were to racial concepts. As Rüdiger Hachtmann reminds those marvelling at the Beveridge-style elements of the AWI's wartime plans, the DAF repeatedly articulated the vision that in future all German workers would become skilled workers – leaving the unskilled work on the conveyor belt to be carried out by racial inferiors who were intellectually and spiritually 'better equipped' to carry out this deadening, repetitive work.[81] On women, let us not forget Hitler's wartime response to Robert Ley's wage equality initiative: 'It is the goal of National Socialism, a goal which must be achieved once and for all when we have returned to peace-time, that basically only the man earns the wages . . . '[82]

This has led some authors, such as Wolfgang Zöllitsch, to write of a 'Teilmodernisierungskonzept'.[83] 'Partial modernisation', if it is merely a descriptive term, is perfectly acceptable. But as an analytical concept it undermines the notion of a coherent 'syndrome' of development on which the modernisation paradigm depends. For what we then really want to know is in what areas and to what degree some objective developmental logic was forcing the Nazis (or might, if the Nazis had lasted longer, have forced them in the future) to pursue modernisation. If the Nazis were in fact freely able to choose – a bit of western-style consumerism here, some barbaric racial policies there – then we would have to conclude that modernisation, or indeed any kind of developmental paradigm, was of little help in explaining what was going on. On the other hand if, as Michael Prinz has suggested, and as seems plausible, there *were* powerful developmental pressures acting on the Nazis – some of them anticipated in their ideology, some of them happily or resignedly acquiesced to once the Nazis were in power – it is precisely the complexity and unevenness of these pressures, the balance in Nazi ideology

---

[79] On all this, see Frei's excellent discussion in 'Wie modern', pp. 380ff.

[80] Ute Daniel, ' "Kultur" und Gesellschaft. Überlegungen zum Gegenstandsbereich der Sozialgeschichte', *GG*, vol. 19, no. 1 (1993), pp. 69–99.

[81] Hachtmann, *Industriearbeit*, pp. 83–4.

[82] Rüdiger Hachtmann, 'Industriearbeiterinnen in der deutschen Kriegswirtschaft 1936 bis 1944/45', *GG*, vol. 19, no. 3 (1993), pp. 332–66, here p. 360.

[83] Zöllitsch, *Arbeiter*, p. 241.

between responding to developmental exigencies and wilful, idiosyn-
cratic ideas, which is interesting and which the global concept of 'modernisation' obscures. The recent approach to modernisation has thus
raised crucial questions about the social function of Nazi ideology which
the classical paradigm, with its blanket assumptions of Nazi irrationality,
did not; but it cannot answer the questions it has raised.

Many of the above criticisms cannot be levelled at Peukert's
approach. For Peukert, Nazi racism is at the centre and its horrific distinctiveness is fully acknowledged. And let us also dismiss the simplistic
but commonly made criticism that, because other nations were modern
and did not have a Holocaust, 'modernity' logically cannot provide an
adequate explanation of Nazi racism and the Holocaust. There are two
obvious responses to this. In the first place, Peukert would argue that
Weimar Germany was *more* modern than other states, that it experienced the shock of the new with an intensity not undergone by other,
more slowly modernising societies. Thus it was, as it were, a 'surfeit' of
modernity that paved the way for Nazism. A second response is that
although it is true that something other than modernity must account
for the fact that Germany rather than, for example, Britain, experienced
a Holocaust, this is of secondary significance compared with the contribution made by modernity to the Holocaust. In other words, any
advanced industrial society is far closser to a potential Holocaust than
was, say, nineteenth-century Germany. It is not illogical to argue that
Nazi racial policy was quintessentially modern and only secondarily
German.

Nevertheless, the modernity thesis does have serious weaknesses. In
the first place, like older modernisation approaches and like so many
theories about modernity generally,[84] the way the modern crisis has been
conceptualised marginalises the importance of the international situation. The only exception to this general rule in Peukert's work is that
the difficult shifts in the international division of labour during the
interwar period – which contributed so much to European nations'
economic difficulties – have been incorporated into his definition of a
modern capitalist crisis. Yet it is clear that the whole way of thinking
about the nation, the way in which the crisis was understood, as well
as the failure of the Weimar order to deal with its own internal problems,

---

[84] A point made by Antony Giddens in his *The Consequences of Modernity* (Stanford, 1990,
page references here to Polity Press paperback edn, Cambridge, 1991), pp. 63–5; see
also Dean Tipps' criticism of modernization theory that 'Any theoretical framework
which fails to incorporate such significant variables as the impact of war, conquest,
colonial domination, international political and military relationships, or of international trade and the cross-national flow of capital cannot hope to explain either the
origins of . . . societies or the nature of their struggles.' Tipps, 'Modernization', p. 212.

was crucially tied up with a European balance of power problem that the First World War had intensified rather than solved. 'Versailles' needs to be close to the centre of any explanation of Weimar's crisis and Nazi ideology.

On a broad theoretical level, of course, sophisticated theories of modernity now acknowledge the rivalry between nation-states as a crucial ingredient of the modern experience;[85] to that extent, acknowledging the significance of the international situation docs not negate the idea of Weimar's crisis of Nazi ideology being 'modern'. But once it is defined in this very open way, in which a wide variety of very different international situations are possible, it is clear that modernity *per se* no longer provides a very useful explanation of the Nazi phenomenon. Moreover, once we build the relationship between nation-states into our definition of modernity, then it becomes increasingly difficult to see as modern a regime whose inability to live among its neighbours and whose reckless expansionism condemned it to such a rapid demise.

In the second place, the notion of the modern crisis tends to obscure the way Nazism was tied to its particular epoch, rather than to immanent characteristics of modern society. However abhorrent Ernst Nolte's attempts to relativise the Holocaust,[86] he is correct in seeing the epochal experiences of total war and the Bolshevik success in Russia as crucial factors in shaping National Socialism.[87] Bolshevik success could not, as Nolte now seems to believe, conceivably point the way to Auschwitz but it was surely crucial in creating the 'totalitarian temptation'. And the emergence of violent, activist politics could not have taken place without the shock of total war conjoined with Germany's strange post-war situation of being almost bereft of an army at a time of great internal upheaval. Defining the epoch, rather than modernity *per se*, seems crucial.

A third limitation to Peukert's approach is its relative neglect of intellectual and cultural traditions in shaping perceptions of and responses to the crisis. German illiberalism may not be proof of backwardness but neither was it simply the product of particular kinds of modern problems. Instead, as historians make the 'linguistic turn', it is becoming increasingly clear how important for the actors in any particular society and period is the inheritance of national (or sub-national) ways of seeing

[85] E.g. Giddens, *Consequences*.
[86] See, for example, Ernst Nolte's pieces 'Between Historical Legend and Revisionism? The Third Reich in the Perspective of 1980' and 'The Past that Will not Pass: a Speech that Could Be Written but not Delivered', both reprinted in translation in *Forever in the Shadow of Hitler? Original Documents of the Historikerstreit, the Controversy Concerning the Singularity of the Holocaust* (New Jersey, 1993), pp. 1–15 and 18–23.
[87] Ernst Nolte, *The Three Faces of Fascism* (London, 1965).

and feeling. One very obvious example was the distinctively ethnic rather than territorial fashion in which the German nation was conceptualised. Another was the fact that freedom was interpreted by many groups in German society as a corporate rather than an individual concept.[88] A less obvious but no less important feature of German political culture as it evolved in the course of the nineteenth century was that because the Prussian and Imperial regimes were so strongly defined by fatherly authority, fears about the collapse of public order became entwined with fears about loss of virility.[89] All these examples provide instances of inherited ways of seeing or feeling which played a powerful role in shaping National Socialism and providing it with support.

The problem with the old notion of the *Sonderweg* was its implication that only Germany had a special path. But if the *Sonderweg* is taken to mean that Germany, like other nations, had its own particular set of intellectual, cultural and emotional traditions which continued powerfully to shape the modern experience, then it ought to be rescued. As the emphasis on *emotion* and *discourse* here implies, the *Sonderweg* also needs rescuing from an older kind of narrowly intellectual *Geistesgeschichte* which produced the kind of intellectual lineage that, in Pierre Ayçoberry's words, required Hitler to have read Fichte.[90] It is time for a modern *Geistesgeschichte* to be brought back to bear on twentieth-century German history.

Closely linked to this neglect of Germany's emotional inheritance is the fact that the modernity argument is far too rationalistic in its approach to explaining National Socialism. The crucial limitations of any such approach are surely provided by the Holocaust. It is hard to take seriously the argument put forward by Aly, Heim and colleagues that the Holocaust can be accounted for by the economics of *Lebensraum* and the drive to reduce unnecessary welfare burdens. As many authors have shown, the Holocaust often ran counter to economic logic; on the occasions when economic forces were allowed to dictate policy, the result was to slow down or limit the killing.[91] Thomas Sandkühler and

[88] Thus, for example, entrepreneurial 'freedom' meant freedom for entrepreneurs as a group to regulate their affairs independently of state intervention, rather than free competition, or freedom of the individual.

[89] See Nicolaus Sombart, *Die deutschen Männer und ihre Feinde. Carl Schmitt – ein deutsches Schicksal zwischen Männerbund und Matriarchatsmythos* (Munich, 1991); Mark Roseman, 'Generation Conflict and German History', in Roseman (ed.), *Generations in Conflict*, pp. 1–46.

[90] Ayçoberry, *Nazi Question*, p. 194.

[91] Ulrich Herbert, 'Arbeit und Vernichtung', in Dan Diner (ed.), *Ist der Nationalsozialismus Geschichte? Zu Historisierung und Historikerstreit* (Frankfurt/Main, 1987), pp. 198–236.

Hans Walter Schmul have recently shown that, true enough, IG Farben's willingness to move into Poland to take advantage of cheap labour was a decisive prerequisite for the expansion of Auschwitz; but on the other hand, the management of Auschwitz was characterised by a continual conflict between economic motives and ideology, with the latter frequently triumphant. The fact that 2,757 skilled Jewish armaments workers were deportted to Auschwitz from their vital jobs in Berlin and then worked to death as unskilled construction workers or murdercd outright provides one of thousands of such examples.[92]

IV

What is left of Ralf Dahrendorf's thesis that Nazi Germany unwittingly achieved a revolutionary modernisation of German society? A quick glance at the literature makes clear that, unlike the previous discussion, the debate over this question is only secondarily a conceptual one. Instead, the basic facts are in dispute, with many historians arguing that National Socialist policy had no long-term legacy at all (other than the crushing military defeat it brought upon Germany). The lack of consensus on the facts persists in part because there are still so many gaps in our knowledge. But those gaps themselves persist because the question of National Socialist impact is such a hard one to answer. The absence of institutional continuity in the transition from Weimar to Third Reich and again to the postwar period, particularly in the political and cultural sectors, makes the monitoring of any sort of continuous process of change in, say, public policy, political culture or collective behaviour almost impossible. So we have usually to make do with contrasts between the patterns of behaviour that emerged in postwar Germany (particularly western Germany)[93] and those that existed in Weimar, and to seek explanations for these contrasts. But the problem here, given the many discontinuities that divided pre-1933 from post-1949 Germany, is that there is no easy rule of thumb which would enable us to isolate the consequences of Nazi policy from those, say, of defeat or Allied intervention or of the fact that West Germany existed in a very different international situation from that of Weimar or (and here the challenges are even more formidable) from changes which could have been expected to take place in the intervening period no matter what regime was in power.

---

[92] Thomas Sandkühler and Hans Walter Schmul, 'Noch einmal: die I.G. Farben und Auschwitz', *GG*, vol. 19, no. 2 (1993), pp. 259–67, here p. 265.

[93] Because open historical enquiry into East German society is still in its infancy it was not possible to include the Soviet Zone and GDR in this account.

These difficulties notwithstanding, a number of analysts have ventured into the arena. Recently, Dahrendorf's work has been subjected to a blistering critique from Jens Alber who argues that the Nazi era either left German society fundamentally unchanged or made only temporary dents on longer-term trends. As Alber shows, a large number of key social indicators – of urbanisation, employment structure, secularisation (as expressed by cross-denominational marriages) – indicate considerable continuity.[94] In other areas, the Nazis clearly broke from the long-term trend of modernisation. This was evident in elite recruitment, for example, where the lower-middle class enjoyed a brief heyday before the trend to greater professionalisation revived in the postwar era. (In fact, Alber's conclusions, which draw on Wolfgang Zapf's work in the 1960s,[95] are somewhat outdated here. Recent work has shown the many tendencies towards greater professionalisation within the Third Reich and also – in the second half of the 1930s – the growing emphasis on academic qualifications even in organisations such as the SS which had had the most open recruitment patterns.[96] However, this does not gainsay that the National Socialists provided no radical modernising impulse themselves.) Even where the Nazis did mount a 'modernising' challenge to traditional institutions, Alber argues that these were fully restored in the postwar era. The renewed importance of family and church provides two examples.

In keeping with Alber's conclusions, many other historians have challenged the view that West German society in the early 1950s was very different from Weimar. Jürgen Falter had dubbed the Federal election of 1949 the last Weimar election[97] because of the close correlations between voting patterns in the late 1920s and early 1930s and those pertaining in 1949. Other authors have pointed out how much of older German culture was still to be found or was revived in the late 1940s and 1950s. It was only in the course of that decade, so they argue, that the pace of social change picked up.[98]

Ranged against these works, however, is a growing and equally impressive literature claiming that the National Socialists did indeed

---

[94] Jens Alber, 'Nationalsozialismus und Modernisierung', *Kölner Zeitschrift für Soziologie und Sozialpsychologie*, vol. 41 (1989), pp. 346–65; here pp. 351–3.
[95] Wolfgang Zapf, *Wandlungen der deutschen Elite. Ein Zirkulationsmodell deutscher Führungsgruppen 1919–1961* (Munich, 1965).
[96] See Prinz, 'Soziale Funktion moderner Elemente', pp. 309f.; Herbert Ziegler, *Nazi Germany's New Aristocracy: the SS Führerkorps 1922–1939* (Princeton, 1989).
[97] Jürgen Falter, 'Kontinuität und Neubeginn. Die Bundestagswahl 1949 zwischen Weimar und Bonn', *Politische Vierteljahresschrift*, vol. 22 (1981), pp. 236–63.
[98] Axel Schildt and Arnold Sywottek, ' "Wiederaufbau" und "Modernisierung". Zur Westdeutschen Gesellschaftsgeschichte in den fünfziger Jahren', *Aus Politik und Zeitgeschichte*, no. 6–7 (1989), pp. 18–32.

generate profound and lasting social change. Such change is most frequently seen as taking place at the level of the perceptions, experience and outlook of the population – 'eine Revolution der Sichtweisen, Einstellungsmuster und Wahrnehmungsformen – eine braune Kulturrevolution der Köpfe' – as Mallmann and Paul put it,[99] and in the institutional trappings, habits of association and norms pertaining to different milieux and sub-cultures. Two sets of social identities, in particular, have been seen as involved in such changes. On the one hand, a number of authors have argued that the homogeneity and narrow horizons of Germany's provinces, such as the Saar, the Ruhr and Bavaria were decisively broken by the nationalising impact of the Nazis.[100] On the other hand, and sometimes overlapping with the above, a growing body of work argues in different ways that important changes to the culture and identity of the working class took place in the Third Reich. The common theme is the evolution of a more unified and open culture and, implicitly or explicitly, an explanation is thus being given for the stability of democracy in the Federal Republic.

Juxtaposing these conclusions and the approach of Alber it seems that the regime achieved (and, indeed, attempted) relatively few changes to the structure of society, other than its remarkable efficiency in eliminating those unwanted minority groups it defined as racially undesirable. The structures of class society survived unscathed; inequalities in wealth, life chances and power remained largely undiminished. At the same time, however, it profoundly disrupted established perceptions, patterns of behaviour and allegiances in ways which allowed new kinds of identity and public interaction to be created in the postwar era. That is to say, it changed consciousness and culture without corresponding changes to the underlying social structure.

Is that really possible? Many authors have doubted that the Nazis could have made enduring changes to consciousness and culture if fundamental social structures were left intact. The idea of a link between social structure and political superstructure was as axiomatic for the classical modernisation theorists as for Marxist sociologists. Jens Alber, too, assumes that the lack of 'real' social change meant that whatever myths the Nazis were able to disseminate must have died with them (indeed, he assumes, to my mind wrongly, that this is also David

---

[99] Klaus-Michael Mallmann and Gerhard Paul, *Herrschaft und Alltag: ein Industrierevier im Dritten Reich* (Bonn, 1991), p. 162.

[100] As well as Mallmann and Paul on the Saar, see for Bavaria Martin Broszat *et al.* (eds.), *Von Stallingrad zur Währungsreform* and Broszat's brief remarks in Institut für Zeitgeschichte (ed.), *Alltagsgeschichte*, for the Ruhr Karl Rohe, *Vom Revier zum Ruhrgebiet. Wahlen, Parteien, politische Kultur* (Essen, 1986), esp. pp. 32–9.

Schoenbaum's position).[101] Yet what the example of the Third Reich demonstrates is the importance of the intervening mechanisms and institutions which interpret, and thus construct, social reality.

In the first place, as Dahrendorf originally pointed out, the Nazis destroyed with unparalleled thoroughness the organisational basis of political life. Not just the party organisations but the whole cultural network became more and more attenuated or was eradicated altogether. This disruption was particularly crucial in urban areas where, as Karl Rohe says, such organisations had played a decisive role in the transmission of cultural and political identity.[102] Terror and surveillance meant that it was dangerous even in the privacy of one's own home to try to communicate countervalues to the younger generation. At the same time, the Nazis constructed their own organisations – particularly effectively for the younger generation – and carried them into the deepest provincial hinterland in a way in which political organisations and youth groups had previously failed to do. True, the Nazi changes lasted only twelve years but what recent oral history work has shown is that never before had a generation been subjected to such a homogeneous and distinct socialisation as the Hitler Youth generation.[103] This would make the transmission of older traditions and values very difficult in the postwar period.

Alongside this institutional disruption came the symbolic and linguistic construction of a national community. Like the consumer public in relation to a modern advertising campaign, the German public remained sceptical about the overt claims of Nazi propaganda but 'bought' some of the underlying message. Few workers, for example, believed that the Nazis were acting selflessly for the good of the *Volksgemeinschaft*. But the idea that there *was* a *Volksgemeinschaft* and that the workers had an important place in it passed subliminally into general perceptions, not least because it appealed successfully to concerns about personal status that had left many workers feeling excluded from Weimar society.[104] Recent work has shown how successfully the Nazis invested Socialist discourse and symbols with new national and *völkisch* meanings.[105] Of

[101] Alber, 'Nationalsozialismus und Modernisierung', p. 355; see above, p. 202.
[102] Rohe, *Vom Revier zum Ruhrgebiet* and see Mark Roseman, 'Political Allegiance and Social Change: the Case of Workers in the Ruhr', in John Gaffney and Eva Kolinsky (eds.), *Political Culture in France and Germany* (London, 1991), pp. 173–206.
[103] See Reese, 'The BDM Generation' and Alexander von Plato, 'The Hitler Youth Generation and its Role in the Two Post-war German States', in Roseman (ed.), *Generations in Conflict*, pp. 210–26.
[104] Frei, 'Wie Modern' and Mai, ' "Warum steht der deutsche Arbeiter zu Hitler?" '.
[105] Eberhard Heuel, *Der umworbene Stand. Die ideologische Integration der Arbeiter im Nationalsozialismus 1933–1939* (Frankfurt/Main, 1989), pp. 586ff.; Wolfgang Eggerstorfer, *Schönheit und Adel der Arbeit. Arbeitsliteratur im Dritten Reich* (Frankfurt/Main, 1988).

course, the *Volksgemeinschaft* was not just about symbols and signs. For young workers, in particular, Hitler Youth, Nazi sport organisations, mobility opportunities in the army and so on – coupled with the simultaneous destruction of the labour movement – offered limited but new kinds of individual opportunity that challenged older collective modes of interest representation. The biographical analysis of postwar workers and labour leaders has revealed how strongly their self-perception was influenced by these new experiences.[106]

Against this kind of emphasis on change Jens Alber might well point to the many restorations or continuities in social forms and public and political culture between Weimar and the early years of West Germany. Yet it was surely only natural that any changes the Nazis had wrought would find overt manifestation in the postwar era only gradually. Dahrendorf himself explicitly acknowledged in his study the reconfessionalisation of German society after 1945[107] and the revived significance enjoyed by the family.[108] There was an understandable harking back to the familiar and the familial. 'In times of turmoil and political change', as Jeffrey Herf has recently observed, 'the orientation to the world offered by still-intact political traditions and meaningful interpretations of reality are precious resources to which people tenaciously cling'.[109] Moreover, as we have seen it was the younger generations who were particularly affected by National Socialism. It would take time before they were in a position to assert themselves or become in statistical terms the dominant generation.[110]

In short then, the balance of recent research is tending to confirm some of Dahrendorf's observations whilst challenging his conceptual framework. Nazi Germany did seriously disrupt the transmission of an older culture and it did in many ways facilitate the integration into a national political culture both of regional subcultures and, crucially, of the working class. Other more ambivalent changes might be noted in relation to the position of women. On the other hand, it is hard to sustain the view that profound structural changes in society had taken place or that many of the changes in political culture were a symptom of 'modernisation'. If we take Dahrendorf's definition of the active and conscious citizen, the young workers of the postwar era with their aversion to politics were actually less 'modern' than their Weimar

---

[106] Alexander von Plato, *'Der Verlierer geht nicht leer aus.'* *Betriebsräte geben zu Protokoll* (Berlin and Bonn, 1984); Plato, 'The Hitler Youth Generation'.

[107] Dahrendorf, *Gesellschaft*, p. 465.

[108] *Ibid.*

[109] Jeffrey Herf, 'Multiple Restorations: German Political Traditions and the Interpretation of Nazism, 1945–1946', *Central European History*, vol. 26, no. 1 (1993), pp. 21–56.

[110] A point made by Rohe, *Vom Revier zum Ruhrgebiet*, p. 37.

predecessors. Instead, the real story of Nazi impact is about the replacement of one set of political cultures and subcultures by another.

When the Nazi impact is defined in this way it is clear that it was
only in retrospect, once the very varied potentialities of the Nazi era
had been reshaped and filtered out by the postwar circumstances, that
the 'westernising' effects became dominant ones. In the first place there
were many facets to the Nazi project that were simply suppressed in
the postwar years. Moreover, the uses to which the population put its
experiences of the Third Reich after 1945 were heavily influenced by
the fact that those experiences were in many respects contaminated. It
was often not possible to talk about them in public. For the individual
too, much as one might try and rescue something positive from the
previous twelve years, there was a growing acceptance that crimes of
the utmost barbarity had been carried out in the name of the German
people. There was no 'intact' interwar experience that could be carried
untroubled into the postwar era.[111] It was thus only in a refracted and
submerged condition, which owed as much to postwar conditions as to
the original experiences themselves, that memories of the Nazi era could
be integrated into and could influence behaviour and perceptions in the
postwar era.

V

When we reflect on the changing character of the modernisation paradigms brought to bear on understanding the Nazi question we begin to
be aware that the ways in which successive generations of historians
have conceptualised the 'modern' are themselves strongly influenced by
the experience of Nazism and the Holocaust. This is true not just of
historians of Germany but of all the western theorists of modernity.
Auschwitz is so enormous a fact that it has impinged on all of our consciousness – and its impact continues to evolve. In the postwar era, the
defeat of Nazism clearly had a double impact on the way modernity was
understood in the West. In the first place, it meant that many of those
aspects of interwar western society which had revealed unwelcome parallels with the Nazis were quietly buried – the racism, the distrust of
democracy and the advocacy of an elitist technocracy. This made
Nazism seem all the more isolated and incomprehensible in terms of
the, now sanitised, modern tradition. Secondly, the fact that Nazism
had been defeated allowed confidence in the superior character of the
US path of social development. The Holocaust had been stopped and

---

[111] Lutz Niethammer, ' "Normalisierung" im Westen. Erinnerungsspuren in die 50er
Jahre', in Diner (ed.), *Ist der Nationalsozialismus Geschichte?*, pp. 153–84.

it was understandable that it should now be marginalised under the general heading of Nazi barbarity.

Gradually, however, the Holocaust has seeped into our sense of the present. It has produced a powerful mood of leave-taking from the certainties of the modern, and triggered an understandably bitter attack on the shibboleths of our former confidence.[112] As we now see, ethnocentricity was from the start the shadow side, if not of the enlightenment ideas *per se*, then of the way they came to be applied. (Because of this, classical modernisation theory *itself* seems now in some respects linked to the same spirit that led to the Holocaust. In a reaction to Nazism, modernisation theorists dropped the racism of older western evolutionism: they talked of ' "modernity" rather than "civilisation", "tradition" rather than "barbarism" '.[113] Under the surface, though, modernisation theory remained just as ethnocentric as its evolutionist forebear.) Moreover, it is not just the marginalisation of the 'other' that now seems suspect in the modern western tradition; what had seemed so safe, so neutral – technology, bureaucracy and so on – are, it is now clear, not uninvolved in the tragedy.

In other words, when we look at the evolving attempts to apply concepts of modernity to understanding Nazi Germany we realise we are dealing with an example of that inflexivity of knowledge which Antony Giddens sees as one of the constituent elements of the modern.[114] Concepts of modernity evolve under the impact of the Nazi experience and are then reapplied to help understand that experience. As the impact of Nazism has gradually revealed to western society the 'Holocaust in the modern', so we as historians have begun to understand what is modern about the Holocaust.

Yet it is clear that the learning process is not a linear one. In each intellectual wave there has been an emotional over-reaction, be it because of defensive reactions against what we might otherwise learn from the Holocaust, be it because the process of rethinking modernity was associated at each step with a particular juncture in the Cold War. Both the old modernisation theory and the new critical paradigm contain their own kinds of blindness. In particular, the postmodernist leave-taking from the old certainties of modernity is, for all its qualities, both flawed and dangerous.

Its flaws are clearly evident in the way National Socialism has been characterised by recent literature as a 'pathology of the modern'. The

---

[112] Eric Santner, *Stranded Objects. Mourning, Memory and Film in Postwar Germany* (Ithaca and London, 1990), pp. 7ff.; Jean-François Lyotard, 'Ticket to a New Decor', which appears in translation in *Copywright*, vol. 1, no. 10 (1987), pp. 14–15.
[113] Tipps, 'Modernization', p. 206.
[114] Giddens, *Consequences*, pp. 36–45.

problem is less that National Socialism is being linked to modernity than that the modern is being too closely identified with the 'rational'. The immense power of nationalism in contemporary eastern Europe reminds us that a key element of modernity is the emotive power of imagined communities. The Weberian emphasis on science and rationality is in many ways now surely outdated, ignoring all that we have learned from Freud and his successors about the motives and needs which drive human beings. The culture which generated National Socialism was shaped, as we have seen, by powerful anxieties about boundaries and identities, about the fragility of the public order, about the potency and vigour of German masculinity. All these, quite as much as the spirit of science, provided animus and murderous purpose. In one of his last works, Detlev Peukert, though sticking with his interpretation of 'science' as explanation, explicitly acknowledged this complex bundle of factors and – without perhaps noting their full significance – acknowledged too the collective feelings and emotions, such as the search for wholeness, for ways of dealing with death, which had shaped the yearning for *Volksgemeinschaft*.[115]

Even the very broad argument that the enlightenment saw the birth of a drive for domination and control seems hard to sustain. John Gillingham, in the context of English history, for example, has recently traced the intellectual invention of 'otherness' back to William of Malmesbury in the twelfth-century.[116] The human roots of the Holocaust evidently lie deep; the specific character of the enlightenment is more negated than confirmed.[117]

Let us also not forget that in interwar Europe to be 'modernist' was often to seek to go 'beyond rationality'. As even a passing glance at modernism shows, those who in the 1920s regarded themselves as being modern or avant-garde often eschewed reason, seeking some truer meaning, some higher truth than the dry dictates of orderly thought. Commenting on Lyotard, Frederic Jameson has written recently of 'all the affect (depth, anxiety, terror, the emotions of the monumental) that marked high modernism'.[118] Many modernists were drawn to Fascism on this basis. And though it was Italian Fascism that was particularly attractive to the modernist intellectual, there was, as Jeffrey Herf reminds us, more than a little of this anti-rational modernism in the

[115] Detlev Peukert, 'The Genesis of the "Final Solution" from the Spirit of Science', in Thomas Childers and Jane Caplan (eds.), *Reevaluating the Third Reich* (New York and London, 1993), pp. 234–52, here pp. 240ff.
[116] John Gillingham, 'The Beginnings of English Imperialism', *Journal of Historical Sociology*, vol. 5, no. 4 (1992), pp. 392–409.
[117] A point made well by Herf, *Reactionary Modernism*, p. ix.
[118] Frederic Jameson, 'Foreword' to Lyotard, *The Postmodern Condition*, p. xviii.

attitudes of the Nazis themselves to moral scruples, to action, violence and death.[119] Thus the impulses behind National Socialism and the motives for its most distinctive 'achievement' – the Holocaust – can never be reduced to the formula of a search for the rational society. They lie as much in Bloch's 'medieval streets' as in the 'spirit of science'.

[119] Herf, *Reactionary Modernism*.

SUGGESTIONS FOR FURTHER READING

William Sheridan Allen, *The Nazi Seizure of Power. The Experience of a Single German Town* (rev. edn, London, 1984).

Pierre Ayçoberry, *The Nazi Question* (London, 1981).

Omer Bartov, *Hitler's Army. Soldiers, Nazis, and War in the Third Reich* (Oxford, 1991).

David Beetham, *Marxists in the Face of Fascism* (Manchester, 1983).

Richard Bessel (ed.), *Life in the Third Reich* (Oxford, 1987).

Renate Bridenthal, Atina Grossmann and Marion Kaplan (eds.), *When Biology Became Destiny: Women in Weimar and Nazi Germany* (New York, 1984).

Martin Broszat, *The Hitler State. The Foundation and Development of the Internal Structure of the Third Reich* (London and New York, 1981).

Michael Burleigh and Wolfgang Wippermann, *The Racial State. Germany 1933–1945* (Cambridge, 1991).

Jane Caplan (ed.), *Nazism, Fascism and the Working Class: Essays by Tim Mason* (Cambridge, 1995).

Anthony L. Cardoza, *Agrarian Elites and Italian Fascism: the Province of Bologna 1901–1926* (Princeton, 1982).

Thomas Childers and Jane Caplan (eds.), *Reevaluating the Third Reich* (New York and London, 1993).

Paul Corner, *Fascism in Ferrara 1915–1925* (Oxford, 1975).

David Crew (ed.), *Nazism and German Society 1933–1935* (London and New York, 1994).

Victoria De Grazia, *The Culture of Consent: Mass Organization of Leisure in Fascist Italy* (Cambridge, 1981).

How Fascism Ruled Women: Italy, 1922–1945 (Berkeley, Los Angeles and Oxford, 1992).

David Forgacs (ed.), *Rethinking Italian Fascism: Capitalism, Populism and Culture* (London, 1986).

Norbert Frei, *National Socialist Rule in Germany. The Führer State 1933–1945* (Oxford, 1993).

Roger Griffin, *The Nature of Fascism* (London, 1993).

Ian Kershaw, *The Nazi Dictatorship. Problems and Perspectives of Interpretation* (3rd edn, London, 1993).

MacGregor Knox, *Mussolini Unleashed, 1939–1941. Politics and Strategy in Fascist Italy's Last War* (Cambridge, 1982).

Tracy H. Koon, *Believe, Obey, Fight. Political Socialization of Youth in Fascist Italy, 1922–1943* (Chapel Hill and London, 1985).

Claudia Koonz, *Mothers in the Fatherland: Women, the Family and Nazi Politics* (New York, 1986).

Walter Laqueur (ed.), *Fascism. A Reader's Guide* (Harmondsworth, 1976).

Stein Ugelvik Larsen, Bernt Hagtvet and Jan Petter Myklebust (eds.), *Who Were the Fascists? Social Roots of European Fascism* (Oslo, 1980).

Adrian Lyttelton, *The Seizure of Power: Fascism in Italy 1919–1929* (2nd edn, London and Princeton, 1988).

Charles S. Maier, *The Unmasterable Past. History, Holocaust and German National Identity* (Cambridge, Mass. and London, 1988).

Tim Mason, *Social Policy in the Third Reich. The Working Class and the 'National Community'* (Providence and Oxford, 1993).

Hans Mommsen, *From Weimar to Auschwitz* (Cambridge, 1991).

Philip Morgan, *Italian Fascism 1919–1945* (Basingstoke, 1995).

Franz L. Neumann, *Behemoth. The Structure and Practice of National Socialism 1933–1944* (New York, 1966).

R. J. Overy, *War and Economy in the Third Reich* (Oxford, 1994).

Luisa Passerini, *Fascism in Popular Memory: The Cultural Experience of the Turin Working Class* (Cambridge, 1987).

Detlev J. K. Peukert, *Inside Nazi Germany. Conformity, Opposition and Racism in Everyday Life* (Harmondsworth, 1989).

Nicos Poulantzas, *Fascism and Dictatorship* (London, 1974).

Roland Sarti (ed.), *The Ax Within: Italian Fascism in Action* (New York, 1974).

Jonathan Steinberg, *All or Nothing. The Axis and the Holocaust 1941–1943* (London, 1990).

Jill Stephenson, *Women in Nazi Society* (London, 1975).

Edward R. Tannenbaum, *The Fascist Experience: Italian Society and Culture 1922–1945* (New York, 1972).

Doug Thompson, *State Control in Fascist Italy. Culture and Conformity, 1925–43* (Manchester, 1991).

Henry A. Turner, Jr. (ed.), *Nazism and the Third Reich* (New York, 1972). *Reappraisals of Fascism* (New York, 1975).

Perry R. Willson, *The Clockwork Factory: Women and Work in Fascist Italy* (Oxford, 1993).

Stuart Woolf (ed.), *The Nature of Fascism* (London, 1968).

INDEX

Milan, 8, 44, 49, 57, 59, 87, 115, 186
militarisation, 150–2, 158
militarism, 21
military, *see* armed forces
military training, *see under* training
militias, *see* citizens' militias
miners, 57, 71
Ministry of Food and Agriculture
(German), 97
Ministry of the Interior (German), 98,
103–4, 106, 109
Ministry of Justice (German), 103, 106,
108–9
misogynism, 84–5, 93
'mixed marriage', 101, 104
modernisation, 9, 10, 14–15, 21, 88–9,
165–7, 170–1, 173, 182, 191–4, 196,
198–205, 207, 209–18, 221–2,
225–6
modernisation theory, 75, 167, 197–200,
202–6, 209, 212–15, 217–18, 223,
227
modernism, 228
modernity, 18, 27, 75, 94, 138–9, 158,
197–9, 203–7, 212–16, 218–20,
226–8
Molise, 193
Moltke, Helmut Graf von, 121
Monarchism, Monarchists (Italian), 189,
192
monarchy (German), 116–17
monarchy (Italian), 114, 117, 124–5,
128, 130, 167, 182–4, 188
monetarist policies, 171–2
Montecatini fertiliser works, 54
morale, in wartime, 58–9
morality, moral values, 25, 27–30, 38
see also bourgeois values
Moro, Aldo, 186
Mosca, Gaetano, 15, 20
Mother Cross, 99, 109
motherhood, 69, 79–80, 82, 87, 94–5
Mothers' and Children's Relief, *see*
Hilfswerk Mutter und Kind
Movimento Sociale Italiano (MSI), 165,
186, 188–90, 192–5
see also Alleanza Nazionale
Mühlberger, Detlef, 43
Muslim influences, 87, 92
Musso, Stefano, 46
Mussolini, Benito, 6, 8, 10, 15, 45, 48,
50, 57–9, 82, 86, 92, 113–14,
124–6, 128, 165–70, 176–7, 180,
182–3, 185, 192
cult of, 82, 178
decision to go to war, 168

economic and financial policies of,
170–3, 175
ideology of, 124, 168

Napoleon, 119, 121
National Agency for Maternity and
Infancy, *see* ONMI
national community, 7, 13
see also racial community
national community (*Volksgemeinschaft*),
see racial community
National Democratic Party of Germany
(Nationaldemokratische Partei
Deutschlands, NPD), 194
'National Economy/Domestic Economy',
97
National Fascist Party (PNF), 17, 49, 51,
125–6, 166–7, 169–70, 175–6, 178,
188
membership of, 19–20, 125, 180–1
support for, 170
National Socialism, 3–9, 12, 14, 27, 41,
62–3, 65, 70, 73, 95, 197–8, 200–2,
206, 212–13, 225, 227–9
ideology of, 62, 68, 72, 75, 108, 124,
131, 137, 155–6, 159, 162, 200,
205–8, 212–13, 216–19
support for, 72, 220
National Socialist German Workers' Party
(NSDAP), 35, 126, 141, 150, 156,
178
activism of members, 34, 37
membership of, 19–20, 26, 125
National Socialist Organisation of
Women, *see* NS-Frauenschaft
National Women's Leadership, *see*
Reichsfrauenführung
nationalism, 24, 42, 60
nationalists, 14
Natoli, Claudio, 43–4
Nazism, *see* National Socialism
'Negroes', 101
Nemec, Gloria, 90, 92
neo-Fascism, 10, 165, 182, 184–6,
188–90, 194
neo-Fascists, 166–7, 186, 196
see also Alleanza Nazionale; Movimento
Sociale Italiano
neo-Nazism, 194
neo-realism, 176
Neumann, Franz, 38, 61, 62, 67, 72, 137
New Economic Policy (NEP), 15
New Right, 77
New Social Movements (Italy), 195
newsreels, 142, 157–8, 160
Niethammer, Lutz, 214
Nolte, Ernst, 23n., 25, 219